AI, IoT, and Blockchain Breakthroughs in E-Governance

Kavita Saini
Galgotias University, India

A. Mummoorthy
Malla Reddy College of Engineering and Technology, India

Roopa Chandrika
Department of Information Technology, Malla Reddy College of Engineering and Technology, India

N.S. Gowri Ganesh
Saveetha Engineering College, India

A volume in the Advances in Electronic Government, Digital Divide, and Regional Development (AEGDDRD) Book Series

Published in the United States of America by
    IGI Global
    Information Science Reference (an imprint of IGI Global)
    701 E. Chocolate Avenue
    Hershey PA, USA 17033
    Tel: 717-533-8845
    Fax: 717-533-8661
    E-mail: cust@igi-global.com
    Web site: http://www.igi-global.com

Library of Congress Cataloging-in-Publication Data

Names: Saini, Kavita, 1976- editor. | Gowri Ganesh, N. S., 1971- editor. |
    Mummoorthy, A., 1983- editor. | Chandrika, Roopa, 1976- editor.
Title: AI, IoT, and blockchain breakthroughs in e-governance / edited by:
    Kavita Saini, N.S. Gowri Ganesh, A. Mummoorthy, and Roopa Chandrika.
Description: Hershey, PA : Information Science Reference, [2023] | Includes
    bibliographical references. | Summary: "The goal of this book is to
    clearly define and emphasize various AI algorithms, as well as new IoT
    and blockchain breakthroughs in the field of e-governance. The
    discipline of data analytics, security is on the verge of reaching new
    heights, thanks to the introduction of AI capabilities. Every chapter
    will cover blockchain technology, ML and DL algorithms, their origins,
    problems and benefits and various government use cases, to clearly
    explain the growing power of AI and security algorithms for the
    development and operation of e-governance applications. A thorough
    in-depth understanding of AI algorithms through real use case
    application can help to kindle interest in research. Students, scholars,
    bureaucrats, industrialists in and scientists interested in AI ,
    cybersecurity and blockchain can greatly benefit from this book"--
    Provided by publisher.
Identifiers: LCCN 2022056316 (print) | LCCN 2022056317 (ebook) | ISBN
    9781668476970 (hardcover) | ISBN 9781668477014 (paperback) | ISBN
    9781668476987 (ebook)
Subjects: LCSH: Electronic government information--Security measures. |
    Public administration--Data processing. | Computer security. |
    Blockchains (Databases) | Internet of things. | Artificial intelligence.
Classification: LCC JF1525.A8 A43 2023 (print) | LCC JF1525.A8 (ebook) |
    DDC 352.3/802854678--dc23/eng/20221230
LC record available at https://lccn.loc.gov/2022056316
LC ebook record available at https://lccn.loc.gov/2022056317

This book is published in the IGI Global book series Advances in Electronic Government, Digital Divide, and Regional Development (AEGDDRD) (ISSN: 2326-9103; eISSN: 2326-9111)

British Cataloguing in Publication Data
A Cataloguing in Publication record for this book is available from the British Library.

All work contributed to this book is new, previously-unpublished material. The views expressed in this book are those of the authors, but not necessarily of the publisher.

For electronic access to this publication, please contact: eresources@igi-global.com.

Advances in Electronic Government, Digital Divide, and Regional Development (AEGDDRD) Book Series

Zaigham Mahmood
University of Derby, UK & North West University, South
Africa

ISSN:2326-9103
EISSN:2326-9111

Mission

The successful use of digital technologies (including social media and mobile technologies) to provide public services and foster economic development has become an objective for governments around the world. The development towards electronic government (or e-government) not only affects the efficiency and effectiveness of public services, but also has the potential to transform the nature of government interactions with its citizens. Current research and practice on the adoption of electronic/digital government and the implementation in organizations around the world aims to emphasize the extensiveness of this growing field.

The Advances in Electronic Government, Digital Divide & Regional Development (AEGDDRD) book series aims to publish authored, edited and case books encompassing the current and innovative research and practice discussing all aspects of electronic government development, implementation and adoption as well the effective use of the emerging technologies (including social media and mobile technologies) for a more effective electronic governance (or e-governance).

Coverage

- E-Citizenship, Inclusive Government, Connected Government
- Online Government, E-Government, M-Government
- ICT within Government and Public Sectors
- Adoption of Innovation with Respect to E-Government
- Case Studies and Practical Approaches to E-Government and E-Governance
- Current Research and Emerging Trends in E-Government Development
- Urban Development, Urban Economy
- Public Information Management, Regional Planning, Rural Development
- Frameworks and Methodologies for E-Government Development
- E-Governance and Use of Technology for Effective Government

IGI Global is currently accepting manuscripts for publication within this series. To submit a proposal for a volume in this series, please contact our Acquisition Editors at Acquisitions@igi-global.com or visit: http://www.igi-global.com/publish/.

Titles in this Series

For a list of additional titles in this series, please visit: www.igi-global.com/book-series

IGI Global
PUBLISHER of TIMELY KNOWLEDGE

701 East Chocolate Avenue, Hershey, PA 17033, USA
Tel: 717-533-8845 x100 • Fax: 717-533-8661
E-Mail: cust@igi-global.com • www.igi-global.com

Table of Contents

Detailed Table of Contents

Chapter 1
    Bramha S. Tripathi, Indian Institute of Technology, Delhi, India
    Ritu Gupta, Galgotia University, India

Nowadays, industry 4.0 is very popular technology for industrial automation & rapid development of electrical and electronics technology, information technology, or advanced manufacturing technology. In this research concluded the challenges of cyber security and AI based industry 4.0, and discusses the key emerging technologies like internet of things, cloud computing, cyber security, artificial intelligence, etc., for making an industry 4.0 revolution. In this research the analysis of major issues and potential solution to key emerging technologies of new world is presented. This research gives the all-industrial revolution comparison analysis to growth of manufacturing industries and its benefits of different revolution. In this research paper give the analysis of why industry 4. 0 is best for the advanced manufacturing for growth of industries. This chapter provides a holistic view of cyber security and artificial intelligence in the industry 4.0 landscape, identifying and analyzing its fundamental concept, challenges, and ongoing future trends.

Chapter 2
    Prithi Samuel, SRM Institute of Science and Technology, India
    Reshmy A. K., SRM Institute of Science and Technology, India
    Sudha Rajesh, SRM Institute of Science and Technology, India
    Kanipriya M., SRM Institute of Science and Technology, India
    Karthika R. A., SRM Institute of Science and Technology, India

E-government is the effective and efficient delivery of high-quality information and governmental services to citizens and/or other governmental and non-government entities. Both the service provider and the citizens using the services will gain from big data analysis. Market Research indicates that 75% of government agencies are using big data to enhance the standard of living for individuals. Big data analytics gives a perspective into the effectiveness of government programmes and policies. In order to gauge public sentiment and comprehend citizens' thoughts and attitudes about government programmes, forecasting and prescriptive analysis suggests the optimal course of action. This chapter will provide a brief overview of key topics to help readers fully comprehend how big data is used across the government department.

Chapter 3

Vishal Venkataramani, Sri Sivasubramaniya Nadar College of Engineering, India
Ramdhanush Venkatakrishnan, Sri Sivasubramaniya Nadar College of Engineering, India
Chamundeswari Arumugam, Sri Sivasubramaniya Nadar College of Engineering, India

IoT usage growth expands in the wild range because of smart digital India in India. The government is funding various projects for boosting the expansion at a large level to promote smart digital India. Many start-up companies are flourishing due to the expansion of government policies in promoting smart digital India. Many public and private companies were improving their skill set to expand the government requirements. Here, for this chapter, the two case studies, satellite based IoT and solid waste management are discussed. The current trends, techniques, technologies, architectures, solutions, applications and issues were discussed. The recent advancement pertaining to these fields, comparison of the properties, and technology evolution were discussed elaborately to get a glimpse of smart digital India.

Chapter 4

Kavita Saini, Galgotias University, India
Arnav Tyagi, Galgotias University, India
Akshat Antal, Galgotias University, India

Blockchain is an acquired information framework that incorporates a square chain. Blockchain capacities as a common record or as an overall record keeping arrangement of all exchanges on an incorporated blockchain. Blockchain is a successful framework for putting away and taking care of records of exchange at its center. All the more explicitly, blockchain is a typical, extremely durable record of circulated trades working from connected trade squares and putting them away in a high level data set. Blockchain relies upon developed cryptographic strategies to permit any member in an organization to convey, (for example, putting away, trading, and showing information), without earlier certainty between the collections. All members become mindful of participation with the blockchain and permit framework affirmation before information is incorporated, working with trustless coordinated exertion between associations. Blockchain is virtual digital money Bitcoin's spine innovation.

Chapter 5

J. Brintha Jei, SRM Dental College, India
S. Behin Sam, Dr. Ambedkar Government Arts College (Autonomous), India

Smart health care depends on emerging technologies like electronic health records, along with internet of things, artificial intelligence, mobile communications, cloud computing, etc. This helps to create various systems like health management systems and medical service systems. This chapter includes: (1) development of smart health care using machine learning and blockchain technology; (2) uses of machine learning and blockchain technology with smart healthcare applications; (3) impact of smart healthcare applications on human health; (4) features of smart healthcare applications; and (5) limitations.

Chapter 6

Jyothi K. C., Vellore Institute of Technology, India

Neelu Khare, Vellore Institute of Technology, India

The technology boom in Industry 4.0 has resulted in the generation of large volume of medical data. Smart healthcare systems have burgeoned with the convergence of blockchain, machine learning, and internet of things (IoT). The amalgamation of privacy-preserving blockchain technology and predictive diagnosis by machine learning models produces an enhanced healthcare system. This chapter aims to shed light on the machine learning algorithms and blockchain technologies currently used in the healthcare industry. The advantages of opting for blockchain for preserving data integrity and privacy are highlighted. A few applications and steps involved in implementing blockchain and machine learning in healthcare, as well as the challenges faced while doing so, are discussed. Finally, a theoretical blockchain-machine learning internet of medical things(IoMT) framework is proposed, drawing from the recent research advancements.

Chapter 7

Prithi Samuel, SRM Institute of Science and Technology, India

Jayashree K., Panimalar Engineering College, India

Babu R., SRM Institute of Science and Technology, India

Vijay K., Rajalakshmi Engineering College, India

The usage of artificial intelligence (AI) technologies that depend on massive volumes of data, which are frequently made available through IoT, is thus directly related to the creation of smart governments. In order to increase the effectiveness of governance and the standard of living for citizens, Internet - of - things enabled AI technologies can be used in several important areas of smart government. In order to provide fulfilled government functions, AI and its subdomain innovations have the opportunity to address a number of current organizational inadequacies. In this chapter the foundations, benefits, and challenges implementing these technologies in the public sector or government are discussed. Following that, the various AI, Ml technologies and IoT frameworks for smart governance are explored. Then the focus is on the applications and use cases of IoT, AI and machine learning for smart governance.

Chapter 8

Lokeswari Y. Venkataramana, Sri Sivasubramaniya Nadar College of Engineering, India

Shomona Gracia Jacob, University of Technology and Applied Sciences, Nizwa, Oman

VenkataVara Prasad D., Sri Sivasubramaniya Nadar College of Engineering, India

R. Athilakshmi, SRM Institute of Science and Technology, India

V. Priyanka, Sri Sivasubramaniya Nadar College of Engineering, India

K. Yeshwanthraa, Sri Sivasubramaniya Nadar College of Engineering, India

S. Vigneswaran, Sri Sivasubramaniya Nadar College of Engineering, India

In many applications where classification is needed, class imbalance poses a serious problem. Class imbalance refers to having very few instances under one or more classes while the other classes contain sufficient amount of data. This makes the results of the classification to be biased towards the classes containing many numbers of samples comparatively. One approach to handle this problem is by generating synthetic instances from the minority classes. Geometric synthetic minority oversampling technique (G-SMOTE) is used to generate artificial samples. G-SMOTE generates synthetic samples in the geometric region of the input space, around each selected minority instance. The performance of the classifier is compared after oversampling using G-SMOTE, synthetic minority oversampling technique and without oversampling the minority classes. The work presents empirical results that show around 10% increase in the accuracy of the classifier model when G-SMOTE is used as an oversampling algorithm compared to SMOTE, and around 30% increase in performance over a class imbalanced data.

Chapter 9

Aswini J., Saveetha Engineering College (Autonomous), Anna University, Chennai, India
Malarvizhi N., Vel Tech Rangarajan Dr. Sangunthala R&D Institute of Science and Technology, India
Siva Subramanian, S.A. Engineering College (Autonomous), Anna University, Chennai, India
Gayathri A., SIMATS School of Engineering, Saveetha Nagar, India

In recent years, augmented reality & virtual reality (AR/VR) has been seen as a technology with huge potential to give companies an operational and competitive advantage. But despite the use of new technologies, companies still face challenges and cannot immediately achieve performance. In addition, companies must adopt attractive technologies and analyse the areas where these technologies can be adopted, which emphasizes the importance of establishing appropriate e-government practices. This study explores how AR/VR governance is applied to support the development of sustainable AR/VR applications and analyse the negative impacts based on application domains. The study illustrates what practices are used to obtain information that helps engage technologies by overcoming obstacles with recommended actions that lead to desired results. The research helps to identify the most important scopes and limitations of AR/VR in e-governance.

Chapter 10

Newlin Rajkumar, Anna University, Coimbatore, India
Alfred Daniel, Karpagam Academy of Higher Education, Coimbatore, India
Jayashree S., KgiSL Institute of Technology, India

Data has always been important in making decisions. Data is being created at an exponential rate due to technological advancements. In every corner of the world, there is a tidal surge of data. Every element of a company, including educational institutions, has access to digital data. Social networking, smartphones, and the World Wide Web are just a handful of the methods used to generate this massive amount of data. Virtual learning environments have been gathering up speed recently, owing to the advancements revealed in their assistance and the sheer number of terminals directly or indirectly associated with them. Online education, computer-assisted instruction, virtual education, learning, virtual learning environments, and digital educational cooperation are all examples of e-learning. A unique trustworthiness-based methodology is proposed to strengthen data security in computer-supported collaborative learning environments, taking into account the vital security-related concerns in e-learning.

Chapter 11

Vipin Jain, Teerthanker Mahaveer University, India
Mohit Rastogi, Teerthanker Mahaveer University, India
J. V. N. Ramesh, Koneru Lakshmaiah Education Foundation, India
Anshu Chauhan, Teerthanker Mahaveer University, India
Pankhuri Agarwal, Teerthanker Mahaveer University, India
Sabyasachi Pramanik, Haldia Institute of Technology, India
Ankur Gupta, Vaish College of Engineering, Rohtak, India

Banks cannot afford to be complacent in their operations. Due to the dramatic changes brought about by improvements in computer technology (IT) as well as competitive intensity from FinTech businesses, they must re-evaluate their competing advantages. A major point of emphasis in this essay is that banks must not abandon relationship banking that encourages direct interaction with bank clients. Orienting relationship banking on the long term simplifies incentives while also supporting bank clients' long-term requirements and objectives. However, because to the availability of IT-driven economy of scale as well as rivalry by FinTech start-ups and IT corporations, banks may be tempted to enter the transaction banking business. In this context, the paper evaluates the importance of distance, AI, and behavioural inclinations in the decision-making process. The suggestions for banking stability are analyzed in detail. The authors believe that relationship banking has the potential to reduce its disadvantages, but it should conform to the newer facts to flourish.

Chapter 12

Kannadhasan Suriyan, Study World College of Engineering, India
Nagarajan R., Gnanamani College of Technology, India
Manjushree Kumari J., Gnanamani College of Technology, India
Jisha Chandra C., Gnanamani College of Technology, India

Medical image collaboration may be accomplished for medical practise and education by bringing the idea of CSCW to the medical imaging field. Medical pictures may be examined and diagnosed by groups of people, and individuals can talk about them on a chat system while exchanging visual image data on their terminals. The process of generating visible pictures of inside body structures for scientific and medicinal research and therapy, as well as a visible view of the function of internal tissues, is known as medical imaging. The goal of this procedure is to identify and treat disorders. This procedure generates a database of the organs' normal structure and function, making it simple to spot abnormalities. Organic and radiological imaging, using electromagnetic energy (X-rays and gamma), sonography, magnetic scopes, and thermal and isotope imaging are all part of this process.

Chapter 13

B. Satheesh Kumar, Karpagam Academy of Higher Education, Coimbatore, India
K. Sampath Kumar, Galgotias University, India

Patients can control, share, and manage their health records with family, friends, and healthcare professionals utilizing electronic health records (EHRs), which use an open channel, or the Internet. When a lot of data is available, DL methods show promise in these health applications. A distributed blockchain-based

IoT system would benefit greatly from these ideas. This research proposes novel technique in Healthcare Data Based Feature Selection and Classification Using Blockchain and Machine Learning Architectures. The network has been secured using centralized blockchain sensor network. Here the input sensor-based healthcare data has been collected and processed for noise removal and smoothening. Then the processed data feature has been selected using Greedy Mixed Forward Colony Optimization feature selection. The suggested framework's superiority is supported by security research and experimental findings using the IoT-Botnet and ToN-IoT datasets. Proposed technique attained acc of 95%, precision of 85%, recall of 76%, F1 score of 63%, sec rate of 95%, DT Rate of 85%.

Preface

In recent years, there has been a growing trend towards the integration of artificial intelligence (AI), the internet of things (IoT), and blockchain technology in e-governance. These breakthroughs are transforming the way governments operate and deliver services to citizens.

AI can be used to automate and streamline various government processes, from citizen services to regulatory compliance. For instance, chatbots powered by AI can help citizens access information and services easily, while predictive analytics can help governments identify areas that require immediate attention.

The IoT, on the other hand, can be used to monitor and manage various assets, including vehicles, buildings, and public infrastructure. This can help governments optimize their operations, reduce costs, and improve service delivery. Additionally, the data generated by IoT devices can be used for predictive maintenance and other analytical purposes.

Blockchain technology is also playing a critical role in e-governance. Blockchain provides a secure, tamper-proof platform for storing and sharing data, which can help governments to enhance transparency, reduce fraud, and increase trust in public institutions. Additionally, blockchain can be used to streamline various processes, including voting, identity management, and property registration.

Overall, the integration of AI, IoT, and blockchain technology in e-governance is providing governments with new ways to enhance service delivery, improve efficiency, and increase transparency. As these technologies continue to evolve, we can expect to see even more innovative solutions emerging in the e-governance space.

AI, IoT, and blockchain breakthroughs in e-governance are transforming the operations of various governments around the world. For example, in the United States, several government agencies are using AI-powered chatbots to help citizens access services and information more efficiently. In addition, IoT devices are being deployed to monitor public infrastructure, such as bridges and highways, and provide real-time data to improve maintenance and safety.

In Europe, governments are using blockchain to improve transparency and reduce fraud in public procurement processes. Estonia, for example, has implemented a blockchain-based system for voting and land registration, which has greatly increased efficiency and security in these areas. IoT devices are also being used in Europe to improve energy efficiency and reduce carbon emissions.

In Asia, governments are leveraging AI and blockchain to improve citizen services and enhance data security. In China, for instance, the government has implemented a blockchain-based system for tracking food safety, while AI-powered chatbots are being used to provide customer service in various industries. In India, the government is exploring the use of blockchain for identity management and improving the efficiency of public services.

In Africa, governments are using AI, IoT, and blockchain to enhance healthcare services and improve agricultural productivity. For example, AI-powered chatbots are being used in Kenya to provide medical advice and support to citizens, while IoT devices are being deployed to monitor soil moisture and temperature to improve crop yields.

Overall, the integration of AI, IoT, and blockchain in e-governance is a global trend that is transforming the operations of governments around the world. As these technologies continue to evolve, we can expect to see even more innovative solutions emerging in e-governance, which will benefit citizens and governments alike.

The target audiences of this book are decision makers of the government, researchers, research scholars and general technical onlookers.

The impact of AI, IoT, and blockchain breakthroughs in e-governance on decision-makers in the government is significant. These technologies have the potential to transform the way governments operate and deliver services to citizens, which can lead to better decision-making and improved outcomes. For instance, AI-powered predictive analytics can help decision-makers identify areas that require immediate attention, such as potential public health outbreaks or infrastructure maintenance needs. This can lead to more effective resource allocation and better outcomes for citizens.

In recent years, there have been significant breakthroughs in the application of these technologies in e-governance, which refers to the use of digital technologies to enhance the efficiency, transparency, and accountability of government processes.

Researchers and students in this area of study can explore the potential applications of these technologies in e-governance, and work to develop new solutions that can improve the efficiency, effectiveness, and transparency of government services including:

AI in E-Governance: AI can be used to automate repetitive tasks, analyze data, and make predictions, which can help governments make more informed decisions. Researchers can study the use of AI in areas such as healthcare, transportation, and public safety, as well as its potential for improving citizen engagement and participation.

IoT in E-Governance: IoT refers to the network of physical devices connected to the internet, which can collect and share data. Researchers can investigate how IoT can be used to improve infrastructure management, environmental monitoring, and emergency response, among other areas.

Blockchain in E-Governance: Blockchain is a distributed ledger technology that can be used to create secure and transparent digital records. Researchers can explore the use of blockchain in areas such as voting, identity management, and supply chain management, as well as its potential for improving transparency and reducing corruption.

While the target audience can explore these topics, this book can benefit the readers in the chapter of this book:

Industry 4.0 has the potential to transform the manufacturing industry, improve productivity, reduce costs, and create new opportunities for businesses. However, it also presents some challenges and potential issues that need to be addressed to fully realize its benefits. Industry 4.0 presents significant opportunities for businesses, but also challenges that need to be addressed. Chapter1 deals with these challenges, manufacturers can fully realize the benefits of Industry 4.0 and drive innovation and growth in the manufacturing sector.

Big data analytics is becoming an essential tool for e-governance, as it helps government agencies analyze vast amounts of data to make informed decisions and improve the delivery of services to citizens. Big data analytics is transforming e-governance, allowing government agencies to make more informed decisions, improve the delivery of services, and enhance citizen engagement and participation. As more data becomes available and analytical tools become more sophisticated, the use of big data analytics in e-governance is expected to increase significantly in the coming years. Chapter 2 addresses the need for the big data in various sector for the implementation of egovernance in the Government sector and also the research challenges of the AI and big data algorithms.

Blockchain technology is known for its innovative features, such as high security, decentralization, and sealing properties, which allow all members to accept linkage and transmission at an incredibly low cost. By leveraging peer-to-peer communication between IoT devices, transaction security can be further strengthened while ensuring convenience and precision for users. Chapter 3 focuses on two case studies, satellite-based IoT and solid waste management, and examines the latest trends, techniques, technologies, architectures, solutions, applications, and issues in these areas.

Chapter 4 discusses DApps, which are an improved version of traditional applications, as they can potentially become self-sustaining assets by allowing their partners to invest in DApp development. These applications use the Ethereum blockchain for data storage and smart contracts for their application logic. Smart contracts are a set of rules that are publicly available and run precisely according to those rules. To support the development of DApps, Ethereum application development companies that offer affordable hourly rates for entrepreneurs, SMEs, and established enterprises. Chapter 5 discusses the use of blockchain technology in healthcare allows for secure patient record keeping, with exclusive access keys for both doctors and patients. This enables patients to access their health records safely and conveniently, at any time. Patient records contain vital information such as health reports, prescribed medications, health outcomes, and ongoing monitoring of the patient's health. While blockchain has the potential to revolutionize the entire medical sector, the challenge lies in persuading healthcare providers to embrace and adopt the technology on a wider scale. Similarly, although machine learning has significant benefits for healthcare, its implementation in the industry requires a careful and deliberate approach.

The integration of blockchain, machine learning, and the Internet of Medical Things (IoMT) presents several challenges such as scalability, power consumption during the mining process, implementing complex deep learning algorithms on big data, and a few security vulnerabilities. However, the advantages of this integration far outweigh the drawbacks. The smart healthcare systems benefit greatly from the data integrity, efficiency, speed of processing transactions, and security provided by blockchain technology. Additionally, machine learning algorithms' predictive analytics only enhance the healthcare industry's capabilities. Blockchain technology's transparency and decentralization properties provide a means of tracing decision-making processes, thus alleviating the obscurity of black-box machine learnings. Overall, Chapter 6 deals with the integration of blockchain, machine learning, and the IoMT is revolutionizing the healthcare industry.

AI and its subdomain innovations have the potential to enable effective government functions. Intelligent (AI) technologies are directly linked to the development of smart governments with the data available through IoT. IoT-enabled AI technologies in several key areas of smart government can increase the efficiency of governance and improve citizens' standard of living. Chapter 7 discusses the foundations, benefits, and challenges of implementing these technologies in the public sector or government and also explores various AI, ML technologies, and IoT frameworks for smart governance. Chapter 8's objective is to shed light on the machine learning algorithms and blockchain technologies currently employed in the healthcare industry. The chapter also discusses a few applications and steps involved in implementing blockchain and machine learning in healthcare, as well as the challenges encountered while doing so. A case study around medical data has been discussed where class imbalance plays a significant issue in classification. A solution to handle the imbalance problem is focused like techniques in generating synthetic instances from the minority classes. Geometric Synthetic Minority Oversampling Technique (G-SMOTE), a technique is used to generate artificial samples. G-SMOTE generates synthetic samples in the geometric region of the input space.

Companies often face challenges in implementing new technologies and may not see immediate improvements in performance. To effectively adopt new technologies, it is important for companies to establish appropriate e-government practices and identify areas where these technologies can be applied. Chapter 9 examines how AR/VR governance can be used to support the development of sustainable AR/VR applications and analyzes the potential negative impacts of these technologies in various application domains. The chapter identifies best practices for obtaining information and engaging with AR/VR technologies to overcome obstacles and achieve desired results. It also identifies the most significant opportunities and limitations of AR/VR in e-governance.

Digital data is now ubiquitous, permeating every aspect of a company, including educational institutions. The proliferation of social media, smartphones, and the internet has resulted in an overwhelming amount of data. Data has always been a critical component in decision-making, and with advancements in technology, the rate of data creation has skyrocketed. Virtual learning environments have gained momentum due to their assistance and the sheer number of terminals associated with them. E-learning encompasses online education, computer-assisted instruction, virtual education, learning, virtual learning environments, and digital educational cooperation. To address security concerns in computer-supported collaborative learning environments, a novel trustworthiness-based methodology is proposed in Chapter 10. The methodology discoursed data security in e-learning by addressing vital security-related issues.

Chapter 11 highlights the need for banks to reassess their competitive advantages in light of advancements in computer technology and competition from FinTech companies. While banks should not abandon relationship banking, which involves direct interaction with clients and supports their long-term requirements and objectives, they may be tempted to enter the transaction banking business due to the availability of IT-driven economy of scale and competition from FinTech start-ups and IT corporations. The writing evaluates the role of distance, AI, and behavioural inclinations in decision-making, and provides recommendations for banking stability. The research in this chapter shows that relationship banking can overcome its disadvantages by adapting to changing realities.

Medical imaging is an essential tool in medical research, diagnosis, and treatment of diseases. It involves the creation of visual images of internal body structures and the function of internal tissues. The primary objective of medical imaging is to detect abnormalities in the body and to diagnose and treat various medical conditions. Chapter 12 discusses collaborative technologies to revolutionize medical imaging. The images generated are used to create a database of the normal structure and function of organs, making it easier to detect abnormalities. Collaborative technologies and Computer Supported Cooperative Work (CSCW) have the potential to collaborate medical experts remotely on the analysis and diagnosis of medical images.

The use of electronic health records and Deep Learning methods is becoming increasingly important in healthcare applications. Electronic Health Records (EHRs) allow patients to access and share their health information with others, which can improve the quality of care they receive and help healthcare professionals make better-informed decisions. EHRs can also facilitate communication between healthcare providers and patients, making it easier for patients to ask questions, receive advice, and manage their health more effectively. However, ensuring the privacy and security of EHRs is crucial to prevent unauthorized access or data breaches. Chapter 13 addresses the issue of healthcare data management and classification using machine learning and blockchain technologies. The use of blockchain technology ensures the security and privacy of the data, and the application of machine learning algorithms improves the accuracy and efficiency of the classification process. A solution that aims to improve the security, privacy, and trust management of cloud-based EHRs, and to prevent harmful assaults and server non-repudiation is proposed in the chapter.

Dr. N.S. Gowri Ganesh, one of the editors of this book, worked at C-DAC, a scientific society of the Government of India, recognized the significance of books related to the latest technological implementations in the government sector for its stakeholders. We believe that this book will be useful for research scholars, the teaching community, and government officials involved in decision-making.

Kavita Saini
Galgotias University, India

A. Mummoorthy
Malla Reddy College of Engineering and Technology, India

Roopa Chandrika
Department of Information Technology, Malla Reddy College of Engineering and Technology, India

N. S. Gowri Ganesh
Saveetha Engineering College, India

Chapter 1
A Survey on Cyber Security and AI–Based Industry 4.0:
Advances in Manufacturing Technology and Its Challenges

Bramha S. Tripathi
https://orcid.org/0000-0001-9690-0545
Indian Institute of Technology, Delhi, India

Ritu Gupta
https://orcid.org/0000-0003-4616-3262
Galgotia University, India

ABSTRACT

Nowadays, industry 4.0 is very popular technology for industrial automation & rapid development of electrical and electronics technology, information technology, or advanced manufacturing technology. In this research concluded the challenges of cyber security and AI based industry 4.0, and discusses the key emerging technologies like internet of things, cloud computing, cyber security, artificial intelligence, etc., for making an industry 4.0 revolution. In this research the analysis of major issues and potential solution to key emerging technologies of new world is presented. This research gives the all-industrial revolution comparison analysis to growth of manufacturing industries and its benefits of different revolution. In this research paper give the analysis of why industry 4. 0 is best for the advanced manufacturing for growth of industries. This chapter provides a holistic view of cyber security and artificial intelligence in the industry 4.0 landscape, identifying and analyzing its fundamental concept, challenges, and ongoing future trends.

DOI: 10.4018/978-1-6684-7697-0.ch001

INTRODUCTION

Industry 4.0 is the current trend new revolutionary technology of automation and advanced manufacturing. It includes cyber security, Digital twin, Artificial intelligence, Internet of things, cloud computing, product design, robotics, and advanced system integration techniques. Industry 4.0 concept based on the innovation of "fourth industrial revolution", whose main objective is the integration and speed of production processes with use of advanced information technologies. It combines advanced manufacturing methods with new era digital technologies and different communications protocol technology. The fourth industrial revolution makes it possible to produce a product with superior quality and at a cost comparable to that of mass-produced items. The technical foundation for this notion is provided by intelligent, digitally interconnected systems and production methods. Industry 4.0 also describes the full life cycle of a product, starting with its conception and continuing through its development, manufacturing, use, and maintenance, and concluding with its recycling. (Federal Government of Germany, n.d.).

The industrial perspective has been changing over the past few years as a result of these distracting technical advancements. The Industry 4.0 concept supports a number of cutting-edge technological advancements that have an impact on both manufacturing products and its processes, going beyond the significance of conventional manufacturing transformation and smart, intelligent machines. This integration of the digital and physical worlds enables the production of advanced and intelligent products.

The combination of Web advancements and cutting-edge developments in the field of "smart" objects (machines and items) appears to result in a contemporary main worldview shift in mechanical generation, based on the premise of a sophisticated digitalization within industrial facilities. Future-generation manufacturing frameworks that are calculated and effective are depicted, along with situations where individual things are in charge of their own manufacturing planning. Usually intended to achieve bulk production costs while maintaining the ability to produce individual things in batches of one. This yearning for the future led to the creation of the term "Industry 4.0," which refers to a planned "4th mechanical revolution" and is a memory of program versioning.

Manufacturing sectors are taking a significant amount of interest in the innovative revolution in industries that is also known as the advanced manufacturing system Industry 4.0. For manufacturing industries all over the new world, operational manufacturing efficiency, productivity, and customized characteristics are absolutely necessary (Ervural & Ervural, 2017).

The traditional manufacturing industry is undergoing a revolutionary change as a result of the digitalization of manufacturing, which is being aided by advancements in sensors, artificial intelligence, robotics, and networking technology. This change is prompting a rethinking of manufacturing as a service. Concurrently, there is a movement in demand away from the production of goods in large quantities and toward the production of things on an individual, batch-by-batch basis (Federal Government of Germany, n.d.).

As a result, the Fourth Industrial Revolution, as it is known, began. There are three primary stages in I4.0: First, industrial asset sensors that collect data closely resembling human emotions are used to acquire digital records and concepts. Fusion of sensors is the name given to it. The second step is the implementation of the data's analytical capability through analysis and sensor-based data visualization. Signal processing, as well as optimizing, visualizing, cognitive calculations, and high-efficiency computations, are just a few of the many background processes that are carried out. An industrial cloud supports a service system in order to manage the massive amount of data. Third, aggregate data must be turned into meaningful outputs employing additive manufacturing, autonomous robots, digital design, and simulation in order to translate information into action. Before being transformed into meaningful knowledge in the industrial cloud, raw data is processed using programs for data analysis (Lezzi et al., 2018).

Conventional machines must be converted into automated machines in order to enhance their overall performance and maintenance management with the interaction of their surroundings. Building an open, intelligent manufacturing platform for industrial networks of information is the aim of Industry 4.0. Real-time data monitoring, tracking of product status and positions, and holding of instructions to control production processes are the three main requirements of Industry 4.0.

The purpose of the paper is to close this conceptual, research, and industry 4.0 problem gap. The authors of this article discuss many Industry 4.0 revolutions, design concepts, elements, and problems that businesses should consider while implementing Industry 4.0 solutions.

Figure 1. New revolutionary technology for advance manufacturing: Industry 4.0

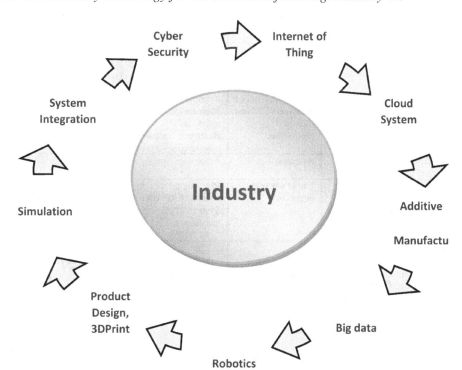

REVOLUTION HISTORY

The term "Industries 4.0" refers to the fourth industrial revolution, which is now taking place. Three earlier industrial revolutions occurred before this one in the history of the human race (Hermann, 2016).

1st Industrial Revolution introduces the machines into production by the end of the 18th century (1760-1840). In this 1st industrial revolution concept based on manual production with use of steam-powered engines and water as a source of power. This is called industry 1.0. In this Technology firstly adopted agriculture & textile industry by the British Industries.2nd Industrial Revolution focused on the development of a number of management programs that allowed for an increase in the efficiency and effectiveness of manufacturing facilities while also introducing pre-existing systems like telegraphs and railroads into industries using electricity as a power source. Industry 2.0 refers to this from the years 1870 to 1940. 3rd Industrial Revolution introduces the industries leaning on digital technologies in manufacturing. This revolution is called industrial 3.0 between 1950 -1980. This revolution allows the creation of software systems to connect electronic hardware, as well as integrated systems like material needs planning & supply chain management's formalization. Change from analogue and mechanical systems to digital ones is what is known as the "Digital Revolution" in this sector of the economy. The third revolution greatly aided the advancement of computers, information technology, and communication technology (Hermann, 2016).

Table 1. Comparison of the industries 1.0, 2.0, 3.0, 4.0 in various parameters

Parameter	Industry 1.0	Industry 2.0	Industry 3.0	Industry 4.0
Year of Inventions	1760-1840	1870-1940	1950-1980	2000
Based Technology	methods used in manufacturing that use steam and water.	Electrically powered manufacturing techniques enabled more advanced machinery and increased production.	Manufacturing processes using digital technologies. Which allows development of software systems to interface the electronic hardware Integrated systems	Intelligent machines, storage systems, and production facilities used in manufacturing can initiate activities, control one another, and share information without the need for human intervention.
Principal	Division of Labour	Assembly line	Automated Support	Smart Production
System Used	Mechanization of manufacturing with the help of power form	Use of electrical energy	PLC/Digital controls,ERP/MRP System, IT & automation	Cyber-Physical system, Smart Factories, IoT etc.
Example of use technology				
Efficiency of production	Low	Medium	Medium	High
Advantage	Industry 1.0 made the revolution of industry grow tremendously with a faster engine, transporting more goods in a shorter amount of time	very important role in Industry 2.0 by making auto cheaper and mass production and affordable for consumers	Industry 3.0 has boosted automation and productivity significantly to lower operational expenses for organizations.	Supply and demand must increase for Industry 4.0 of the Internet of Things (IoT) to be made possible by the rapid advancement of technology. The workforce's productivity generates the supply.

However, different experts' views of what Industry 4.0 actually means vary. The various definitions of Industry 4.0 provided by various researchers.

4

Table 2. Industry 4.0 definition by different researchers

Mrugalska & Magdalena (2017)	Kagermann, Wahlster & Johannes (2013)	Sharma and Gidwani (2019)	Schumacher, Erol & Sihn (2016)	Qin, Liu & Grosvenor (2016)
Modern and more advanced equipment and tools with cutting. Edge software and networked sensors can be utilised to plan, predict, adapt, and regulate societal outcomes and economic models to develop another phase of value chain industry.	Industry 4.0 uses cutting-edge technologies and communications technology to accelerate the growth of the industrial automation sector.	The idea of Industry 4.0 has been considered as a new dimension by the manufacturing industries, and several of them have already embraced it in a variety of ways.	There is industry 4.0, a cutting-edge technology. A new era of production methods is being ushered in by service, automation, artificial intelligence, robots, the internet of things, and additive manufacturing. A phenomena known as Cyber-Physical Production Systems appears as the line between reality and virtual reality blurs (CPPS).	The adoption of the most cutting-edge technologies will simplify the processes of collecting and analysing data. The Industry 4.0 operating capability that is interoperable offers a sustainable manufacturing environment.

DESIGN CONCEPT OF INDUSTRY 4.0

Industry 4.0 design principles enable easy-to-use advanced manufacturer systems and known information to explore a future transition to Industry 4.0 technologies. These are following conceptual design principal follow the industry 4.0:

Figure 2. Design concept of revolutionary technology for advance manufacturing: Industry 4.0

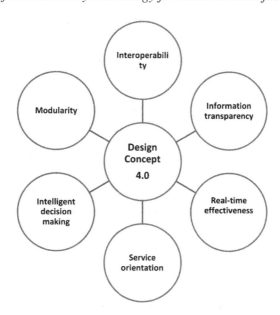

Concept of Industry 4.0

Interoperability

This concept of Industry 4.0 based on a product or system, whose interfacing and communication between human or system can be easily understood, to work with other products or systems without any restrictions. It involves accessing real-time data that leads the way to a new approach like IoT, Cloud, 3d Printing i.e. can improve their production operations.

Information Transparency

This concept based on the term of virtualization of the system. It means ability of system information build a virtual copy of real world for upgrading or improving the digitalize functionality of the smart manufacturing system. This virtualization helps to manage easily growing complexity reduce equipment downtime and optimize processes of the system.

Real-Time Effectiveness

This concept based on the collecting real time data store and analysis data. It is used for internal mechanisms such as machine failure in a production line, where the system will identify the problem and preload tasks onto other operational systems, in addition to industry market research. This concept will be helpful for the system flexibility and the optimization of advanced manufacturing system.

Service-Orientation

This idea assumes that assistance systems can help people by gathering and presenting data that is clear enough to help them make decisions and solve urgent problems quickly.

Intelligent Decision Making

This concept based on the self-decision making capability according to the environment condition & increase the bulk product with the demand of the product. This concept focuses the technology of artificial intelligence and resolves the various effects like self-diagnosis, configuration, and optimizations of the advanced manufacturing system according to working environment condition.

Modularity

This concept based on the ability to customize the product to a new market requirement. A sophisticated manufacturing system must be able to quickly and easily adjust to unforeseen changes and market trends.

Component of Industry 4.0

"Industry 4.0" is the fourth industrial revolution, academics and researcher still facing the difficulty to accurate definition of this approach and also its relevant component which component define the why it is called industry 4.0 revolution . Hermann, Pentek, and Otto set out to research the key elements of industry 4.0 for their review (Hermann & Otto, 2015). The following components included in revolution of industry 4.0.

Figure 3. Industries 4.0 components (as identified in the 51 publications under analysis)
Source: Hermann and Otto (2015)

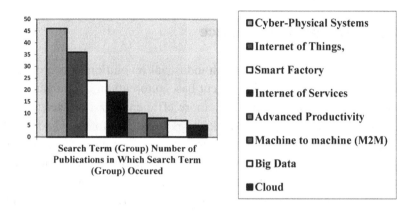

Cyber-Physical Systems (CPS)

Smart industrial systems and production plants need to be protected from cyber security threats more than ever as a result of Industry 4.0's increased connection and adoption of industry-standard communications protocols. Therefore, comprehensive identification and access management of devices and users, as well as secure, dependable communications, are necessary. Cyber Physical Systems (CPS) are automated systems that link computing and communication infrastructures with operations in physical reality (Federal Government of Germany, n.d.; Hermann, 2016). The emphasis in CPS is on networking several devices, in contrast to traditional embedded systems, which are developed as standalone units (Hermann, 2016). The CPS concept is combination of different technologies that provide the facilities of communications and integration between physical (machines, humans and other components) and different advanced computational technology (Lee et al., 2015). CPS is providing the Industry 4.0-enabled manufacturing environment that offers real-time data collection, analysis, and transparency across every aspect of a manufacturing operation. CPS Define the following concept:

- Cyber capability in physical components & different domain
- Provide the cyber and physical security
- Multiple scale of different networking
- Identifying the vulnerabilities of a CPS

Before tackling the security issues, the Industrial IoT's system assets (system components) should be identified. In the business world, an asset is a sensitive and priceless resource. Any IoT system's primary elements are its system hardware, software, services, and service data (including the buildings, machinery, etc.). The following benefits can be attained when the industrial assets have been located, which are generally associated with cybersecurity issues (i.e., in the contexts of I4.0).

- defining the system's inherent weaknesses that affect its security;
- defining the system's cyber threats;
- identifying the risks associated with cyberattacks;
- defining the countermeasures to deal with cybersecurity issues.

Internet of Things and Internet of Service

This is the very Import component to create fourth industrial revolution .it is a concept of integrating advanced manufacturing system, artificial intelligent base automation, and advanced system and data analytics to help make every worker and industry more efficient. First IoT term used by Germany's Industry 4.0 strategy has observed that we will make more use of the Internet and Internet of things for interactions between human and machines enabling intelligent manufacturing and producing the fourth revolution. The IoT includes different advanced sensors, communication module like GSM, GPS etc., laser scanners and other arbitrary objects, which can be connected to the Internet according to recognize protocol, for information interchange and communication in order to understand intelligent identification, location, tracking, system monitoring and system management (Zhou et al., 2015). Internet of service is one of the important components in the fourth industrial revolution. Internet of service concept based on the functionality of web services, social networks, interactivity, web services and service-oriented ecosystem.

Internet of service acts as "service merchants" to provide services through the internet according to the different types of digitalization services. They are available and on demand around business models, partners and any setup for services. This technology provides the network infrastructure to support a service-oriented ecosystem. IoS consists of participants, infrastructure services, business models and services themselves. Services are offered and merged into value-added services from different vendors, and communications via various communication channels. This approach allows different variants of distribution in the value Chain (Hercko, 2015).

Smart Factory

Smart Factory one of the popular components of fourth industry revolutions. It is the logical connection of Specific production steps, from preparing stages to actuators in the field. In industry 4.0, advanced manufacturing system and its machinery part will be adept to increase production processes through self-optimization; systems will freely modify to the condition of the system, development of the product design and network environment, which allows production of highly customized, flexible, and efficient products. Its basic objective is fed on the basis of information obtained online, so every moment possible to determine the condition, Status and position of the device. These systems observe their tasks on the basis of information from the real world as location or condition of the manufacture system, the information from the virtual world as electronic documents, drawings or simulation models. Only because the smart industries have more features than the conventional ones, as shown in Table 2 (Gröger, 2018), can this potential be realized. With these new additions, the plant is now more flexible and may alter without requiring human input to accommodate different product requirements. To adapt to the changing environment of manufacturing, the machines may negotiate and work together.

This is crucial in order to satisfy the demands of varied items made on the same production line. This has become more and more important in recent years as the emphasis has shifted from conventional mass production to customized customer -driven products, which necessitate that the same production line be capable of producing a variety of commodities. This is the smart factory's most notable main objective. Industry 4.0 has enormous potential, and more and more works are discussing how to use it (Behrendt et al., 2020).

Figure 4. Smart and traditional factories
Source: Gröger (2018)

Smart factory	Multiple Resources
	Adaptive Routing
	Strong convergence
	comprehensive connection
	Self-Organized
Traditional factory	Small Number of Fixed Resources
	Fixed Routing
	floor control network operation
	Separate Layers
	Separate Control

ARTIFICIAL INTELLIGENCE

The science and engineering of creating intelligent devices, particularly intelligent computer program, is known as artificial intelligence (John McCarthy). Because this technology is utilized in so many aspects of daily life, artificial intelligence has fundamentally altered our way of living. Industry 4.0 has recently undergone major improvements due to artificial intelligence (AI). Industries are concentrating on enhancing product uniformity, productivity, and lowering operational costs, and they hope to do this by collaborating with people and robotics. Hyper-connected production processes in smart industries are dependent on many devices that communicate via AI automation systems by capturing and processing all data types. Modern manufacturing can be transformed in significant ways by the use of intelligent automation technologies. AI delivers relevant information to aid in decision-making and alert the user of technical inaccuracies. Based on their aim to incorporate IoT devices and connected machines into their equipment, industries will process data transmitted from those devices using AI Technologies. It gives businesses the capacity to thoroughly track all of their end-to-end operations and procedures.

The promise of artificial intelligence in the fourth industrial revolution is the availability of pertinent data, computer power, and algorithms. It makes advantage of digital technology that have improved our intelligence and productivity and changed the way we interact, learn, shop, and play. With the development of computing systems that can see, hear, learn, and reason, artificial intelligence is opening new potential to enhance healthcare and education, combat poverty, and build a more sustainable future (https://aissmscoe.com/artificial-intelligence-and-its-impacts-on-industry-4-0-and-healthcare/). Industrial 4.0 AI stands out in five specific ways:

- **Data:** Requires large amount of data that comes from a range of units, products, regimes, etc.
- **Making Decisions:** Offer the industrial environment's often low tolerance for error, handling ambiguity is crucial. Efficiency is especially crucial for complex optimization issues.
- **Algorithms:** It demands the integration of cognitive, digital, and physical knowledge, model deployment, governance, and management.
- **Objectives:** Through a combination of factors like scrap reduction, higher quality, enhanced operator performance, industrial AI primarily focuses on concrete value creation.
- **Infrastructures:** Real-time processing capabilities for hardware and software are highly prioritized, enabling industrial-grade reliability.

Industry 4.0 AI research challenges can be divided into three categories:

Figure 5. Industry 4.0 AI research challenges

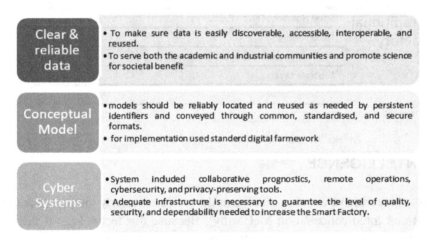

Five broad dimensions can be used to group the enabling technologies for industrial 4.0 AI: data, analytics, platforms, operations, and human-machine technology. Below is a description of these five dimensions:

- **Data Technique:** At every stage of the production process, more and more data is generated as a result of digitalization. These data can come from various sources at various levels of abstraction and can be structured, unstructured, or mixed.
- **Analytics Technique:** This technique is necessary to convert the unprocessed data obtained by Data technique into knowledge and, as a result, additional value for businesses. This integrates data processing at various levels, from the edge to the cloud, utilizing real-time data streams, and machine learning to enable continuous progress through self-learning processes and self-optimization.

- **Platform Technique:** Act as catalysts for the other technologies, allowing for the connection of multiple elements whether at the edge, fog, or cloud levels. Given the requirement for greater flexibility and agility, it is crucial that this technology include self-reconfiguration and self-organization capabilities.

- **Operations Technique:** The transition from analytical knowledge to actionable information supplied by decision-support systems requires the use of this technique. Combining operation technique with the prior technologies enables an operational change from experience-driven to data-driven production with improved operational maintenance and management.

Big Data

In 4th Industry revolution, big data refers to large sets of structured or unstructured system data that can be compiled, stored, organized, and analyzed to reveal patterns, trends, associations, and opportunities through the rapid development of the Internet. In industry 4.0, workshop equipment within the CPS will integrate sensor data and enterprise information systems. During this process, large volumes of data will be uploaded to a cloud computing data center to store, analyze, and form decisions, which will guide the production process. Big data and analysis will bring a range of benefits to manufacturing companies, such as optimizing processes, reducing costs, and improving operational efficiencies (Hermann & Otto, 2015). Industry-connected smart equipment have the capacity to produce enormous amounts of data. Data is collected from a wide range of sources, including advanced technologies, various flora, and the goods produced in the factories. Possibly, industrial big data both independently and in conjunction with other platforms, including as well as on-premise, cloud, and mobile/edge devices systems. Additionally, data visualization and analysis aid in the extraction of relevant insights from the data. The most popular are listed below (Jagatheesaperumal, 2021).

Figure 6. Analytical techniques used for industrial big data

Descriptive Analytics:	Predictive Analytics:	Prescriptive Analytics
• It relates to the interpretation and analysis of historical business data, enabling firms to more thoroughly examine and comprehend changes through time and their causes[27]. • Data aggregation and data mining are the two primary data collection methods used when gathering data for descriptive analysis[27].	• It enables sectors, companies, and organization to take the initiative by foreseeing future occurrences using data from the past[26]. • Predictive maintenance, product cost, lifetime, and failure prediction are some important uses. Industries might use historical and present data to accurately machine patterns, machine learning and other advanced analytic technologies[26].	• It enables sectors, companies, and organisations to base choices on historical data. • Predictive and prescriptive analysis are closely related, and the former uses the latter to determine a plan of action based on predictions given by predictive analytics methodologies. Prescriptive analytics are replacing predictive analytics in big data applications in contemporary industries [28].

M2M

This component based on the principal of machine-to-machine communication that appears between two separate machines through wireless or wired networks. It covers the interaction between many sophisticated manufacturing systems connected to the internet. These physical items have computing capabilities built in, allowing them to collect information about all linked systems and communicate it with other connected industrial systems.

1. **Machine Learning:** The ability for computer systems to learn and advance on their own through the use of artificial intelligence is provided by the machine learning process.
2. **Artificial Intelligence:** This idea is predicated on a computer's capacity to carry out operations and come to its own conclusions, both of which would require some degree of human intellect.

Advanced Productivity

Advanced products integrated into modern manufacturing process flows are able to self-development, collecting and storing data and communicate within the industrial environment. Now days advanced products don't only provide their identification, also explain their status and previous lifecycle. They are able to new era of computing algorithms and machine learning technologies, which composes them adept at processing productions stages resulting in the completed product and also forthcoming maintenance operations (Hermann, 2016).

With the advent of Industry 4.0, additive manufacturing techniques will be increasingly employed to create small quantities of bespoke goods with advantageous constructions, such intricate, lightweight designs. Systems for decentralized, high-performance additive manufacturing will shorten delivery routes and cut inventory levels. With the use of additive manufacturing techniques like fused deposition method (FDM), selective laser melting (SLM), and selective laser sintering, production should be quicker and less expensive (SLS)().3D Printing and Additive Manufacturing (AM): In 4th industry revolution, 3D Printing & additive manufacturing is one of the essentially tools. The implementation of advanced production skills for the purpose of integrating different digital technologies plays an important role in the competitiveness of the economy. The enterprise capacity of 3D printers is set to play an increasing role in the production of small series personalized products (Tay et al., 2018).

Cloud Computing

In 4th industrial revolution, Cloud Computing technology is an important factor in growth of digital transformation. This technology provides the connection between Data, Manufacturing system and Human. Data becomes valuable thing for industries, and its role will become a vital thing in the fourth coming future. Cloud computing refers to the practice of using interconnected remote servers hosted on the Internet to store, manage, and process information. Nowadays, advanced manufacturing systems are starting to adopt the latest Cloud Computing technology that can help you to overcome the challenges in the fourth industrial revolution such as application portability, dynamic routing, and Centralized platform administration (Hermann & Otto, 2015).

CHALLENGES OF INDUSTRY 4.0

Industry 4.0 is currently a vision for the future since it encompasses a wide range of topics and challenges, including security, standardization, automation and digitalization, employment, and privacy concerns (see in Figure 4). The development of smart gadgets, employment, big data analysis and processing, digital production, and privacy are some of the science and technology challenges that we primarily explore in this paper. For the manufacturing industry sector, there are numerous problems and difficulties in implementing industry 4.0. These issues and challenges are often brought on by Industry 4.0's still high implementation costs and a lack of awareness. A few of the challenges that come with adopting industry 4.0 in the industrial sector, particularly the manufacturing business, include financial constraints, low productivity, high labor costs, high logistical costs, and a lack of research and specialists in doing so (Broto & Indiarto, 2021). Here is a basic description of these difficulties.

Figure 7. Different challenges of Industry 4.0

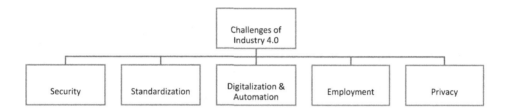

Security

In 4th industry revolution, Digital security is most challenging aspect of implementation. In deployments of industry 4.0 we use internet of service, internet of thing and cloud computing. They are stored the data information. For security of data leaks, cyber theft and security breaches must also be put into consideration, because this problem creates industrial loss and its reputation.

Standardization

Such for the development of industry 4.0, we needs globally norms and standards for common understanding. This industry 4.0 approach offer the opportunity to use the development of new technical systems across industries and sectors. There is no such thing as "Global standard for advanced manufacturing system". For creation of Initiatives for new global standards should be based on market requirement, driven by industry and other stakeholders. This is the import challenges for industry 4.0 development. This can be helping to create Collaboration between standards bodies and play the important role for mutual understanding of the different industry sectors.

Employment

For adoption of new technology and advanced manufacturing production, we need acquire different skills worker. This may improving the salary rate of employee but lack of new technology skill worker the important challenges in industry 4.0. we need to improved and trained the employee skill quality accordingly.

Privacy

This is the very crucial challenges of industry 4.0. This is not only the customers concern but also the manufacturer. The reason is this, an interconnected industry, manufacturer need to data collection and analysis. This can appear to be a threat to the customer's privacy. Different small- and large-scale businesses will have to make their way to a more transparent atmosphere by sharing their data going forward. So overcome this challenge bridging the gap between the customer and manufacturer and creates the global privacy rules for industry.

Opportunities in Industry 4.0

Figure 8. Opportunities in Industry 4.0

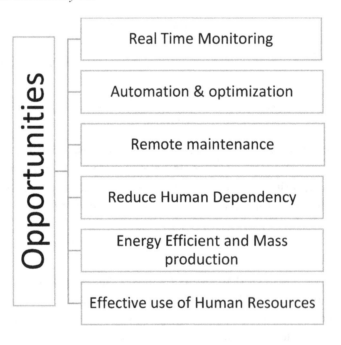

Future industrial developments The Future of Industry 4.0 focuses on important developments and how they affect modern smart industries, including those that move beyond Industry 4.0 and towards Industry 5.0. One of the fundamentally important elements of implementing Industry 4.0 is the industry's internal cultural transformation. To successfully implement smart manufacturing processes, this calls for strong leadership that is committed to altering the management process and investing in the innovative technological researcher and learner (Jagatheesaperumal, 2021).

- **Infrastructure Innovation in the Industrial Sector:** As concern about automated decision-making by intelligent industrial machines using AI develop, the necessity for reliable machines is becoming more crucial. Explainable artificial intelligence has evolved into a transparent strategy for predicting needs in the automated sector with the full adoption of Sector 4.0.
- As the smart industries advance towards Industry 5.0 and beyond, the IIoT will have a substantial impact on critical industrial sectors that control manufacturing, power, and chemicals. IIoT devices also improve status monitoring, cut manufacturing costs, increase production productivity, and offer more secure solutions.
- **Reconfigurable Factories:** Manufacturing procedures can be made flexible and rearranged in accordance with client demands and expectations. At a cost that is affordable for consumers, the product cycle of goods is adjusted to client needs with improved serviceability and scalability.

BENEFITS AND ACTION AREA OF INDUSTRY 4.0

Industry 4.0 offers a clever strategy for business expansion and a unique source of product value creation, particularly for advanced manufacturing industries. These are following benefits of industry 4.0.

1. Self-optimize production facilities
2. Customer-oriented facilities
3. Creates innovation opportunities
4. Improved productivity and efficiency
5. Higher revenues generation
6. Pushing in new technologies research for helping in education improvement and skilled labor
7. **Reduces Costs:** Due to facilities of proper utilization of resources, faster manufacturing, better quality, less machinery uses reason for reducing the cost of the products.

For analyzing the scheme of action, content was collected that described their main aims that is strategic guidelines, bases, preliminary areas, preliminary task, action plan. Finally, these following areas were listed.

- **Innovation and Research:** To develop leading-edge technologies and make advanced manufacturing system-based test beds.
- **Education and Training Facilities:** To coordinate and organize different workshop, conference for teaching of engineering students, and developed skilled manpower.
- **Advanced Infrastructure Modification:** With support the different digital technologies of SME enterprises and develop advanced production system.
- **Creating Business Environment:** To create different policies for support of various managements that is most impacted by the industry 4.0.

- **Develop Global Standards and Norms:** To standardize M2M communication and develop advanced production system for different industry. These methods provide the chance to leverage the creation of new technical systems across many industries and sectors.
- **Cyber Security and Network Security:** Secure production data security, cyber security and network system security.
- **Industry Showcasing:** To promote national industrial excellence abroad via different research showcase, conferences, magazine article, annual meet-up.

Figure 9. Benefits of Industry 4.0

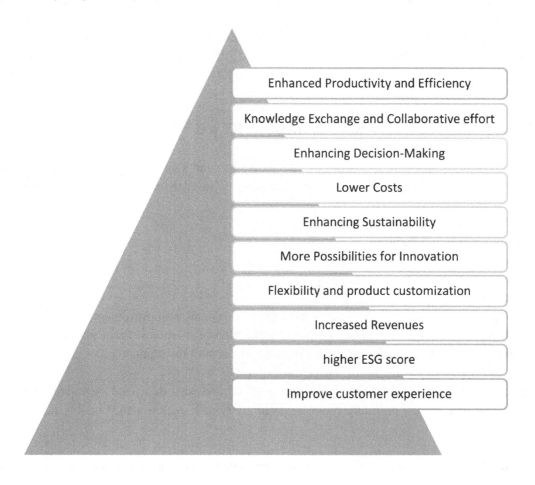

CONCLUSION

The fourth industrial revolution will integrate the physical and digital worlds in order to boost productivity and improve manufacturing. The literature review work adds to the continuing conversation around Industry 4.0 in both the scientific and professional communities. The research work establishes a common understanding of the phrase "Industry 4.0" by establishing a definition, which is necessary for an intelligent scientific conversation on the subject. Academics can discover, describe, and choose Industry

4.0 scenarios in the framework of additional investigations thanks to the design principles developed from the four fundamental Industry 4.0 components and its problems.

In this paper, we were able to come to the concluding remarks and conclusions. The future success of industries depends on digitization. A key factor is how quickly different industries adopt digitization. Organizations must become more adaptable to technological disruption, which is not solely dependent on technological advancements but also on staff members' capacity to adapt to changing working conditions and procedures. Employees must always stay up to date with technological advancements in order to keep up with the ever-changing environment. Operational excellence, which enables the creation of entirely stable, trustworthy, and predictable processes, is a requirement for smart industry applications. To reduce variations, enhance process capabilities, carry out predictive maintenance, and achieve zero defects and scheduled downtime, data analytics and the six-sigma approach are utilized. The goal of this study project was to provide an overview of the benefits, problems, and significance of Industry 4.0. When a company chooses to adopt this new method of producing, all of the organization's processes are affected by the connection of people, things, and systems that creates dynamic, real-time optimized, and self-organizing value creation networks across companies. This is what we tried to demonstrate in our review of the current and future features of the concept of Industry 4.0.

REFERENCES

Ahmad, K., Maabreh, M., Ghaly, M., Khan, K., Qadir, J., & AlFuqaha, A. (2020). Developing future human-centered smart cities: Critical analysis of smart city security, interpretability, and ethical challenges. arXiv preprint. doi:10.1111/deci.12451

Araz, O. M., Choi, T.-M., Olson, D. L., & Salman, F. S. (2020). Role of analytics for operational risk management in the era of big data. *Decision Sciences*, *51*(6), 1320–1346. doi:10.1111/deci.12451

Behrendt, A., Odenwälder, P., Müller, N., & Schmitz, C. (2020). *Industry 4.0 Demystified—Lean's Next Level McKinsey*. McKinsey. https://www.mckinsey.com/business-functions/operations/our-insights/industry-4-0-demystified-leans-next-level (accessed on 9 January 2020).

BMBF-Internetredaktion. (2016). *Zukunftsprojekt Industrie 4.0 - BMBF*. Bmbf.de.

Brad, S., Murar, M., & Brad, E. (2018, March). Design of smart connected manufacturing resources to enable changeability, reconfigurability and totalcost-of-ownership models in the factory-of-the-future. *International Journal of Production Research*, *56*(6), 2269–2291. doi:10.1080/00207543.2017.1400705

Broto, L. M. & Indiarto, B. (2021). Issues and Challenges in Implementing Industry 4.0 for the Manufacturing Sector. *Indonesia International Journal of Progressive Sciences and Technologies*, *25*, 650-658.

Ervural, B., & Ervural, B. (2017). Overview of Cyber Security in the Industry 4.0 Era. *Industry 4.0: Managing The Digital Transformation*, 267–284.

Federal Government of Germany. (n.d.). *Information on Industrie 4.0*. Federal Government of Germany. www. bmwi.de/ Redaktion/ DE/Dossier /industrie -40.html

Giraldo, J., Sarkar, E., Cardenas, A. A., Maniatakos, M., & Kantarcioglu, M. (2017). Security and privacy in cyber-physical systems: A survey of surveys. *IEEE Des. Test, 34*(4), 7–17. doi:10.1109/MDAT.2017.2709310

Gröger, C. (2018). Building an industry 4.0 analytics platform. *Datenbank-Spektrum: Zeitschrift fur Datenbanktechnologie: Organ der Fachgruppe Datenbanken der Gesellschaft fur Informatik e.V, 18*(1), 5–14. doi:10.100713222-018-0273-1

He, S., Ren, W., Zhu, T., & Choo, K.-K. R. (2020, February). BoSMoS: A BlockchainBased Status Monitoring System for Defending Against Unauthorized Software Updating in Industrial Internet of Things. *IEEE Internet of Things Journal, 7*(2), 948–959. doi:10.1109/JIOT.2019.2947339

Hercko, J. (2015). Industry 4.0 – New Era Of Manufacturing. In Conference: InvEnt. Demänovská.

Hermann, M. P. & Otto, B. (2015). *Design Principles for Industrie 4.0 Scenarios: A Literature Review.* Technische Universität Dortmund Fakultät Maschinenbau Audi Stiftungslehrstuhl Supply Net Order Management.

Hermann, P. O. (2016). *Design Principles for Industrie 4.0 Scenarios.* Academic Press.

Jagatheesaperumal, S. (2021). The Duo of Artificial Intelligence and Big Data for Industry 4.0. *Review of Applications, Techniques, Challenges, and Future Research Directions.*

Lasi, H., Hans-Georg, K, Fettke, P., Feld, T., & Hoffmann, M. (2020). Industry 4.0. Business & Information Systems Engineering, 4 (6), 239-242.

Lee, J., Bagheri, B., & Kao, H. A. (2015). A cyber-physical systems architecture for industry 4.0-based manufacturing systems. *Manufacturing Letters, 3*, 18–23. doi:10.1016/j.mfglet.2014.12.001

Lezzi, M., Lazoi, M., & Corallo, A. (2018). Cybersecurity for Industry 4.0 in the current literature: A reference framework. *Computers in Industry, 103*, 97–110. doi:10.1016/j.compind.2018.09.004

Rehse, J.-R., Mehdiyev, N., & Fettke, P. (2019). Towards explainable process predictions for industry 4.0 in the dfki-smart-lego-factory. KIKunstliche Intelligenz, 33(2), 181–187. doi:10.100713218-019-00586-1

Tay, L., Te Chuan, A. H., Aziati, N. (2018). An Overview of Industry 4.0: Definition, Components, and Government Initiatives. *Journal of Advanced Research in Dynamical and Control Systems.*

Wang, S., Wan, J., Li, D., & Zhang, C. (2016). Implementing Smart Factory of Industrie 4.0: An Outlook. *International Journal of Distributed Sensor Networks, 12*(1), 3159805–3159810. doi:10.1155/2016/3159805

Zhou, K., Liu, T., & Zhou, L. (2015). Industry 4.0: Towards Future Industrial Opportunities and Challenges. In *12th International Conference on Fuzzy Systems and Knowledge Discovery*. IEEE. 10.1109/FSKD.2015.7382284

Chapter 2
AI–Based Big Data Algorithms and Machine Learning Techniques for Managing Data in E–Governance

Prithi Samuel

SRM Institute of Science and Technology, India

Reshmy A. K.

 https://orcid.org/0000-0001-5835-5232

SRM Institute of Science and Technology, India

Sudha Rajesh

SRM Institute of Science and Technology, India

Kanipriya M.

SRM Institute of Science and Technology, India

Karthika R. A.

SRM Institute of Science and Technology, India

ABSTRACT

E-government is the effective and efficient delivery of high-quality information and governmental services to citizens and/or other governmental and non-government entities. Both the service provider and the citizens using the services will gain from big data analysis. Market Research indicates that 75% of government agencies are using big data to enhance the standard of living for individuals. Big data analytics gives a perspective into the effectiveness of government programmes and policies. In order to gauge public sentiment and comprehend citizens' thoughts and attitudes about government programmes, forecasting and prescriptive analysis suggests the optimal course of action. This chapter will provide a brief overview of key topics to help readers fully comprehend how big data is used across the government department.

DOI: 10.4018/978-1-6684-7697-0.ch002

INTRODUCTION

E-governance has become more and more important as customers have become familiar with the idea of their data obligations. It consists of a number of measures, standards, guidelines, and procedures that enable businesses to use the data properly and responsibly. Their usage of data must be productive and efficient in pursuing their goals. A comprehensive business intelligence and information analytics solution called a big data analytics framework uses both traditional and big data. Data is gathered by the government's analytical engine from a variety of sources, including the world wide web, social networks, devices, machinery logs, and other datasets maintained by various government departments. This causes the amount of transaction data generated by e-government to expand dramatically, increasing the need for big data analytics. They are transformed and presented in an analyzer-friendly way by this analytical engine. In this sense, e-governance includes duties and procedures for ensuring that data utilised by an organisation is secure and of high quality. Transactional data is increasing dramatically as a result of global and Indian e-Governance initiatives, making it challenging to examine such a massive number of data housed across numerous sites using conventional data mining methods. The government will be able to make better judgments thanks to it, and the public will receive timely and accurate information. In terms of efficient service delivery, result rather than output determines whether an e-Government project succeeds. The vast majority of the states and governments in India are concentrating on harnessing emerging technology to provide citizen services, improve the effectiveness of how the government functions, and find new methods to raise money. "Big Data Analytics" is a significant revolutionary innovation that affects both corporations and the governments. An integrative business intelligence and information analytics solution called a big data analytics software uses both traditional and big data. Data is gathered by the government's aeronautical engineer from a variety of sources, including the web, social networks, detectors, machinery records, and other datasets maintained by various government agencies. This causes the rate of transaction data generated by e-government to expand dramatically, increasing the need for big data analytics. They are transformed and presented in an analyzer-friendly way by this difference engine. Market Research reveals that 75% of government agencies are using big data to enhance the standard of living for individuals. Big Data Analytics offers insights into the effectiveness of administration practises and initiatives. In order to gauge public sentiment and comprehend citizens' thoughts and attitudes about government programmes, prescriptive and anticipatory analysis suggests the optimal course of action. Structured and unstructured data are the two types of big data. Structured data provides information that is typically kept in manual processes or enterprise applications, such as real estate taxes, construction permits, criminal backgrounds, and car records. Social networking, emails, movies, photos, and other types of unstructured data are examples.

Through citizen-government integrations, AI has the potential to improve e-governance assistance. For instance, the government of Andhra Pradesh in India collaborated with Microsoft to develop Kaizala, an AI-assisted app. Kaizala served as a citizen-government interaction, directing citizen questions to the proper government organization. The app may also be utilized by the government to provide computer-controlled notifications to its inhabitants. As a result of these AI-assisted interfaces, authorities can better regulate their citizens.

The vision of e-Governance (Picciano 2012) is to "Make all Public Services more accessible to the ordinary citizen in his local area, through widely accepted delivering services channels and achieve effective, consistent and trustworthy data at minimal expense. The primary goal of e-Governance is to achieve five primary objectives (Alshomrani & Qamar, 2013): a strategic framework, improved public service, slightly elevated and cost-effective governmental agencies, participation of citizens in democratic principles, and organizational and administrative legislative change. In India, the Department of Electronics and Information Technology (DeitY) and the Dept of Administrative Reforms and Public Grievances (DARPG) have developed the National e-Governance Plan (NeGP) (NeGP Website, 2014). More than 1000 eGovernance facilities have mostly been accessed via NeGP, according to NeGP. The e-taal (Electronic Transaction Aggregation and Analysis Layer) is a government web website that offers statistics on electronic payments performed by citizens participating in e-Governance projects. As per the e-taal, Indians completed over 350 million e-transactions in the previous year.

Illusion of E-Governance

Democracy should emphasize a personally responsible and open government, idealised zero corruption, a strong legal system, liberal values, and tolerance of various viewpoints. The executive, legislative, and judicial branches of government should be separate and autonomous in order to best uphold these principles. The support and simplification of democratic accountability or operations for the government, managers/administrators, citizens, and corporate entities is the strategic goal of e-Government. All parties can be connected through ICT usages, and processes and events can be supported. Other goals include improving administration's efficiency, responsiveness, and accountability while meeting society's demands and expectations through improved political services and communication between the public, private sector, and government. According to Akinfenwa (2014), the goals of e-Government are to reduce wasteful paper use and storage capacity by converting important records and documents to electronic files, enhance efficiency and productivity, boost administrative process efficiency, and minimise the organisational burden placed on staff.

Role of AI and ML in E-Governance

AI ensures that data reaches the intended recipient without being intercepted by cybercriminals using man-in-the-middle, spear spam email, malware, adware, and any other cyber - attacks. AI, in essence, is democratizing data governance. For example, in intelligent automated discovery, AI is used to analyze behavioral data collected during information processing. Recordings are inferred from behavioral data in this circumstance. Businesses can detect anomalies by incorporating AI into their processes. For example, if a data centre suffers a breach, the organisation can persuade an AI-based solution to recognize any cyber-attack. It must go across algorithms for machine learning and absorbs massive amounts of information for this purpose. As a consequence, whenever a cyberattack begins to emerge, AI can detect the template and inform the authorities before sensitive information is compromised. This also implies that AI can significantly improve data privacy, conformance, and reliability. As a result, businesses can make sure that they possess a 24/7 shield who, unlike human resource management, can continuously monitor their transmitted data.

Depending on the industry, various sources generate a variety of information. Many organisational government agencies have been exploring ways to use data to improve their operational processes. Sales personnel, for example, can benefit from studying customer preferences. Many organisations now use predictive analytics to enhance the effectiveness of their operational processes. Correspondingly, manufacturing companies are heavily investing in artificial intelligence for analytics. They hope to accomplish this by identifying industry requirements and adapting their manufacturing techniques consequently.

Benefits of AI Based Big Data Algorithms and ML In E-Governance

Law Enforcement

A key role in any governmental architectural style is the effective policing and regulation of the law. AI system integration can improve and digitise current features and capabilities for better law enforcement implications. Law enforcement is developing and giving in-depth knowledge about the legal violations taking place in the contemporary world. This includes the use of face recognition, voice recognition, unmanned aerial vehicles, battle droids, automated proto automobiles, prescriptive modelling, and cyber defence. These systems aid in quickly containing and resolving problems.

Automating Routine Tasks

Paperwork is a necessary component of most governmental institutions in underdeveloped and developing nations. It can be time-consuming and occasionally nerve-racking to assign, perform, and pass files between departments when they are necessary for making crucial decisions. Therefore, implementing repetitive tasks reduces paperwork, speeds up query responses, and gives government agencies more time to work on other issues related to development.

Modernizing Security and Privacy Mechanisms

The government has data on the populace, officials, businesses, etc. To prevent malfunctions of private information, this information must be secured and shielded from fraudsters. By incorporating machine learning algorithms that detect interruptions in the database file and protect the data from cyber criminals, integrating AI systems can aid in computerising and security protocols.

Rapid Crisis Reaction

Due to internal structural hierarchical processes, governments' responses, and actions during emergencies (natural calamities or significant industrial accidents) may be delayed. The government can predict the climate and other factors that aid in taking action in advance with the help of automated systems powered by predictive analytics and AI.

Challenges and Obstacles of AI Based Big Data Algorithms and ML In E-Governance

Incremental Data Influence

There's a rationale for how some data now is known as "big data." Data production and retrieval have increased at an increasing rate. Computer technology is exploding. The number of data-storage devices has grown. These devices progressed from laptops and desktops in the 1990s to smartphones and tablets by the end of the 2000s. With the growth of IoT, an increasing number of devices are becoming internet-connected, including wearable technology, fitness bands, fridges, TVs, home surveillance systems, and even wall clocks. Whereas these changes are welcomed, the influence of this information explosion on organisations requires careful consideration. They require a dependable infrastructure capable of handling all of this data.

Upgrade from Enterprise Systems

Enterprise systems cannot meet modern information requirements and must be phased out. Moreover, the transition to modern models is difficult. You must create a platform for the innovative system that incorporates adaptability, confidentiality, and conformance.

Observance of the Framework

The effective implementation of AI is dependent on having significant exposure to all sources of data. Statistics must be free of bias and comprehensive, and your data-related functional areas must follow your data governance mechanisms.

Ethical Implications and Responsibilities of E-Governance

GDPR (General Data Protection Regulation) and CCPA (California Consumer Privacy Act) are two recent guidelines aimed at improving user data. They establish a set of minimal level requirements that must be adhered to. Failure to comply with their requirements may lead to serious ramifications.

Some of the most innovative data-driven organisations have gone over and above these regulatory requirements in terms of how they interact with consumers and their data. Examine the performance of Io-Tahoe, a company that provides intelligent data discovery solutions. It recognised the importance of PII (personal identifiable information) security, but it now actively assists its customers in working with confidential documents such as PII.

However, GDPR remains the low-bar for the vast majority of businesses. At the moment, AI has incredibly low ethical standards. Despite the fact that many SEC registrants have raised concerns about AI's vulnerabilities, it is clear that business owners are not concentrating on or investing in this area.

Organizations in regulated industries are attempting to address AI ethics as well as data governance. Their position has elevated them to the status of facto representatives in AI ethics. Nonetheless, efforts to develop a sustain for AI ethics in the United States are hindered by a lack of data security and data governance. As a result, a few analysts claim that Europe would be the first to develop an AI ethics legislation structure within the next 5 years. Besides deciding to take one's AI morality sincerely, users can increase public confidence in one's firm. One's artificial intelligence systems must:

- Every person should be fairly treated.
- Individuals must be engaged and empowered.
- Operate effectively and consistently
- Appreciate for privacy and security of information
- Implement computational responsibility.

AI and Big Data Governance

The use of artificial intelligence is quickly growing throughout numerous industries. This technology is driving continuous advances in the decision-making processes and overall performance of numerous sectors. It also helps to increase customer understanding, service quality, and risk prediction and prevention.

It is necessary for enterprises to develop a comprehensive data governance framework in order to realise the full potential of their data.

As consumer awareness of their data rights increases, data governance becomes increasingly important. It includes a set of performance measures, benchmarks, guidelines, and procedures that give companies the tools they require to utilize correct information ethically. Their use of data must be effective and efficient while they are continuing to pursue their objectives. Thus, data governance comprises duties and methods for the security and quality of an organization's utilised data.

Data governance is the collection of procedures designed to effectively manage data. Enterprise data availability, usability, integrity, and security must be ensured by appropriate policies. In machine learning, data governance procedures ensure that all organisational stakeholders have access to high-quality data at all times.

Gradients of Data Quality

As in computer science, the adage "garbage in, garbage out" holds true in machine learning. This implies that even the most sophisticated machine learning model will perform badly if fed poor-quality data. How then would one measure data quality prior to its actual use? A data quality evaluation method begins with the definition of a list of data dimensions. Data dimensions are original data characteristics that can be assessed against predetermined standards. Among the most prevalent data dimensions are:

Accuracy

It determines the reliability of a dataset by comparing it to a known, reliable reference dataset. If refers to a single data field and is typically associated with the amount of outliers generated by database errors, sensor malfunctions, improper data gathering tactics, etc.

Timeliness

It is the delay between data generation and acquisition and its use. Data utilised after it was obtained may be obsolete or no longer reflect the physical phenomenon it is attempting to explain.

Completion

It refers to the proportion of available data, or the absence of missing information.

Consistence

When identical data located in separate storage places can be regarded equivalent, it is consistent (equivalent can have several meanings from perfect match to semantic similarity).

Integrity

High-integrity data adheres to the syntax (format, type, range) of its description, as specified by a data model, for instance.

AI'S FUNCTION IN DATA GOVERNANCE

In an effort to gain a competitive advantage in data analytics, firms are constantly searching for effective solutions. If AI is configured with data governance policies, you can extract the most value from your data. AI assists data management in determining which practises are ineffective and which are successful.

Based on the associated industry, several data sources offer a vast array of information. Numerous organisational departments have sought to leverage data to improve operations. For instance, sales departments that investigate consumer trends can gain valuable insights. Numerous businesses have adopted predictive analysis to improve the efficacy of their company operations.

Similarly, manufacturing facilities are investing extensively in AI for analytics. They intend to identify industry requirements in order to change their manufacturing methods accordingly.

AI is employed for maintenance purposes as well. When quality is compromised owing to a certain machine, analytics identifies the underlying problem. Management is then responsible for determining whether predictive maintenance is required.

With the addition of AI, firms can discover irregularities. For instance, organizations could indeed train an Intelligence approach to recognize any cyber-attack if a cloud infrastructure experiences a breach. It uses algorithms from machine learning and utilizes a sizable amount of data to accomplish this. As a result, when a cyber-threat arises, AI can spot the pattern and notify the appropriate parties before data is hacked. This implies that a significant portion of privacy protection, conformance, and security controls can be automated using AI. As a result, companies can guarantee that expressing personal data transmission are monitored by a guard who, in contrast to human resources, is accessible around-the-clock, every day of the week.

AI makes sure that information reaches its target without being tampered with by cybercriminals using man-in-the-middle, javelins spam email, computer viruses, trojan horses, and any other type of cyberattack. Democratizing AI is democratising data governance. In automated process discovery, for instance, AI is used to examine behavioral data created during data processing. Behavioral data are derived in this manner into digital recordings.

Policies and Guidelines

Data Governance Strategies

With a proper data governance plan, a business can enjoy the following benefits:

- Data governance enhances data quality. It provides a standard to ensure that data is uniform, comprehensive, and correct.
- Data governance enables enterprises to discover the location of essential entity data through a useful capability. This facilitates seamless data integration.

- A 360-degree vision can be utilized by businesses to comprehend clients and other commercial firms.
- Data governance involves ensuring they own a framework that is effective for complying with laws like HIPAA and GDPR or regulatory requirements like PCI DSS (Payment Card Industry Data Security Standards).

In a data-driven and automated world, data governance enhances data management by introducing the human element. It develops norms of behaviour and best practices for data management. Consequently, topics that are normally disregarded in data, such as compliance, security, and legal, are addressed effectively.

Consider the following recommendations for formulating effective data policies:

Connect Data Policies TO Their Respective Business Contexts

This will increase the perception of their significance and motivate compliance.

Align Data Policies With a Structured Measurement Structure

Teams responsible for data governance should create metrics for each data policy in order to quantify the impact of each policy on business goals and other intended outcomes. A measuring framework provides the techniques and instruments necessary to evaluate and quantify the degree to which data sets conform to predefined standards. This will facilitate the work of data stewards to standardise implementation, monitoring, and correction.

Determine the Reach of Data Policies

The scope of a data policy defines both its organisational and technical context. Consider whether each data policy applies to the entire organisation, a single business unit, or a specific workgroup. Determine technically if it pertains to the complete data model, particular tables, or individual data items.

Big Data Framework for E-Governance

Improved openness, accountability, efficiency, and efficacy in the next generation of e-government and healthcare could lead to more intelligent governance. It enables businesses to resolve issues successfully by utilising the advantages of information through big data analysis. Big Data is now prevalent and has a big impact on many global industries.

The majority of components are taken from reputable frameworks of several countries that successfully implemented big data in e-government in order to lower risk of big data projects and help government agencies understand clearly about the steps of big data implementation to take advantage of its benefits for effective governance (Dwivedi et.al, 2019). The Big Data for E-Government framework, often known as BDFEG, is depicted in Figure 1 below. Its layers and components are summarised below.

Servers, operating systems, networking systems, storage systems, user interfaces, and other elements are included in the platform layer.

Figure 1. A big data framework for e-governance (BDFEG)

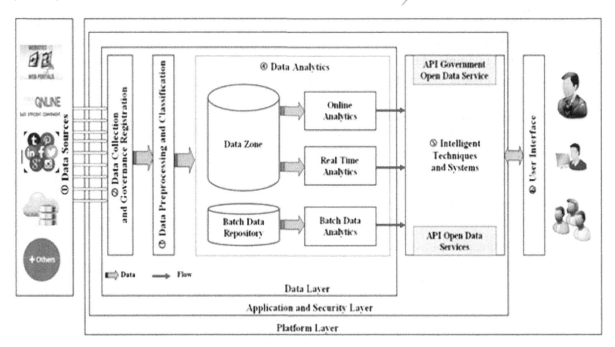

Data collection and governance registration, data preparation and categorization, and data analytics are the three primary parts of the data layer. This layer offers both real time and batch processing options for data. The following is a succinct overview of the major elements of the data layer:

First, intelligent approaches encompass platforms or architectures as well as advanced data processing techniques (data mining, machine learning, deep learning, etc). (web services, microservices). They will be applied in the future to create intelligent systems.

After doing data analysis and applying intelligent approaches, intelligent systems will then be constructed. They include expert systems, recommendation systems, expert systems for making predictions, and other similar systems.

Additionally, this component offers two different types of API (Application Program Interface). The API government open data service helps government organisations create intelligent systems, while the API open data service aids corporations, universities, hospitals, healthcare providers, and developers, among other sectors.

The BDFEG's physical implementation will make more sense of the application and security layer's systems of applications and safety-assuring solutions. The most significant element in this layer is specifically intelligent approaches and systems, which it refers to following data analysis as vital parts.

Data sources (such as internal databases, websites/portals, online public service systems, statistical systems, financial systems, social networks, and so forth) are accessed during the first step of data collection and governance registration.

Data collection in the first stage will be cleaned in the second step through data pre-processing and classification. This component is in charge of formatting input data so that it is ready for analysis.

Finally, there are two distinct categories of directories in business intelligence. The data region serves to store data gathered from electronic services (internet sites, public online services, social networking sites, etc.), whereas the bulk data archive is utilized to store data sources in DBMSs. (such as Hadoop HDFS, NoSQL, and other systems). Three different types of analytics are also included in the component: batch, internet, and real-time analytics. Additionally, this component includes three additional types of data analytics. To handle newly created data, real-time analytics and website traffic are commonly used.

Big Data Dimensions for E-Governance

The theoretical basis for the many facets of e-governance is shown in Figure 2.

Figure 2. E-governance dimensions

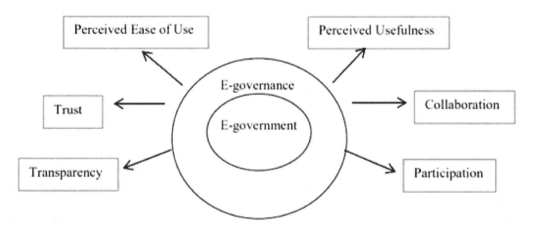

A subset of e-governance is referred to as e-government. The primary goal of e-government should be to enable e-governance; it should not only be a way for the government to disseminate information, share information among agencies, and facilitate online transactions. Perceived usability, perceived utility, and trust in government websites all have a big impact on e-government. E-government then contributes to the larger idea of e-governance, which calls for cooperation from government representatives in order to transform official websites into a platform for democratic discourse, citizen participation, and transparency in order to ensure the success of e-governance initiatives. Therefore, the six aspects of e-governance are used to evaluate it: PEOU, PU, collaboration, trust, participation, and transparency.

The PEOU measures how much a person thinks the system would operate automatically. In other words, how simple it would be to pick up the new system, use it, and become proficient at it while evaluating how clear, comprehensible, flexible, and controllable it is.

Perceived usefulness (PU) measures how much people think a certain system would improve their ability to accomplish their jobs. PU is the citizen's perception of the extent to which government websites can assist them in finding all the information they need and finishing their work more quickly. PU also depends on the e-government services provided, such as filing tax returns and applying for a new passport or provisional licence.

Trust is the belief in the government's dependability and integrity when delivering services online. For people to conduct business online and divulge personal information, trust is a key factor. The lack of trust could result in a rejection of electronic governance and significant disruptions to its ongoing usage.

In order for citizens to receive seamless public services without having to comprehend the complex structure of government, the collaboration dimension gauges the degree to which technology may be used to combine information and services across various government departments. Collaboration aims to improve front-office public service delivery, back-office productivity, and overall governmental interoperability.

The notion of governing with people is the foundation of participation. It entails the use of the Internet to include the public in government decision-making. It encapsulates the degree to which people believe they are a member of a democracy in which they believe their opinions are valued and taken into account when making choices.

By enabling numerous persons to express their opinions at any time that is convenient for them and at a lower coordination cost than in the traditional citizen engagement process, online participation makes citizen engagement simple, quick, and efficient. Citizens now receive input from government officials thanks to the development of information and communication technology, and decision-making is more open and transparent. This brings us to the final e-governance dimension, transparency.

The following are the main advantages of using big data analytics in e-governance projects:

Governments should improve the availability of information and services online for business analytics.

- Creating process transparency
- Performance tracking and visualisation
- Predicting societal demands
- Obtaining knowledge and insights to improve current initiatives and launch new ones.
- Providing better services to citizens.

Data Science in E-Governance

E-governance always refers to good governance, which is the provision of services to the public. The service is also reasonably priced. The government must prioritise and fully utilise information and communication technology (ICT) in order to improve service delivery. The goal is no longer just process automation or conversion from a manual to a computerised system. To boost throughput, machine learning, data mining, and artificial intelligence will also be used in e-government. In order to analyse services, their effects on society, and their sustainability for the socioeconomic development of the country, big data and its analysis are also used.

The epidemic Covid-19 has struck the world in a horrifying way, and nearly all of the governments are working extremely hard to protect both their economies and the safety and security of their population. The advantages of data science and artificial analysis can be investigated during such periods. Data has made it possible to track Covid-19 patients, the source of transmission, and potential outcomes; this is a prime example of data science in the modern era. The availability of open data on websites like Kaggle gives academics the chance to create various solutions and enhance them.

The Government of India is utilising data in order to develop analytical frameworks and broaden its e-Governance projects throughout the entire nation, realising the importance of data as a national resource. Even in India's hinterland, smartphone penetration and data consumption are rising, giving the government more tools to create evidence-based policies, better target welfare programmes for the underprivileged, and digitally enlighten residents with data-driven information.

As evidence of this, the government decided to geotag the entire agriculture industry, which is the backbone of India's economy and the primary source of income for millions of people, in order to increase its security and profitability. Using remote sensing and data analysis, its potent software, Forecasting of Agriculture outputs using Satellite, Agro-meteorology and Land-based observations (FASAL), enables farmers to forecast the yield of important crops and thereby boost their revenue for a better life.

Government may make extensive use of data science. By utilising predictive causal analytics, prescriptive analytics, and machine learning, it can assist in obtaining valuable knowledge and information from vast amounts of data in order to improve government decision-making or in giving the insights needed to make data-driven decisions. Through enhanced predictive analytics, for instance, the government can use the data to address implementation gaps, identify overlaps, target the appropriate recipients, and contribute to wise policy making.

Only data that has passed quality control without substantial issues is suitable for consumption by third parties and for use in machine learning model development.

We spend a considerable amount of time assessing data quality. We use a continuous approach to data monitoring, beginning with data collection, cleaning, and transformation and continuing through data integration and model construction. This 'whole pipeline' strategy expedites the creation and debugging of our models and ensures their superior performance. When a model fails to perform as planned, the data scientists who adhere to our technique know precisely what to modify.

Obviously, the true value of data rests in its contribution to an organization's decision-making processes. Implementing a data governance structure ensures the quality of an organization's data, which is a prerequisite for adopting artificial intelligence for business processes.

Data governance is an absolute necessity for any organisation. Because accurate information always leads to sound conclusions.

AI AND BIG DATA USE CASES IN E-GOVERNANCE

Big Data is a key idea in Industry 4.0 since it helps to improve governance's usefulness and productivity. Big data analytics (BDA) offers benefits to both businesses and governments through a variety of intelligent systems, including intelligent monitoring, intelligent decision-support, and intelligent prediction systems (Jadhav et.al, 2018). The use of big data is essential for intellectual power. Intelligent governance models and procedures might be affected in a "game-changing" way by the new technology and goods. While such technologies may be "game-changing," which is a huge problem for all stakeholders in governmental and commercial information systems.

The underlying platform for IoT and AI application development and use is BDA. For example, intelligent technological tools can decipher conversation, audio, and handwriting. BDA will therefore help generate future AI systems and other intellectual schemes. They can use some intellectual techniques, such as machine learning, deep learning, and other similar ones, to learn by themselves through contact with people or other systems. BDA is still problematic, however, due to current noteworthy restrictions, such as the need for very influential processing computers, the on-going study of innovative tools for storing and processing large and unstructured databases, and the ever-increasing demand for highly accurate prediction systems among humans.

Social Welfare Schemes

Reaching the appropriate people at the appropriate time is the main difficulty for public welfare programmes. This is made increasingly harder in nations with large populations, like India. However, these programmes' reach may be expanded by AI-powered systems. For instance, in the government's mid-day meal programme, process automation technologies can guarantee that food reaches the beneficiaries on schedule while machine learning and supply chain management can forecast the inventory.

Predictive Policies and Surveillance

Although the efficacy and fairness of AI in predictive policing are still debatable, it offers benefits when applied properly. Palantir's law enforcement solution, for instance, may geo-search the area around interesting places and predict where and when the next crimes would happen.

Governments may aid in the identification of criminals by using AI surveillance, where ML algorithms analyse the photos, videos, and data captured on CCTVs. However, racial profiling and examples of human rights violations are clogging up the ethical side of AI-powered monitoring. After receiving a lot of criticism, IBM really ceased creating or selling face recognition technologies for mass monitoring.

Documentation

The simplest method to embrace AI is in this way. This comprises the extraction and entry of correspondence, legal papers, certifications, and invoices. For government workers, automating content creation using NLG may save up a lot of time so they can concentrate on other crucial tasks. The conversion of official documents into several languages is made simple by AI. For instance, Korea utilised AI-based real-time translation services for the 2018 Winter Olympics in PyeongChang.

Military Intelligence

The planning, initiation, integration, and development of new AI capabilities are carried out by specialised departments or agencies in many nations. Examples include the UK's AI Council, the Strategic Council for AI Technologies in Japan, and the US's National Science and Technology Council. Unmanned combat aerial vehicles, or UAVs, are autonomous military drones that are often used in the military (UCAV). For instance, in Nagorno-Karabakh, Azerbaijan utilised drones to attack Armenia.

Predicting Natural Calamities

AI-powered systems are able to track forest dryness, forecast wildfires, analyse earthquake magnitude and patterns, record rainfall, simulate flooding, utilise seismic data to predict volcanic eruptions, and forecast hurricanes using satellite imagery. AI can aid in our readiness for catastrophes and prevent the tragedies that force majeure may bring about.

Other Use Cases

- The Chabot's can be used to plan meetings, giving directions for the requests to the concern department, appointing support and responding to FAQs.
- The appropriate social media posts for opinions from the residents can be analysed using data analytics on the usefulness of the amenities.
- High prioritized calls can be arranged using speech processing technologies and ML algorithms.
- Personalized tutoring is provided in government schools
- Social media posts related to dangerous roadways can be tracked and respond right away.
- Instance recognition can also materialize using NLP practises.

APPLICATION AREAS OF BIG DATA IN E-GOVERNANCE

The goal of e-Government is to "Make all Public Service available towards the Common Person in his Local area, through Pervasive Delivering Services Channels and achieve effective, consistent and trustworthy data at minimal expense," according to the statement of vision of the concept (Picciano, 2012). A legislative framework, improved government service, high-quality and premium governmental agencies, civilian interaction in participatory democracy, and organizational and administrative restructure are the five major objectives of e-Government (Alshomrani, 2013) that it aims to achieve.

EDUCATION

By empowering teaching assistantships, internship opportunities, and some other aspects of the functional application of abilities that earn students real-world opportunity to be exposed, or otherwise—most educational establishments merely barely scratch the surface of supplemental skill development. The next dilemma is to find the best and most beneficial internship opportunities, which is a "mini-scale job seeking" in and of itself (Pereira, et.al, 2018). Upskilling the educator according to their strengths and choosing the appropriate technical skills is intelligent instruction.

Nevertheless, work placements are much simpler to obtain in just about any company than a teaching assistantship, and the business world is aware of the necessity for students to acquire actual experience. Therefore, it makes sense to investigate the extra abilities that aid students in getting aware of the difficulties of the corporate sector.

- Tracking students: identifying the diverse elements that influence their achievement.
- School Location: Choosing and planning the location that will be preferable for an university.
- Administration: Organising and evaluating school authorities is part of administration.

HEALTHCARE

Healthcare is one of the quickest industries of the economy over the past ten years, and with the threat of epidemics like the coronavirus eruption on the trend, the sector is expected to continue to grow.

Companies from all over the world are relying on cutting-edge methods like AI, deep learning, and Big Data to keep ahead of the quantity demanded for health - care products and services (Chui et.al, 2017).

The use of AI in healthcare will be enormous. The global market is expected to reach $8 billion by 2026, and there is a significant overlap between big data analytics and artificial intelligence (AI), where visual information is optimised to effectively alleviate practical issues in industry and society.

Preclinical Studies in the Pharmaceutical Development

Able to conduct effective medical testing is one of the major obstacles in pharmaceutical research. A report conducted in Patterns in Pharmacological Sciences found that it can currently take up to 15 years to develop a new, cardiovascular drug to market. Additionally, the price ranges from $1.5 to $2 billion. Clinical studies take up about half of that moment, many more of which end in failure. Nevertheless, investigators can choose the appropriate patients who will take part in the experimental studies using AI technology (Jeffcock Peter, 2017). They can also more efficiently and precisely regulate their healthcare reactions, which will save them time & expense.

The Standard of Electronic Medical Records (EHR)

Any health practitioner will unquestionably mention burdensome EHR systems when asked what the scourge of their existence is. Clinical observations and patient data were historically manually recorded by clinicians, and no two did it in precisely the same way. They would frequently wait until shortly after the doctor encounter, which encouraged human error. Conversely, conversations with health care workers, diagnostic procedures, and effective treatments can be enhanced and substantiated more precisely and almost instantly with AI- and deep learning-backed speech recognition technologies.

Public and Safety

Numerous regulatory norms that influence citizens' daily lives are rarely found in software standards or artificial intelligence (AI), but rather in corporate (and monopolistic) configurations where researchers and entrepreneurs work. The dangers of giving AI and ML the power to make public and private decisions are not yet fully understood by policymakers. To recognize the potential benefits and to reduce the risks of these intersections, all nations must comprehend the influence of machine learning and smart modelling techniques in government policy configuration and reaction. With the assistance of data and AI, good policy can ensure that the social sciences are entering a "golden age," where contextual complexity and numerical explanations are brought to a new level.

RESEARCH CHALLENGES OF AI BASED BIG DATA ALGORITHMS FOR E- GOVERNANCE

Increasing Transparency and Complexity

Algorithms can carry out basic math operations or very intricate reasoning processes. Both humans and computer programmes are capable of processing algorithms. Although algorithms have been around for a while, they are now a more and more crucial component of computer programmes. Invading daily activity governance in this way, algorithms grow more autonomous and covert. Many different types of notations, such as natural, arithmetic, or computer, can be used to express algorithms (Rahaman et al, 2021)

Combining Data and Algorithms

It is important to figure out how to unlock algorithms so that they can be truly co-produced and have the transparency that we demand with our other organizational systems. What obstacles exist specifically to democratizing consumer experience with data and algorithms to ensure openness and transparency? Giving users the choice over how much data they share, with whom they share it, how that data is organised, and other factors would be part of this engagement.

Computer-Driven Governmentality

In a graphic design, those who are in charge of data gathering and heuristic operation are the ones in control. The utilization of data and algorithms simultaneously raises the dangers of security lapses, ongoing operations, and privacy violations. The public looks to the government to protect their privacy, maintain the availability of the Internet, and secure the databases where their personal information is kept. Public safety can be increased, and society can be improved with the help of sensors, data, and algorithms.

CONCLUSION

So much government entities are beginning to use AI and deep learning techniques to increase their systems and products as a result of recent advancements in these fields. The adoption of such technologies is hampered by a wide range of issues, including a lack of experts, computation power, trust, and AI interpretability. It can be easier to foster confidence and trust and encourage the adoption of such cutting-edge techniques if there is clear communication about the use of AI and safeguards are in place to preserve the scheme and its users. Given the simplicity of providing financial services across borders, policymakers and the sector should engage in a multidisciplinary dialogue. Findings from the analysis point to a widespread adoption of machine learning techniques in the public sector, which are quite intriguing.

REFERENCES

Alshomrani, Q. (2013). Cloud based e-Government: Benefits and Challenges. *International Journal of Marketing and Sales Education*, 4(6), 15–19.

Chui, K. T., Alhalabi, W., Pang, S. S. H., Pablos, P. O. D., Liu, R. W., & Zhao, M. (2017). Disease Diagnosis in Smart Healthcare: Innovation, Technologies and Applications. *Sustainability*, 9(12), 2309. doi:10.3390u9122309

Dwivedi, A., Pant, R.P., Khari, M., Pandey, S., & Pande, M. (2019). E-Governance and Big Data Framework for e-Governance and Use of Sentiment Analysis. SSRN doi:10.2139/ssrn.3382731

Jadhav, B., Patankar, A. B., & Jadhav, S. B. (2018). A Practical approach for integrating Big data Analytics into E-governance using Hadoop. *2018 Second International Conference on Inventive Communication and Computational Technologies (ICICCT)*, Coimbatore, India. 10.1109/ICICCT.2018.8473353

NeGP Website. "About NeGP". NeGP Website. Retrieved 17 July, 2014.

Pereira, G. V., Charalabidis, Y., Alexopoulos, C., Mureddu, F., Parycek, P., Ronzhyn, A., & Wimmer, M. A. (2018). Scientific foundations training and entrepreneurship activities in the domain of ICT-enabled governance. In *Proceedings of the 19th Annual International Conference on Digital Government Research: Governance in the Data Age,* (p. 98). ACM. 10.1145/3209281.3209316

PeterJ. (2017). https://blogs.oracle.com/bigdata/machine-learningtechniques

Picciano, A. G. (2012). The Evolution of Big Data and Learning Analytics in American Higher Education. *Journal of Asynchronous Learning Networks*, *16*(3), 9–20. doi:10.24059/olj.v16i3.267

Rahaman, Md.Mahbobor & Haque, Afruza & Hasan, Md. (2021). *Challenges and Opportunities of Big Data for Managing the E-Governance. 1.* 490-499.

Chapter 3
Recent Trends in IoT as Part of Digital India

Vishal Venkataramani
Sri Sivasubramaniya Nadar College of Engineering, India

Ramdhanush Venkatakrishnan
Sri Sivasubramaniya Nadar College of Engineering, India

Chamundeswari Arumugam
Sri Sivasubramaniya Nadar College of Engineering, India

ABSTRACT

IoT usage growth expands in the wild range because of smart digital India in India. The government is funding various projects for boosting the expansion at a large level to promote smart digital India. Many start-up companies are flourishing due to the expansion of government policies in promoting smart digital India. Many public and private companies were improving their skill set to expand the government requirements. Here, for this chapter, the two case studies, satellite based IoT and solid waste management are discussed. The current trends, techniques, technologies, architectures, solutions, applications and issues were discussed. The recent advancement pertaining to these fields, comparison of the properties, and technology evolution were discussed elaborately to get a glimpse of smart digital India.

INTRODUCTION

IoT applications have been adopted in industries on a large scale in India. Starting from agriculture, health monitoring systems, wearables, transport companies, energy monitoring systems, etc., they are adopted in industries. Smart metering (Ashish, 2021) is upcoming digital technology in India. It is targeted to replace 250 million conventional meters for digital transformation in the country. Challenges to ensure the trust of these resources in terms of security, reliability, and finance are much awaited. Manufacturers are setting up targets to ensure the connectivity of this meter for reliable usage alongside prevention from data breaches and hacking with built-in encryption and digital authentication mechanisms.

DOI: 10.4018/978-1-6684-7697-0.ch003

Industries started using IoT-based counting systems (Niranjane et al., 2022) in the manufacturing environment that uses IR sensor, microcontroller, and Node MCU to count multiple product production. To save water resources in the reverse osmosis process, an IoT device (Dudhpachare et al., 2022) embedded with ESP32, and DTH11 sensors were used. Indian pharma IoT (Rakshit & Srivastava, 2021) with internet-connected wearables for health monitoring is a boom to digital India. IoT with sensors was used to measure the temperature, humidity, and weight of beehives in a beehive monitoring system (Pandimurugan et al., 2021). A lot of challenges in the IoT domain were discussed and the applicability of blockchain with SHA256 for sharing of data is detailed (Teli et al., 2022). A secure signature technique on legitimate documents using IoT smart devices was proposed (Meshram et al., 2021). An automation library management system to detect the user and book automatically using RFID and microcontroller (Devi et al., 2021) is a time-saving system in digital India. IoT was applied in the healthcare domain to classify diseases (Kansal et al., 2022) using images. A smart digital board was designed to display the weather data, temperature, humidity, air speed and pollution (Dhule et al., 2021).

IoT has been used in many domains across the states in digital India. Many technologies are emerging in digital India for improving the production and ease the customer interaction to use it. ESP32 sensor, DTH11 sensor, IR sensor, microcontroller, Node MCU, RFID, etc., are used to develop many products. The developed products are commercially available in the Indian market for citizens. Thus, to get more technical insights of two IoT products that exist in the Indian market, is taken up for discussion in this chapter.

The objective here is to explore the two products that are available in the Indian market. Satellite based IoT and solid waste management is taken up in this study. An introduction to satellite based IoT devices, technology, solution providers, cost, performance measures, applications were discussed to get an insight on this product in digital India. Then, trends in solid waste management, generic model, architecture, solutions, technologies used, applications, and issues were discussed.

RECENT TRENDS IN SATELLITE BASED IoT FOR SMART DIGITAL INDIA

Satellite objects that orbit the Earth, along with IoT devices can be linked together in different ways. One is the way satellites act as a source of wireless connection to IoT devices. The network formed through this connection allows valuable information to be communicated even in adverse conditions of the world. Moving towards smart digital India, it is important to understand this mode of connection. A satellite connection is established with a fairly simple process of signal transmission. A signal from the satellite orbiting the Earth is sent to a dish/modem installed at ground level. This is done with the help of radio waves, which are ideal for communication since they can change direction through refraction/reflection. This data is then fed to the satellite from the modem and then back to the modem at ground level setting up a network. In the case of connecting an IoT device, the device through the help of a satellite antenna transmits data that connects to the network. This network allows the user to view the data sent by virtue of it being delivered to the data center.

In some parts of the world, not all resources to get internet connections exists. It is then that the use of satellite-based communication is required. In places where these land-based services are underdeveloped, satellite connection is the more advantageous option. In remote areas such as polar regions, oceans, deserts or forests, there is a need for the IoT sensors used in these regions to connect to the Internet. Since a terrestrial network is rather difficult to set up in these areas, satellite connectivity can be opted (Routray et al., 2019). Goods being shipped from one part of the world to another requires a tracking device to ensure that the products are sent safely. Here the only way to track the movement of the goods is with the help of satellites. Satellite connection to IoT devices is represented in Figure 1. From Table 1, it can be concluded that WLAN is the better mode of connection to the Internet overall.

Figure 1. Satellite connection to IoT devices

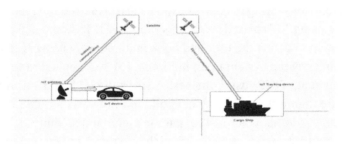

Table 1. Difference between satellite internet and WLAN

Satellite Internet	WLAN
Distribution points over 20,000 miles from Earth.	The distribution point is about 10 miles from the access point.
High latency	Low latency
Speed is slower than WLAN	Very High speed.
Available Everywhere	Not available everywhere
Weather can affect speed	Weather has no effect on the connection
Cost is high	Less expensive than satellite connection

Approach of Companies in India Towards Satellite Internet

Now that the groundwork for the potential of satellite internet is laid, it is necessary to look at the companies in India who seek to venture into the implementation of satellite internet in India. In (PTI, 2021), SIA-India has identified how satellite internet can connect to IoT devices. SatCom Industry Association (SIA-India) offer satellite communication ecosystem in India. They strive to make use of the various satellite bands which are useful for IoT connectivity. It is also to be noted that SIA-India looks to improve on the underlying factors of cost, speed and throughput which hinder satellite connection. They serve as application solution providers for the national and international. Figure 2 represents wireless Internet Vs satellite internet.

Other companies such as in (Hemant Mishra/Mint, 2022), talk about the ageing company that is BSNL and the ever-growing company that is Jio. Both have received an upvote from The Department of Telecommunications to begin the offering of satellite internet in India. The importance of high-speed internet in remote locations of India (Kaur, 2022) is emphasized without any need for fiber-optic infrastructure. This serves as a groundbreaking motive for the future of satellite internet in India. Jio has always looked to provide services that are easily accessible at an affordable price as well, which is why it stands as a strong competitor among others in providing satellite internet to India. Finally, in the form of another competitor, comes Elon Musk-led Starlink (Kashyap, 2022), it can be observed that StarLink had already tried to establish a satellite connection in India in 2021, but was made to cancel the pre-bookings that were made available to the people due to regulatory reasons. However, it seeks to come back stronger, where the estimated market for satellite internet in India is seeded to be around 13 billion. Table 2. provide the comparison of Jio vs StarLink vs BSNL.

Figure 2. Wireless internet vs satellite internet [distance]

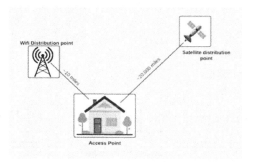

Table 2. Jio vs StarLink vs BSNL [satellite internet properties]

	Jio	**StarLink**	**BSNL**
Cost	High	Very High	Low
Throughput	Upto 100Gbps	50-200Mbps	100 Mbps
Technology used	GEO,MEO	LEO	LEO/VSAT

Performance Measures of Satellite-Based Internet

Latency: Naturally, in the case of satellite internet, the distance between the access point and the distribution point is over 22000 miles as stated in Table 1. Hence, there is said to be high latency involved in the case of satellite internet. In (Schell, 2021), it can be noticed that high latency acts as a hindrance to the connection established, making it feel delayed which is why there is a need to overcome this issue. One such solution to this issue is the use of Low-Earth Orbit (LEO) satellites which are located only a few hundred kilometers from Earth. In (Leyva-Mayorga et al., 2020), the advantages of LEO satellites are given, enumerating why they are the ones used in 5G communications around the world. One such application is in (ETTelecom, 2022), where Nelco, a Tata group company andTelesat demonstrated a "fiber-like performance" with a 35 ms latency round trip which is staggeringly impressive.

Throughput: Throughput is the actual amount of data that is successfully transmitted over the communication network. It is represented as kbps, Mbps or Gbps. Higher throughput along with latency is key for any connection. In (Chatterfee, 2022) Hughes Communications India (HCI), is one of the providers who offer high throughput and speed data. In (Routray & Mohammed, 2019), a well-rounded assessment of satellite IoT integration is provided where the reliability of the connection, coverage of the IoT networks as well as security of the connection are dealt with.

Weather: While weather serves as an uncontrollable factor, certain satellite frequency bands tend to work better regardless of weather conditions. Given in (Schell, 2021), even a slight change in the weather condition can affect the stability of our connection. This is because satellite signals are meant to travel through the various layers of the atmosphere. To tackle this predicament, in (LotusArise, 2020), the satellite spectrum properties are listed. Certain bands such as C-band are less susceptible to rain fade than other bands. Because all the different types of satellite connectivity's work the same from the earth, the type of satellite used depends on how the satellite's position will help the solution from the air. This enables companies like in (PTI, 2021) to make use of such frequency bands depending on the condition of the atmosphere.

Figure 3. Satellite spectrum properties

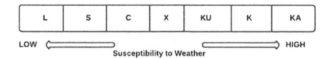

Cost: As the competition for providing satellite services to the remote areas of India gradually increases the cost will also decrease as companies will be keener on providing cost-effective services as the popularity of the service increases. Figure 3 shows the satellite spectrum properties.

Applications of Satellite Based IoT

In Routray et al. (2020), given the role of Satellite internet being used to connect to the IoT devices in military services. By military services, it means the measures taken in the protection of borders and real-time defense. In order to operate on these actions, there is a need to use smart systems. It is also elaborated in Routray et al. (2020), why satellite based IoT provides the better solution to handle these tasks. It considers the advantages that have already been documented in the form of accessibility and reliability (Routray & Mohammed, 2019). In Routray et al. (2020), the other forms of satellite technologies such as LEO, Geostationary Earth Orbits (GEO) (Leyva-Mayorga et al., 2020) and its properties have been explained in detail.

In a similar context to Routray et al. (2019) deals with Mission Critical applications in general and the usage of satellite based IoT. In Routray et al. (2019), a review of other applications of satellite IoT is provided such as in the field of Smart Agriculture, Healthcare, Air Navigation Systems, etc. The performance measures of satellite connectivity given have already been taken into consideration while implementing them in these domains. This gives a good idea of the future applications of satellite connectivity after being able to improve on the compromised factors.

IoT TRENDS IN SOLID WASTE MANAGEMENT

Solid waste management is one of main application in digital India to clear the garbage. But why is IoT relevant here? The answer lies in why the current systems need improvement. The market for smart city applications is only growing by the day (Tele2, 2021). The amount of solid waste generated across the globe is steadily rising, and so are the expenses required to dispose and manage the waste generated. Thus, there is a growing necessity to track the information regarding the generation and handling of waste. Optimizing the process of garbage disposal can save a lot of time and effort (Sequeira, 2020), ultimately contributing to a better environment. All fall under the umbrella of the digital India campaign, by rapidly progressing and solving social issues through novel technological solutions.

Model for an IoT Solution

With the base motivation for IoT solutions to solid waste management covered, the next topic of interest is implementation. The basic design of the system is that multiple bins are connected to a network, and through this network, relay information about the bin levels, the state of the waste accumulated etc. Using this data can give a better understanding of the problem and can be used to devise a more efficient and effective solution. By devising a better solution, the goal is to end up with a device that can measure the necessary data and keep tracking while staying connected to a network. The device also needs to be compact and financially feasible. There are three major steps while trying to design such a device:

Step 1: Connect the device to a network
Step 2: Collect data from the bins
Step 3: Relay data from the bins to the network

Figure 4. A pictorial representation of an IoT network

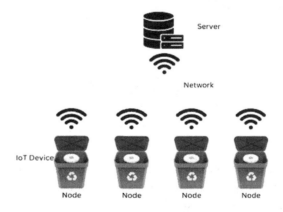

Figure 4. represents a pictorial view of an IoT network. Breaking it down, the first step is to connect all the bins to a network. To do this, a network interface is needed. This interface will need to handle

establishing a connection with other bins and create a secure channel for data transfer. The next step is to sense the status of the waste. This entails the need for a sensing unit. The sensing unit must contain different kinds of sensors to accurately track the garbage. Sensors of different kinds can be used, each with its own function. The types of data that can be gathered are many, including temperature, toxicity, humidity, and bin capacity. The choice of sensors depends on the specifics of the problem to be solved. The next and final step is to relay the data perceived from the sensors to the network. To do this, a communication unit is needed. This unit must be able to transfer data back and forth between the network unit and the sensing unit. Thus, the use of analog-to-digital converters and receiver-transmitter systems is abundant here. Putting together all the steps gives a model for a generic IoT solution. Figure 5 shows a conceptual diagram of the genetic architecture of such an IoT device.

While the model suggested in Figure 5 is a generic model, there are other works that propose different architectures for the same IoT solution. Research done in (Pardini et al., 2019) suggests a model with 5 layers and it shown in Figure 6. Each model has a different role to play and combined, they form a larger and complete system. The purpose of each layer is briefly listed below:

Perception Layer: This layer is like the sensing unit as proposed before. It contains a variety of sensors, collects information at the physical level, and transmits them to higher layers through secure channels.

Network Layer: Receives data from the perception layer and relays it to the upper layers by passing it through a network established by using one of many protocols. These protocols are typically wireless in nature.

Middleware Layer: It consists of a set of sublayers to manage the different parts of the IoT system. This layer may interact with both software and hardware components. Thus, it needs to communicate with both kinds of subsystems.

Figure 5. The model architecture of an IoT device

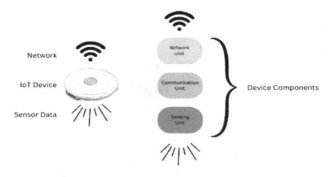

Application Layer: The application layer is an entirely software-made layer wherein it provides services to the users above and provides a user interface for access to the entire network. This layer is built on top of the previous layers and can provide a bird's eye view of the working of the system.

Business Layer: This business layer is a more niche service that generates reports, graphs, statistics, and analytical data that are important to the solution itself. It makes using the IoT device easier and enables a more data-driven approach to solving the same problem. New insights can be drawn when utilizing the business layer as it provides value in making high-level business decisions.

Figure 6. A 5-layer model for an IoT solution to solid waste management

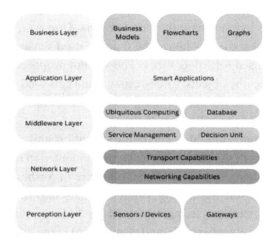

Another 3-layered architecture is depicted in Akram et al. (2021), with a structure very similar to the generic model proposed before. It consists of 3 layers and it is represented in Figure 7.

Perception Layer: Consists of sensors and actuators that help to gauge physical data and send signals about the status of the waste being tracked.

Network Layer: Transmits information to and from the network, acting as a bridge between the individual node and the network.

Application Layer: Provides a range of services to customers or end users who can draw insights and improve the efficiency of the management of solid waste.

Figure 7. A 3-layer model to implement an IoT solution for solid waste management

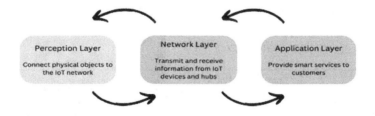

Implementation of The Model's Components

Having discussed the general structure of an IoT device, it is necessary to look at each component of the structure in detail to gain a deeper understanding of the working of the system. Revisiting the 3 layered architecture discussed at the beginning of the section, the analysis of each layer is done below.

First is the sensing unit. The sensing unit gathers information about the environment. This implies it requires a lot of sensor nodes. Research in Vishnu et al. (2021) suggests the use of an ultrasonic sensor, the MB1010 LV-MaxSonar-EZ. It can provide serial output, analog voltage, and pulse width. As an alternative, infrared sensors can also be used. The primary difference is that ultrasonic makes use of sound waves, and infrared uses light to sense the same objects. However, ultrasonic is more accurate at finding data like distance and shape and is hence the majorly used sensor. Either can be integrated into Arduino, which is commonly used for IoT devices. The system proposed by Akram et al. (2021) uses proximity sensors for sensing nearby objects, force-resistive and cell-load sensors to measure weight and pressure in the bins, and moisture sensors for gauging the wetness of the waste, all factors that contribute to computing the urgency level of the collection of waste.

The next part is the communication unit. The communication unit acts as a manager between the sensory and networking sections of the device. It can be implemented in many ways. The most common one, however, is using a host microcontroller. The architecture of Vishnu et al. (2021) uses analog-to-digital converters (ADC) to convert the analog voltage signals into digital form. UARTs (universal asynchronous receiver-transmitters) are frequently used for bidirectional communication with other units of the IoT device. Arduino, Raspberry Pi, and Atmega are some examples of controllers that also have inbuilt sensor nodes. This part of the device controls and manages the operation of all the other units and subsystems of the rest of the device. It understands the different kinds of data passed on in the network and transmits them in an appropriate format for the required component.

The next section is the networking unit. This is the most impactful section of the device, as it is critical to enabling the entire network, forming the backbone of the IoT device. The connection to the network is done by a wifi module. The most used is LoRaWAN (Long Range WAN). It can provide long-range communications, much broader ranges compared to wifi and Bluetooth. Its significance is even more when the location is remote and other networks are unstable. Vishnu et al. (2021) makes use of the RN2903 transceiver modules to send data over long distances with lower power consumption. LoRaWAN resists interference by using a Chirp spread spectrum modulation. The research in Akram et al. (2021) analyzes the performance of LoRaWAN on several parameters such as bit rate, signal-to-noise ratio, etc. It also talks about the hardware implementation of a LoRa gateway. Other wireless technologies such as GSM, Zigbee, CDMA2000 EV-DO, and RFID are also growing in popularity and usage as alternatives to LoRaWAN. Table 3. provides a detailed comparison of these technologies.

Table 3. A comparison of wireless technologies used

Parameter / Technology	GSM	Long Range WAN (LoRaWAN)	Zigbee	Bluetooth	WiFi
Wireless Network	Wide Area Network	Low-Power Wide Area Network	Personal Area Network	Personal Area Network	Local Area Network
Operating Band	900–1800 MHz	433/869/915 MHz	868/915 MHz and 2.4 GHz	2.4 GHz	2.4 GHz/5 GHz
Data Rate	172 Kbps	50 Kbps	20, 40, 100, and 200 kbps	2 Mbps	11-54 Mbps
Limitation	High power consumption	Data rate, network capability	Line of Sight (LOS)	Short-range communication	Short-range communication

In addition to the connectivity of the nodes in the network, there are GPS modules in each node depending on the specific problem at hand. If the physical location of data is important to the problem being solved, the GPS modules are also included in the networking unit. They help add a new worldview of looking at the statistics involved in the problem. This becomes especially relevant in the context of real-time garbage collection.

Example Architectures in Existing Research

To sum it up, below depicted are some system designs that incorporate all the individual units together. This creates a larger, more cohesive device for tracking garbage data. The system proposed by Vishnu et al. (2021) is discussed as an example. The sensors used are ultrasonic in nature and are connected to an Analog to Digital Converter (ADC). The power module is used by the device to self-sustain without depending on an external battery. It is constructed using solar panel modules. A GPS module is also present to enable physical tracking of the bins and geolocation data. The LoRaWAN module and all the other components are interconnected using the ATmega 2560 microcontroller as the host.

Another such example is provided in Akram et al. (2021). It shows the block diagram of a LoRaWAN based gateway, used to establish a connection between various nodes (bins) in the network. It uses the Atmega 328P as the host microcontroller. In addition to LoRaWAN, it also uses WiFi modules. Voltage converters are being used instead of analog to digital converters. One more system proposed by Singhvi et al. (2019) uses Arduino as a controller to interface with sensors and GPRS (General Packet Radio Service) modules. It also suggests the use of GSM based techniques to create the network needed for IoT processing. The system also uses ultrasonic sensor nodes and gas sensors to sense the toxicity of the garbage bin under consideration.

Applications and Issues

The applications for IoT-based solutions for solid waste management are many. Even within solid waste management, there are many issues that can be tackled by the design of an IoT solution. The garbage collection routines can be optimized, and the bin levels can be monitored efficiently. The real-time evaluation of the waste in bins can be used to run analytic tests and provide insight into the patterns of data output from different localities. This in turn can improve the response and mitigation of climate change. Also, using data collected by these IoT devices can be deployed with the assistance of a smartphone app that can allow for more transparent waste handling between the citizens and the government. The scope for managing waste will only become more valuable over time, as dealing with waste holds the future of the global response toward climate change.

Even though the implementation of IoT solutions for solid waste management has been discussed extensively, these solutions must be incorporated into everyday life. A lot of Indian research has gone into devising a solution, but the corresponding deployment of these systems must be met. The number of initiatives taken towards smart waste management needs to increase, to push the goals of Digital India further. The more action taken, the more efficient the waste collection will be. The integration of IoT with solid waste management is still a work in progress, and this issue needs more attention than ever. The need for businesses and government-aided schemes dedicated to this issue is high. Only with effective implementation can the benefits of the IoT solution be realized.

DISCUSSION

With a lot of implementation details and specifics discussed by existing work, the task of identifying potential future scope becomes pertinent. Soon, people in India will be able to harness IoT devices even in remote areas with the help of satellite connections. The demand for satellite connections is predicted to increase fourfold in the upcoming years due to its eminent potential. On the front of solid waste management, there is a plethora of academic research being performed, and the number of applications is steadily increasing. However, the rate at which policies are being framed to accommodate these changes in the respective domains needs to increase. This must become a key objective of the Digital India initiative, as the positive benefits of doing so multiply exponentially.

CONCLUSION

In summary, the trends on the Internet of Things pertaining to Digital India applications have been discussed. Among the possible applications, the ones in focus include Satellite based IoT and Solid Waste Management. In Satellite-based applications, the services provided by this mode of connection regarding IoT, along with businesses in India that provide the same along with its recent applications have been discussed extensively. As far as solid waste management is concerned, existing research trends were discussed, along with a generic model for any future work pertaining to the same. The ramifications of solid waste management on climate change were also highlighted, pointing out the urgency in bringing the solutions discussed to effect.

REFERENCES

Akram, S. V., Singh, R., AlZain, M. A., Gehlot, A., Rashid, M., Faragallah, O. S., El-Shafai, W., & Prashar, D. (2021). Performance Analysis of IoT and Long-Range Radio-Based Sensor Node and Gateway Architecture for Solid Waste Management. *Sensors (Basel)*, *21*(8), 2774. doi:10.339021082774 PMID:33920008

Akram, S. V., Singh, R., Gehlot, A., Rashid, M., AlGhamdi, A. S., Alshamrani, S. S., & Prashar, D. (2021). Role of Wireless Aided Technologies in the Solid Waste Management: A Comprehensive Review. *Sustainability*, *13*(23), 13104. doi:10.3390u132313104

Ashish, S. (2021). Now is the time for smart meter adoption in India. *Times of India*. https://timesofindia.indiatimes.com/blogs/voices/now-is-the-time-for-smart-meter-adoption-in-india/

Chatterfee, A. (2022). India gets its first High Throughput Satellite Broadband Service. *The Hindu*. https://www.thehindu.com/sci-tech/technology/india-gets-its-first-high-throughput-satellite-broadband-service/article65889436.ece

Devi, P. D., Mirudhula, S., & Devi, A. (2021). Advanced Library Management System using IoT. In *Fifth International Conference on I-SMAC (IoT in Social, Mobile, Analytics and Cloud) (I-SMAC)*, (pp. 150-154). IEEE. 10.1109/I-SMAC52330.2021.9640697

Dhule, C., Agrawal, R., Dorle, S., & Vidhale, B. (2021) Study of Design of IoT based Digital Board for Real Time Data Delivery on National Highway. In *6th International Conference on Inventive Computation Technologies (ICICT)*, (pp. 195-198). IEEE. 10.1109/ICICT50816.2021.9358560

Dudhpachare, A. K., Kuthe, T. V., Lalke, C. V., Wyawahare, N. P., Agrawal, R., & Daigavane, P. (2022). Process of RO's Wastewater Reuse & Water Management in Society by Using IOT Automation. In *International Conference on Applied Artificial Intelligence and Computing (ICAAIC)*, (pp. 1546-1550). IEEE. 10.1109/ICAAIC53929.2022.9792805

ETTelecom. (2022). *Tata's Nelco, Telesat successfully conduct LEO satellite internet trial in India.* ETTelecom. https://telecom.economictimes.indiatimes.com/news/tatas-nelco-telesat-successfully-conduct-leo-satellite-internet-trial-in-india/91640942

Hemant Mishra/Mint. (2022). DoT okays BSNL to provide satellite-based services using gateway installed in India. *Mint.* https://www.livemint.com/companies/news/dot-okays-bsnl-to-provide-satellite-based-services-details-here-11652010859939.html

Kansal, I., Popli, R., Verma, J., Bhardwaj, V., & Bhardwaj, R. (2022) Digital Image Processing and IoT in Smart Health Care -A review. *International Conference on Emerging Smart Computing and Informatics (ESCI)*, 1-6. 10.1109/ESCI53509.2022.9758227

Kashyap, H. (2022). *Elon Musk's Starlink Applies for DoT Licence To Bring Satellite Broadband To India. INC 42.* inc42.com/buzz/elon-musks-starlink-applies-dot-licence-bring-satellite-broadband-india/#:~:text=The%20competition%20within%20India's%20%2413,satellite%2Dbased%20broadband%20to%20India

Kaur, J. (2022). *Jio Gets DoT Nod To Launch Satellite-Based Broadband Services: Report.* INC 42. https://inc42.com/buzz/jio-gets-dot-nod-to-launch-satellite-based-broadband-services-report/

Leyva-Mayorga, I., Soret, B., Roper, M., Wubben, D., Matthiesen, B., Dekorsy, A., & Popovski, P. (2020). LEO Small-Satellite Constellations for 5G and Beyond-5G Communications. *IEEE Access : Practical Innovations, Open Solutions*, 8, 184955–184964. doi:10.1109/ACCESS.2020.3029620

LotusArise. (2020). *Satellite Frequency Bands: L, S, C, X, Ku, Ka-band.* Lotus Arise. https://lotusarise.com/satellite-frequency-bands-upsc/

Meshram, C., Obaidat, M. S., Tembhurne, J. V., Shende, S. W., Kalare, K. W., & Meshram, S. G. (2021). A Lightweight Provably Secure Digital Short-Signature Technique Using Extended Chaotic Maps for Human-Centered IoT Systems. *IEEE Systems Journal*, 15(4), 5507–5515. doi:10.1109/JSYST.2020.3043358

Niranjane, V., Shelke, U., Shirke, S., & Dafe, S. (2022). IoT based Digital Production Counting System. In *International Conference on Electronics and Renewable Systems (ICEARS)*, (pp. 452-455). IEEE. 10.1109/ICEARS53579.2022.9752399

Pandimurugan, V., Mandviya, R., Gadgil, A., Prakhar, K., & Datar, A. (2021). IoT based Smart Beekeeping Monitoring system for beekeepers in India. In *4th International Conference on Computing and Communications Technologies (ICCCT)*, (pp. 65-70). IEEE. 10.1109/ICCCT53315.2021.9711901

Pardini, K., Rodrigues, J. J. P. C., Kozlov, S. A., Kumar, N., & Furtado, V. (2019). IoT-Based Solid Waste Management Solutions: A Survey. *Journal of Sensor and Actuator Networks*, 8(1), 5. doi:10.3390/jsan8010005

PTI. (2021). SIA-India for unleashing full potential of all satellite bands for IoT. *Economic Times*. https://economictimes.indiatimes.com/tech/tech-bytes/sia-india-for-unleashing-full-potential-of-all-satellite-bands-for-iot/articleshow/82219179.cms

Rakshit, P., & Srivastava, P. K. (2021). Cutting Edge IoT Technology for Smart Indian Pharma. In *International Conference on Advance Computing and Innovative Technologies in Engineering (ICACITE)* (pp. 360-362). IEEE. 10.1109/ICACITE51222.2021.9404627

Routray, S. & Mohammed, H. (2019). *Satellite Based IoT Networks for Emerging Applications*. Springer.

Routray, S. K., Javali, A., Sahoo, A., Sharmila, K. P., & Anand, S. (2020). Military Applications of Satellite Based IoT. In *Third International Conference on Smart Systems and Inventive Technology (ICSSIT)* (pp. 122-127). IEEE. 10.1109/ICSSIT48917.2020.9214284

Routray, S. K., Tengshe, R., Javali, A., Sarkar, S., Sharma, L., & Ghosh, A. D. (2019). Satellite Based IoT for Mission Critical Applications. In *2019 International Conference on Data Science and Communication (IconDSC)* (pp. 1-6). IEEE. 10.1109/IconDSC.2019.8817030

Schell, A. (2021). *Fixed Wireless Internet vs. Satellite Internet: What Are The Differences*. Upward Broadband. https://www.upwardbroadband.com/fixed-wireless-internet-vs-satellite-internet-what-are-the-differences/#:~:text=However%2C%20satellite%20and%20fixed%20wireless,tower%20that%20broadcasts%20these%20services

Sequeira, N. (2020). IoT Applications in Waste Management. *IoT For All*. https://www.iotforall.com/iot-applications-waste-management

Singhvi, R. K., Lohar, R. L., Kumar, A., Sharma, R., Sharma, L. D., & Saraswat, R. K., Singhvi, R. L., Lohar, A., Kumar, R., Sharma, L. D., & Saraswat, R. K. (2019). IoT BasedSmart Waste Management System: India prospective. In *4th International Conference on Internet of Things: Smart Innovation and Usages (IoT-SIU)* (pp. 1-6). IEEE. 10.1109/IoT-SIU.2019.8777698

Teli, T. A., Yousuf, R., & Khan, D. A. (2022). Ensuring Secure Data Sharing in IoT Domains Using Blockchain. In *Cyber Security and Digital Forensics: Challenges and Future Trends* (pp. 205–221). Wiley. doi:10.1002/9781119795667.ch9

Tele2. (2021). The Role of IoT in Smart Waste Management. *Tele2*. https://tele2iot.com/article/the-role-of-iot-in-smart-waste-management/

Vishnu, S., Ramson, S. R. J., Senith, S., Anagnostopoulos, T., Abu-Mahfouz, A. M., Fan, X., Srinivasan, S., & Kirubaraj, A. A. (2021). IoT-Enabled Solid Waste Management in Smart Cities. *Smart Cities*, 4(3), 1004–1017. doi:10.3390martcities4030053

Chapter 4
The Blockchain–Empowered Application:
DApp

Kavita Saini
Galgotias University, India

Arnav Tyagi
Galgotias University, India

Akshat Antal
Galgotias University, India

ABSTRACT

Blockchain is an acquired information framework that incorporates a square chain. Blockchain capacities as a common record or as an overall record keeping arrangement of all exchanges on an incorporated blockchain. Blockchain is a successful framework for putting away and taking care of records of exchange at its center. All the more explicitly, blockchain is a typical, extremely durable record of circulated trades working from connected trade squares and putting them away in a high level data set. Blockchain relies upon developed cryptographic strategies to permit any member in an organization to convey, (for example, putting away, trading, and showing information), without earlier certainty between the collections. All members become mindful of participation with the blockchain and permit framework affirmation before information is incorporated, working with trustless coordinated exertion between associations. Blockchain is virtual digital money Bitcoin's spine innovation.

INTRODUCTION

Decentralized applications (dApps) are advanced applications or projects that exist and run on a blockchain or distributed (P2P) organization of PCs rather than a solitary PC (Zheng, Xie, Dai, Chen, & Wang, 2017). DApps (additionally called "dapps") are outside the domain and control of a solitary

DOI: 10.4018/978-1-6684-7697-0.ch004

power. DApps—which are frequently based on the Ethereum stage—can be produced for an assortment of purposes including gaming, money, and online media (Dutta & Saini, 2021).

- Decentralized applications—otherwise called "dApps" or "dapps"— are advanced applications that sudden spike in demand for a blockchain organization of PCs as opposed to depending on a solitary PC.
- Since dApps are decentralized, they are liberated from the control and obstruction of a solitary power.
- Advantages of dApps incorporate the protecting of client security, the absence of control, and the adaptability of improvement.
- Downsides incorporate the possible powerlessness to scale, challenges in fostering a UI, and troubles in making code adjustments.

UNDERSTANDING DECENTRALIZED APPLICATIONS (DAPPS)

A standard web application, for example, Uber or Twitter, runs on a PC framework that is possessed and worked by an association, giving it full authority over the application and its operations. There might be different clients on one side, however the backend is constrained by a solitary association (Koo et al., 2018).

DApps can run on a P2P organization or a blockchain network. The basic structure is shown in Figure 1. For instance, BitTorrent, Peak, and Popcorn Time are applications that sudden spike in demand for PCs that are essential for a P2P organization, by which numerous members are devouring substance, taking care of or cultivating content, or at the same time filling the two roles (Christidis & Devetsikiotis, 2016).

With regards to digital currencies, DApps run on a blockchain network in a public, open-source, decentralized climate and are liberated from control and impedance by any single power. For instance, a designer can make a Twitter-like DApp and put it on a blockchain where any client can distribute messages. When posted, nobody—including the application makers—can erase the messages.

Characteristics Of DAPP

DAPP's regularly have the accompanying qualities:

- They run on the blockchain
- Their code is made open-source works independently with next to no individual or gathering controlling most of tokens
- They produce DAPP tokens to offer some incentive to their contributing hubs
- Clients are conceded admittance to them in return for tokens
- Diggers are compensated with tokens when they effectively add to the biological system

Figure 1. Basic structure of Dapp

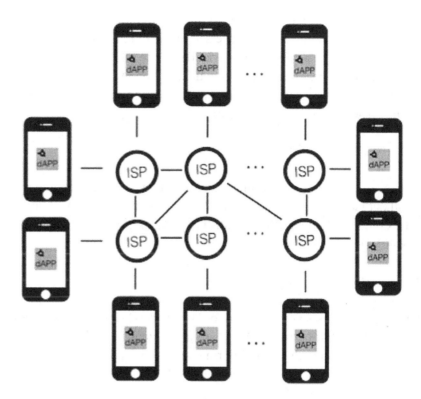

Security

Progressed level of safety is the critical advantage of a Dapp (Raj et al., 2020). As it is run on the blockchain as explained in Figure 2, the information is circulated to every one of the hubs in the organization. Moreover, exchanges that happen on the blockchain are lastingness; it implies that all exchanges are stacked up forever and can't be meddled with, bringing about safer information assurance (Saini, 2020).

Figure 2. Security

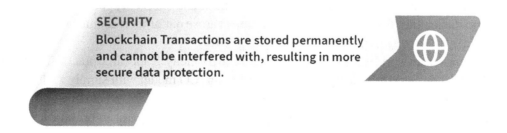

Further Developed Information Straightforwardness

The second and most significant advantage of Dapp is information straightforwardness. In the Circulated Application, the information is put away on a dispersed organization that implies the information exist on different PCs simultaneously (Yusuf & Surjandari, 2020). The information is just open for the clients who are accessible on the circulated network. So the information put away on the disseminated record is more straightforward and nobody can eradicate or distort the information record without the consent of all members in the organization (Wang et al., 2019).

Improved Monetary Productivity

The Blockchain innovation permits both business and people make their exchanges straightforwardly to the end client without including any center man (Zheng, Xie, Dai, Chen, & Wang, 2017). It permits individuals to be less reliant upon monetary establishments/bank just as it improves the monetary productivity of the country (Koo et al., 2018).

Quicker and Less Expensive

Decentralized framework dispenses with the need for an outsider, bringing about quick and less expensive exchanges (Datta, 2017). Furthermore, Dapps are impervious to vacation and actual blackouts, as there is no focal server farm to store the entire information. So the client can make exchanges whenever in speed and savvy way with next to no issue (Saini et al., 2021).

Key Elements of Dapp

Decentralized applications (dApps) are one of the greatest possible employments of blockchain innovation, as they open up entirely different choices for buyer and business-centered items with usefulness that hasn't been seen previously (Koo et al., 2018).

Towards the finish of 2018, a group set off to examine and concentrate on the territory of dApp improvement with expectations of unraveling the present status of this essential market. They at first amassed a rundown of 1,624 dApp improvement projects yet simply figured out how to track down contact data for 900 tasks Of this pool, 160 undertakings finished up our full 40-question review (Dutta & Saini, 2021). The objective was to isolate current realities from hypotheses and reports on what's going on in the dApp market. They needed to know the number of dynamic dApp projects there are, what they're doing, and what challenges they face when assembling their dApps.

What they found is that the dApp people group is youthful and energetic, yet it faces various quick and longer-term difficulties. Four central matters of interest arose out of their examination. DApps were bootstrapping in 2018 (Zheng, Xie, Dai, Chen, & Wang, 2017).

In 2017, the blockchain world was loaded up with trust and publicity. It appeared practically any thought that utilized blockchain could raise a ton of capital through an ICO model with simply a whitepaper and a fantasy. While a large number of the famous stages and ventures in the blockchain world were made out of this promotion, not many buyer centered dApps, for example, games or informal communication applications, were made during this time (Dutta & Saini, 2021).

As the publicity died down all through 2018, however, dApps were being dispatched. In spite of cruel economic situations right around 3/4 (72%) of the activities that finished our study were begun in 2018, and 41 percent were begun over the most recent a half year (Dutta & Saini, 2021).

Concerning subsidizing, 2017's dApps were for the most part self-supported (38%) or financed by token deals (31%), while VC contributed projects make up just 24% of our responders. In 2018, the quantity of self-financed dApps multiplied to almost 68%, with 47% of groups having 3-5 individuals and just a little part got subsidizing through symbolic deals (10%) or VC venture (16%).

What this tells us is that dApps are comprised of more modest groups that can dispatch a thought rapidly and with negligible subsidizing, similar as the beginning of versatile application improvement, where a little group could bootstrap an extraordinary buyer application thought, construct a client base, then, at that point, raise financing.

DApps are depending on 'unified' arrangements … for the present.

We'd love to envision that the decentralized upheaval blockchain has made will happen out of the blue, however the framework for this innovation is as yet being fabricated. We observed that dApp engineers are utilizing brought together answers until further notice and expecting the chance of changing to decentralized ones later on. Incorporated parts like stockpiling, information base, or backend are being utilized by 65% of tasks. 43% have somewhere around one decentralized part other than a brilliant agreement. 68% show they may utilize decentralized capacity or data set later on. Client onboarding and training are by a wide margin the greatest obstacles.

The main issue dApp designers announced was a general low measure of clients in the crypto/ blockchain world. Almost 10 years later the beginning of the digital money world with the dispatch of Bitcoin, openness convenience actually stay the biggest impediments to development (Raj et al., 2020). Exercises that may appear to be instinctive to the no-nonsense crypto fan, for example, making a wallet or saving your private key (secret word), are significant obstacles to the normal client. The way that there is no secret word recuperation choice is an issue for most customers, and crypto ignorance remains determinedly high.

This issue is pervasive that 78% of respondents said it was the significant road obstruction to reception of dApps (Saini, 2020). Making a wallet, buying cash, and understanding private keys, exchanges, and gas are gigantic boundaries to client development (Kumari & Saini, 2019).

They can't at any point lose (or change!) that secret key or probably they'll for all time lose admittance to everything. That is a hard sell without some genuinely great onboarding devices," one respondent composed (Kumari & Saini, 2019).

Furthermore, dApp engineers revealed low generally DAU (every day dynamic clients) for their applications, which isn't shocking given the issues with onboarding and instructing new client (Christidis & Devetsikiotis, 2016).

Numerous dApp producers are wagering on games.

We found a shockingly high pervasiveness of gaming-centered dApp projects among our respondents. Of the returned reviews, 27% of tasks said they are centered around some type of gaming dependent on blockchain innovation. While this probably won't agree with the fantasies of blockchain devotees, it's awesome information for the momentary development of the business. Around the world, gaming is a billion dollar industry and is an area that might actually see the most noteworthy development rate given current usership (Christidis & Devetsikiotis, 2016). As opposed to trusting everybody will awaken one day and conclude they're prepared to give a shot blockchain, it's a good idea to wager that clients will enter the blockchain space because of experience with an application (Yusuf & Surjandari, 2020). Furthermore given there are a great many more video gamers and card sharks than there are legal advisors and lenders, games are the most recognizable of applications (Kumari & Saini, 2019).

Generally, our discoveries spell greater than not for the dApp business (Zheng, Xie, Dai, Chen, & Wang, 2017). While we essential got some information about the specialized difficulties, the general opinion appeared to be that development will come once gives like UX are improved. Also, many undertakings are drawing nearer to tackling this issue. Crypto proficiency isn't an unrealistic fantasy however an expected reality assuming that engineers put legitimate consideration and assets toward making dApps usable to blockchain rookies (Christidis & Devetsikiotis, 2016). All together for the dApp market to accomplish a higher pace of reception, these ventures should zero in on the client venture and the client experience. All things considered, taking a gander at the PC business (or even the cell phone industry), it wasn't until UX further developed that we saw monstrous development from ordinary clients (Dutta & Saini, 2020).

THE ANATOMY OF A FLOW DAPP

The graph beneath traces the parts of a normal dapp based on the Stream blockchain. While numerous dapps are organized in an unexpected way, this engineering presents essential ideas that will be examined all through this aid.

1. **Dapp Client:** The dapp customer is the interface through which clients associate with your dapp. Web and portable applications are normal instances of dapp customers.
2. **Smart Contract:** A savvy contract is an assortment of code, conveyed to a super durable area on the blockchain, that characterizes the center rationale for a dapp.
3. **User Account:** A client account is a record on the blockchain that stores the advanced resources possessed by a solitary client.
4. **Transaction:** An exchange is a piece of code submitted to the blockchain that changes the condition of at least one client records and savvy contracts. All exchanges start from somewhere around one client account. By and large, an exchange passes information between a client account and a brilliant agreement.
5. **State Query:** A state inquiry is a solicitation made to the blockchain that profits data about the condition of your dapp's brilliant agreements.
6. **User Wallet:** A client wallet is programming or equipment that controls admittance to a client's record on the blockchain. The application customer commonly interfaces with the client's wallet to send exchanges to the blockchain.
7. **Flow Client Library (FCL):** The Flow Client Library is a structure that gives a standard interface to associate customer applications and client wallets. Fig. 3: shows the flow of DApp in detail.

Figure 3. A flow DApp

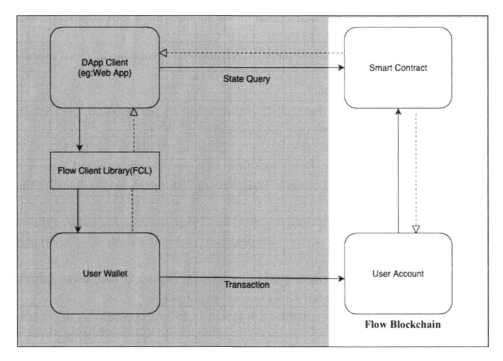

BUSINESS MODEL OF DAPP

What qualifies a task as a Decentralized Application?

The application should be totally open-source, it should work independently, with no substance controlling most of its tokens, and its information and records of activity should be cryptographically put away in a public, decentralized square chain.

The application should produce tokens as indicated by a standard calculation or set of rules and potentially convey a few or each of its tokens toward the start of its activity. These tokens should be vital for the utilization of the application and any commitment from clients ought to be compensated by installment in the application's tokens.

The application might adjust its convention because of proposed upgrades and market input yet all progressions should be chosen by larger part agreement of its clients.

What is the lawful substance and what do they do?

Token issuance is ordinarily finished by a non-benefit which deals with the advancement of the code. This non-benefit won't ever get monetary advantages from the product and may have the accompanying liabilities:

- Issuance of beginning tokens
- Holding of designer tokens
- Overseeing abundance installments
- Setting the course of the venture to be created

There could be no other lawful substances required. Proprietors of tokens don't should be addressed by an organization. A supporter of the improvement of the undertaking doesn't need a particular lawful element by the same token.

The non-benefit can settle on choices completely decentralized permitting a "proof of stake" casting a ballot instrument to decide any choice.

What does the coin issuance resemble?

Tokens are given by the white paper that facilitates the organizers musings and fuses local area input. A few classifications for which tokens may are being given:

- **Kickstarter (Crowdsale):** An underlying one-time offer of tokens is a typical approach to at first asset a DApp. The cash raised will be saved into the establishment which will utilize that to foster the venture.
- **Engineer Pool:** A part of the tokens can be saved for designers chipping away at the venture. As the market sets a valuation for the venture, the designer pool will acquire it's esteem and can draw in supporters of the undertaking.
- **Premine:** It is ideal to keep away from premining a token. Networks hate this methodology. If a premine is done it is prescribed to have a significant explanation.
- **Client Conduct (Mining):** Client Conduct dispersion of tokens boosts hubs to contribute assets to the DApp. In Bitcoin, there is a square award like clockwork. This motivating forces supporters of give hashing capacity to the DApp.

Similarly, DApps need to decide how to boost the organization to contribute the necessary asset. This is the main piece of the symbolic circulation. Extra time hashing power will be completely compensated with exchange charges on Bitcoin anyway proportional to that the square prize gives the motivation.

What are the tokens precisely?

The tokens object is to permit admittance to a PC framework. For instance, an individual should claim some measure of bitcoins to have any exchange on Bitcoin. The bitcoins permitted the person to utilize a PC framework. The benefit of utilizing this framework might change extra time yet come up short on the basic elements of a value security.

There are no fundamental resources that can be addressed by the tokens, there aren't profits and no value in anything is claimed by having a token.

Centralised vs. Decentralised App

A centralized application is possessed by a solitary organization. The application programming for a brought together application dwells on at least one server constrained by the organization. As a client, you'll collaborate with the application by downloading a duplicate of the application and afterward sending and getting information to and from the organization's server.

A decentralized application (otherwise called a dApp or dapp) works on a blockchain or shared organization of PCs. It empowers clients to take part in exchanges straightforwardly with each other rather than depending on a focal power. The client of a dApp will pay the engineer a measure of digital money to download and utilize the program's source code. The source code is known as a brilliant agreement, which permits clients to finish exchanges without uncovering individual data.

Notable instances of centralized applications are Twitter, Facebook, Instagram, and Netflix. Banks and other monetary foundations utilize concentrated applications to permit their clients online admittance to their records (Christidis & Devetsikiotis, 2016).

Peepeth, an interpersonal organization choice to Twitter, is an illustration of a decentralized application (Dutta & Saini, 2021). Cryptokitties is a dApp game that permits clients to trade virtual felines. MakerDAO is a decentralized credit administration supporting the stablecoin Dai and permits clients to open a collateralized obligation position (CDP).

ADVANTAGES OF DAPP

Large numbers of the upsides of dApps revolve around the program's capacity to shield client security. With decentralized applications, clients don't have to present their own data to utilize the capacity the application gives. DApps utilize savvy agreements to finish the exchange between two unknown gatherings without the need to depend on a focal power (Kumari & Saini, 2019).

Advocates keen on free discourse bring up that dApps can be created as elective web-based media stages (Christidis & Devetsikiotis, 2016). A decentralized online media stage would be impervious to restriction in light of the fact that no single member on the blockchain can erase messages or square messages from being posted (Datta, 2017).

Ethereum is an adaptable stage for making new dApps, giving the foundation expected to engineers to zero in their endeavors on tracking down creative utilizations for computerized applications This could empower fast sending of dApps in an assortment of enterprises including banking and money, gaming, web-based media, and internet shopping.

WORKING OF DAPP

Dapps have their backend code (shrewd agreements) running on a decentralized organization and not a unified server. They utilize the Ethereum blockchain for information stockpiling and brilliant agreements for their application rationale. A brilliant agreement resembles a bunch of decides that live on-bind for all to see and run precisely as per those guidelines.

Smart Contract

A Smart Contract is a bunch of rules written to decide how members or partners can take an interest. Aids programmed sending of the agreement and is generally appropriated. Shrewd Agreements resemble contracts like in reality however they are advanced. It is a little PC program put away on Blockchain. As a savvy contract dwells in Blockchain it accordingly can't be compromised and disposes of the requirement for any focal power.

The two players might consent to specific advanced agreements and when more is met the understanding is naturally applied. Anyway, brilliant agreements ought not be contrasted with legitimate agreements in the present yet there is a future chance of lawful agreements as long as specific conditions are met.

Smart Contracts are like agreements as in reality however are advanced in many fields. A little PC program put away on Blockchain. The savvy contract stays on Blockchain so it can't be hindered and disposes of the requirement for any focal power (Datta, 2017). All gatherings to the understanding consent to specific agreements carefully and when certain principles are met the arrangement is naturally upheld. Anyway, shrewd agreements ought not be contrasted with lawful agreements in the present however there is a future chance of legitimate agreements as long as specific conditions are met.

Be that as it may, Smart Contracts ought not be contrasted with lawful agreements as of now, however they might become lawful agreements later on assuming specific standards are met. There are numerous far-reaching utilization of lawful agreements as brilliant agreements acknowledged by courtrooms once explicit legitimate necessities are characterized and followed.

Functions of Smart Contracts

A Smart Contract is a mechanized exchange convention that executes the provisions of an agreement. With the assistance of rise of blockchain innovation, brilliant agreement can implement or self-execute authoritative provisions.

It doesn't need the requirement for a focal power, general set of laws, or an outside implementation instrument. Brilliant agreements render exchanges recognizable, straightforward, and irreversible.

It is answerable for:

- Working with
- Confirming
- Uphold or self-execute authoritative statements
- Upholding the arrangement or an understanding.

The motivation behind utilizing Blockchain innovation is to keep the exchanges altered evidence and straightforward without the mediation of any focal power. When some lawful principles are determined and followed, we might encounter an inescapable use of lawful agreements in type of savvy contracts acknowledged by courtroom. It is completely accomplished as the data composed on a square can never be changed by anybody. Here, every exchange must be confirmed by the all members, in this way restricting the need of government or bank. One of the Instances of Straightforward Agreements is A basic advanced worth trade like Bitcoins or Litecoin to somebody.

Traditional Contracts vs. Smart Contracts

We should check out a guide to see how Smart contracts work that you might be acquainted with Kickstarter a huge gathering pledges stage. Item groups can go to Kickstarter to do a task and put out an objective of subsidizing and begin gathering cash from other people who trust in the thought. Kickstarter is really an outside organization that lives between item gatherings and patrons which implies the two of them need Kickstarter's trust to deal with their funds appropriately.

Assuming that a venture is effectively financed by the undertaking group they anticipate that Kickstarter should give them their cash, then again fans need their cash to go to the task assuming they are supported or get a return when it has not accomplished its objectives. Both the item group and its backers need to depend on Kickstarter yet with Smart contracts we can construct the very framework that doesn't need an outer organization like Kickstarter so we should make a shrewd agreement. With this we can orchestrate a brilliant agreement to hold every one of the assets got until a specific point project patrons would now be able to move their cash through a Smart contract assuming that the undertaking gets full financing the agreement passes consequently.

Ethereum

Ethereum is one of the blockchain based appropriated figuring stage. It is a worldwide, open-source stage for decentralized applications. On Ethereum one can compose code that controls some advanced qualities which runs precisely as customized, and is available anyplace on the planet.

Ethereum gives the Ethereum Virtual Machine (EVM) to produce Ether by running the code of Smart contracts on the pubic hubs present on the organization, which is transferred by its maker.

For making the code for Smart Contracts, Solidity, an OOP language is utilized.

This UI is known as a decentralized application or a Dapp. This server separates the blockchain from the convention administrations. Truffle IDE gives a neighborhood climate to gather different parts of a DApp. In this part, Smart Contract will be carried out and further arrangement on Decentralized Application for two contextual analyses.

Benefits

This stage gives openings on new plans of action and worth creation for big business. The stage is planned to lessen the expense of trust and coordination between business parties. Where business network responsibility assumes a significant part in business, it Worked on something similar and supportive in functional effectiveness. The stage is similarity with public fundamental net or permissioned, private organizations and seriously future-verification your business.

LIMITATIONS OF DAPP

The utilization of dApps is as yet in the beginning phases, and hence it is trial and inclined to specific issues and questions. There are questions regarding whether the applications will actually want to scale viably, especially if an application requires huge calculations and over-burdens an organization, causing network clog.

The capacity to foster an easy-to-use interface is another worry. Most clients of applications created by conventional brought together foundations have a usability assumption that urges them to utilize and communicate with the application. Getting individuals to change to dApps will expect designers to make an end-client experience and level of execution that rivals currently well-known and set up programs.

The test of doing code adjustments is one more impediment of dApps. Once conveyed, a dApp will probably require progressing changes for the motivations behind making improvements or to address bugs or security chances. As per Ethereum, it tends to be moving for engineers to make required updates to dApps in light of the fact that the information and code distributed to the blockchain are difficult to alter.

Pros:
- Advances client security
- Opposes oversight
- Adaptable stage empowers dApp improvement

Cons:
- Test, will be unable to scale
- Challenges in fostering an easy-to-understand interface.
- Hard to make required code changes

CONCLUSION

Because of blockchain innovation, applications have developed into DApps. DApps are the better version of older applications as they can possibly become self-supporting assets by permitting their partners to put resources into DApp improvement. Soon, DApps will be liked over right now accessible conventional applications for a very long time, for example, installments, stockpiling, distributed computing, and so forth. The progression of blockchain reception is unavoidable, which will bring about various current works on becoming outdated.

In spite of the fact that it has been a moderately brief time frame since Ethereum dispatched, blockchain is acquiring and greater prominence every day. Countless organizations from assorted enterprises are thinking about utilizing appropriated record innovation to determine their issues. For that reason, smart contracts are turning out to be progressively well known on the grounds that they empower various gatherings to perform exchanges without outsider go-betweens. Many individuals ask themselves which organization will be most appropriate for executing their thoughts into the real world.

Ethereum application advancement organization in India can give business visionaries, SMEs, set up ventures administrations at a reasonable hourly rate. Notwithstanding, nobody can work with all blockchains, so every task requires its novel methodology.

We trust you found this chapter accommodating. Decentralized applications in blockchain are progressive innovation and will immediately become one of the most popular arrangements among undertakings. You can gain by this chance by turning into a blockchain proficient. Get a blockchain course to get familiar with every one of the fundamental abilities for becoming one.

REFERENCES

Androulaki, E. (2018). Hyperledger Fabric: A Distributed Operating System for Permissioned Blockchains. In *Proceedings of the 13th EuroSys Conference, EuroSys 2018*. ACM. 10.1145/3190508.3190538

Christidis, K., & Devetsikiotis, M. (2016). Blockchains and smart contracts for the internet of things. *IEEE Access: Practical Innovations, Open Solutions*, *4*, 2292–2303. doi:10.1109/ACCESS.2016.2566339

Datta, S. P. A. (2017). Cybersecurity-Personal Security Agents for People, Process, Atoms & Bits. *Journal of Innovation Management*, *5*(1), 4-13.

Dutta, S., & Saini, K. (2020). Blockchain and Social Media. In Blockchain Technology and Applications (pp. 101-114). Auerbach Publications. doi:10.1201/9781003081487-6

Dutta, S., & Saini, K. (2021). Securing Data: A Study on Different Transform Domain Techniques. *WSEAS Transactions on Systems And Control, 16*, 110–120. doi:10.37394/23203.2021.16.8

Dutta, S., & Saini, K. (2021). Statistical Assessment of Hybrid Blockchain for SME Sector. *WSEAS Transactions on Systems And Control, 16*. doi:10.37394/23203.2021.16.6

Koo, D., Shin, Y., Yun, J., & Hur, J. (2018). Improving Security and Reliability in Merkle Tree-Based Online Data Authentication with Leakage Resilience. *Applied Sciences (Basel, Switzerland), 8*(12), 2532. doi:10.3390/app8122532

Kumari, K., & Saini, K. (2019). CFDD (CounterFeit Drug Detection) using Blockchain in the Pharmaceutical Industry. *International Journal of Engineering Research & Technology, 8*(12), 591-594.

Nakamoto, S. (2008). *Bitcoin: A peer-to-peer electronic cash system*. Bitcoin.

Raj, P., Saini, K., & Surianarayanan, C. (Eds.). (2020). *Blockchain Technology and Applications*. CRC Press. doi:10.1201/9781003081487

Saini, K. (2020). Next Generation Logistics: A Novel Approach of Blockchain Technology. In *Essential Enterprise Blockchain Concepts and Applications*. CRC Press.

Saini, K., Roy, A., Chelliah, P. R., & Patel, T. (2021). Blockchain 2.O: A Smart Contract. In *International Conference on Computational Performance Evaluation (ComPE)*, (pp. 524-528). IEEE. 10.1109/ComPE53109.2021.9752021

Wang, W., Hoang, D. T., Hu, P., Xiong, Z., Niyato, D., Wang, P., Wen, Y., & Kim, D. I. (2019). A Survey on Consensus Mechanisms and Mining Strategy Management in Blockchain Networks. *IEEE Access : Practical Innovations, Open Solutions, 7*, 22328–22370. doi:10.1109/ACCESS.2019.2896108

Yusuf, H., & Surjandari, I. (2020). Comparison of Performance Between Kafka and Raft as Ordering Service Nodes Implementation in Hyperledger Fabric. *Int. J. Adv. Sci. Technol., 29*(7), 3549–3554.

Zheng, Z., Xie, S., Dai, H., Chen, X., & Wang, H. (2017). An Overview of Blockchain Technology: Architecture, Consensus, and Future Trends. In *Proc. - IEEE 6th Int. Congr. Big Data*. IEEE. 10.1109/BigDataCongress.2017.85

Chapter 5
Application of Machine Learning and Blockchain Technology for Smart Healthcare Applications

J. Brintha Jei
SRM Dental College, India

S. Behin Sam
Dr. Ambedkar Government Arts College (Autonomous), India

ABSTRACT

Smart health care depends on emerging technologies like electronic health records, along with internet of things, artificial intelligence, mobile communications, cloud computing, etc. This helps to create various systems like health management systems and medical service systems. This chapter includes: (1) development of smart health care using machine learning and blockchain technology; (2) uses of machine learning and blockchain technology with smart healthcare applications; (3) impact of smart healthcare applications on human health; (4) features of smart healthcare applications; and (5) limitations.

INTRODUCTION

Due to abrupt advance in medical field the attention has been shown towards smart healthcare applications. This smart healthcare applications uses wireless network, portable devices, medical persons to receive, process and investigate the medical happing's. Information of each and every patient can be grasped by the medical professionals at any point of time and in any part of the universe. This helps to make the diagnosis and planning of treatment immediately for the patients. Blockchain technology works under specific rules to identify the transactions made by the patients, manages storage, summons automation, and further added applications. Machine learning is the prime technology involves in investigation, intelligent discernment, and creative healthcare analyses. Machine learning is software-based method, it uses predetermined set of technologies and theories like statistical and linguistic strategy to analyse liberated text or sound. It is of two types; they are unsupervised learning and supervised learning.

DOI: 10.4018/978-1-6684-7697-0.ch005

SMART HEALTH CARE

Smart healthcare applications are defined as a stream which includes acquisition of data, computing and networking technologies, data privacy, processing of data and dissemination of data. Medical management in healthcare involves three key components:

1. The medical team includes doctors, nurses, administration, and technicians
2. Emergency oriented services
3. Health and health related service users like patients

E-health is defined as "an emerging field in the intersection of medical informatics, public health and business, referring to health services and information delivered or enhanced through the Internet and related technologies". As a whole this term signifies not only the development in technology, but also involves the state of mind, global thinking, improve local and regional health by using communication technology and information.

Blockchain was introduced by Satoshi Nakamoto in 2009 for designing and developing cryptocurrency, Bitcoin. This technology is used in wide areas like finance, banking, education, healthcare, media, power sector, governance, logistics etc. This maintains a distributed ledger technology which removes the third party to authenticate the transaction.

Figure 1. Diagram of blockchain

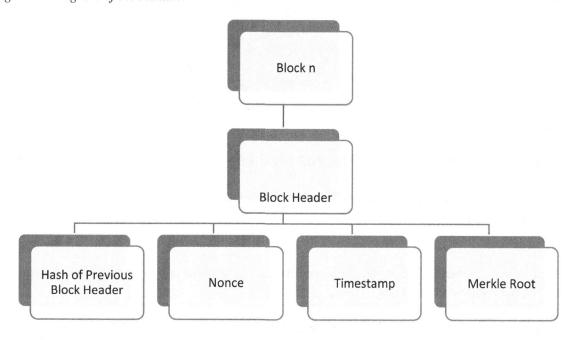

BLOCK STRUCTURE

Figure 2. Distributed digital ledger

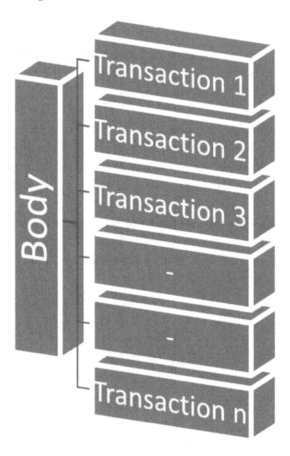

The distributed digital ledger is maintained by the Block chain by using the blocks. Each block consists of

- Data- purpose of blockchain will command the type of data
- Hash- will identify the block and its components
- Previous hash- communicates current block to previous block

Block chain structure includes various layers like presentation layer, consensus layer, networking layer, data layer, infrastructure layer.

Electronic Health Record: Healthcare Blockchain

They ensure access to health records by the healthcare providers and by their patients. Single source of accurate medical records can be maintained. Medical insures can directly access the medical records and the time, cost and intermediary can be avoided

Table 1. Layers of blockchain

Layers of blockchain	Function
Presentation layer	Chaincode User interface Smart contract
Consensus layer	Proof of stake Prime proof of work Proof of work Proof of activity
Networking layer	Peer to peer
Data layer	Blockchain authentic data are stored and managed Data signature
Infra structure layer	Verifies transactions Classify into blocks Telecast in the network

Characteristic Features of Blockchain in Healthcare

1. Secures electronic health record
2. Drugs can be traceable and ensure safety
3. Manage the human organ supply chain
4. Maintains privacy in bio-informatics
5. It streamlines the patient care and avoid mistakes
6. It is the digital backbone to interface with ML

Uses of Blockchain

1. Medical health care data can be owned by patients themselves
2. Data is transparent
3. Data can be verified
4. Trusted data can be obtained
5. Decentralization of health data
6. Improved data privacy
7. Improved data security

Blockchain Healthcare Operating System

Figure 3. Blockchain healthcare operating system

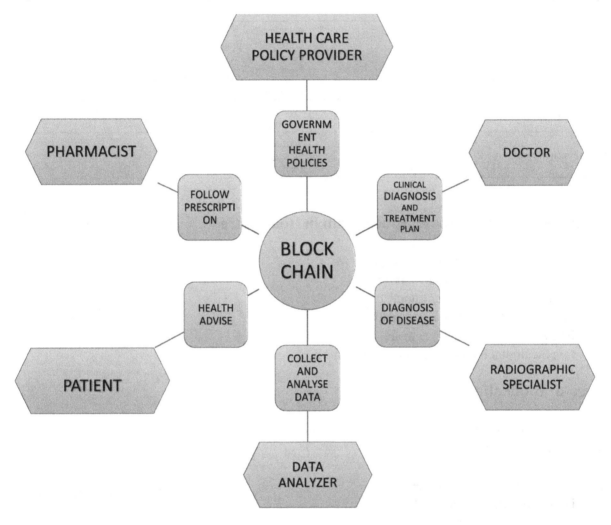

MACHINE LEARNING

Machine Learning (ML) is a field that came through artificial intelligence. It is mainly associated with developing and designing algorithms which helps to enhance the computers to work based on empirical data. ML plays a significant role in smart health by improving the ML algorithms, improved methods to capture data, enhancing computer networks and customization based on user's requirement. It also improves the healthcare services by giving proper medical diagnosis, early diagnosing the diseases and analysis the disease condition. ML has the ability to classify the patients into groups based on risk factor. As ML uses various probabilistic, statistical and optimization methods.

Significance of Machine Learning in Health Care

1. Helps in enhancing diagnosis
2. Support in making clinical decision
3. Provide guidance to maintain patient lifestyle
4. Maintain patient stratification based on health condition
5. Predictive investigation can be made
6. Maintains administrative process

Advantages of Machine Learning in Health Care

1. Self-regulated routine work is carried out by virtual nursing
2. ML helps the physician for diagnosing and treatment planning
3. By providing virtual assistance helps the patient to obtain the basic health care guidance
4. New advancements and innovation of pharmaceutical drugs by ML reduce the research cost and time
5. Helps to improve the resource management of organisations and hospital by enabling automation of administrative backstopping
6. ML helps the doctors to make correct decision and helps to enhance patient outcomes
7. Helps the organisation to stretch-out their treatment without compromising the quality of the treatment
8. Reduce the risk and mortality of the patients by diagnosing serious disease, conducting surgeries with robotic assistance and early identification of patients with high risk
9. ML allows extraction of faster health data from important patient cases and satisfies the medical professionals
10. ML consolidates the health data of the health organisations and make them to govern the refined data.

Block chain technology with machine learning will enhance the ability of the nation with early warning monitoring for infections/ diseases of epidemic in nature. This helps to reduce the mortality and morbidity rate by reducing health treats to public and maintains universal health security.

Machine Learning Facilitated Blockchain in Public Health

Table 2. ML facilitated blockchain and its functions

	ML facilitated BC	**Function**
1.	Artificial neural network	• It helps to overcome time consumption procedure. • Maintains personal health records • Requires less human involvement • Involves in medical imaging in radiology department • Helps to recognise text and voice
2.	Decision tree	• Used by medical physicians to make decisions more accurately • It is patient friendly
3.	Naive Bayes	• Enhances the ability and certainty of smart healthcare contracts • Can build and share continuously updated health care data to public block chain using smart healthcare contracts • Maintain the healthcare data like cardiac disease, diabetes mellitus and cancer.
4.	K-Nearest Neighbor	• Used to compare available patient cases • Very effectual in finding cardiac cases • Can be used to build-up smart models to help in accurate diagnosing of cardiac problems
5.	K-Means Clustering	• Based on the spread profiles it line-up chronic kidney disorder patients • Used for pattern disclosure in smart health care data
6.	Random Forest	• Used to track, control and limit the dissemination of infections in intensive care unit
7.	Support Vector Machine	• It creates boundary of the multifaceted area of the input data and helps to segregate similar data into numerous segments. • Prevents hospital readmission and death by forecasting cardiac patient drug loyality
8.	Deep Learning-Enabled Blockchain Technologies for Public Health	• Provide large amount of information about patient cases • It is a universal decentralized database which can be verifiable.
9.	Recurrent Neural Networks	• It maintains secrecy and safety of the patients healthcare medical data • Patients health record cannot be seen without their concern • Also make a track of the given medical prescriptions and medical happenings.
10.	Deep Autoencoder	• Provides excellent results based on tasks of unsupervised learning
11.	Deep Belief Network	• Can give good result with tasks of supervised and unsupervised learning • It acts as a realm for electroencephalography.
12.	Deep Convolutional Neural Network	• Used for image capturing and processing • Helps to detect lung scan of COVID-19 infected patient. It also helps to differentiate the scans of normal lung and viral pneumonia affected lung
13.	Deep Generative Models	• To generate medical image, to analyse and process medical image • To impute cell gene
14.	Deep Reinforcement Learning	• Medical parametric image analysis, register image and to detect anatomical landmarks

Challenges of ML in Healthcare

- Lack of clean organised health data among organizations as most of the datasets are noncompatible among the healthcare organisations.

- Existing biases in ML can creep in and amplify the machine learning algorithms which is trained by humans
- Lack of strategy of ML create high impact on conventional medical health care workflow
- ML healthcare is a complex technology so it requires outstanding technical expertise and deep knowledge of medical science.

Figure 4. Machine learning in healthcare

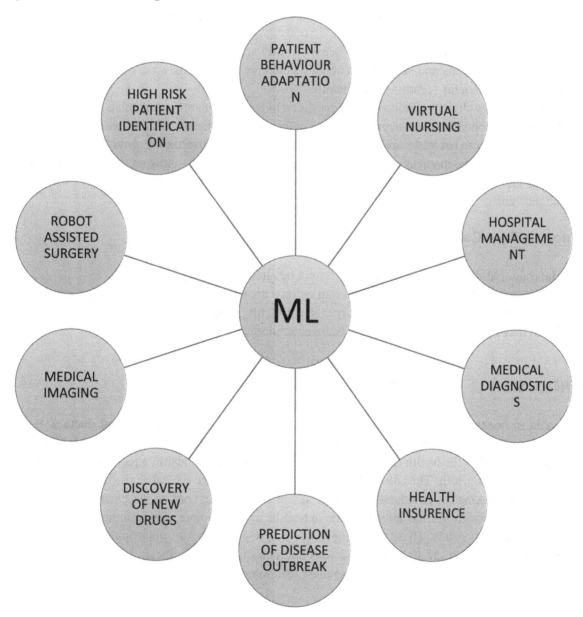

Issue Solving Blockchain and Machine Learning

- All authorised users will have a copy of their shared health record. This helps to prevent the problem in acquiring health data. These data's can be fed to ML models though this trustable and reliable results can be obtained.
- The models can be skilled with the real health data and this helps to enhance the accuracy and efficacy of them and hence reduces the amount to be paid to the chief authority.
- The training can be given to the models based on the doctors treatment, advices and suggestions given to other patients whom having similar clinical symptoms and problems. This makes them to provide lifestyle advices for the patients.
- The trained model uses the language processing software and identify the disease and can provide the treatment options and suggestions about health care professionals, thus it can clear the basic doubts of the patients regarding their health.
- It also provides clinical opinions and suggestions to the healthcare professionals.
- The trained models involves in predicting the outbreak of the disease when the patients test reports are added in these networks and can provide suggestion to the healthcare providers.
- If the details of the medical equipment's and machines are added to this network, it monitors the details and predict the need for changing the equipment or removal and replacing of the part of the machines.

Things to Take Care

- The transaction details once recorded it cannot be altered
- The copy and the past record of all the transactions are stored in this technology, so there may be increase in the size of database and may create difficulty in handling the database in near future.
- There may be mistakes when the details are entered manually

CONCLUSION

Blockchain in healthcare helps to maintain patients records with exclusive keys and doctors. It also connects the users to their health records at any point of time in a safer way without any problem. The patient record includes the health report, pharmacological drugs used, health outcomes and continuous track of that patients health. Thus blockchain has the ability to change the entire medical sector but the only problem is making the healthcare providers should embrace and utilize the blockchain technique in a wider level. Though ML has huge benefits in healthcare, implementation of in healthcare requires a slow and careful approach. These technologies provide huge number of opportunities to be utilized. This helps in eliminating the in-between persons and commission. Healthcare profession is in direct contact with the life of the patient, so by using these technologies the morbidity rate can be reduced and the life span of the patient can be enhanced.

ADDITIONAL READING

Alabdulatif, A., Khalil, I., & Saidur Rahman, M. (2022). Security of Blockchain and AI-Empowered Smart Healthcare: Application-Based Analysis. *Applied Sciences (Basel, Switzerland)*, *12*(21), 11039. doi:10.3390/app122111039

Cornelius, C. A., Qusay, H. M., & Mikael, E. (2019). Blockchain technology in healthcare: A systematic review. *Health Care*, *7*(2), 56. doi:10.3390/healthcare7020056 PMID:30987333

Du, X., Chen, B., Ma, M., & Zhang, Y. (2021, January 12). Research on the Application of Blockchain in Smart Healthcare: Constructing a Hierarchical Framework. *Journal of Healthcare Engineering*, *6698122*, 1–13. doi:10.1155/2021/6698122 PMID:33505644

Khedkar, V.S. & Patel, S. (2021). Diabetes prediction using machine learning: A bibliometric analysis, *Library Philosophy and Practice, 4751.*

Li, Y., Shan, B., Li, B., Liu, X., & Pu, Y. (2021, August 13). Literature Review on the Applications of Machine Learning and Blockchain Technology in Smart Healthcare Industry: A Bibliometric Analysis. *Journal of Healthcare Engineering*, *9739219*, 1–11. doi:10.1155/2021/9739219 PMID:34426765

Oladimeji, O. (2023). Machine Learning in Smart Health Research: A Bibliometric Analysis. *International Journal of Information Science and Management*, *21*(1), 119–128. doi:10.22034/ijism.2022.1977616.0

Pardakhe, N. V., & Deshmukh, V. M. (2019). Machine Learning and Blockchain Techniques Used in Healthcare System. *2019 IEEE Pune Section International Conference (PuneCon)*, Pune, India. 10.1109/PuneCon46936.2019.9105710

Vyas, S., Gupta, M., & Yadav, R. (2019). Converging Blockchain and Machine Learning for Healthcare. *2019 Amity International Conference on Artificial Intelligence (AICAI)*, Dubai, United Arab Emirates. 10.1109/AICAI.2019.8701230

Yu, H., Sun, H., Wu, D., & Kuo, T. T. (2020, March 4). Comparison of Smart Contract Blockchains for Healthcare Applications. *AMIA ... Annual Symposium Proceedings - AMIA Symposium. AMIA Symposium*, *2019*, 1266–1275. PMID:32308924

Chapter 6
Convergence of Machine Learning and Blockchain Technology for Smart Healthcare Applications

Jyothi K. C.
Vellore Institute of Technology, India

Neelu Khare
Vellore Institute of Technology, India

ABSTRACT

The technology boom in Industry 4.0 has resulted in the generation of large volume of medical data. Smart healthcare systems have burgeoned with the convergence of blockchain, machine learning, and internet of things (IoT). The amalgamation of privacy-preserving blockchain technology and predictive diagnosis by machine learning models produces an enhanced healthcare system. This chapter aims to shed light on the machine learning algorithms and blockchain technologies currently used in the healthcare industry. The advantages of opting for blockchain for preserving data integrity and privacy are highlighted. A few applications and steps involved in implementing blockchain and machine learning in healthcare, as well as the challenges faced while doing so, are discussed. Finally, a theoretical blockchain-machine learning internet of medical things(IoMT) framework is proposed, drawing from the recent research advancements.

INTRODUCTION

Role of Healthcare in E-Governance

The past decade has witnessed a tremendous growth of data and several research advancements to handle the influx of information. Countries have invested thousands of dollars in information technology to build and efficient system for storage, structuring and processing of big data, for efficient governance.

DOI: 10.4018/978-1-6684-7697-0.ch006

Thus, digitalization begat the inception of E-governance. E-governance is the use of Information and Communication Technology (ICT) for enabling government services, transfer of information, communication transactions across different organizations. Supply Chain Logistics, elections and finance are a few among the multitude of e-governance initiatives. One prominent but challenging sector is the healthcare industry.

SMART HEALTHCARE

The increased population density, limited resources, geographical barriers to access healthcare services puts a strain on medical service providers as well as patients (Subash et al., 2008). The importance of accurate, prompt e-medical diagnosis is stressed even more, in the wake of the COVID-19. Health is the fundamental factor for overall human well-being. It is estimated that smart healthcare systems will generate billions of dollars in revenue.

Smart healthcare is a system designed using technologies such as wearable devices, IoT, and mobile internet to dynamically access and transfer information between patients and healthcare providers (hospitals, clinical research centers, etc.) and to interactively monitor and respond to the medical environment intelligently.

IoT-connected devices like wearables, skin sensors, home monitoring tools and more, enable richer medical insights into symptoms and health trends, new levels of remote care, and greater control to patients over their care and treatment.

Smart healthcare incorporates Internet of Medical Things (IoMT), wearable devices, cloud computing, machine learning and blockchain and other technologies. It covers a gamut of medical services ranging from drug testing to disease diagnosis and dynamic treatment. These are primarily executed using machine learning algorithms.

MACHINE LEARNING

Machine Learning (ML) is a subset of Artificial Intelligence (AI) which enables computers to emulate human thinking pattern, without explicitly being programmed. Its definition and origin dates to 1959 and was popularized by the Pioneer in the field of Artificial intelligence and the famous inventor of the Checkers self-playing program. Tom Michell defines machine learning functionally as "A computer program is said to learn from experience E with respect to some class of tasks T and performance measure P if its performance at tasks in T, as measured by P, improves with experience E."

To define machine learning in layman's terms, it is basically the ability to make computers think like humans. For example, when shooting a basketball, the first attempt results in the ball lands a few inches from the backboard. After altering the shooting stance, the ball bounces off the backboard. Eventually after adjusting the shooting force, position, zoning in on the target, the ball falls in the hoop. Thus, the result improves by learning from each trial. Replicating similar cognitive thinking processes in computers is what machine learning aims to do, and Alan Turing brings the question "can machines do what we (as thinking entities) can do?" to light in his paper "Computing Machinery and Intelligence".

Machine learning is commercially applied in forecasting the weather, detecting fraudulent transactions, and predicting the remaining useful life of industrial machinery with the aid of statistical algorithms and machine learning models. For example, the temperature, humidity, rainfall data collected over the past few months is fed into the machine learning model. The model then identifies the hidden pattern through correlation analysis, feature extraction and so on to predict if it will be sunny tomorrow. The more convoluted and well-known implementation of this use case is the Google weather forecast.

The field of data analytics, where machine learning techniques are used for predicting the business outcome, based on historical data is known as predictive analytics. Data scientists, engineers, and business analysts unveil the hidden patterns and produce reliable insights about the future trends and events, to facilitate businesses.

Often, we come across suggestions for friends or followers while browsing social media. By comparing user data, age, gender, geographical location, and by matching the characteristics of existing connections with others, new suggestions are provided. This is implemented using an information filtering system, known as the recommendation engine. These engines are widely used for product recommendations as well.

Machine learning predictions for real world cases, where external factors affect the outcome or cognitive reasoning and explanation are required for a particular decision, hamper the 100% accuracy score of the model. However, problems like "Does this file contain a virus?" and "Will this customer default on his or her credit card repayment?" can be resolved using machine learning techniques.

Figure 1. Machine learning roadmap

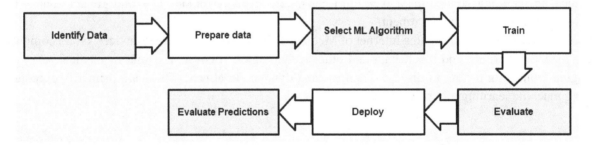

Types of Machine Learning

Machine learning is broadly classified into four categories *viz.* Supervised Machine Learning, Unsupervised Machine Learning, Semi-Supervised Machine Learning and Reinforcement Learning, based on the type of data fed into the model, and the algorithms used to achieve the desired outcome.

Supervised Learning

In supervised learning, the machine learning algorithm fed data where the target variable is associated with numeric or string tags or classes for training. The model identifies and correlation between the factor variables and these tags, also known as labels. It then applies the logic to map the associated label to the new example data loaded into it. The concept of supervised learning can be compared to how a child learns alphabets. She associates the names of the alphabets to the shape, sounds and lines or curves of each alphabet. Then, when given a letter, she notices the features and maps it to the alphabet names(labels) stored in her memory and thus, identifies it.

Figure 2. Stages of a supervised learning problem

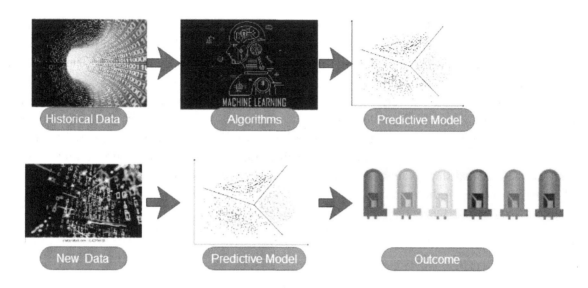

Unsupervised Learning

Unsupervised learning is when the algorithm learns from data which is unlabeled, i.e., no tags associated with the target response. The algorithm categorizes the data according to the identical and dissimilar features it observes. These algorithms are beneficial especially when restructuring of data is required. The model can be used to generate new dataset with independent features, extracted from the unlabeled dataset, that can serve as input for a supervised machine learning model. An example of unsupervised learning is distinguishing horses and humans. The model learns patterns and uses the features identified such as skin color tone, facial features, and body shape to label them as "human" or "horse". (Figure 3) represents an unsupervised learning mechanism for identification of cats and dogs.

Figure 3. Unsupervised learning mechanism for identification of cats and dogs

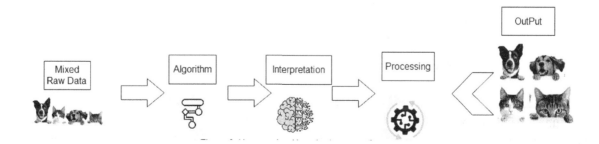

Semi- Supervised Learning

As the name suggests, semi-supervised learning is the intermediary between supervised and unsupervised learning. A semi-supervised algorithm is trained on unlabeled and labeled data. This aims to maximally utilize the available data, as unlabeled data are vast in volume compared to annotated data. The unlabeled similar data are clustered using an unsupervised learning algorithm based on the degree of similarity. The labels are then assigned with reference to the labelled data, on which the semi-supervised model is trained on. This approach is similar to learning to ride a bicycle. In the beginning, you ride with training wheels attached till you get comfortable with peddling and braking. Once the training wheels are removed, someone pushes you from behind while peddling until you can balance yourself. Finally, after learning all the essential steps, you start riding the bicycle yourself, but you figure out when to brake, pedal faster depending on the road conditions and obstacles on the way. (Figure 4) is an example of semi-supervised learning where the ML model classifies fruits.

Figure 4. Semi-supervised learning example

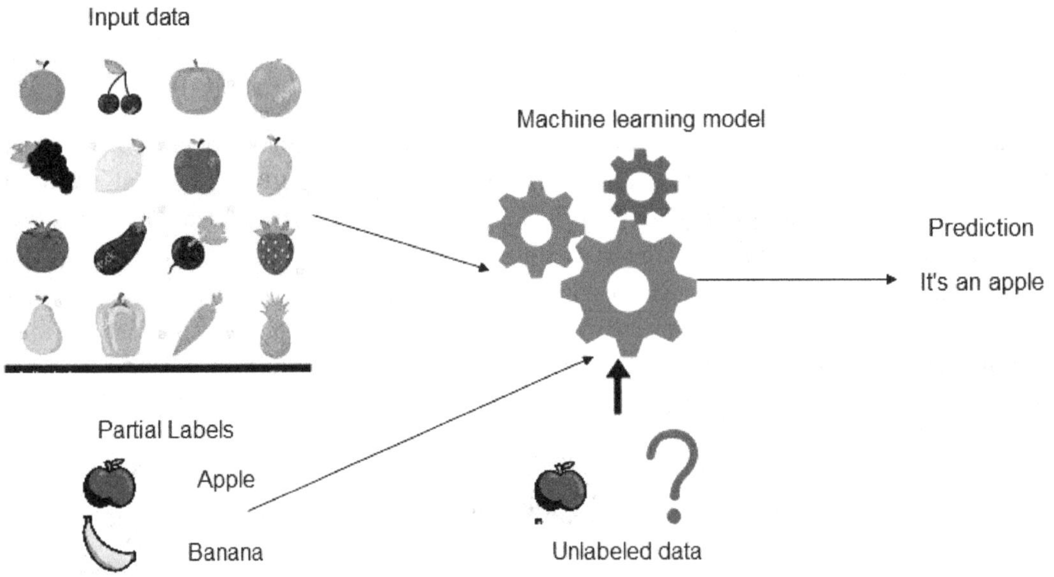

Reinforcement Learning

Reinforcement learning is the process of training the "agent", i.e., the model to achieve a target with the aid of punishments and rewards along with the unlabeled data. The feedback mechanism "punishes", i.e., penalizes the model's scores when a wrong decision is made and gives incentives, increments the score when the model makes a correct decision. This is akin to trial-and-error experiments, in real world terms. The application lets the model know of the results of its actions, for example in the case of navigating a maze, whether the path leads to a dead-end or not. Amazon's Deep Racer provides a cloud, car-racing platform where you train an autonomous racing car to compete in virtual and physical leagues.

Figure 5. Reinforcement learning process diagram

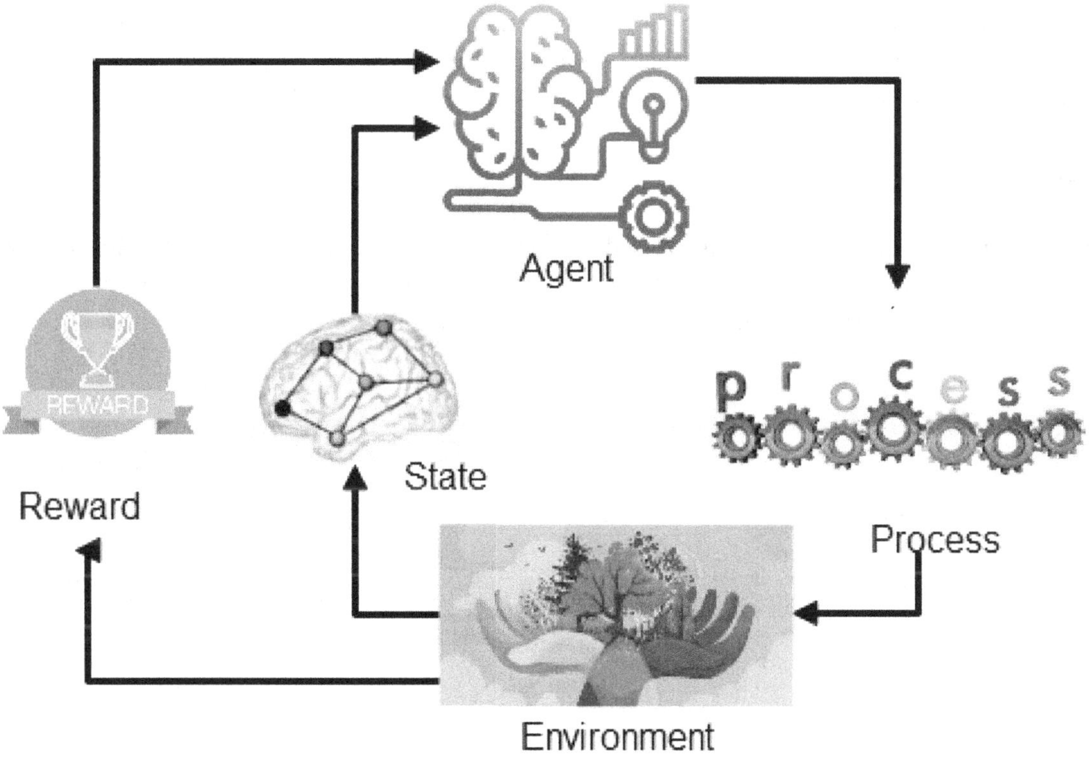

Classification of Machine Learning Based on The Desired Target

Machine learning can be classified into regression, classification, clustering, association, positive reinforcement, and negative reinforcement based on the target outcome.

Regression

Regression algorithms are subdivision of supervised learning where the target variable is in continuous format. Estimating the healthcare costs based on demographic and patient health records, prediction blood glucose values are examples of regression.

Classification

Like regression, classification also comes under supervised learning however, the target variable is discrete, in the form of tags or classes, not continuous in nature. Detecting if a tumor is malicious or benign is a classic classification problem statement.

Clustering

Clustering is a type of unsupervised learning where the unlabeled data is segregated into different groups or "clusters" based on the degree of similarity among the input data points. Clustering is widely used for disease and patient subtypes identification (Martin-Gutierrez et al., 2021).

Association

Association rule learning is also a supervised learning method which finds dependencies among the input variables as to maximize the profit generated. Association rule mining has been used to decipher the nature of amino acids in protein sequences. (Gupta et al., 2006)

Figure 6. Flowchart of types of machine learning

Machine Learning Algorithms in Healthcare

Machine learning is applied to eclectic electronic health record (EHR), e.g., patient health records, routine clinical data, imaging data, and digital clinical research data (e.g., omics data) for disease diagnosis and prognosis, drug discovery and designing dynamic treatment regimens (DTRs). Below are a few popular machine learning techniques used in healthcare.

Support Vector Machine

Support vector machine (SVM) creates most optimal decision boundary that divides an n-dimensional input into several classes. This decision boundary, known as the hyperplane, is used to classify the new data fed into the model during testing. Support vector machines are used for both classification and regression problems. (Ali et al., 2022) proposed a smart healthcare system to classify vocal disorders using SVM.

Figure 7. Graph of classification results of SVM model

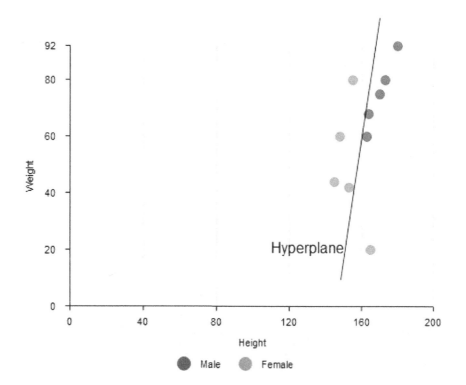

Artificial Neural Networks

Artificial neural networks (ANN) are modelled on the connectivity of neurons in the human brain. They are comprised of an input layer, multiple hidden layers and an output layer. Each layer contains neurons connect to the next layer (feed forward direction) via "weights", which are akin to dendrites and axons connecting the neurons in the brain. The number of input features and output labels(classes) decide the number of the neurons in the input layer and the output layer respectively. ANNs are popular in predicting Alzheimer's or diagnosing general diseases from EMR data (Ferdous et al., 2020).

Logistic Regression

Logistic Regression is a statistical machine learning algorithm which outputs the probability of occurrence(likelihood) of an event. It implements the sigmoid function which plots an S-shape curve, ranging from 0 to 1. Logistic regression has been found to perform well in binary classification tasks, for example heart failure prediction as demonstrated by Ambesange et al (2020) and Nishadi (n.d.).

Random Forest

Random Forest is an ensemble classifier and is implemented a collection of decision trees trained on various subsets of data and the final output is the average of the results of the single decision trees. The use of multiple classifiers aids in minimizing bias, preventing overfitting and making the model robust to outliers. A popular application of random forest in medical diagnosis is breast cancer prediction., (Octaviani & Rustam, 2019).

Figure 8. Workflow of random forest for generic prediction task

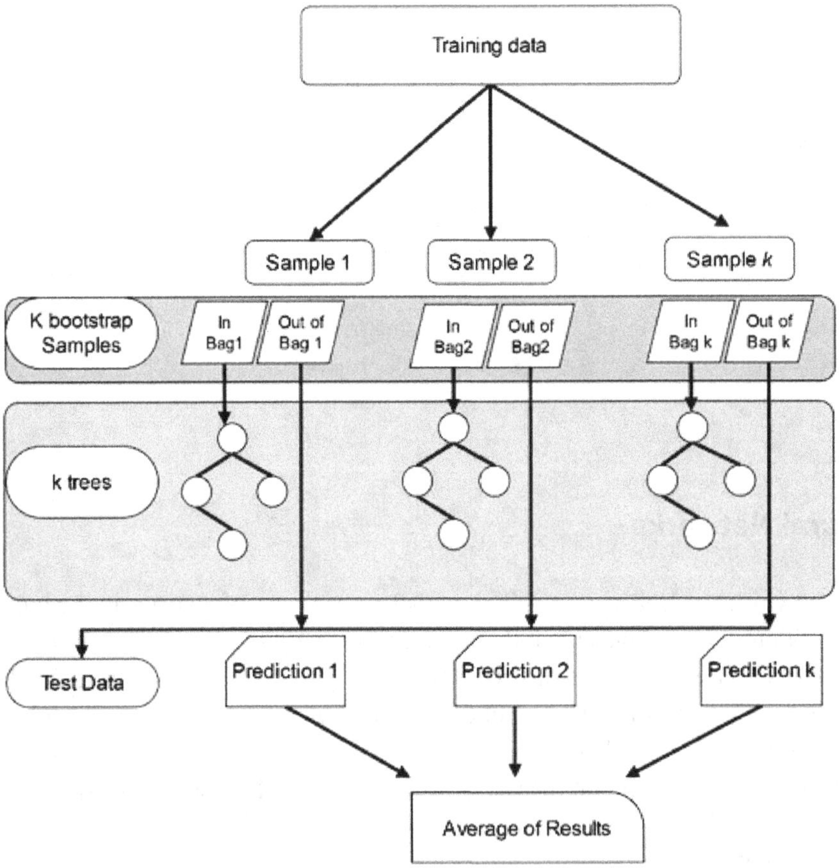

Recent Trends in Machine Learning Applications in Smart Healthcare

While the integration of Internet of Things (IoT) sensors and machine learning models is widely used in the transportation, banking and e-commerce sectors, the implications of the IoMT-ML techniques in the healthcare industry is of greater magnitude. A few applications are prediction systems, recommendation systems, living assistance, medical data aggregation and secured analysis.

Disease Prediction

The discovery and diagnosis of diseases are sped up with the aid of machine learning algorithms and also are beneficial commercially, as patients can receive diagnosis virtually by just sending their electronic health records. One such up-and-coming application that P1vital is planning to launch is PReDicT (Predicting Response to Depressive Treatment) device which monitors the patients' emotional responses to anti-depressive treatments for 1 week and forecasts the effectiveness of treatment (Simon et al., 2019). Machine learning has also been proven to be more accurate in diagnosing rare diseases as compared to experienced doctors. For example, Cedars-Sinai developed an artificial intelligence (AI) tool to predict the occurrence of a heart attack based on computed tomography angiography (CTA) images. The model diagnoses precisely in 5-6 seconds as opposed to the expert diagnosis which takes 25-30 minutes on an average.

Patient Health Monitoring

With the prevalence of diseases and burgeoning population world-wide, AI virtual assistants can be used to tackle the problem of personalized treatments for all. For example, Sense.Iy uses a virtual reality nurse to monitor vital signs such as weight, blood pressure and oxygen as well as answer any queries from the patients. The patients' records are stored by the embedded AI, which is then, transferred to doctors. IBM Watson provides multiple treatment options based on a patient's history using machine learning models.

Medical Imaging and Diagnosis

Medical imaging refers to the process of generating images of the human body, organs and tissues, using various tools. When medical imaging is combined with AI, the machine learning algorithms can be used for assessing the images and diagnosis, for the models catch minute anomalies, which are missed by the naked eye. The integrated technology also has the added advantages of storing and sending the results of the ML models for EHR record maintenance of patients and validation of the results by radiologists respectively, and thus has been used commercially. For example, Quantx's Quantitative Insights provides a diagnostic system for predicting breast cancer and similarly Arterys' cardiac MRI automates the cardiac analysis process using the trained ML models.

BLOCKCHAIN

Blockchain technology, one of the leading technologies introduced in the Industry 4.0, has transformed a plethora of businesses and organizations, in an era seeking privacy, security and interoperability .(Alla & Soltanisehat, 2018) The distributed ledger technology was first introduced by Satoshi Nakamoto in 2008, for the Bitcoin cryptocurrency's transactions. ('Oberhaus, 2018) and has since then been integrated in various sectors, including finance and governance. Let us take the traditional banking system as an example to understand how blockchain can be integrated in society. In this model, the banks are the central authorities which decide upon the transaction regulations- time taken to process a transaction, charge per transaction and so on. On replacing the banks with the blockchain, the transactions are validated by several computers or "nodes" on the network. Therefore, there is no single authority making the decisions and this "decentralized" property earned blockchain its "distributed ledger" alias. (Figure 9) represents the transaction process on a one-to-one basis, i.e., without the intervention of a third-party.

Figure 9. Transaction process on a one-to-one basis

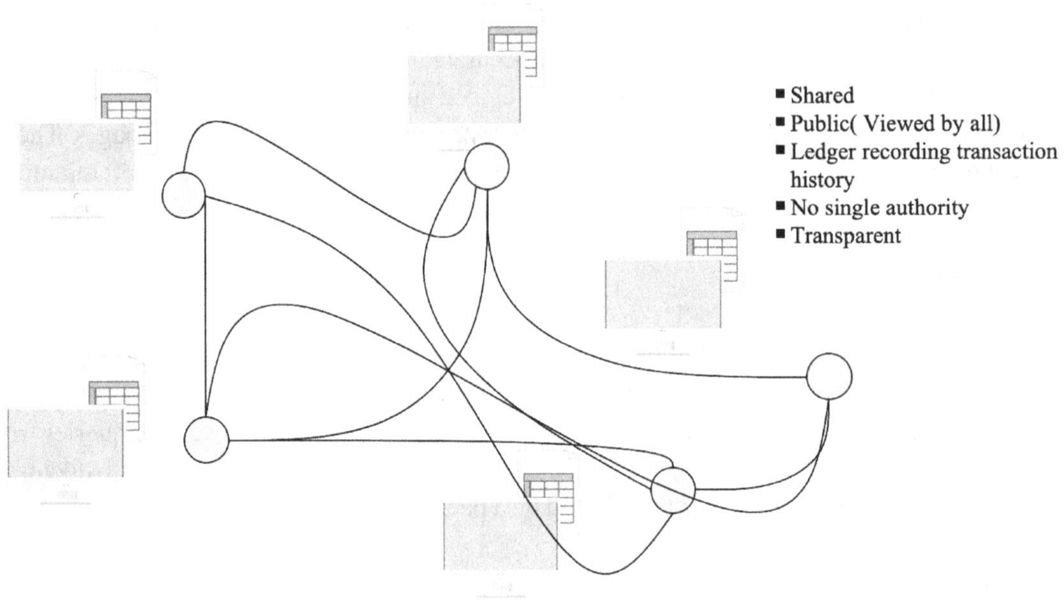

- Shared
- Public(Viewed by all)
- Ledger recording transaction history
- No single authority
- Transparent

Blockchain in Healthcare

The rapid developments in Internet-of-Things (IoT) and big data technologies has generated a massive volume of electronic medical records(EMR) data, which are more convenient for data storage and access. Thus, it is necessary to ensure that the data is secure and unbreachable. In order to achieve this, several hospitals have reduced data sharing which led to the scattering of EMR data across various medical institutes and thereby, impeding medical research.(Adamu et al., 2020) To preserve data integrity and privacy while not compromising on interoperability, blockchain is proposed as a solution for sharing medical data due to its decentralized, tamper-proof nature.(Varma Kakarlapudi et al., 2021).A few application scenarios for blockchain in healthcare are blockchain-based storage and access, and combining blockchain with Internet of Medical Things(IoMT). One among many successful real-world blockchain applications is BlockRx, which integrates medical data from various biomedical institutes using a combination of blockchain technology and iSolve's digital ledger technology (Hosseini Bamakan et al., 2021).

Blockchain Overview

Blockchain is essentially a chain where data blocks, recorded over a period, are cryptographically linked to their previously validated data blocks. The nodes or computers in the blockchain network are responsible for validating transactions on the block.

There are three types of blockchain architecture which are as follows:

Private Blockchain

Private blockchains have control over who can participate in the network. Only by invitation from the owners and authentication of identity and related information, can participants become members in the network. The network operator(s) or the owners can also decide permissions for users to execute consensus protocols that determine mining rewards and allows only select users to maintain the ledger. Additionally, owners of the network can modify and delete the entries on the blockchain apart from being responsible for validation.

Permissionless Blockchain

Also referred to as public blockchain, permissionless network is open to all individuals or organizational nodes. The transactions can be validated by any member in the network and similarly, any node can participate in consensus algorithms for mining, e.g., Bitcoin, Etherium.

Permissioned Blockchain

Permissioned blockchain is also referred to as hybrid blockchain, for they are a mix between private and public. In this network, all the nodes involved in the blockchain are known and the authorization to access the data is relatively less strict compared to private blockchain. Only, the respective organizations verify every transaction in the network. A few examples are Hyperledger Fabric and Ripple which are also private blockchains.

Figure 10. Blockchain architecture

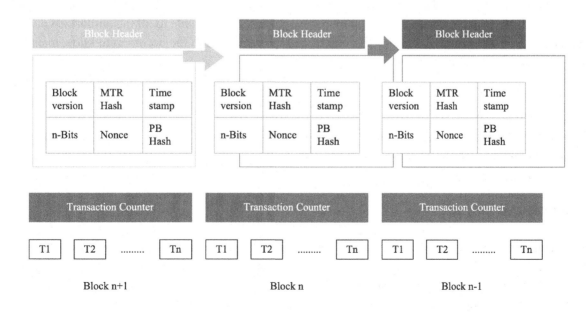

The blockchain is a series of blocks, containing transaction information. Each block consists of a header and transaction counter. The first block in the chain is the parent or genesis block and the hash value of this block is stored in next block's header, and the next block's hash value is stored in the subsequent block and so on. The block header comprises of the following information:

- Block version: Block version is a collection of the validation rules.
- Merkel Tree Root (MTR) Hash: MTR Hash provides the hash value of all transactions in a particular block.
- Time stamp: stores the current time in seconds.
- n-Bits: target threshold of a valid block hash
- Nonce: Nonce is a 4-byte field, used for generating the hash value. It starts from 0 and increases whenever a hash value is calculated.
- Parent block hash contains the previous block's hash value.

The transaction counter is used to keep track of the number of transactions in a block, which depends on the block size and size of each transaction. For trustworthy communication and authentic transactions, digital signatures based on asymmetric cryptography mechanism are used (Aung & Tantidham, 2017).

Some key features of blockchain which are advantageous for implementation in healthcare are as follows:

Immutability

Transactions published on a blockchain network are immutable and cannot be modified. The data blocks are also linked to each other through hash values, and any modifications done in one block will result in the change in hash values of the other blocks and thus, we can easily determine if the data has been tampered with. The sequential addition of data is useful in analyzing patient records. The precompiled records (transactions published on the network) provide information such as disease history and treatment fees which can be used to forecast the duration of treatment, cost and so on. Another application is drug traceability. Since the transactions published on the block are visible to all the authorized parties, medicine buyers can simply scan the QR code of a drug (published in the network) to know manufacturer's details, origin of production, etc.

Consensus

Consensus protocol is the process where a group of active nodes come to an agreement or "consensus" before publishing a transaction on the network. This feature is beneficial for ensuring the integrity and privacy of patient records.

Decentralized Storage

The decentralization ensures that there is no central authority governing the transactions in the network and the ledger records are transparent, including permissioned blockchains which provide less transparency but still reveal the general information of a transaction. The interplanetary file system (IPFS) of blockchain can be implementing in storing EHR records. The protocol basically creates a single hash for one file, which ensures that all versions of that file across the network are identical. The hash values allow users to access data on websites but since, websites change regularly and blockchain files are immutable, the website addresses are mapped to the DNS.

Security

Blockchain adds security via two layers: decentralization and cryptography. The decentralization ensures that there is no single point of failure, so even if one node is faulty or hacked the original data stored in the other nodes are preserved. Cryptography consists of complex mathematical algorithms which provide security by encrypting all information on the blockchain. The input data is passed through a mathematical algorithm and the output produced is random but of a fixed size, along with a hash value. The hash value acts as the unique identifier and tampering one hash results in the tampering of all hashes, which is nearly impossible. The security property is most optimal for ensuring the privacy and integrity of EMRs. A few characteristics attributing to the uniqueness of blockchain compiled from (A et al., 2017; Chang et al., 2019; Underwood, 2016), are listed in Table 1.

Table 1. A compilation of blockchain features identified from literature

Authors	Features identified
(Underwood, 2016)	Immutability, transparency and trust
(A et al., 2017)	Self-sovereignty, transparency, provenance, trust, immutability, disintermediation, collaboration
(Chang et al., 2019)	security, resilience, unalterable evidence, out of the box, no single point of failure, immutability, transaction history/traceability, data privacy, synchronization, dynamic consent, personal data storage clouds enabling individual access, self-executing contractual states, multilevel de-identification and encryption technologies, data integrity

Blockchain Applications in Healthcare

Patient-Centric Electronic Health Records (EHRs)

Electronic health record comprises of a patient's health related information, clinical notes, and laboratory results, in digital format. EHR resolved the issues found in paper-based medical records such as low efficiency and errors in reports. These systems are primarily used for data storage, scheduling of appointments and lab tests, billing all of which further enhance patient care. However, they also come with the risk of data breaches, unsynchronized information and lack of interoperability (Shahnaz et al., 2019). Blockchain poses a solution for the before-mentioned problems. A few benefits of blockchain-enabled EHR systems are: (i) patients can view their records after updates and have control to authorize the necessary medical practitioners to access their records. (ii) Patients and medical insurance providers can communicate directly without the need of an intermediary, thereby saving time and money. (iii) A single source of truth is maintained, i.e., all changes made to a patient's EHR is synchronized across all departments or hospitals. Medical Chain, one of the leading examples for this integration, provides smart healthcare by implementing blockchain technology for the maintenance of EHRs.

Smart contracts for medical insurance and supply chain management

Health insurance protects the assets of an individual from loss due to medical emergency and accidents, and based on the type of insurance acquired, covers doctor visits, surgical expenses and so on. The traditional method for insurance claims is susceptible to minor errors such as misspelling of a patient's name, or the claim was not sent and so on. Automation of the process will rectify these problems and blockchain is one way to implement this. Smart contracts, blockchain-based technology, smooth the settlement process by making the insurance claims transparent to both the patient and insurer. Moreover, these smart contracts can also be used in the healthcare sector among medical practitioners and pharmaceutical companies for authenticating identities, logging contract details and so on. HealthVerity and Chronicled are some healthcare companies which employ the smart contract mechanism.

Challenges in Blockchain

Currently blockchain based healthcare systems are centralized on a small scale. To further expand this, enabling the platform to support multiple fund providers, health ministries and medical research institutes will promote large-scale collaboration and ultimately, enhance the end users' experience.

To continue making blockchain technology an accomplishment, multiple fund providers, healthcare researchers, and health ministries will need to collaborate for the transformation of the healthcare sector, as it will significantly help end users, (Bhattacharya et al., 2019) There are several major blockchain security challenges and preventions, a few of which are listed below: (Wenhua et al., 2023)

51% of Attacks

Miners are responsible for validating the transaction and when a group gains monopoly in the network, the entire blockchain ledger gets rigged and corrupt. A 51% attack is an attack where a group of miners control more that 50% of the hash mining rate in the blockchain network. These attacks often occur early in the network when there are few miners thereby, modifying the entire blockchain. One preventive measure for 51% attack is to increase the hash rate by improving the mining pool monitoring.

Sybil Attacks

In a sybil attack, the entire blockchain network crashes due to flooding by a large number of fake network nodes, created by hackers. Using appropriate consensus algorithms and keeping an eye on nodes which forward blocks from one user only can prevent sybil attacks.

Routing Attacks

Routing attacks are caused when hackers leverage an account's anonymity to intercept data sent to internet service providers (ISP). This exposes confidential data without the user's awareness. To minimize routing attacks, users must use strong and regularly updated passwords, ensure that security routing protocols with certificates are implemented.

Endpoint Vulnerabilities in Blockchain

This refers to exploitation of vulnerabilities at the user-end of blockchain network. For example, hackers might obtain the user's password by tracking user behavior and target devices. Regular inspection of system(time, location and device access) and not storing blockchain keys as text files locally in devices are a few measures to prevent endpoint vulnerability attacks.

AN IOMT- ML-BLOCKCHAIN BASED FRAMEWORK FOR HEALTH MONITORING

From (Muneer & Raza, 2022) and (Qureshi et al., 2022) the key layers and processes are identified and described for a blockchain, IoT and machine learning integrated platform for health monitoring. An architecture diagram of the framework is presented in Figure 11.

Figure 11. Layers of theoretical framework

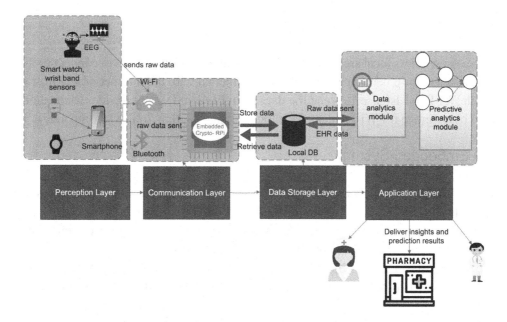

Perception Layer

This is the base layer which contains all the IoT sensors, monitoring equipment and wearable devices (wristbands, smart watches, and electroencephalogram (EEG) headsets). The devices provide the following data: (a) step count and pulse rate recorded by the wristband; (b) SPO2, steps count, heart rate, sleep time and quality, stress indexes which are measured by the smart watch; (c) impulses of the brain neurons (provided by the EEG headsets) which indicate abnormal brain states and cognitive diseases (Alzheimer's, Parkinson's, Epilepsy).

Communication Layer

A gateway is a hardware component used as a channel for communication and information transfer across the network(s). Common gateways used for short-range transmission are wireless sensors, radio-frequency identifier (RFID), Bluetooth and Wi-Fi and gateways for lengthy information exchange include cloud, blockchain and telecommunications technologies.

The following gateways are implemented in this framework:

Bluetooth

This wireless technology is a short-range wireless communication system which securely transfers information between two or more mobile devices and computers using UHF (ultra-high bandwidth 2.4 GHz) electromagnetic radiation. Bluetooth is a personal area network (PAN) with a coverage area of ranging from more than a kilometer to less than a meter. Here, the Bluetooth transfers the raw data (from the wearable devices) to embedded system for blockchain implementation (Raspberry Pi 4) using the smartphone as an intermediary.

Wi-Fi

Wi-Fi is a type of a wireless local area network (LAN) technology that allows to connect mobile devices, computers, and other equipment (printers and video cameras) with the internet or amongst themselves. Like Bluetooth, Wi-Fi is also used to send the data from EEG and sensor devices to the embedded system. The area of coverage for Wi-Fi spans for a longer range (within 70 feet), compared to Bluetooth.

Blockchain Embedded System

The system is designed on Raspberry Pi 4(RPi 4) which was chosen as the multiprocessor embedded platform due to its low cost and low power consumption (less than two watts). The security is implemented in two levels: (a)encrypting the incoming data;(b) using a consensus mechanism, Proof-of-Work(PoW) for mining. A Raspberry crypto platform was used for the above tasks.

Each patient executes a private blockchain system and decides who to grant access to among the medical service providers (doctors, nurses, and pharmacists). Thus, a doctor can participate in multiple blockchain networks.

The public and private keys are generated during encryption and assumed in the smart contract to authenticate and authorize the user. Upon examining the certificate, we can find out if the ledger has been tampered with or not, thereby maintaining transparency. Using these key pairs, the encrypted data is decrypted for analysis and diagnosis with the patient's consent. A more detailed explanation of the Ethereum crypto architecture and the features of the blockchain are explained below.

Ethereum-Crypto Architecture

The architecture comprised of two components:

Raspberry Pi 3(RPi 3): This embedded hardware, known as the "master", executes nodes which are responsible for encrypting the transactions. It also creates a multitude of blocks. RPi 3 sends the data received from RPi 4(via Wi-Fi) to the daughter board, Field Programmable Gate Arrays (FGPA), for encryption.

Figure 12.

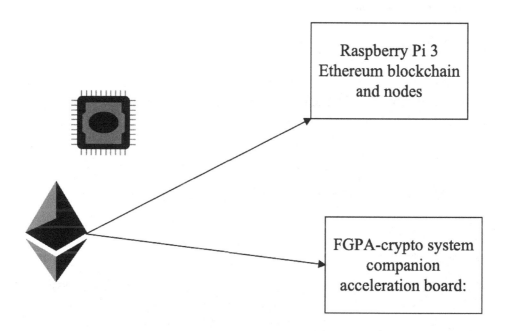

FGPA Board

FGPAs are known for optimizing the performance of a hardware accelerated PoW consensus algorithms constrained by real-time delivery of results and low power consumption. (Ktari, Jalel and Abid, 2008) (Tien Tuan Anh, D and Ji, W and Gang, C and Rui, L and Blockbench, 2017) The companion acceleration board runs encryption and mining blockchain function by implementing Keccak algorithm, which is used for achieving PoW consensus. During encryption of the data, the public-private key pairs are generated. The encrypted and mined data are sent back to RPi 3 and saved to secure the blockchain and maintain data confidentiality. The permissioned Ethereum-RPi architecture is presented in (Figure 12).

Proof of Work Algorithm

The blockchain uses this decentralized mechanism to ensure that all the nodes are in consensus before publishing a transaction on the network, i.e., block. The basic concept is that the first node which solves a "computationally intensive" problem gets to validate its block. The PoW algorithm is widely used in cryptocurrency mining.(Bitcoin, n.d.) A permissioned Ethereum blockchain is used in combination with PoW to maintain the confidentiality and security of data.

The Keccak encryption algorithm which enables customization of hardware accelerators, is a 256-bit cryptographic hash function used by the Ethereum blockchain. After finding the nonce, a random value, solution for the Keccak problem, the block along with the nonce value is mined. These values are combined and encrypted into the hash value.

Then, the hash is compared with the target value (T.V). If the hash<T.V, then the result is correct else incorrect. In case of an error, one must restart the process by inserting a new nonce. The obtained hardware accelerators are embedded on the FGPA board to speed up the PoW computation. For further details, please refer to (Ktari et al., 2022).

Data Type and Access

The data acquisitioned is compiled into a collection of records in digital format, electronic health records (EHR), before adding them to the blockchain. These data are shared between the doctors and patients. The public and private keys generated are used to access EHR through the process of encryption and decryption.

Figure 13. Flow chart of access process

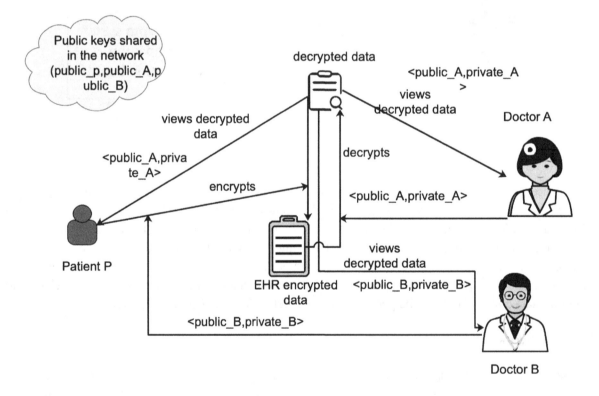

1. The patient authorizes doctor A and adds him to the blockchain to access the encrypted EHR data. The public keys of the members in the network and shared and visible to all.
2. Doctor A decrypts the data using her public and private keys.
3. The patient then uses A's public-private key pair to view the decrypted data.

4. The patient encrypts the data with B's public-private key pair.
5. B decrypts the data using his private key and the public key of the patient.
6. This process is repeated for all the authorized medical personnel.

Storage Layer

The data storage layer is associated with user administration, information management, data processing, storage analytics, stream analytics and security protocol. User administration refers to the management of members where the patient is the admin or master node, and the rest are authorized participant nodes. The RPi data(raw) is received in the raw format from the communication layer which the storage layer forwards to the data analytics module in the application layer for data processing. The transformed data, in the form of EHR, is stored in a local database which can be accessed using a web server hosted on RPi 4. MongoDB, a NoSQL database, supports variety of data types and it can be hosted on RPi as well.

Storage analytics caches the large volume of data in RAM to speed up querying and decision-making processes. Stream analytics is the instantaneous analysis of data, also known as, data-in-motion analysis. In this framework, 1-D data is sent to the RPi-Crypto module every five minutes for encryption and transaction validation. The more complex 2-D data is stored in the local database. Although blockchain addresses most security concerns (transparency, data integrity, secure authorization access, data confidentiality and reliability), Security Socket Layer Business Applications Interfaces (SSL API) can be implemented to ensure communication security.

Application Layer

The application layer consists of the data analytics and predictive analytics modules. These use ML and deep learning (DL) models to transform the data(structuring), extract features (correlation analysis, dimensionality reduction, etc.,) and deliver insights for diagnosis and treatment (predicting the progression of a tumor, evaluating the psychological health status of a patient and abnormal heart condition prognosis (Sarhaddi et al., 2021).

CONCLUSION

There are still some limitations in implementing blockchain-machine learning integrated IoMT frameworks. These include scalability, power consumption (during mining process as well as implementing complex deep learning algorithms on big data) and a few security vulnerabilities. However, the benefits of this integration outweigh the cons. The data integrity, efficiency, speed of processing transactions and security brought by blockchain along with the predictive analytics of machine learning algorithms, only enhance the smart healthcare systems. Furthermore, the obscurity of the black-box machine learnings can be alleviated by blockchain. Blockchain brings explainability to machine learning models with its transparency and decentralization properties, providing a route to trace the decision processes of the models. On an overall perspective, the blockchain-machine learning-IoMT integration has revolutionized the healthcare industry and is continuing to improve day by day.

REFERENCES

A, G., AF, C., & A, I. D. S. (2017). *Blockchain in Education* (Issue KJ-NA-28778-EN-N). Publications Office of the European Union. doi:10.2760/60649

Adamu, J., Hamzah, R., & Rosli, M. M. (2020). Security issues and framework of electronic medical record: A review. *Bulletin of Electrical Engineering and Informatics*, 9(2), 565–572. doi:10.11591/eei. v9i2.2064

Ali, Z., Imran, M., & Shoaib, M. (2022). An IoT-based smart healthcare system to detect dysphonia. *Neural Computing & Applications*, 34(14), 11255–11265. doi:10.100700521-020-05558-3

Alla, S., & Soltanisehat, L. (2018). *Blockchain Technology in Electronic Healthcare System.*

Ambesange, S., Vijayalaxmi, A., & Sridevi, S., Venkateswaran, & Yashoda, B. S. (2020). Multiple Heart Diseases Prediction using Logistic Regression with Ensemble and Hyper Parameter tuning Techniques. *2020 Fourth World Conference on Smart Trends in Systems, Security and Sustainability (WorldS4)*, 827–832. 10.1109/WorldS450073.2020.9210404

Aung, Y. N., & Tantidham, T. (2017). Review of Ethereum: Smart home case study. *2017 2nd International Conference on Information Technology (INCIT)*, 1–4. 10.1109/INCIT.2017.8257877

Bhattacharya, S., Singh, A., & Hossain, M. M. (2019). Strengthening public health surveillance through blockchain technology. *AIMS Public Health*, 6(3), 326–333. doi:10.3934/publichealth.2019.3.326 PMID:31637281

Bitcoin. (n.d.). *Frequently Asked Questions*. https://bitcoin.org/en/faq

Chang, S. E., Chen, Y.-C., & Lu, M.-F. (2019). Supply chain re-engineering using blockchain technology: A case of smart contract-based tracking process. *Technological Forecasting and Social Change*, *144*, 1–11. doi:10.1016/j.techfore.2019.03.015

Ferdous, M., Debnath, J., & Chakraborty, N. R. (2020). Machine Learning Algorithms in Healthcare: A Literature Survey. *2020 11th International Conference on Computing, Communication and Networking Technologies (ICCCNT)*, 1–6. 10.1109/ICCCNT49239.2020.9225642

Gupta, N., Mangal, N., Tiwari, K., & Mitra, P. (2006). Mining Quantitative Association Rules in Protein Sequences. In G. J. Williams & S. J. Simoff (Eds.), *Data Mining: Theory, Methodology, Techniques, and Applications* (pp. 273–281). Springer Berlin Heidelberg. doi:10.1007/11677437_21

Hosseini Bamakan, S. M., Ghasemzadeh Moghaddam, S., & Dehghan Manshadi, S. (2021). Blockchain-enabled pharmaceutical cold chain: Applications, key challenges, and future trends. *Journal of Cleaner Production*, *302*, 127021. doi:10.1016/j.jclepro.2021.127021

Ktari, J., Frikha, T., Amor, N. Ben, Louraidh, L., Elmannai, H., & Hamdi, M. (2022). *IoMT-Based Platform for E-Health Monitoring Based on the Blockchain.*

Ktari, Jalel and Abid, M. (2008). A Low Power Design Methodology Based on High Level Models. *ESA*, 10--15.

Martin-Gutierrez, L., Peng, J., Thompson, N. L., Robinson, G. A., Naja, M., Peckham, H., Wu, W., J'bari, H., Ahwireng, N., Waddington, K. E., Bradford, C. M., Varnier, G., Gandhi, A., Radmore, R., Gupta, V., Isenberg, D. A., Jury, E. C., & Ciurtin, C. (2021). Stratification of Patients With Sjögren's Syndrome and Patients With Systemic Lupus Erythematosus According to Two Shared Immune Cell Signatures, With Potential Therapeutic Implications. *Arthritis & Rheumatology (Hoboken, N.J.)*, *73*(9), 1626–1637. doi:10.1002/art.41708 PMID:33645922

Muneer, S., & Raza, H. (2022). *An IoMT enabled smart healthcare model to monitor elderly people using Explainable Artificial Intelligence (EAI). 1*(June), 16–22.

Nishadi, A. S. T. (n.d.). Predicting Heart Diseases in Logistic Regression of Machine Learning Algorithms by Python Jupyterlab. *International Journal of Advanced Research and Publications* . https://www.kaggle.com

'Oberhaus, D. (2018, August 28). *The World's Oldest Blockchain Has Been Hiding in the New York Times Since 1995*. VICE.

Octaviani, T. L., & Rustam, Z. (2019). Random forest for breast cancer prediction. *AIP Conference Proceedings*, *2168*, 020050. doi:10.1063/1.5132477

Qureshi, A., Batra, S., Vats, P., Singh, S., & ... (2022). A Review of Machine Learning (ML) in the Internet of Medical Things (IOMT) in the Construction of a Smart Healthcare Structure. *Journal of …*, *13*.

Sarhaddi, F., Azimi, I., Labbaf, S., Niela-Vilén, H., Dutt, N., Axelin, A., Liljeberg, P., & Rahmani, A. M. (2021). Long-Term IoT-Based Maternal Monitoring: System Design and Evaluation. *Sensors (Basel)*, *21*(7), 2281. Advance online publication. doi:10.339021072281 PMID:33805217

Shahnaz, A., Qamar, U., & Khalid, A. (2019). Using Blockchain for Electronic Health Records. *IEEE Access: Practical Innovations, Open Solutions*, *7*, 147782–147795. doi:10.1109/ACCESS.2019.2946373

Simon, J., Perić, N., Mayer, S., Deckert, J., Gorwood, P., Pérez, V., Reif, A., Ruhe, H., Veltman, D., Morriss, R., Bilderbeck, A., Dawson, G., Dourish, C., Dias, R., Kingslake, J., & Browning, M. (2019). PMH21 cost-effectiveness of the predict test: results and lessons learned from a European multinational depression trial. *Value in Health*, *22*, S684. doi:10.1016/j.jval.2019.09.1495

Subash, C., Mahapatra, Das, R., & Patra, M. (2008). *Current e-Governance Scenario in Healthcare sector of India.*

Tien Tuan Anh, D., Ji, W., Gang, C., Rui, L., & Blockbench, A. (2017). Framework for Analyzing Private Blockchains. *Proceedings of the 2017 ACM International Conference on Management of Data*, Chicago, IL, USA, 14–19.

Underwood, S. (2016). Blockchain beyond Bitcoin. *Communications of the ACM*, *59*(11), 15–17. doi:10.1145/2994581

Varma Kakarlapudi, P., Mahmoud, Q. H., & Systematic, Q. A. (2021). *healthcare A Systematic Review of Blockchain for Consent Management*. doi:10.3390/healthcare

Wenhua, Z., Qamar, F., Abdali, T.-A. N., Hassan, R., Jafri, S. T. A., & Nguyen, Q. N. (2023). Blockchain Technology: Security Issues, Healthcare Applications, Challenges and Future Trends. *Electronics (Basel)*, *12*(3), 546. doi:10.3390/electronics12030546

Chapter 7
Artificial Intelligence, Machine Learning, and IoT Architecture to Support Smart Governance

Prithi Samuel

SRM Institute of Science and Technology, India

Jayashree K.

Panimalar Engineering College, India

Babu R.

(iD) https://orcid.org/0000-0003-0891-7190

SRM Institute of Science and Technology, India

Vijay K.

Rajalakshmi Engineering College, India

ABSTRACT

The usage of artificial intelligence (AI) technologies that depend on massive volumes of data, which are frequently made available through IoT, is thus directly related to the creation of smart governments. In order to increase the effectiveness of governance and the standard of living for citizens, Internet - of - things enabled AI technologies can be used in several important areas of smart government. In order to provide fulfilled government functions, AI and its subdomain innovations have the opportunity to address a number of current organizational inadequacies. In this chapter the foundations, benefits, and challenges implementing these technologies in the public sector or government are discussed. Following that, the various AI, Ml technologies and IoT frameworks for smart governance are explored. Then the focus is on the applications and use cases of IoT, AI and machine learning for smart governance.

DOI: 10.4018/978-1-6684-7697-0.ch007

INTRODUCTION

Emerging automation exists today are changing the method of person's employability as well as their way of life, and have unexploited impending towards revolutionizing governance.

Smart Governance a Nutshell

Smart Governance facilitates governments towards achieving enriched governance, societal enclosure, civilian assignation, and financial progression. Smart governance trends are in the fields of Information Communication Technology, Social Listening, and Internet of Things.

Information Communication Technology

Citizen prospective within constructing an information-based environment working assignation remains the principal creeds attributed to SMART governance. ICT enables instantaneous interface among persons as well as foremost experts transmuting the provision based on data plus amenities. The aforementioned huge civilian familiar amenities

Social Listening

Societal mass media remains a remarkable mediocre for foremost activities towards reaching to the peoples by way of nearly seventy to eighty percent of them partake being there on podiums such as Facebook, Instagram, as well as WhatsApp. Keeping a strong societal mass media existence marks government group accessible as well as simply available.

Internet of Things (IoT)

IoT application benefits officers tenuously control facilities like streetlights, waste disposal management, and the water supply chain. By setting up sensors across the city for different services and collecting data at a centralized control center and disbursing the services accordingly. However, the IoT governance model should be transparent and collaborative with shared responsibility between the agencies and citizens.

AI, ML, and IoT for Smart Governance

AI, ML, and DRL initiate important solicitation in the arena of healthiness intellect, that had advanced as of with improved information rapidity, enhanced devices, higher Smooth uses, as well as cloud facilities. Recent municipalities remain experiencing digital conversion by the use of IoT plus AI centered tools. Smart Transportation denotes towards transport structure which would make use of leading-edge devices, controller schemes, as well as ICT (Zhu et al., 2018). Maintainable ITS (Zhao et al., 2017) entails constant observing and estimating of city transportation movement information.

Benefits of AI, ML, and IoT for Smart Governance

AI would simplify the method of collecting as well as hoarding administration statistics concerning the section towards the peoples as well as industries. AI supports peoples as well as industries towards participating in the progressions based on policymaking, previously evolving or executing some different rule or strategy. AI provides preeminent approach towards eliminating fraud through powering the amenities. It is also make sure pellucidity in the data conversed.

Lenience accessibility of management facilities 24*7 for each resident with the use of online submissions.

Challenges and Obstacles of AI, ML, and IoT for Smart Governance

Three main challenges of IoT, AI and ML in smart governance are Mindscaping, Speculation, Security and Privacy, Interoperability, Privacy and Ethical concerns.

Mindscaping

Requesting an administration towards adopting a different structure remains arduous. To elicit the sanction of the administration as well as the public would be the primary stage towards movement as of with e-government toward smart- administration. Mindscaping is the method of Cogentin the persons towards accepting a variant. Since smart-governments are open, transparent, collaborative, community-engaged, and citizen-centric in nature, convincing the people is a minor concern. The foremost concern is to change the perspective of the administration.

Speculation

Present technical possessions have to be improved to make way for up-to-date IoT systems. Telecom systems remain a significant measure of every administration.

Security and Privacy

The foremost challenge is security and privacy. Big IoT systems in canny administrations remain by serious threat of security attacks.

Interoperability

The structure of IoT AI solicitations consists various principal components, such as sensing system which will gather data across originating out of the persons, entity, and the environment, plus systems that is aimed at storage as well as to process information, altogether of that uses several tools Al-Besher (2022). Moreover, the organization can remain interoperable by way of several new organizational apps. Furthermore, the amount of tools can root problems by means of conservation facilities plus maintainable.

Privacy and Ethical Concerns

In the medical management field gathering information about individuals and the possession about the individual information plus the aids of their handling accompany towards privacy and ethical concerns. (Alexopoulos et al.,2019)

Opportunities of AI, ML, and IoT for Smart Governance

IoT solicitations' existence remains towards managing and examining real-time information which will collaborate by means of ML and workings toward assisting cities, peoples, as well as governments. The mesh mash of great rapidity, robust, small potential capability of being connective and tools like IoT, ML and AI that would permit the change toward defensible smart municipalities. Intellectual parking schemes, Communal welfare, smooth road traffic management and canny road lamps are the various solicitations of Iot and ML in smart municipalities.

MODULARIZING SMART GOVERNMENT WITH ARTIFICIAL INTELLIGENCE AND MACHINE LEARNING

AI and ML Based Automated Smart Government

The combined effect of four simple techniques, such as semantic web, multi-agent systems, autonomic computing, and AI techniques, could arouse toward emerging an innovative podium which would assist to perceptive web in order to enhanced e-government businesses as well as facilities (Al-Mushayt, 2019).

MI and AI Application Benefits for the Public Sector

Governments use AI for generating further precise forecasts as well as towards simulating multifaceted system to facilitate testing by means of a variety of strategy option (Yulu Pi, 2021) The first benefits of AI are effectiveness as well as enactment assistances denote toward increasing administration operations' efficiency. Next, threat detection as well as observing trepidations building threat detection further operative with the use of AI. AI aimed at communal control possibly accompany towards financial profits, includes building e-government amenities as well as schemes further cost-effective. Amenity welfares could accomplish as a result of enlightening the eminence of communal amenities, (Cynthia 2019)

Applications of Machine Learning in Government

ML algorithms are enhancing numerous aspects of everyone lives. It also provides better compute control, custom-made tablets, AI based chat bots and etc. Nowadays communal region front-runners utilize ML aimed at administration initiative, services as well as operation. Towards gaining essential insight of strategy information, to filter resident strategy information ML techniques have been widely used. The applications of ML in government sectors are as shown in Figure 1.

Figure 1. Applications of ML in government sector

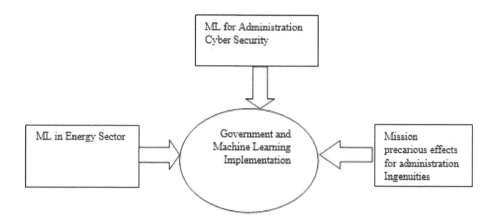

ML in Energy Sector

Administration agency is currently collaboratively working with ML expert for implementing ML solutions in the direction of benefiting the power segment. ML algorithms are used for multifaceted prediction toward being done by means of great accurateness thus, in effect enlightening higher authority administration's verdict creation. furthermore, it as well provides immense latent now enabling utilities towards changing at a more rapidly rate all along the complete value sequence.

ML for Administration Cyber Security

There are various attacks such as electronic mail safety, accomplice intimidation, ransom ware etc.in the computer. These attacks gave rise to various threats to administration hence the administration is binding a variety of hurdle towards overcoming the security challenge. Thus the administration agency is currently acclimating towards analytics-driven method toward safe keeping. within this method, administration agency would influence ML, also facilitate a flexible retort. ML techniques moreover make possible the progress of vibrant properties aimed at employing real-time intellect that supports in identifying ransomware intimidations in actual.

Mission Precarious Effects for Administration Ingenuities

Administration organizations are frequently imposed by the tough task of giving people by means of further proficient, operative, as well as translucent facilities devising exacting plus reducing financial plan. Administration organizations could use ML techniques to increase operative efficacies by means of interpreting datasets, detection of anomaly, and buildingforecastsaroundimminentmeasures.ML could be aimed at attaining intuitions from inclusive communal data, towards delivering precise analysis resultant from the data, as well as towards developing smart product.

IOT-ENABLED AI AND ML SYSTEMS FOR SMART GOVERNMENT

IoT (Internet of Things) and AI (Artificial Intelligence) can be used in combination to create smart government systems. IoT devices can gather data from various sources, such as cameras, sensors, and other connected devices. This data can then be analysed using AI algorithms to gain insights and make decisions. Examples of IoT-enabled AI and ML systems for smart government include:

Smart traffic management systems that use cameras and sensors to detect traffic congestion and adjust traffic signals accordingly.

- Intelligent waste management systems that use sensors to track the level of waste in garbage bins and optimize garbage collection routes.
- Predictive maintenance systems that use IoT sensors to monitor the condition of public infrastructure such as roads, bridges, and buildings and predict when maintenance is needed.
- Smart energy management systems that use IoT devices to monitor and control energy usage in government buildings.
- Overall, IoT-enabled AI and ML systems for smart government can help improve efficiency, reduce costs, and enhance the overall quality of public services.

IoT enabled smart government refers to the use of Internet of Things (IoT) technology to improve the efficiency and effectiveness of government operations and services. This can include the use of IoT sensors and devices to monitor and manage public services such as transportation, energy, and waste management. It can also include the use of IoT technology to improve communication and collaboration between government agencies and with citizens. Examples of IoT enabled smart government include the use of smart traffic lights to optimize traffic flow, the use of smart water meters to improve water management, and the use of IoT-enabled cameras to enhance public safety. Overall, the goal of IoT enabled smart government is to improve the quality of life for citizens while also reducing costs and increasing efficiency for government agencies.

In response to the rapid advancement of digital technology, smart government has been envisioned as an adaptive development of e-government to improve citizen involvement, accountability, and interoperability (Gil-Garcia, Zhang, & Puron-Cid, 2016). Through the use of intelligent technologies, which serve as catalysts for innovation, sustainability, competitiveness, and liveability, governments have attempted to cope with complex and uncertain situations and attain resilience, leading to the birth of the term "smart government" (Scholl & Scholl 2014). The usage of intelligent (AI) technologies that rely on massive volumes of data, which are frequently made available through IoT, is thus directly related to the creation of smart governments.

We first examine the difficulties in developing and integrating these technologies in the public sector in this guest editorial for the special issue on IoT and AI for Smart Government. After reviewing several IoT and AI frameworks for smart governance and smart cities, we then suggest a research framework that adds to the literature by incorporating both IoT and AI components and incorporating the answer to the problems that have been discovered. The suggested framework describes the IoT and AI research topics and problems for smart government. We then give a brief summary of each of the six papers included in this special issue.

The integration of Internet of Things (IoT) and Artificial Intelligence (AI) and Machine Learning (ML) systems is transforming the way governments operate and provide services to citizens. These technologies have the potential to improve efficiency, reduce costs, and enhance the quality of services. IoT-enabled systems allow for the collection and analysis of data from various sources, such as sensor networks, cameras, and other devices. This data can then be used by AI and ML systems to make decisions and predictions, leading to smarter and more efficient government operations.

One example of an IoT-enabled AI system is the use of smart cameras for traffic management. These cameras use AI algorithms to analyze traffic patterns and adjust traffic signals accordingly, reducing congestion and improving traffic flow. This can lead to improved air quality and reduced fuel consumption, as well as saving time and money for citizens. Another example is the use of IoT-enabled systems for public safety. Smart cameras and sensors can be used to detect and prevent crime, while AI and ML systems can be used to analyze data and predict crime patterns. This can lead to improved safety for citizens and reduced crime rates.

In addition, IoT-enabled systems can be used to improve the delivery of public services. For example, sensors can be used to monitor the condition of infrastructure, such as bridges and roads, and alert authorities to potential problems before they become critical. This can lead to improved safety for citizens and reduced costs for government. Overall, IoT-enabled AI and ML systems have the potential to revolutionize the way governments operate and provide services to citizens. By leveraging the power of these technologies, governments can improve efficiency, reduce costs, and enhance the quality of services.

Conceptual Framework

A conceptual network, also known as a semantic network, is a type of graphical representation that is used to organize and represent knowledge. It is a collection of concepts and the relationships between them. The concepts are represented as nodes or vertices in the network, and the relationships are represented as edges or arcs that connect the nodes. Conceptual networks are used in a variety of fields, including artificial intelligence, cognitive psychology, and natural language processing. They are particularly useful for representing knowledge that is complex and multi-dimensional, such as the relationships between different concepts in a specific domain.

One of the key benefits of using a conceptual network is that it allows for the representation of knowledge in a way that is easy to understand and navigate. By visualizing the relationships between concepts, it is possible to see how different pieces of knowledge are connected and how they relate to one another. This can be especially useful for knowledge management and information retrieval. Another benefit of conceptual networks is that they are flexible and can be easily updated as new information becomes available. This makes them a valuable tool for organizing and representing knowledge in fields such as research, where new information is constantly being discovered.

There are several different types of conceptual networks, including hierarchical networks, associative networks, and semantic networks. Each type has its own specific characteristics and is used for different purposes. For example, hierarchical networks are used to represent knowledge that is organized into a hierarchical structure, while associative networks are used to represent knowledge that is based on associations between concepts.

Conceptual networks have been used in a variety of fields, including artificial intelligence, cognitive science, and education. They are often used to represent knowledge in a specific domain, such as a particular subject area in education or a specific industry in business. In artificial intelligence, conceptual networks are used to represent knowledge in a machine-readable format, allowing for the creation of intelligent systems that can understand and reason about the information they are provided.

To create a conceptual network, one must first identify the key concepts or pieces of information that are relevant to the topic at hand. These concepts are then organized into a graph or diagram, with connections and relationships between the concepts represented by lines or arrows. The connections can represent various types of relationships, such as cause and effect, similarity, or hierarchy.

One common method for creating a conceptual network is to start with a central concept, or "root" concept, and then add related concepts to the network as branches or nodes. The connections between the concepts can be based on various criteria, such as similarity, importance, or relevance to the overall topic.

Conceptual networks have a wide range of applications in various fields, including:

Education

Conceptual networks can be used to create visual aids for teaching and learning. They can help students understand the relationships between different concepts, making the material more accessible and easier to understand.

Business

Conceptual networks can be used to represent the relationships between different business concepts, such as products, services, and customers. This can help companies understand the relationships between different elements of their business and make more informed decisions.

Artificial Intelligence

Conceptual networks are used to represent knowledge in a machine-readable format, allowing for the creation of intelligent systems that can understand and reason about the information they are provided.

Conceptual networks are a powerful tool for organizing and visualizing complex information. They can help make complex concepts more understandable and accessible, and can be used in a wide range of applications in various fields. With the help of advanced technology and software, creating a conceptual network has become much easier, and it is expected that the use of conceptual networks will continue to grow in the future.

IoT In Improving Citizens' Engagement with Public Services

An IoT project aimed at improving citizens' engagement with public services could involve the use of connected devices, such as smart sensors and cameras, to gather data and provide real-time information to both citizens and government officials. The data could be used to improve the delivery of public services, such as waste management, traffic management, and emergency response. The project could also include the development of mobile applications and web portals for citizens to access information and provide feedback on public services. Additionally, the project could explore the use of block chain technology to securely store and share data, and to ensure transparency and accountability in the delivery of public services.

The Internet of Things (IoT) has the potential to revolutionize the way citizens engage with public services. By connecting devices, sensors, and networks, IoT can provide real-time data, automate processes, and improve communication between citizens and government agencies. One of the key benefits of IoT in public services is the ability to gather real-time data from various sources. For example, smart traffic sensors can provide real-time traffic data to city officials, allowing them to optimize traffic flow and reduce congestion. Smart parking sensors can also be used to provide real-time information on parking availability, making it easier for citizens to find parking spots.

IoT can also be used to automate processes, such as waste management and energy consumption. Smart waste bins can be equipped with sensors that can detect when they are full and automatically schedule a pickup. Smart buildings can use IoT to monitor and control energy consumption, reducing costs and improving energy efficiency. Furthermore, IoT can also improve communication between citizens and government agencies. For example, a smart city platform can provide citizens with real-time information on public services, such as transportation, waste management, and emergency services. Citizens can also use the platform to report issues, such as potholes, and track the status of their reports.

In conclusion, IoT has the potential to greatly improve citizens' engagement with public services. By providing real-time data, automating processes, and improving communication, IoT can make public services more efficient and responsive to citizens' needs. Governments should invest in IoT to improve citizens' engagement with public services and enhance the overall quality of life in the community.

The concept of citizen engagement basically entails giving individuals the technology they need to stay in touch with governmental organisations, such as educational institutions or healthcare facilities. Enhancing chances for community people to voice their thoughts, offer suggestions, and participate more actively in local decision-making is the main goal of citizen engagement.

The Role IoT Plays in Citizen Engagement

The way governments interact with their constituents has changed as a result of the Internet of Things. It not only enables them to better respond to their constituents, but it can also increase accountability and openness in general and safeguard civil freedoms. Cities can become smarter than ever before when social media, the most popular method of public involvement, is combined with IoT devices, which gather data from cars, buildings, homes, and other objects. Civic leaders can utilise this data to better determine where resources are most required because cities are constructed around activity centres that produce vast volumes of data.

IoT devices can also be used to track and report on vital services like water availability, public transportation, paved surfaces, power grid operation, and more. This gives government officials the real-time data they need to make crucial decisions that enhance infrastructure reliability and people's quality of life while also assisting them in ensuring that these systems are operating at their best.

IoT also involves linking people to one another and establishing thriving communities, so it's not only about connecting people and their representatives. IoT allows a community-wide discussion that promotes action and creativity by giving people a forum to express their ideas and views. Governments can use the Internet of Things to collect data and get input from citizens in real-time about events that are happening and topics that are important to them.

Benefits of Citizen Engagement for Citizens

Higher Satisfaction

Cities become more effective when citizens are involved. A city's residents become more engaged with their community when they are included in decision-making processes, which improves communication and transparency and raises citizen satisfaction. Because they can recognise themselves in the policies, citizens are also more motivated to improve their town and feel more invested in it.

Real-Time Updates

Cities and local governments can give citizens access to real-time information about their communities through the use of IoT, including city notifications and updates on topics like public safety, crime statistics, weather, and more. IoT actually makes it easier for people to acquire detailed information from a variety of sources at once, allowing them to better personalise their decision-making procedures based on solid information. For instance, networked light bulbs might instantly notify authorities when a streetlight goes out or a fire hydrant breaks on a residential street. The same technology might also enable people to locate specific problems in their neighbourhood so they can respond appropriately and, if necessary, modify their regular habits.

Quick Issue Resolution

Quick issue resolution occurs when locals can report issues immediately from their smartphones. This makes municipal governments more effective while also keeping the populace content. By using IoT technology in your city, you will be able to keep track of where and when repairs are required, preventing time and money waste.

Integrative Public IoT Framework for Smart Government

The Internet of Things (IoT) has been rapidly growing in recent years, and it is expected to continue its growth in the future. IoT technology enables the interconnection of various devices and systems, enabling the collection and sharing of data in real-time. This technology has the potential to revolutionize the way governments operate, from improving public services to enhancing citizen engagement. In this paper, we propose an integrative public IoT framework for smart government, which aims to provide a holistic approach to implementing IoT in government. The IoT has been widely adopted in various industries, such as manufacturing, healthcare, and transportation. However, its implementation in government has been limited. The government sector faces unique challenges when implementing IoT, such as data privacy and security, regulatory compliance, and lack of standardization. These challenges need to be addressed to ensure the successful implementation of IoT in government.

Integrative Public IoT Framework

The proposed framework is based on four key pillars: governance, infrastructure, services, and citizen engagement. These pillars work together to create a comprehensive approach to implementing IoT in government.

Governance

This pillar focuses on creating a governance structure that ensures data privacy and security, regulatory compliance, and standardization. The governance structure should include a dedicated team responsible for managing the IoT infrastructure and services, as well as a set of policies and procedures to ensure data privacy and security.

Infrastructure

This pillar focuses on the physical and virtual infrastructure that supports the IoT ecosystem. The infrastructure should include a robust network, data storage, and processing capabilities to support the collection and sharing of data in real-time.

Services

This pillar focuses on the development and deployment of IoT-enabled services that improve public services and citizen engagement. These services should be designed to meet the needs of citizens and should be easy to use and accessible.

Citizen Engagement

This pillar focuses on engaging citizens in the IoT ecosystem. This can be achieved through various means, such as public consultations, citizen feedback, and online platforms. Citizen engagement is important to ensure that the IoT ecosystem is designed to meet the needs of citizens.

APPLICATIONS AND USE CASES IN BUILDING SMART GOVERNANCE

The improvement of city life is a priority for governments as urbanisation trends increase. They make every effort to get metropolitan areas ready for the influx of people. This results in the creation of cutting-edge infrastructure. The purpose of cutting-edge technology initiatives is to improve comfort. They can also make the most of the time people spend performing monotonous chores. For instance, enduring traffic congestion, operating building systems, completing tasks in shopping centres, and so forth.

Many people think that intelligent structures are a thing of the future and there is no need to worry about them. However, reality reveals the revers and the same is illustrated with some sample scenarios.

Singapore: The Smart Nation initiative was started by the Singaporean government. The government created the "Green Mark Scheme" as a part of this endeavour. Making 80% of city buildings green and environmentally friendly is one of the plans' objectives. By improving building efficiency and the energy system, this will be accomplished.

Aragon: In a similar vein, Aragon began its transition to smart infrastructure in 2019. Their government made the decision to create Smart City Zaragoza in order to reduce energy consumption by 20%. They weren't expecting the outcomes they got. The idea of a "smart city" assisted Aragon in reducing its energy use by 30%.

Therefore, smart buildings are a future concept that is beginning to take shape now. The prospects are endless for a building manager. They typically aim to optimise building management, practise sustainability, and cut costs. Facility managers who are looking for ways to impress their clients or building inhabitants may also find it fascinating. Last but not least, real estate developers will be intrigued by smart building technologies. It's a strategy for differentiating their offerings from those of the competition.

Additionally, there is now more research available on building technology solutions. Some of the scenarios are given below.

Government Services

IoT and advanced analytics can help make governance efficient for people by focusing on the services and benefits provided and the beneficiaries (Ameren Ahmad, 2023). There are a number of important services and documents required to enable citizens to claim various benefit schemes, sorted and registered there. There is a web-based system of the government that digitally provides documents such as ration card, residency certificate, caste certificate, aadhar card, driver's license, pan card.

While these systems are not convenient for either party, they do provide a cost-effective and accessible solution literally anywhere without losing records. Some aspects of governance involve document verification processes such as online KYC. We are digitizing by utilizing the IoT system. In banking, the move to online banking has made it easier to maintain a consolidated record of transactions across all platforms with a single user ID and password. There are smart cameras on the road connected to systems that can alert people to speeding and other road errors, and services such as online FIR (First Information Report) and cybercrime surveillance only pave the way for law enforcement. It's not an IoT-only aspect of, but it also makes it ubiquitous.

For example, web-based system, like the Delhi government's E-District, plans to provide door-to-door services to citizens, and only this will work through the internet and integrated systems.

Another web-based platform, My Gov, uses a "conversation," "do," and "dissemination" strategy to involve citizens in governing. The Public Distribution System (PDS) Portal in India is designed to be a one-stop information source for PDS, which is of particular relevance to the general public. The underpinning of smart governance is ICT, or information and communication technology. This type of technology offers a way to enhance interagency cooperation and to efficiently and sustainably supply services. With the help of ICT, an information-based ecosystem has been developed that can make use of smart governance to interact and work with both enterprises and citizens. Interaction on social media and analytics - Social media can be used as a tool for effective smart government to the extent that cities use it to talk less and listen more.

Law Enforcement

Any governance architecture must have functions for regulation and law enforcement. Integrating AI technology can improve and automate current skills to better uphold the law. RoboCop, drones, autonomous prototype cars, predictive analytics, and cyber defence are just a few of the law enforcement agencies that have evolved to supply a plethora of information concerning legal violations in the modern world. These systems aid in quicker problem detection and resolution.

Automating Routine Tasks

Paperwork is a crucial component of the majority of emerging and impoverished nations' political systems. When important choices are at stake, allocating, using, and sharing files across departments can be laborious and stressful. Therefore, automating regular processes minimises paperwork, speeds up response times to enquiries, and gives government employees important time to concentrate on other development-related issues.

Rapid Disaster Relief

Due to internal structural hierarchical processes, governments' responses to and actions in the event of emergencies (natural disasters or significant industrial accidents) may be delayed. Governments can forecast weather and other variables using predictive analytics and automated AI systems, allowing for quicker decision-making.

Public Infrastructure Conservation

The upkeep of public infrastructure using digital platforms promotes efficient and successful operations. And it encompasses each and every platform developed to deal with the issue of creating a better nation. The advantages of maintaining an AI-driven public platform are numerous. People may easily obtain information on all government services, respond to public questions in a timely manner, and request any service they need whenever they need it.

By combining public, commercial, and government practises onto one platform, eGovernance and AI are digitising government services and applications. Legal implications and decision-making have never been simpler. The dynamics of governance are shifting due to automation and digital disruption. Applications are being revitalised and reinvigorated by emerging technologies to make them more socially conscious in light of shifting ecosystem policies. By making government activities more transparent across the board, e-governance connects citizens and governments. The governance profile will change and the service will be the best through altering the culture of using technology to create better technology.

Public Relations

Public relations play a vital role in the smart city development. Some of the primary factors to be dealt with are discussed below.

Healthcare

Health care is an important responsibility of governments and the healthier and healthier the population becomes, directly or indirectly proportional to the growth of the country. In governance, IoT tools are used by governments to keep track of registered users. And not to mention the relevant authorities who strictly require citizens to register on the platform. IoT can help achieve this by enabling users to get real-time status updates by connecting to a central user interface that is used to communicate data from users for real-time updates and collection, and allows for efficient control in situations. It can also be used in reverse to update population needs and generate data from lagging areas with inadequate medical facilities so that services can be provided.

Example

The Aarogya Setu app was launched by the government as a tool to protect people from the Covid pandemic and take corrective action safely while allowing them to get the latest updates in real time. This included contact tracing and self-assessment, along with the ability to update details of current cases and reduce cases due to illness.

This updated the details of his nearby Covid-19 hotspots, categorized into zones such as red, green and orange. Not only that, the application also provided his Covid test lab available nearby for those who needed it.

Now the application brings up a tab for his web initiative for another government called Cowin, which is the booking of vaccination sites for different age groups. This allows residents to find the nearest medical center where they can get vaccines, find the right slot based on real-time availability dates and times, and maintain a profile record of vaccination doses. Also Delhi government application 'Delhi Fights Corona' is doing its best to ensure real-time availability of treatment, oxygen and ventilators at this time when all hospitals are flooded with such cases.

Healthcare is therefore a highly digitized sector, in which smooth governance, functioning software and big data are guaranteed, which governments use for things like vaccine supply chains and bed planning which is illustrated in Figure 2. Sending real-time updates to the population during a pandemic is all a product of the Internet of Things.

Education

Education is another factor for successful governance that IoT addresses. Smart classrooms, smart boards, anywhere-accessible online learning materials, and web-based distance learning pedagogies are now commonplace for people.

Figure 2. Smart City equipped smart healthcare process

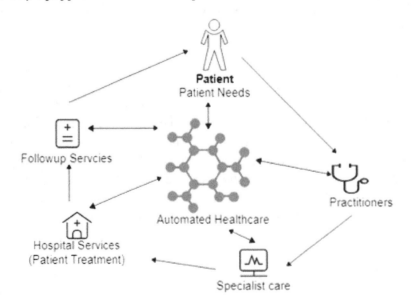

The internet and smart devices allow schools and teachers to digitally record children's progress so they can track it all at once. Education is an integral part, and to follow such a concept, there are several open portals successfully operating through centralized web systems that make education freely accessible.

Example: e-pathshala is one of his applications with downloadable e-books of the NCERT syllabus that can be accessed from all devices. CBSE Saransh is an application used by parents and teachers to analyze student performance to take corrective action. This somehow encourages parents who can't make it to their child's school to leave a track record of using only smartphones.

Startup India App allows users to get updates from the authorities on start-up so they know when is the right time to start and access all the benefits and services offered. The National Scholarship Portal is one such portal aimed at simplifying the scholarship process, understanding beneficiary applications, sanctions, details, verification processes, and more. There are several education-based applications that combine smart class functionality with portals that only work with IoT and advanced analytics to streamline governance.

Domestic Security

As they conduct business, companies transfer sensitive data between systems. On the other side, cybersecurity offers a variety of hardware and software solutions to protect information and information processing or storage systems. Information protection becomes more crucial as its scope and complexity expand. Social security numbers and financial information are two of the most important of these. Cybersecurity refers to defending systems, networks, and software from online threats. gaining access to, changing, or destroying confidential data, extorting money from customers, or interfering with corporate processes.

Cyberattacks often target processes. One of the issues in today's society is implementing cyber-security appropriately and effectively because both the number of gadgets and hackers' creativity have grown. Cybersecurity defends against harmful assaults on computers, servers, mobile devices, and electronic systems (Ismagilova et.al. 2022). Its role can be summed up as defending against threats to the devices that people use, the data they contain, and their identities. Without cyber security, businesses are unable to protect themselves from hacking and data breaches, making them an easy target for attackers. Due to the growth of worldwide communications and the usage of cloud services to store private and sensitive data, security threats are rising. In general, cyber-security threats are divided into three categories: (a) Cyber-crime (b) Cyber-attack and (c) Cyber-terrorism. Figure 3 summarizes the various collaterals Enterprise solutions available.

Renovating Privacy and Security Mechanism

Governments have data about the general population, elected officials, companies, and other groups. To avoid personal information being misused, this information needs to be secured and protected from scammers (Chen Ma, 2021). By incorporating machine learning algorithms that can detect interruptions in digital databases and shield information from cybercriminals, the incorporation of AI systems aids in automating and securing information. The various security issues to be addressed are given in Figure 4

Figure 3. Enterprise security solutions

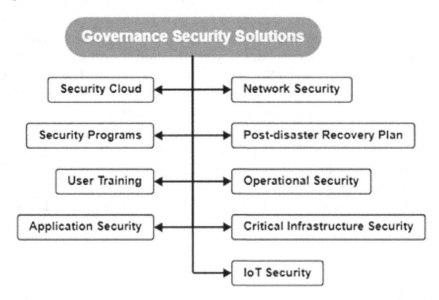

Figure 4. Various Security Challenges

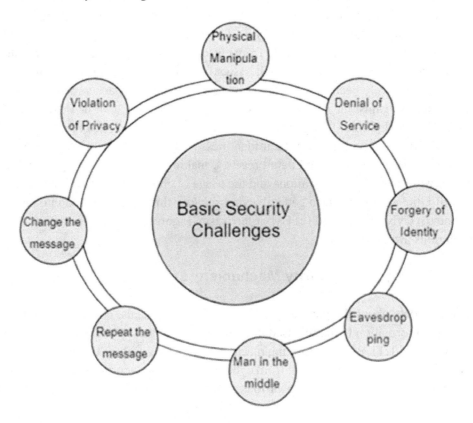

Transportation

In contemporary traffic management systems, planners aim to make the best use of already installed infrastructure and cutting-edge technology. In this sense, improving network efficiency as well as enhancing human and vehicular safety and cutting down on journey time are some of the main objectives of traffic management systems. The transportation network needs effective systems to service the transportation industry and, on the other hand, good management of these systems in order to accomplish the aforementioned purpose. The most significant benefits of employing smart transportation systems are their ability to decrease traffic congestion, increase safety, save time, use less fuel, and provide better service. The monitoring and recording systems for violations, the meteorological status information system, the driver warning system, the vehicle information system, the ease with which the law can be swiftly and effectively implemented by the police, and the improvement of social security are some of the notable components of this system. There are four categories into which smart transportation systems can be categorised: location-based services, cooperative traffic efficiency, active road safety to enhance road safety, and global internet services. Vehicular Ad hoc networks are a component of a smart transportation system that is made up of lots of fast cars.

RESEARCH CHALLENGES OF AI, ML AND IOT FOR SMART GOVERNANCE

The Internet of Things (IoT) and Artificial Intelligence (AI) have the potential to revolutionize the way public sector organizations operate, providing new opportunities for efficiency, cost savings, and improved service delivery. However, the adoption of these technologies in the public sector is not without its challenges. One of the biggest challenges facing the adoption of IoT and AI in the public sector is the lack of standardization and interoperability. Many IoT devices and systems are built using proprietary technologies, which can make it difficult for different devices and systems to communicate with one another. This can limit the ability of public sector organizations to take full advantage of the benefits of IoT and AI.

Another challenge is the lack of skilled personnel to design, implement and manage IoT and AI systems. The public sector often lacks the resources and expertise to effectively utilize these technologies, which can make it difficult to fully leverage their potential benefits. Data privacy and security are also major concerns in the adoption of IoT and AI in the public sector. IoT devices and systems collect and transmit large amounts of data, which can make them vulnerable to hacking and other cyber threats. Additionally, AI systems rely on large amounts of data to function, which can create significant privacy concerns for citizens.

The cost of implementing IoT and AI systems is also a significant challenge for public sector organizations. IoT devices and systems can be expensive to purchase and maintain, and AI systems require significant computational power and storage capacity, which can be costly. This can make it difficult for public sector organizations to justify the costs of these technologies, particularly in the face of budget constraints.

Finally, the public sector often operates in a highly regulated environment, which can make it difficult to adopt new technologies. Many public sector organizations are subject to strict regulations and compliance requirements, which can make it difficult to implement IoT and AI systems without violating these regulations.

In conclusion, the adoption of IoT and AI in the public sector is not without its challenges. These include lack of standardization and interoperability, lack of skilled personnel, data privacy and security concerns, cost, and regulatory compliance. However, with the right policies and strategies in place, public sector organizations can overcome these challenges and harness the power of IoT and AI to improve efficiency, cost savings, and service delivery.

CONCLUSION

The proposed integrative public IoT framework for smart government aims to provide a comprehensive approach to implementing IoT in government. By addressing the challenges of data privacy and security, regulatory compliance, and lack of standardization, this framework can help governments to successfully implement IoT and improve public services and citizen engagement. The framework is designed to be flexible and can be adapted to the specific needs of different governments. It is important for governments to adopt this framework to take advantage of the benefits that IoT technology can offer.

The integration of various IoT devices and sensors in the government system generates a large amount of data that needs to be managed effectively. A centralized platform for data management and analytics will allow for efficient data collection, storage, and analysis, providing valuable insights for decision-making and resource allocation. Blockchain technology can provide a secure and transparent way of managing and sharing data among different government agencies and departments. This will improve data integrity and accountability, and enable efficient and secure data sharing among different government agencies.

Artificial intelligence and machine learning can be used to analyze and make sense of the large amounts of data generated by IoT devices. This will enable the government to identify patterns and trends, and make predictions about future events, enabling more efficient and effective decision-making. A citizen engagement platform will enable citizens to interact with the government through IoT devices and sensors. This will allow citizens to report issues, provide feedback, and access government services, improving communication and transparency between the government and the public.

REFERENCES

Al-Besher, A. & Kumar, K. (2022). Use of artificial intelligence to enhance e-government services. *Sensors, 24*. doi:10.1016/j.measen.2022.100484

Ahmad, A., Ahmad, T., Ahmad, M., Kumar, C., Alenezi, F., & Nour, M. (2023). A complex network-based approach for security and governance in the smart green city. *Expert Systems with Applications, 214*. doi:10.1016/j.eswa.2022.119094

Al-Mushayt, O. S. (2019). Automating E-Government Services with Artificial Intelligence. IEEE Access, 7, 146821-146829. doi:10.1109/ACCESS.2019.2946204

Alexopoulos, C., Lachana A Androutsopoulou, Z., Diamantopoulou, V., Charalabidis, Y., & Loutsaris, M. A. (2019). How Machine Learning is Changing e-Government. ICEGOV '19, Melbourne, Australia.

Gil-Garcia, J. R., Zhang, J., & Puron-Cid, G. (2016). Conceptualizing smartness in government: An integrative and multi-dimensional view. *Government Information Quarterly*, *33*(3), 524–534. doi:10.1016/j.giq.2016.03.002

Ismagilova, E., Hughes, L., Rana, N. P., & Dwivedi, Y. K. (2022). Security, Privacy and Risks Within Smart Cities: Literature Review and Development of a Smart City Interaction Framework. *Information Systems Frontiers*, *24*(2), 393–414. doi:10.100710796-020-10044-1 PMID:32837262

Ma, C. (2021). Smart city and cyber-security; technologies used, leading challenges and future recommendations, *Energy Reports, 7*, 7999-8012. doi:10.1016/j.egyr.2021.08.124

Rudin, C. (2019). *"Stop Explaining Black Box Machine Learning Models for High Stakes Decisions and Use Interpretable Models Instead ."* ArXiv:1811.10154. https://arxiv.org/abs/1811.10154

Scholl, H. & Scholl, M. (2014). Smart Governance: A Roadmap for Research and Practice. *iConference 2014 Proceedings.* . doi:10.9776/14060

Yulu. (2021). Pi Machine learning in Governments: Benefits, Challenges and Future Directions. *eDEM 13*(1), 203-219. http://www.jedem.org doi:10.29379/jedem.v13i1.625

Zhao, Z. Z., Chen, H. P., Huang, Y., Zhang, S. B., Li, Z. H., Feng, T., & Liu, J. K. (2017). Bioactive polyketides and 8, 14-seco-ergosterol from fruiting bodies of the ascomycete Daldinia childiae. *Phytochemistry*, *142*, 68–75. doi:10.1016/j.phytochem.2017.06.020 PMID:28686900

Zhu, L., Yu, F. R., Wang, Y., Ning, B., & Tang, T. (2018). Big data analytics in intelligent transportation systems: A survey. *IEEE Transactions on Intelligent Transportation Systems*, *20*(1), 383–398. doi:10.1109/TITS.2018.2815678

Chapter 8
Geometric SMOTE–Based Approach to Improve the Prediction of Alzheimer's and Parkinson's Diseases for Highly Class–Imbalanced Data

Lokeswari Y. Venkataramana

Sri Sivasubramaniya Nadar College of Engineering, India

Shomona Gracia Jacob

University of Technology and Applied Sciences, Nizwa, Oman

VenkataVara Prasad D.

Sri Sivasubramaniya Nadar College of Engineering, India

R. Athilakshmi

 https://orcid.org/0000-0002-1772-5388
SRM Institute of Science and Technology, India

V. Priyanka

Sri Sivasubramaniya Nadar College of Engineering, India

K. Yeshwanthraa

Sri Sivasubramaniya Nadar College of Engineering, India

S. Vigneswaran

Sri Sivasubramaniya Nadar College of Engineering, India

ABSTRACT

In many applications where classification is needed, class imbalance poses a serious problem. Class imbalance refers to having very few instances under one or more classes while the other classes contain sufficient amount of data. This makes the results of the classification to be biased towards the classes containing many numbers of samples comparatively. One approach to handle this problem is by generating synthetic instances from the minority classes. Geometric synthetic minority oversampling technique (G-SMOTE) is used to generate artificial samples. G-SMOTE generates synthetic samples in the geometric

DOI: 10.4018/978-1-6684-7697-0.ch008

region of the input space, around each selected minority instance. The performance of the classifier is compared after oversampling using G-SMOTE, synthetic minority oversampling technique and without oversampling the minority classes. The work presents empirical results that show around 10% increase in the accuracy of the classifier model when G-SMOTE is used as an oversampling algorithm compared to SMOTE, and around 30% increase in performance over a class imbalanced data.

INTRODUCTION

Learning from class imbalanced data is an important problem for the research community and the industry practitioners. Standard classifiers induce a bias in favor of the majority class during training. This is because the minority classes contribute less to the classification accuracy. Additionally, the distinction between noisy and minority class instances is often difficult. As a result, the performance of the classifiers evaluated on certain metrics suitable for a class imbalanced data is low. It is important to consider that the cost of misclassifying a minority class is frequently much higher than the cost of misclassification of the majority class.

Class Imbalance

An imbalanced learning problem is defined as a classification task for binary or multi-class datasets where a significant asymmetry exists between the numbers of instances under various classes. The dominant class with the highest number of instances is called the majority class while the rest of the classes with insufficient or fewer data are called the minority classes. The Imbalance Ratio (IR), defined as the ratio between the number of instances in the majority class and each of the minority classes, depends on the type of application. The imbalance learning problem can be found in numerous practical domains, such as chemical and biochemical engineering, financial management, information technology (IT), security, business, agriculture, or emergency management.

One approach to handle class imbalance is by modifying the data itself by attempting to re-balance the minority and the majority classes. This can be performed either by removing some instances of the majority class (under-sampling), or by increasing the number of minority class instances (over-sampling). Under-sampling is performed by removing less important patterns, either by random selection or by using some heuristic rules. However, under-sampling is risky as potential important information could be lost. Oversampling is accomplished either by randomly replicating minority class patterns, or by generating new minority class patterns. One disadvantage of replicating minority instances is that the classifier model tends to get over-fitted. The advantage of over-sampling is that it compensates for the shortage of data of the minority class by generating extra data.

Gene Expression Data

The gene expression data plays an important role in encoding proteins which in turn dictates the functions and the status of a particular cell. Therefore, thousands of genes that are present in the gene expression dataset explain the functions of what each cell can perform. Analysis of gene-expression data is in high-demand for the development of prognosis prediction, response to drugs and therapies, or any phenotype or genotype defined independently of the gene expression profile. There are quite a few challenges that can be faced while working with a gene expression dataset. The number of dimensions (features) present in the dataset is usually high. High dimensionality, class imbalance, and high amount of noise in the gene expressions continue to pose as obstacles in the disease diagnosis of a test case. It is essential to extract the meaningful parts of the expression data to suggest therapeutic strategies.

SUPERVISED AND UNSUPERVISED LEARNING

Supervised Learning

Supervised learning is a learning in which the machine is taught or trained using data which is well labeled. After that, the machine is provided with a new set of examples (data) so that supervised learning algorithm analyses the training data (set of training examples) and produces a correct outcome from labeled data. Supervised learning is classified into two categories of algorithms:.

Classification: A classification problem is when the output variable is a category.

Regression: A regression problem is when the output variable is a real value.

Unsupervised learning is the training of machine using information that is neither classified nor labeled and allowing the algorithm to act on that information without guidance. Here the task of the machine is to group unsorted information according to similarities, patterns, and differences without any prior training of data.

Unsupervised learning is classified into two categories of algorithms:

Clustering: A clustering problem is discovering the inherent groupings in the data.

Association: An association rule learning problem discovers rules that describe large portions of your data.

Deep Learning

Deep learning is composed of networks that learn from vast unstructured data and extract relevant information from it and then create patterns that are useful for decision making. Deep learning models can achieve state-of-the-art accuracy, sometimes exceeding human-level performance. Models are trained by using a large set of labeled data and neural network architectures that contain many layers. Deep learning models are trained by using large sets of labeled data and neural network architectures that learn features directly from the data. The various architecture of deep learning includes Deep Neural Networks (DNN), Deep Belief Networks (DBN) which are used for text processing, Convolution Neural Networks (CNN) used for analyzing visual imagery, Recurrent Neural Networks (RNN) and Long Short-Term Memory (LSTM) which are used in speech recognition.

As class imbalance is common in any real time application, the authors in this work have selected healthcare and fraudulent detection through credit card transaction domain to deal and provide solution for class imbalance. As class imbalance affects the model accuracy, the motivation in this current research work is to explore SMOTE and G-SMOTE for solving the problem. The novelty in this current work is to apply G-SMOTE for healthcare data for the first time wherein there is lot of class imbalance between the samples of two different types of diseases and compare the results of SMOTE with G-SMOTE.

RELATED WORK

Deep Learning-based Identification of Cancer or Normal Tissue Using Gene Expression Data

The authors in this work aimed to address the extent to which the machine can learn to recognize cancer. A deep neural network was first trained to predict cancer using various gene selection strategies. Then it was used to identify genes that mostly contribute to classify cancer in the dataset. The performance of the model was compared with other conventional prediction methods. It was observed that the Deep Neural Network (DNN) model trained with the top 3,000 genes of coefficient of variance showed the best average accuracy overall of 97.7%, followed by Support Vector Machine (SVM) with an accuracy of 97.1% (Ahn et al., 2018).

Pros: The deep learning approach not only proved to be a useful tool to accurately predict cancer but also helped to learn important characteristics of cancer.

Cons: There was a performance drop when the model was tested with microarray samples. The accuracy reduction was observed due to the high heterogeneity of the microarray samples.

A Deep Learning Approach for Cancer Detection and Relevant Gene Identification

The authors proposed a deep learning approach for cancer detection and identification of genes critical for diagnosis of breast cancer. A Stacked De-Noising Auto Encoder (SDAE) was used to extract relevant features from the high dimensional expression data. The performance of the extracted features was then evaluated using supervised classification models to verify their usefulness. The highly interactive genes were then observed as useful cancer biomarkers for detection of breast cancer. It was observed that SDAE used along with Support Vector Machine – Radial Basis Function (SVM-RBF) achieved the highest accuracy of 98.26% and highest F-measure of 98.3% whereas SDAE used along with Artificial Neural Network (ANN) achieved the highest sensitivity (Danaee et al., 2017).

Pros: The method was successful in the extraction of the useful genes that enabled
Classification of cancer data. The weights of the model that was useful to extract genes also have the potential to be cancer biomarkers.

Cons: There was a requirement of large datasets for training the classification model.

Discriminative Deep Belief Networks for Microarray-Based Cancer Classification

The authors used a Discriminative Deep Belief Network (DDBN) for cancer data analysis. The network was trained in 2 phases: in the first phase the network weights took initial values by unsupervised greedy layer-wise technique, and in the second phase the values of the network weights were fine-tuned by back propagation algorithm. The model was evaluated against three cancer datasets namely laryngeal, bladder and colorectal cancer. Information Gain was used for gene selection and SMOTE was used for over-sampling the minority class samples. It was observed that DDBN outperformed other conventional methods in all metrics (Karabulut & Ibrikci, 2017).

Pros: The DDBN algorithm can be generalized to perform adequately in other datasets of cancer.

The processing time got reduced and the performance improved due to dimensionality reduction and gene selection.

Cons: The accuracy of the classification model was not very appreciable enough.

This can be understood to the inefficiency of the data pre-processing techniques and due to the high heterogeneity of the microarray samples.

A K-Fold Averaging Cross-Validation Procedure

K-fold Cross Validation (CV) with averaging. The classical K-fold CV model produces predicted values of same size as the input samples fed into it. The averaging technique selects an optimal candidate from each hold-out fold and then takes the average of K such obtained candidates (Karabulut & Ibrikci, 2017).

Pros: The variance of the proposed estimates can be significantly reduced. It gives more stable and efficient parameter estimation procedure. Average Cross Validation (ACV) can be used with penalized model selection method.

Cons: If the value of K is large and the sample size is less, it may cause insufficient fit of data since K-fold ACV performs model selection based on 1/K of the data. So, there should be sufficient samples in the test set.

SMOTE: Learning Vector Quantization Based Synthetic Minority Over-Sampling Technique for Biomedical Data

Over-sampling methods based on Synthetic Minority Over-sampling Technique (SMOTE) have been proposed for classification problems of imbalanced biomedical data. An over-sampling method is introduced to improve the overall effectiveness of SMOTE via vector quantization. Over-sampling method enables to generate useful synthetic samples by referring to actual samples taken from real-world datasets (Nakamura et al., 2013).

Pros: Unlike other methods of classification, SMOTE estimates borderlines between classes which is key to a good classification algorithm.

Cons: While generating synthetic examples, SMOTE does not take into consideration neighboring examples can be from other classes. This can increase the overlapping of classes and can introduce additional noise.

SMOTE is not practical for high dimensional data.

SMOTE: A Comprehensive Analysis of Synthetic Minority Oversampling Technique (SMOTE) for Handling Class Imbalance

The authors presented a theoretical and experimental analysis of the SMOTE method. It is based on generating examples on the lines connecting a point and one of its K –nearest neighbors. It analyses the effect of different factors affecting the accuracy such as size of the training set, dimensions, and the considered number of neighbors K (Elreedy & Atiya, 2019).

Pros: SMOTE can be used for regular balanced classification problems of small sized data. For large sized data, SMOTE achieves better accuracy, so its use is not limited to small sized data or minority class data.

Cons: While generating synthetic examples, SMOTE does not take into consideration neighboring examples can be from other classes. This can increase the overlapping of classes and can introduce additional noise.

SMOTE: Geometric SMOTE – A Geometrically Enhanced Drop-In Replacement for SMOTE

G-SMOTE can be seen as a geometric generalization of the SMOTE algorithm. G-SMOTE defines a flexible geometric region around each minority class instance. G-SMOTE generates synthetic samples in a geometric region of the input space, around each selected minority instance. While in the basic configuration this region is a hyper-sphere, G-SMOTE allows its deformation to a hyper-spheroid (Douzas & Bacao, 2019).

Pros: The tests performed show that G-SMOTE significantly outperforms SMOTE. This can be attributed to the ability of G-SMOTE to generate artificial data in safe areas of the input space and increase the diversity of the generated instances. G-SMOTE parameterizes efficiently the data generation process and adapts to the special characteristics of each imbalanced dataset.

The G-SMOTE implementation is open source and it compatible to Scikit- Learn. An implementation of G-SMOTE is made available in the Python programming language.

Cons: Geometric SMOTE is not very practical for high dimensional data.

A Synthetic Informative Minority Over-Sampling (SIMO) Algorithm Leveraging Support Vector Machine to Enhance Learning From Imbalanced Datasets

A new synthetic informative minority oversampling (SIMO) algorithm was proposed which was integrated with support vector machine (SVM). In this algorithm, first SVM is applied to the original imbalanced dataset, then, minority examples close to the SVM decision boundary; the informative minority examples are over-sampled. Another version of SIMO called weighted SIMO (WSIMO) was also proposed. W-SIMO is different from SIMO in the degree of over-sampling the informative minority examples. In W-SIMO, incorrectly classified informative minority examples are over-sampled with a higher degree compared to the correctly classified informative minority examples (Piri et al., 2018).

Pros: SIMO generates fewer synthetic data points. Therefore, the changes to the original distribution of the data and further computational costs are lower compared to other over-sampling techniques.

SIMO and W-SIMO are not very sensitive to their parameters.

Cons: High computational time when applied to large datasets.

Improving Imbalanced Learning Through a Heuristic Oversampling Method Based on K-Means and SMOTE

A simple and effective oversampling method based on k-means clustering and SMOTE (synthetic minority oversampling technique) was presented, which avoids the generation of noise and effectively overcomes imbalances between and within classes (Douzas et al., 2018).

Pros: Alleviates within-class imbalance. Discourages over-fitting.

Effectively reduces noise generation.

Cons: The model has been proposed only for binary classification tasks.

A Novel Ensemble Method for Classifying Imbalanced Data

The authors proposed a novel ensemble method, which firstly converts an imbalanced dataset into multiple balanced data using random splitting or clustering and then builds several classifiers on these multiple data with a specific classification algorithm. Finally, the classification results of these classifiers for new data are combined by a specific ensemble rule (Sun et al., 2015).

Pros: The proposed method does not change the original class distribution.

It does not suffer from information loss or unexpected mistakes via increasing the minority class instances or decreasing the majority ones.

Cons: The model has been proposed only for binary classification tasks.

Adaptive Semi-Unsupervised Weighted Oversampling (A-SUWO) for Imbalanced Datasets

The over sampling method called Adaptive Semi-Unsupervised Weighted Oversampling (A-SUWO) was proposed for imbalanced binary dataset classification. The proposed method clustered the minority instances using a semi-unsupervised hierarchical clustering approach and determined the size to oversample each sub-cluster using its classification complexity and cross validation. Then, the minority instances were oversampled depending on their Euclidean distance to the majority class. A-SUWO aimed at identifying hard-to learn instances by considering minority instances from each sub-cluster that are closer to the borderline (Nekooeimehr & Lai-Yuen, 2016).

Pros: The proposed model avoids generating synthetic minority instances that overlap with the majority class by considering the majority class in the clustering and oversampling stages.

It determines the sub-cluster sizes adaptively using the standardized average error rate and cross-validation. Avoids over-generalization. It does not ignore isolated sub-clusters.

Cons: The model has been proposed only for binary classification tasks.

From the above literature the following shortcomings were identified in the existing system. (i) Inability to deal with high dimensionality of the gene expressions. (ii) Reduced accuracy due to high heterogeneity of the microarray samples. (iii) Failure of K-fold cross validation due to insufficient test samples. (iv) Introduction of additional noise and increased overlapping of classes when the data is balanced using SMOTE.

(v) Methods like A-SUWO, K-means with SMOTE and Ensemble for classifying imbalanced data have been proposed only for binary classification tasks.

Most classification methods tend to perform poorly on minority class samples. This is because they aim to optimize the overall accuracy without considering the relative distribution of each class. Hence a balanced dataset is important for creating a good prediction model. Hence, the motivation of this research article is as follows.

(i) To enhance the prediction quality and accuracy and build a robust model. This is achieved by dimensionality reduction. (ii) Conventional supervised machine learning methods do not achieve higher accuracy when trained using gene expression data due to its high dimensionality and complexity. A deep neural network achieves improved accuracy compared to other conventional methods.

The Objectives of This Research Work Are as Follows

(1) To perform Feature Extraction using Stacked Autoencoder (SAE) to extract prominent features that is necessary for classifying a sample.
(2) To deal with the class imbalanced data using Geometric Synthetic Minority Oversampling Technique (G-SMOTE) algorithm.
(3) To construct a deep learning-based classification model for disease prediction and to evaluate the constructed model using k-fold cross validation.
(4) To calculate the performance metrics of the constructed model such as accuracy, sensitivity, specificity, precision, recall and F-measure and compare them with the existing results.

Materials and Methods

The datasets namely, the Alzheimer (AD) and Parkinson Dataset (PD) and the Credit card fraud detection Dataset are used for the implementation (GSEA, 2022; GSEA, 2023; UCI, 2016). The former is a multiclass dataset, and the latter is a binary-class dataset. The class distribution, the number of features in each dataset is tabulated below in the Table 1. From the Table 1, it can be seen that the first dataset has a moderate class imbalance, and the second dataset has a high-class imbalance. The former is chosen to prove the robustness of the algorithm for a multi-class dataset and the latter is chosen since there is a high-class imbalance.

Table 1. Dataset description

Dataset	No. of Samples	No. of Features	No. of Classes	Class Distribution	Class Imbalance
Alzheimer and Parkinson Disease	199	1438	3	AD - 74	Moderate
				PD - 37	
				Common - 88	
Credit card fraud detection	284807	31	2	Fraud - 492	High
				Normal - 284315	

GEOMETRIC SYNTHETIC OVERSAMPLING TECHNIQUE(G-SMOTE) TO HANDLE CLASS IMBALANCE

It is important to minimize the misclassification error due to the biasing towards the majority class when a class imbalance dataset is used. Improving the accuracy of prediction is prioritized over the other parameters of efficiency such as the computational time taken to train the data. Datasets with consistent set of samples under each class with class imbalance is obtained. As depicted in Figure1, the first step involves extracting such datasets from a suitable repository. The raw data is then pre-processed to remove noises (if any), fill-in missing values with classical methods, resolve inconsistencies, remove outliers and finally the data is integrated and reduced. Due to the high dimensionality of the gene expression data, it is necessary to reduce the number of features to an appreciable limit since most classifiers tend to perform poor on high dimensional data. Hence, to extract the relevant and most important features, the class imbalanced data is first fed into an Auto encoder, an artificial neural network which extracts features in an unsupervised manner and does dimensionality reduction. A Stacked Auto Encoder (SAE) extracts more robust features from the hidden layers by reconstructing the input from a corrupted version of it. These encoders are stacked to form a deep network by unsupervised pre-training of one layer at a time from the layers below it (Dertat,). When there is a drift between the number of samples in the majority and minority classes, then the data needs to be balanced.

G-SMOTE, a generalization of the SMOTE data generation technique generates synthetic samples in a geometric region of the input space, around each selected minority instance. G-SMOTE selects a safe radius around each minority class instance and generates artificial data within a truncated and deformed hyper spheroid.

By synthetically generating more instances for the minority class, the model will be able to broaden its decision region for minority class (Douzas & Bacao, 2019). The learned features are then fed to a DNN for classification of the re-balanced data using G-SMOTE. The DNN structure consists of an input layer, an output layer and at least one hidden layer. *K*-Fold cross validation technique is used to evaluate the classifier model by partitioning the original dataset into a training set to train the model, and a test set to evaluate it. In *k*-fold cross-validation, the original sample is randomly partitioned into *k* equal size sub-samples. Of the *k* sub-samples, a single sub-sample is retained as the validation data for testing the model, and the remaining *k-1* sub-samples are used as training data. The cross-validation process is then repeated *k* times (the folds), with each of the *k* sub-samples used exactly once as the validation data. The *k* results from the folds can then be averaged or otherwise combined to produce a single estimation. The advantage of this method is that all observations are used for both training and validation, and each observation is used for validation exactly once (Brownlee, 2020), (Geeks for Geeks, 2023). Finally, the predictive performance of the classifier model is assessed and metrics like accuracy, sensitivity, specificity, precision, and F-score are calculated. The obtained results are then compared with SMOTE to estimate the change in the performance.

Data Pre-Processing

Data pre-processing involves transforming the raw data into a useful and efficient format. This is one of the most important phases as it has an impact on the accuracy of the outcome. The datasets extracted often consists of missing values, out-of-range values, and redundant information. Proceeding without screening such problems might produce misleading results. As shown in Figure 2, techniques such as Normalization which scales the data values within the range (0,1), Replacing missing data by the mean/median/most frequently occurring value of the respective column are employed here. Also, if a categorical data is encountered, it is label encoded which involves assigning a numerical value to each category and then they are one-hot encoded which involves converting the numerical value into binary which increases the number of columns equal to the number of categories.

Figure 1. Geometric SMOTE approach for class imbalance

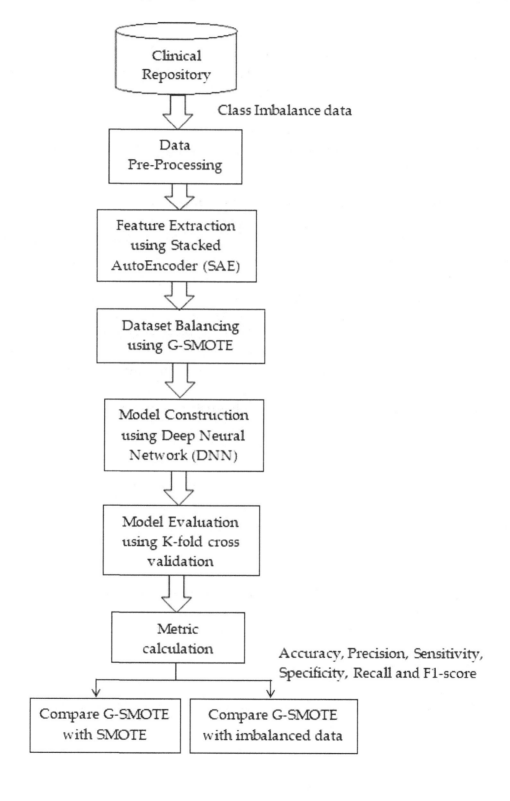

Feature Extraction

If the dataset is highly dimensional, then selecting the features that aids in the prediction will reduce computational cost, helps to identify the important features and might produce better accuracy in the prediction Auto Encoders is a type of artificial neural network used to learn efficient data coding in an unsupervised manner. It also reconstructs the input data. Here stacked auto encoders are used where the output of one encoder is fed into another. The auto encoder model is trained using the input data to obtain a feature vector. This vector is used as an input to the next layer. After training all the hidden layers, back-propagation is used to minimize the cost function and update the weights and bias with training sets to achieve fine tuning (Liu et al., 2018).

SMOTE Algorithm to Balance the Class Imbalanced Data

Data Imbalance refers to class imbalance where there is a major drift in the number of samples under the majority and minority classes. Therefore, balancing is important in order to avoid the prediction results to be biased towards the majority class samples SMOTE algorithm is performed here which over-samples the specified class and produces synthetic samples. As shown in Figure 3, a Sampling Strategy is specified which determines the ratio of the over-sampling or specifies the class to be over-sampled. We can also control the randomization of the algorithm by specifying it in the function's argument. Other optional parameters like number of nearest neighbors can also be specified. SMOTE synthesizes new minority instances between existing minority instances. It generates the virtual records by linear interpolation for the minority class. The synthetic samples are generated by randomly selecting one or more of the k-nearest neighbors for each example in the minority class (Chakrabarty, 2019).

SMOTE Algorithm

Input: Dataset after feature extraction, Sampling strategy for oversampling, Minority class set A, No. of nearest neighbours k, Sampling rate 'N'.
    Output: Over-Sampled Dataset.

1. Shuffle A
2. for each x in A do,
   2.1. Select k nearest neighbours of x by calculating the Euclidean distance between x and every other sample in set A.
   2.2. Select N samples from the k nearest neighbours.
3. Let x_K be a sample from the k nearest neighbours of x and rand(0, 1) be a random number between 0 and 1. The new sample is generated as

$$x' = x + rand(0,1) * |x - x_K|$$

Figure 2. Data pre-processing

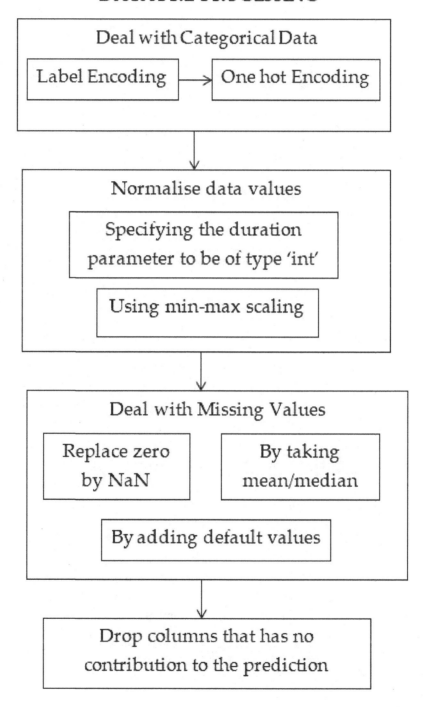

Figure 3. Data balancing using SMOTE

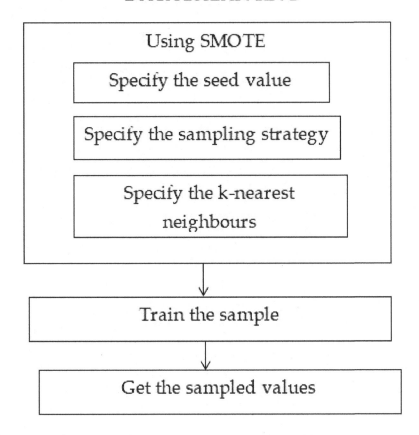

Geometric SMOTE to Balance the Class Imbalanced Data

G-SMOTE algorithm is implemented here as a modification for the SMOTE algorithm. G-SMOTE algorithm is performed here which over-samples the minority class in a safe input region around the minority instances and produces synthetic samples. As shown in Figure 4, a Sampling Strategy is specified which determines the ratio of the over-sampling or specifies the class to be over-sampled. A selection strategy is also specified that decides the input space or the samples from which the k nearest neighbors are to be chosen. We can also control the randomization of the algorithm by specifying it in the function's argument. Other optional parameters like number of nearest neighbors, truncation factor, and deformation factor can also be specified. G-SMOTE extends the linear interpolation mechanism by introducing a geometric region where the data generation process occurs. At the most general choice of hyper-parameters, this geometric region of the input space is a truncated and deformed hyper-spheroid (Douzas & Bacao, 2019).

Figure 4. Data balancing using G-SMOTE

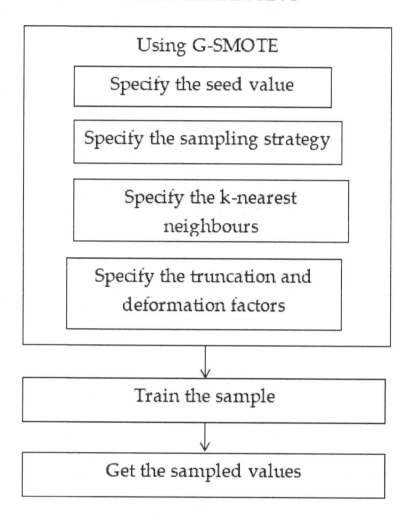

DATA BALANCING

The Main Objectives of G-SMOTE Include:

(1) To define a safe area around each selected minority class instance such that the generated artificial minority instances inside this area are not noisy.
(2) To increase the variety of generated samples by expanding the minority class area.
(3) To parameterize the above characteristics based on a small number of transformations with a geometrical interpretation.

GSMOTE Algorithm

Input: Dataset after feature extraction, sampling strategy for oversampling, Selection strategy, Minority class samples *Smin*, No. of nearest neighbours k, Truncation factor between [-1,1], Deformation factor between [0,1].

Output: Over-Sampled Dataset.

1. Shuffle *Smin*.
2. Specify selection strategy.
3. Repeat until N minority instances are selected,
   3.1. Select a minority instance x from *Smin*.
   3.2. Find k nearest neighbors of x from *Smin*. Let x' be one of them.
   3.3. Calculate the radius of the geometric sphere as R.
   3.4. Generate a synthetic sample *xGenin* the geometric sphere ofradius=1 and centre=0.
   3.5. Transform *xGenby* performing truncation and deformation.
   3.6. Add *xGento* the set of generated samples.

Model Construction

A model is a single, definitive source of information that contains the essential fields and the behaviors of the data being given to it. A Deep Neural Network is used for constructing a model. A stack of layers is then constructed, and the activation function is specified. The model is then compiled and trained to fit the data given to it.

Model Evaluation

It is important to evaluate the constructed model as it is important to determine its performance and to assess how well the model will work in the future and for other sets of data. K-fold cross validation is employed here for model evaluation. This method divides the data into k-folds and the data in each fold is split into training and test sets (Brownlee, 2020). For each fold, the constructed model is fit on the training set, and it is evaluated using the test set. Evaluation score is retained for each fold and an average score is also presented.

EXPERIMENTAL SET UP

Anaconda Navigator

Anaconda Navigator is a desktop graphical user interface (GUI) in Anaconda distribution that allows launching applications. The Navigator can search for packages on Anaconda Cloud or in a local Anaconda Repository and eliminates the need of command-line commands. Also, the navigator helps to the find the required packages, install them in an environment, run the packages, and update them (Anaconda Documentation, 2022).

Jupyter Notebook

Jupyter Notebook is a default application launched by the Anaconda Navigator. It is an open-source web application that allows creating and sharing documents that contain live code, equations, visualizations, and narrative text. Jupyter supports over 40 programming languages, including Python, R, Julia, and Scala. The implementation of this project uses Python with version 3.0 (Jupyter, 2022).

Tensor Flow and Keras

TensorFlow is an end-to-end open-source platform for Machine Learning (ML). It has a comprehensive, flexible ecosystem of tools, libraries and community resources that helps to build and train ML models easily using intuitive high-level APIs like Keras with eager execution, which makes for immediate model iteration and easy debugging (Tensor Flow, 2022).

Command to Install TensorFlow With Pip Python on Windows 10:

python -m pip install –upgrade pip
   pip install tensorflow

Keras is a high-level neural networks API, written in Python and capable of running on top of Tensorflow. It was developed with a focus on enabling fast experimentation. Beyond ease of learning and ease of model building, Keras offers the advantages of broad adoption, support for a wide range of production deployment options. Installation of Keras with tensorflow as backend.

Command to Install Keras

activate tensorflow
   conda install keras

RESULTS

The input dataset was first preprocessed to fill-in missing values by replacing zeroes with *NaN* and then replace each *NaN* in a column by its mean. Normalization was performed to scale the values within the range (0,1). All categorical data in any column was label-encoded and then one-hot encoding was performed. All class labels in the output variable are assigned a unique integer as a result of encoding.

After preprocessing, the input dataset was fed into an Auto encoder to reduce the dimensionality of the data. For the Alzheimer-Parkinson's dataset, the input layer of the encoder consisted of 1438 neurons with the subsequent layers having lesser neurons. The output layer consisted of 100 neurons. The encoder model was trained for 10 epochs. After feature extraction, the dataset with reduced features was oversampled using G-SMOTE by specifying the sampling strategy, sampling selection, number of K-nearest neighbors, random state, truncation factor and deformation factor. Over-sampling using G-SMOTE algorithm resulted in increase in the number of samples from 199 to 264 for Alzheimer and Parkinson dataset, and from 284315 to 568630 samples for credit card fraud detection dataset.

The figures Figure 5 and Figure 6 show how the number of neurons employed in the hidden layers of the DNN impacts the accuracy of the model with two different datasets respectively. For the Alzheimer and Parkinson Dataset with 100 reduced features, the classifier model achieves its optimum accuracy when there are 75neurons in the hidden layers and with respect to the Credit Card Fraud Detection dataset, the maximum accuracy is obtained when there are 10 neurons each in the3 hidden layers of the DNN.

Figure 5. Accuracy vs. number of neurons in the hidden layers for Alzheimer's and Parkinson's dataset

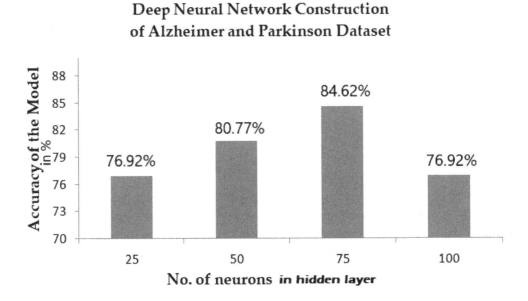

The number of neurons used in the input layer, hidden layers and the output layer and the number of hidden layers deployed in different datasets are tabulated correspondingly in Table 2.

After constructing the DNN model, K-fold cross validation was performed to evaluate the accuracy of the model. K was set to 10.A confusion matrix, (or error matrix), is built to describe the performance of the classification model on a set of test data for which the true values are known. A confusion matrix is a summary of prediction results on a classification problem. It allows the visualization of the performance of an algorithm. The number of correct and incorrect predictions are summarized with count values and broken down for each class. The confusion matrix shows the ways in which the classifier is confused when it makes predictions. Most performance measures such as accuracy, precision, specificity, sensitivity and F1 score are computed from the confusion matrix (Geeks for Geeks, 2023).

A true positive (TP) is an outcome where the model correctly predicts the positive class. A true negative (TN) is an outcome where the model correctly predicts the negative class. A false positive (FP) is an outcome where the model incorrectly predicts the positive class. A false negative (FN) is an outcome where the model incorrectly predicts the negative class.

Figure 6. Accuracy vs. number of neurons in the hidden layers for credit card fraud detection dataset

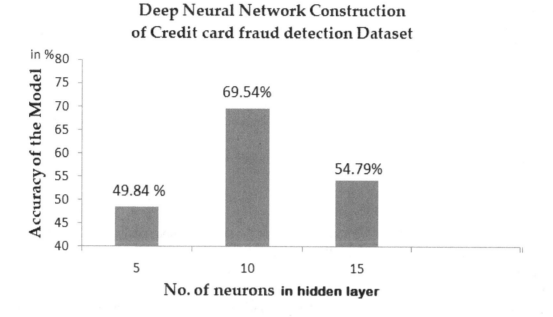

Table 2. Deep neural network description

Dataset	Number of Neurons In			Number of Hidden Layers
	Input Layer	Hidden Layers	Output Layer	
Alzheimer and Parkinson (3 classes)	100	75 each	3	3
Credit card fraud detection (2 classes)	20	10 each	1	3

Accuracy

The classification accuracy rate corresponds to the proportion of observations that have been correctly classified. It is calculated as

Accuracy = (TruePositive + TrueNegative) / (Predicted values)

Precision

Precision is the proportion of true positives among all the individuals that have been predicted to be positives by the model. This represents the accuracy of a predicted positive outcome. It is calculated as

Precision = TruePositive / (TruePositive + FalsePositive)

Sensitivity or Recall

Sensitivity (or Recall), is the True Positive Rate (TPR) or the proportion of identified positives among the positive population. It is calculated as

Sensitivity/Recall = TruePositive / (TruePositive + FalseNegative)

Specificity

Specificity measures the True Negative Rate (TNR), that is the proportion of identified negatives among the negative population.It is calculated as

Specificity = TrueNegative / (TrueNegative + FalsePositive)

F1 Score

F1 score considers both the precision and the recall of the test to compute its value. The F1 score is the harmonic mean of the precision and recall, where an F1 score reaches its best value at 1 (perfect precision and recall) and worst at 0. It is calculated as

F1 score = 2 * (Precision * Sensitivity) / (Precision + Sensitivity)

The above stated Performance metrics were calculated for the Alzheimer and Parkinson dataset and the Credit card fraud detection dataset (STHDA, 2018). The results are presented in the Table 3 and Table 4 respectively.

Table 3. Calculated metrics for Alzheimer's and Parkinson's dataset

Metrics	Results after G-SMOTE
Accuracy (in %)	84.62
Precision (in %)	84.16
Recall or Sensitivity (in %)	86.66
Specificity	0.96
F1 score (in %)	84.49

Table 4. Calculated metrics for credit card fraud detection dataset

Metrics	Results After G-SMOTE
Accuracy (in %)	69.54
Precision (in %)	49.84
Recall or Sensitivity (in %)	100
F1 score (in %)	66.52
Specificity	0

DISCUSSIONS

Comparison of Results Before and After Balancing Using Oversampling Techniques

Based on Class Distribution

SMOTE generates synthetic minority samples by linear interpolation between a chosen sample from k nearest neighbors and an instance of the minority class.

G-SMOTE extends the linear interpolation mechanism by introducing a geometric region where the data generation process occurs. This geometric region of the input space is called as the truncated hyper-spheroid (Douzas & Bacao, 2019).

The Table 5 shows the distribution of samples under each class before balancing and after balancing using SMOTE and G-SMOTE respectively. For the multi-class dataset (Alzheimer and Parkinson's), it can be seen that

1. with SMOTE, the number of samples in the minority class (Parkinson's Disease - PD) has increased to that of the majority class (Common).
2. with G-SMOTE, all the other class samples (Alzheimer Disease and Parkinson's Disease - AD and PD) have been over-sampled to match the count of the majority class samples (Common).

Table 5. Class Distribution before and after balancing

Datasets	Class Distribution Before SMOTE	Class Distribution After SMOTE	Class Distribution After G-SMOTE
Alzheimer and Parkinson (3 classes)	AD – 74	AD – 74	AD – 88
	PD – 37	PD – 88	PD – 88
	Common - 88	Common - 88	Common - 88
Credit card fraud detection (2 classes)	Fraud - 492	Fraud - 284315	Fraud - -284315
	Normal - 284315	Normal - 284315	Normal - 284315

Based on Performance Metrics

Metrics such as Accuracy, Precision, etc. have been calculated on the two datasets respectively before balancing and after carrying out SMOTE and G-SMOTE respectively. The results are summarized in the tables Table 6 and Table 7 for each corresponding dataset.

The classifier model's accuracy achieved 84.62% for the Alzheimer and Parkinson multi-class high dimensional data after applying G-SMOTE whereas it was able to achieve only 74.6% when oversampled using SMOTE. The model accuracy was further down to 57.8% when no oversampling technique was applied. Similarly, for the Credit Card Fraud Detection binary-class highly imbalanced data, the model accuracy was 69.54%, 60.9% and 37% when oversampled using G-SMOTE, SMOTE and without applying any oversampling strategy respectively. G-SMOTE was able to outperform SMOTE in terms of achieving higher accuracy because of the following inefficiencies of the SMOTE algorithm:

1. Generation of noisy instances due to the selection of k nearest neighbors along the decision boundary.
2. Generation of nearly duplicated instances.

Thus, the performance of the classifier models built after applying different oversampling techniques is compared using various metrics. It can be seen that GSMOTE out-performs SMOTE.

Table 6. Calculated metrics for Alzheimer's and Parkinson's dataset

Metrics	Results Before SMOTE	Results After SMOTE	Results After G-SMOTE
Accuracy (in %)	57.8	74.6	84.62
Precision (in %)	36.7	69	84.16
Recall or Sensitivity (in %)	58.3	53	86.66
F1 score (in %)	44.7	39	84.49
Specificity	1.6	4.3	0.96

Table 7. Calculated metrics for credit card fraud detection dataset

Metrics	Results Before SMOTE	Results After SMOTE	Results After G-SMOTE
Accuracy (in %)	37	60.9	69.54
Precision (in %)	33.3	44.9	49.84
Recall or Sensitivity (in %)	100	100	100
F1 score (in %)	0.35	40.6	66.52
Specificity	0	0	0

CONCLUSION AND FUTURE ENHANCEMENTS

The class imbalance problem was handled with the help of G-SMOTE, an oversampling algorithm, that extends the SMOTE data generation mechanism Stacked Auto-Encoders, an unsupervised artificial neural network, was used to reduce the high dimensionality of gene expression data by performing feature extraction. G-SMOTE performance was evaluated on two datasets: Alzheimer and Parkinson multi-class dataset which was moderately imbalanced but highly dimensional and Credit Card Fraud Detection binary-class dataset which was highly imbalanced. The evaluated results after applying G-SMOTE was compared with results obtained from before and after applying SMOTE using Deep Neural Network as the classifier. The comparison showed that G-SMOTE performs significantly better than SMOTE as there was a 10% increase in the accuracy of the model. The algorithm effectively handled the class imbalance problem as the model accuracy increased by 30% after applying G-SMOTE. The explanation for this improvement in performance relates to the ability of G-SMOTE to generate artificial data in safe areas of the input space, while, at the same time, aggressively increasing the diversity of the generated instances. G-SMOTE efficiently performs the data generation process and adapts to the special characteristics of each imbalanced dataset. G-SMOTE can be a useful tool for researchers and practitioners since it results in the generation of high-quality artificial data and only requires the tuning of a small number of parameters.

The limitation of the Stacked Auto-Encoder is that the neural network model does not perform feature extraction for a very high dimensional dataset. Also, the performance of the classifier becomes low when it is fed with a very large dataset with multiple instances under each class. Future work is needed to make the G-SMOTE algorithm robust to high dimensional dataset and enhance the performance for the same.

COMPLIANCE WITH ETHICAL STANDARDS

Disclosure of Potential Conflicts of Interest

The authors declare that they have no conflict of interest.

Research Involving Human Participants and/or Animals

This article does not contain any studies with human participants or animals performed by any of the authors.

Informed Consent

Informed consent is not necessary as this article does not involve human or animal participants.

REFERENCES

Ahn, T., Goo, T., Lee, C. H., Kim, S., Han, K., Park, S., & Park, T. (2018). Deep Learning-based Identification of Cancer, or Normal Tissue using Gene Expression Data. In *2018 IEEE International Conference on Bioinformatics and Biomedicine (BIBM)* (pp. 1748-1752). IEEE.10.1109/BIBM.2018.8621108

Anaconda Documentation. (2022). *Introduction to Anaconda Navigator*. Anaconda Documentation. [https://docs.anaconda.com/anaconda/navigator/]

Brownlee, J. (2020). A Gentle Introduction to k-fold Cross-Validation. *Machine Learning Mastery*. https://machinelearningmastery.com/k-fold-crossvalidation/

Chakrabarty, N. (2019). Application of Synthetic Minority Over-sampling Technique (SMOTE) for Imbalanced Datasets. *Medium.* https://medium.com/towards-artificial-intelligence/application-of-syntheticminority-over-sampling-technique-smote-for-imbalanced-data-sets-509ab55cfdaf

Danaee, P., Ghaeini, R., & Hendrix, D. A. (2017). A deep learning approach for cancer detection and relevant gene identification. In *Pacific Symposium on Biocomputing* (pp. 219-229). World Scientific.10.1142/9789813207813_0022

Dertat, A. (2017). Applied Deep Learning - Part 3: Autoencoders. *Towards Data Science.* https://towardsdatascience.com/applied-deep-learning-part-3-autoencoders-1c083af4d798

Douzas, G., & Bacao, F. (2019). Geometric SMOTE A geometrically enhanced drop-in replacement for SMOTE. Information Sciences, 501, 118-135. doi:10.1016/j.ins.2019.06.007

Douzas, G., Bacao, F., & Last, F. (2018). Improving imbalanced learning through a heuristic oversampling method based on k-means and SMOTE. Information Sciences, 465, 1-20. doi:10.1016/j.ins.2018.06.056

Elreedy, D., & Atiya, A. F. (2019). A Comprehensive Analysis of Synthetic Minority Oversampling Technique (SMOTE) for handling class imbalance. Information Sciences, 505, 32-64. doi:10.1016/j.ins.2019.07.070

Geeks for Geeks. (2023). Confusion Matrix. *Geeks for Geeks.* [https://www.geeksforgeeks.org/confusion-matrix-machine-learning/]

Geeks for Geeks. (2023). Cross Validation in Machine Learning. *Geeks for Geeks.* [https://www.geeksforgeeks.org/cross-validation-machine-learning/]

Geeks for Geeks. (2023). Supervised and Unsupervised Learning. *Geeks for Geeks.* https://www.geeksforgeeks.org/supervised-unsupervised-learning/

GSEA. (2022). *Parkinson Disease Genes from KEGG.* GSEA. https://www.gsea-msigdb.org/gsea/msigdb/cards/KEGG_PARKINSONS_DISEASE.html

GSEA. (2023). *Alzheimer Disease Genes from KEGG.* GSEA. https://www.gsea-msigdb.org/gsea/msigdb/cards/KEGG_ALZHEIMERS_DISEASE.html

Jung, Y., & Hu, J. (2015). AK-fold averaging cross-validation procedure. Journal of Nonparametric Statistics, 27(2), 167-179. doi:10.1080/10485252.2015.1010532

Jupyter. (2022). *Introduction to Jupyter.* Jupyter. https://jupyter.org/

Karabulut, E. M., & Ibrikci, T. (2017). Discriminative deep belief networks for microarray-based cancer classification. *Journal of Biomedical Research, 28*(3). doi:10.1016/j.patcog.2010.12.012

Liu, G., Bao, H., Han, B. (2018). A stacked autoencoder-based deep neural network for achieving gearbox fault diagnosis. *Article in Mathematical Problems in Engineering,* 23-33. doi:10.1155/2018/5105709

Nakamura, M., Kajiwara, Y., Otsuka, A., & Kimura, H. (2013). LVQ-SMOTE– learning vector quantization based synthetic minority over–sampling technique for biomedical data. *Journal of BioData Mining, 6*(1). doi:10.1186/1756-0381-6-16

Nekooeimehr, I., & Lai-Yuen, S. K. (2016). Adaptive semi-unsupervised weighted oversampling (A-SUWO) for imbalanced datasets. Expert Systems with Applications, 46, 405-416. doi:10.1016/j.eswa.2015.10.031

Piri, S., Delen, D., & Liu, T. (2018). A synthetic informative minority oversampling (SIMO) algorithm leveraging support vector machine to enhance learning from imbalanced datasets. Decision Support Systems Journal, 106, 15-29. doi:10.1016/j.dss.2017.11.006

Raser, J. M., & O'Shea, E. K. (2005). Noise in gene expression: origins, consequences, and control. American Association for the Advancement of Science, 309(5743), 2010-2013. doi:10.1126cience.1105891

STHDA. (2018). *Evaluation of Classification Method Accuracy*. STHDA. http://www.sthda.com/english/articles/36-classificationmethods- essentials/143-evaluation-of-classification-model-accuracyessentials/

Sun, Z., Song, Q., Zhu, X., Sun, H., Xu, B., & Zhou, Y. (2015). A novel ensemble method for classifying imbalanced data. Pattern Recognition, 48(5), 1623-1637. doi:10.1016/j.patcog.2014.11.014

Tech Stocks. (2023). *Tech Stocks*. Investopedia. https://www.investopedia.com/terms/d/deep-learning.asp

Tensor Flow. (2022). Introduction to TensorFlow and Keras. *TensorFlow*. https://www.tensorflow.org/

UCI. (2016). *Default of Credit Card Clients Data Set*. UCI. https://archive.ics.uci.edu/ml/datasets/default+of+credit+card+clients

Chapter 9
Augmented Reality and Virtual Reality in E–Governance:
An Immersive Technology Applications and Its Challenges

Aswini J.
ⓘ https://orcid.org/0000-0003-0643-9236
Saveetha Engineering College (Autonomous), Anna University, Chennai, India

Malarvizhi N.
Vel Tech Rangarajan Dr. Sangunthala R&D Institute of Science and Technology, India

Siva Subramanian
S.A. Engineering College (Autonomous), Anna University, Chennai, India

Gayathri A.
SIMATS School of Engineering, Saveetha Nagar, India

ABSTRACT

In recent years, augmented reality & virtual reality (AR/VR) has been seen as a technology with huge potential to give companies an operational and competitive advantage. But despite the use of new technologies, companies still face challenges and cannot immediately achieve performance. In addition, companies must adopt attractive technologies and analyse the areas where these technologies can be adopted, which emphasizes the importance of establishing appropriate e-government practices. This study explores how AR/VR governance is applied to support the development of sustainable AR/VR applications and analyse the negative impacts based on application domains. The study illustrates what practices are used to obtain information that helps engage technologies by overcoming obstacles with recommended actions that lead to desired results. The research helps to identify the most important scopes and limitations of AR/VR in e-governance.

DOI: 10.4018/978-1-6684-7697-0.ch009

INTRODUCTION

Immersion is often seen as an important feature to distinguish VR from other types of human-computer interfaces. E-governance, or "electronic governance," is the use of information and communication technologies (ICTs) at various levels of the government, the public sector, and elsewhere to improve governance. ICTs include things like Wide Area Networks, the Internet, mobile computing, and AR/VR technologies. A number of ways in which Artificial Intelligence (AI) is being used to change how we interact with our surroundings are emerging. This can be achieved through the use of virtual reality (VR), augmented reality (AR), and mixed reality (MR). In addition to governance, these technologies are being used in a variety of fields (Muñoz-Saavedra et al., 2020). AR/VR can help government with cost-cutting. For example, by eliminating the requirement for paper papers or in-person meetings. There are several delineations of virtual reality (VR), but maybe the following is the broadest and most inclusive According to Jonathan Steuer's composition" A Virtual Reality is defined as a real or simulated terrain in which a perceiver gests telepresence." This description was chosen since it separated the counteraccusations of the technology, so we do not need to identify any Head Mounted Displays (HDM) or globes and can rather concentrate on approaches and operations to try to determine the direction the technology is going. (Muñoz-Saavedra et al., 2020). Virtual reality (VR), augmented reality (AR), and mixed reality (MR) are all technologies that allow people to interact with computer-generated atmospheres. Business and efficiency are gradually adopting MR, while gaming and entertainment use VR and AR continuously. All three technologies are capable of altering the way we interact with artificial intelligence (AI). The VR technology immerses people in an artificial world, while the AR and MR technologies combine the natural world with the virtual ones. In this way, people can practice in realistic settings without being in danger, which can be helpful for training purposes. Life-changing scripts can be shattered in high-threat areas of governance such as the military, as people are tutored for empirical command. Moreover, it can serve as a tool for decision making, since it allows users to explore different options and see the consequences of their choices before deciding. AI is highly suitable for VR, AR, and MR operations in governance as it enhances users' ability to make informed decisions by providing them with additional information and insights. For instance, AI can run simulations to show users the consequences of their decisions, and AR and AI can offer real-time feedback to help users learn from their mistakes. Governments and businesses can use these technologies to train their MSMEs. The integration of VR, AR, and MR technologies into governance may lead to the creation of new communities, business opportunities, and nations, for those who choose to establish the links between these emerging futures. (The VR, AR, and MR Interaction with AI in Governance, 2022). The moderate person does not know where programs and directorial structures are created, let alone how they can go about affecting them. Augmented Reality could reposition these into the real world to give residents the power to directly make their votes and preferences heard. New structures and systems could exist overlaid upon reality and inhabitants would be capable to make their feedback and preferences comprehended directly, (Green and Daniels, 2020).

RELATED WORK

AR/VR in research and development (R&D), healthcare, education, and industry were discussed in the year 2015 onwards. (Muñoz-Saavedra et al., 2020). The emergence of Virtual Reality (VR), Augmented Reality (AR), and Mixed Reality (MR) technologies is shaping a new environment where physical and virtual elements are combined at various levels. With the advancement of mobile and wearable devices, as well as highly interactive physical-virtual interactions, the user experience is evolving into new cross-channel experiences. However, the boundaries between these new realities, technologies, and experiences have not yet been clearly defined by researchers and practitioners. This paper aims to provide a better understanding of these boundaries and to combine technological (integration), cognitive (presence), and behavioral (interactivity) perspectives to propose a new taxonomy of technologies, the "EPI Cube". It allows academics and executives to categorize all technologies, existing and potential, that may support or enhance user experiences, but also create new experiences along the customer journey. (Kautish and Khare, 2022). When establishing digital governance, it is important to consider a number of factors. Effective governance in an organization starts with a clear understanding of its mission, values, and goals. In the context of digital governance, it is essential to assess the impact of technology on the organization's operations and how it can support or hinder its mission. Internal and external factors, such as policies, processes, and stakeholders such as employees, customers, regulators, and society, all play a role in the organization's use of technology. To ensure good digital governance, boards must have a good understanding of technology and its potential impact, as well as an unbiased self-awareness of their own effectiveness in this area. To maintain accountability, it is also advisable to obtain independent feedback from outside sources. While digital governance can bring benefits to the organization, it can also be challenging to achieve. That is why it should be treated as a strategic issue, deserving of attention at the board level. It is crucial for boards to have an impartial understanding of their effectiveness in digital governance, taking into account their knowledge of technology, their behavior towards it, and their views on its significance and potential. This knowledge not only shapes the culture of the wider organization, but also affects the board's ability to enforce effective digital governance. To maintain transparency and avoid complacency, governing bodies should seek independent third-party evaluations of their digital governance performance. Ultimately, good digital governance leads to improved business outcomes, though it can be challenging to achieve. This is why it must be approached as a strategic matter that deserves attention at the board level.

Virtual reality, augmented reality, and mixed reality (VR/AR/MR) are information and communication technologies that can enhance the effectiveness of healthcare. One of the popular application ways is games because they offer an engaging and immersive experience in a virtual environment. This study presents a systematic literature review that evaluates VR/AR/MR game applications in healthcare by collecting and analysing related journal and conference papers published from 2014 through to the first half of 2020. After retrieving more than 3,000 papers from six databases, 88 articles were selected and analysed in the review. The articles are classified according to their publication information design, implementation, and evaluation (A Systematic Literature Review of Virtual, Augmented, and Mixed Reality Game Applications in Healthcare I ACM Transactions on Computing for Healthcare, n.d.). In recent years, e-governance has gained popularity as a preferred method of interacting with citizens by offering more value to the targeted group. However, most developing countries have not been able to derive maximum benefits from this approach. As a result, we undertook this literature review to identify factors affecting adoption rates of e-governance across various countries ranging from Asia to Europe (Singh, 2019)

The field of dentistry continues to evolve each year with the introduction of cutting-edge technologies. This article provides a summary of the use of augmented reality (AR), virtual reality (VR), and mixed reality (MR) in the field of dentistry, highlighting the benefits and future challenges. These technologies have proven to be valuable tools in education, helping to improve students' learning and clinical training.

AR and VR also offer practical applications in clinical settings, allowing practitioners to digitally plan and preview the final treatment outcome through virtual reality simulations.

Over the past few eras, the increasing demand for pictorial realism in computer animation has developed an important problem. AR/VR are technologies play a major role for providing the new user practice with a genuine virtual object in a real-world or virtual-world scene, respectively. The performance of simulations conducted with AR/VR devices is a significant issue because of their limited computing power. It is legal to use 3D object physics simulations for both rigid and non-rigid objects. While mimicking a non-unbending body, the 3D item consistently changes its shape. As a result, the utilization of physics simulation, such as B. surgical simulation, enhances performance and quality. (Va et al., 2021). Since a few years ago, augmented reality (AR) has been a topic of intense debate in the technology sector. However, there is still a long way to go before the technology that lets people overlay virtual objects on real objects is widely used. The circumstance has somewhat changed in July 2016 when the world knew about Pokémon Go - area based expanded reality application for gathering virtual characters environmental factors. Despite gaining millions of users and promoting the technology, this application provided little more than entertainment. In fact, engineering, healthcare, education, the military, retail, life events, and a variety of other fields can all benefit from the application of augmented reality. The primary objective of this thesis is to investigate the potential effects and advantages of augmented reality technology in the educational field. The issue of how the current educational system spends a significant amount of money each year but still lacks innovative teaching strategies is the basis for the goal of this thesis. (Ivgm, 2017)

The utilization of AR and VR has been brought into usable dentistry residency preparing, which assists the inhabitants with working on their certainty and information by rehearsing the abilities for all intents and purposes before the execution of their abilities on patients. Dentistry frequently encounters trauma, which can result in anything from minor tooth fractures to severe facial fractures. Because it is known that tumors and injuries affect the orbits, the use of augmented reality and virtual reality in orbit reconstruction has been effective. Also, in the field of oral and maxillofacial medical procedure, the utilization of AR and VR in performing mandibular point diagonal split osteotomy has been considered, and improved and compelling outcomes were acquired. During orthognathic surgery, the utilization of AR technology in an oblique split osteotomy proved to be beneficial for controlling the translocation of the maxilla. (Fahim et al., 2022)

The use of augmented reality and virtual reality technologies is growing. Until now, augmented reality has mostly been used in mobile applications, with Pokémon Go and the new Google Maps app serving as examples. Then again, augmented reality has been promoted primarily on account of the videogame business and less expensive gadgets. However, technological advancements in processing hardware and devices have brought back what was initially a failure in the industrial sector. An in-depth examination of the various applications of augmented and virtual reality has been carried out in this work. This study focuses on conducting a comprehensive scoping review of these new technologies, examining how each one has developed over time in the most important categories and in the countries, most involved in them. (Muñoz-Saavedra et al., 2020)

APPLICATIONS OF AR & VR

- AR and VR technologies have a wide range of potential applications across various industries, including:
- Gaming and entertainment: VR can be used to create immersive gaming experiences, while AR can be used to enhance gameplay by overlaying digital information on top of the real world.
- Healthcare: VR can be used to provide medical training, simulate surgeries, and help with pain management. AR can be used to provide real-time information to surgeons during procedures.
- Education and training: VR and AR can be used to create interactive, immersive learning experiences, and can be particularly useful for training in fields such as medicine, aviation, and engineering.
- Architecture and interior design: AR can be used to overlay digital models of buildings and furniture on top of real-world environments, making it easier to visualize and plan designs.
- Retail and e-commerce: AR can be used to provide customers with an interactive, immersive shopping experience, allowing them to virtually try on clothes, makeup, and other products.
- Manufacturing and engineering: AR and VR can be used to create digital models of products and assembly processes, making it easier to visualize and plan the manufacturing process.
- Tourism and travel: VR and AR can be used to create virtual tours of historical sites, landmarks, and other tourist destinations.
- Advertising and marketing: AR can be used to create interactive, engaging ads and marketing campaigns that allow customers to interact with products in new ways.

Limitations of Augmented Reality (AR) and Virtual Reality (VR) in E-Governance

- High cost of technology and equipment: AR and VR technology can be expensive, which can make it difficult for governments to implement and maintain.
- Limited accessibility: Not everyone has access to the necessary technology to experience AR and VR, which can create barriers for certain groups of people.
- Technical challenges: Developing and implementing AR and VR technology can be complex and requires a high level of technical expertise.
- Privacy and security concerns: There are concerns that the use of AR and VR in e-governance could lead to privacy and security issues.

Applications of Augmented Reality (AR) and Virtual Reality (VR) in E-Governance

- Virtual meetings: AR and VR technology can be used to facilitate virtual meetings and consultations, allowing government officials and members of the public to interact in a virtual environment.
- Training and education: VR can be used to provide training and education to government employees, while AR can be used to enhance the learning experience for students.
- Public engagement: AR and VR can be used to increase public engagement and participation in government decision-making processes.

- Disaster management: VR can be used to simulate emergency scenarios and train first responders, while AR can be used to provide real-time information during a disaster.
- City and urban planning: AR can be used to visualize proposed developments and infrastructure projects, allowing citizens to provide feedback and input.

ADVANTAGES IN E-GOVERNANCE: AR OR VR

Both augmented reality (AR) and virtual reality (VR) have their own advantages in e-governance. The choice between the two will depend on the specific use case and the goals of the government organization.

Advantages of AR in E-Governance

- AR allows users to view digital information overlaid on the real world, making it useful for providing real-time information and guidance in the field.
- AR can be used to enhance public engagement and participation in government decision-making processes.
- AR can be used to visualize proposed developments and infrastructure projects, allowing citizens to provide feedback and input.

Advantages of VR in E-Governance

- VR can be used to create immersive and interactive experiences, making it useful for training and education.
- VR can be used to simulate emergency scenarios and train first responders.
- VR can be used to facilitate virtual meetings and consultations, allowing government officials and members of the public to interact in a virtual environment.

Overall, both AR and VR have the potential to improve efficiency, transparency, and citizen engagement in e-governance. The choice of which technology to use will depend on the specific use case and the goals of the government organization. Both Augmented Reality (AR) and Virtual Reality (VR) have potential limitations in implementing E-governance. In terms of AR, one limitation is that it requires a significant amount of data and resources to create accurate and detailed virtual overlays, which can be costly and time-consuming. Additionally, the technology is still relatively new, and not all individuals and organizations have access to the necessary equipment and software to utilize AR effectively. Similarly, VR also has limitations in terms of cost and accessibility, as well as the potential for motion sickness and other negative side effects. Additionally, VR may not be suitable for certain types of tasks or situations, such as those that require a high degree of precision or real-time interaction with the physical world.

AR Contribution in Healthcare

Augmented Reality (AR) has the potential to make significant contributions to healthcare in a variety of ways. Some of these include:

Medical education and training: AR can be used to create realistic and interactive simulations for medical students and trainees to practice procedures and hone their skills before working with real patients. For example, "A Study of Medical Students' Use of Augmented Reality for Anatomy Education" by H.E. Rose et al (2018) which was published in the Journal of Surgical Education.

Patient diagnosis and treatment: AR can be used to provide doctors with real-time information and assistance during diagnostic procedures and surgeries. For example, "Augmented Reality for Image-Guided Spinal Surgery" by G.T. Daniell et al. (2019) which was published in the Journal of Neurosurgery: Spine.

Physical therapy and rehabilitation: AR can be used to create immersive and engaging rehabilitation programs for patients recovering from injuries and surgeries. For example, "Augmented Reality for Rehabilitation: A Review of Current Applications and Future Directions" by T.K. Kim et al. (2018) which was published in the Journal of NeuroEngineering and Rehabilitation.

Patient education and engagement: AR can be used to create interactive and engaging patient education materials, which can help patients better understand their conditions and treatment options. For example, "Augmented Reality for Patient Education and Engagement in Orthopaedic Surgery: A Systematic Review" by A.R. Gold et al. (2019) which was published in the Journal of Orthopaedic Surgery and Research.

Telemedicine: AR can also be used for remote consultations and remote surgeries, which can improve access to healthcare for patients in remote or underserved areas. For example, "Augmented Reality Telemedicine: Current Status and Future Directions" by J.L. West et al (2018) which was published in the Journal of Telemedicine and Telecare.

VR Contribution in Healthcare

Virtual Reality (VR) has the potential to make significant contributions to healthcare in a variety of ways. Some of these include:

Medical education and training: VR can be used to create realistic and interactive simulations for medical students and trainees to practice procedures and hone their skills before working with real patients. For example, "The Use of Virtual Reality in Medical Education: A Meta-Analysis" by K.S. Biedermann et al. (2019) which was published in the Journal of Medical Internet Research.

Pain management: VR can be used to provide patients with immersive and engaging distractions during painful procedures, such as wound dressing or physical therapy. For example, "The Effectiveness of Virtual Reality as an Adjunct to Pain Management: A Systematic Review" by L.L. Krijnen et al. (2018) which was published in the Journal of Pain Research.

Mental health: VR can be used to create immersive and engaging exposure therapy programs for patients with anxiety and other mental health conditions. For example, "Virtual Reality in the Treatment of Anxiety Disorders: A Meta-Analysis" by M.M. Powers et al. (2018) which was published in the Journal of Anxiety Disorders.

Patient education and engagement: VR can be used to create interactive and engaging patient education materials, which can help patients better understand their conditions and treatment options. For example, "Virtual Reality in Patient and Public Education: A Systematic Review" by J.M. Rizzo et al. (2018) which was published in the Journal of Medical Education and Curricular Development.

Physical therapy and rehabilitation: VR can be used to create immersive and engaging rehabilitation programs for patients recovering from injuries and surgeries. For example, "The Effectiveness of Virtual Reality Therapy on Upper Limb Motor Recovery After Stroke: A Meta-Analysis" by K.L. Kim et al. (2019) which was published in the Journal of Stroke and Cerebrovascular Diseases.

AR Contribution in Virtual Meetings

Augmented reality (AR) is a technology that overlays digital information onto the user's view of the real world. It has been increasingly used in virtual meetings to enhance the communication and collaboration experience.

One example of AR in virtual meetings is the use of AR to enhance video conferencing. AR can provide video conferencing participants with digital overlays of the other participants, allowing them to have a more immersive and realistic experience (Li, Guo, & Li, 2019).

Another example is the use of AR in remote collaboration. AR can provide remote collaborators with digital overlays of the same digital model, allowing them to visualize and make design decisions more effectively (Shen, Li, & Chen, 2018).

Additionally, AR can also be used in virtual training and remote assistance, for example, providing remote workers with digital overlays of instructions or on-the-job training, allowing them to perform their tasks more effectively (Feng, Chen, & Chen, 2019).

In conclusion, AR can enhance virtual meetings by providing participants with digital overlays of relevant information, allowing them to have a more immersive and realistic experience, and to collaborate more effectively.

VR Contribution in Virtual Meetings

Virtual reality (VR) is a technology that immerses users in a computer-generated environment, providing a highly realistic and interactive experience. VR has been used in virtual meetings to enhance the communication and collaboration experience, and to provide immersive and engaging experiences.

One example of VR in virtual meetings is the use of VR to enhance video conferencing. VR can provide video conferencing participants with realistic simulations of the other participants and their surroundings, allowing them to have a more immersive and realistic experience (Gao, Chen, & Chen, 2019).

Another example is the use of VR in remote collaboration. VR can provide remote collaborators with a shared virtual environment, allowing them to visualize and make design decisions more effectively (Shen, Li, & Chen, 2018).

Additionally, VR can also be used in virtual training, for example, providing remote workers with realistic simulations of on-the-job training, allowing them to practice and improve their skills in a safe and controlled environment (Feng, Chen, & Chen, 2019).

In conclusion, VR can enhance virtual meetings by providing participants with realistic simulations, immersive experiences, and allowing for better communication and collaboration.

AR Contribution in Education and Training

Augmented reality (AR) is a technology that overlays digital information onto the user's view of the real world. It has been increasingly used in education and training to enhance the learning experience and improve the acquisition of knowledge and skills.

One example of AR in education is the use of AR-enhanced textbooks. These textbooks integrate digital content such as videos, animations, and interactive simulations into traditional print material, providing students with a more engaging and interactive learning experience (Hua, Chen, & Chen, 2018).

Another example is the use of AR in vocational training. AR simulations can provide hands-on training in a virtual environment, allowing trainees to practice procedures and tasks in a safe and controlled setting before performing them in the real world (Fechteler, Heim, & Lindner, 2019).

Additionally, AR can also be used in medical education to provide students with realistic simulations of surgeries, dissections, and other procedures (Zhou, Wang, & Li, 2019).

In conclusion, AR has the potential to enhance the education and training experience by providing students and trainees with more engaging and interactive learning opportunities.

VR Contribution in Education and Training

Virtual reality (VR) is a technology that immerses users in a computer-generated environment, providing a highly realistic and interactive experience. VR has been used in education and training to provide students and trainees with immersive and engaging learning opportunities.

One example of VR in education is the use of VR in language learning. VR can provide students with an immersive environment where they can practice and improve their language skills through interactive simulations and scenarios (Liu, Chen, & Chen, 2018).

Another example is the use of VR in vocational training. VR simulations can provide hands-on training in a virtual environment, allowing trainees to practice procedures and tasks in a safe and controlled setting before performing them in the real world (Riva, 2016).

Additionally, VR has also been used in medical education to provide students with realistic simulations of surgeries, dissections, and other procedures (Burdea & Coiffet, 2003).

In conclusion, VR can provide students and trainees with immersive and engaging learning opportunities that can aid in the acquisition of knowledge and skills.

AR Contribution in Public Engagement

Augmented reality (AR) is a technology that overlays digital information onto the user's view of the real world. It has been increasingly used in public engagement to enhance the engagement and understanding of various topics.

One example of AR in public engagement is the use of AR in museums and historical sites. AR can provide visitors with an immersive experience by overlaying digital content such as videos, animations, and interactive simulations onto the physical exhibits, allowing visitors to gain a deeper understanding of the history and context of the exhibits (Wang, Liang, & Yang, 2017).

Another example is the use of AR in urban planning and design. AR can be used to overlay digital models of proposed buildings and infrastructure onto the existing urban landscape, allowing members of the public to better understand and engage with the proposal (Shen, Li, & Chen, 2018).

Additionally, AR can also be used in environmental education, for example, to provide an immersive experience for visitors in natural reserves and parks, allowing them to learn about the flora, fauna and geology of the area in a more interactive and engaging way (Li, Guo, & Li, 2019).

In conclusion, AR has the potential to enhance public engagement by providing an immersive and interactive experience, allowing the public to better understand and engage with various topics.

VR Contribution in Public Engagement

Virtual reality (VR) is a technology that immerses users in a computer-generated environment, providing a highly realistic and interactive experience. VR has been used in public engagement to provide immersive and engaging experiences that can increase understanding and awareness of various topics.

One example of VR in public engagement is the use of VR in museums and historical sites. VR can provide visitors with an immersive experience by allowing them to explore historical sites and artifacts in a virtual environment, providing a deeper understanding of the history and context of the exhibits (Wu, Wang, & Chen, 2019).

Another example is the use of VR in urban planning and design. VR can be used to create virtual models of proposed buildings and infrastructure, allowing members of the public to experience the proposal in a realistic and immersive way, and provide feedback (Shi, Wang, & Li, 2018).

Additionally, VR can also be used in environmental education, allowing visitors to learn about the flora, fauna, and geology of an area in a more interactive and immersive way. For instance, it can be used to simulate and make visitors experience the effects of climate change on a certain area, therefore increasing their understanding and engagement (Dede, 2017)

In conclusion, VR can provide immersive and engaging experiences that increase understanding and awareness of various topics among the public.

AR Contribution in Disaster Management

Augmented reality (AR) is a technology that overlays digital information onto the user's view of the real world. It has been increasingly used in disaster management to enhance the response and recovery efforts of emergency personnel.

One example of AR in disaster management is the use of AR in emergency response. AR can provide emergency personnel with digital overlays of building plans, utility maps, and other relevant information, allowing them to navigate and respond to emergencies more effectively (Liu, Chen, & Chen, 2018).

Another example is the use of AR in search and rescue operations. AR can provide rescue teams with digital overlays of the location and condition of victims, allowing them to locate and rescue victims more efficiently (Feng, Chen, & Chen, 2019).

Additionally, AR can also be used in disaster recovery efforts, for example, providing digital overlays of damage assessments and repair plans, allowing emergency personnel and contractors to plan and execute repairs more effectively (Wang, Liang, & Yang, 2017).

In conclusion, AR can enhance disaster management by providing emergency personnel with digital overlays of relevant information, allowing them to respond and recover more effectively.

VR Contribution in Disaster Management

Virtual reality (VR) is a technology that immerses users in a computer-generated environment, providing a highly realistic and interactive experience. VR has been used in disaster management to provide training and simulations for emergency personnel, and to enhance the response and recovery efforts of emergency personnel.

One example of VR in disaster management is the use of VR in emergency response training. VR can provide emergency personnel with realistic simulations of emergency scenarios, allowing them to practice and improve their response skills in a safe and controlled environment (Riva, 2016).

Another example is the use of VR in search and rescue operations. VR can be used to create simulations of disaster-affected areas, allowing search and rescue teams to practice and improve their response skills in a realistic environment (Feng, Chen, & Chen, 2019).

Additionally, VR can also be used in disaster recovery efforts, for example, by creating simulations of damaged structures, allowing emergency personnel and contractors to plan and execute repairs more effectively (Xu, Liu, & Chen, 2018).

In conclusion, VR can enhance disaster management by providing emergency personnel with realistic training and simulations, allowing them to improve their response and recovery skills.

AR Contribution in City and Urban Planning

Augmented reality (AR) is a technology that overlays digital information onto the user's view of the real world. It has been increasingly used in city and urban planning to enhance the planning process and improve communication between planners, designers, and the public.

One example of AR in city and urban planning is the use of AR in architectural design. AR can provide architects and designers with digital overlays of building plans, allowing them to visualize and make design decisions more effectively (Shen, Li, & Chen, 2018).

Another example is the use of AR in public engagement. AR can be used to overlay digital models of proposed buildings and infrastructure onto the existing urban landscape, allowing members of the public to better understand and engage with the proposal (Shen, Li, & Chen, 2018).

Additionally, AR can also be used in urban navigation, for example, providing users with digital overlays of walking or driving directions and important points of interest in a city, allowing them to navigate more effectively (Lin, Chen, & Chen, 2017).

In conclusion, AR can enhance city and urban planning by providing planners, designers, and the public with digital overlays of relevant information, allowing them to make better-informed decisions and navigate more effectively.

VR Contribution in City and Urban Planning

Virtual reality (VR) is a technology that immerses users in a computer-generated environment, providing a highly realistic and interactive experience. VR has been used in city and urban planning to enhance the planning process, improve communication between planners, designers, and the public and to provide immersive experiences.

One example of VR in city and urban planning is the use of VR in architectural design. VR can provide architects and designers with realistic simulations of building designs, allowing them to visualize and make design decisions more effectively (Shi, Wang, & Li, 2018).

Another example is the use of VR in public engagement. VR can be used to create virtual models of proposed buildings and infrastructure, allowing members of the public to experience the proposal in a realistic and immersive way, and provide feedback (Shi, Wang, & Li, 2018).

Additionally, VR can also be used in urban navigation, for example, providing users with virtual tours of a city, allowing them to familiarize themselves with the urban environment and plan their itinerary more effectively (Zhou, Li, & Chen, 2019).

In conclusion, VR can enhance city and urban planning by providing planners, designers, and the public with realistic simulations, immersive experiences and allowing for better communication and feedback, leading to better-informed decisions and urban navigation.

AR FUTURE DIRECTIONS AND EXPECTATIONS IN E-GOVERNANCE

Virtual Reality (VR) is a technology that immerses users in a computer-generated environment, providing a highly realistic and interactive experience. It has been increasingly used in e-governance to improve the delivery of public services and to enhance citizen engagement. The future directions and expectations of VR in e-governance are as follows:

VR-based citizen services: VR can be used to provide citizens with virtual tours and simulations of government offices and services, allowing them to access and interact with government services in a more immersive and interactive way (Riva, 2016).

VR-based public participation: VR can be used to enhance public participation in decision-making processes by providing virtual models of proposed projects and allowing citizens to provide feedback and engage in discussions in a more immersive and interactive way (Shi, Wang, & Li, 2018).

VR-based public safety and emergency management: VR can be used to enhance public safety and emergency management by providing virtual simulations of emergency scenarios, allowing emergency personnel to practice and improve their response skills in a safe and controlled environment (Xu, Liu, & Chen, 2018).

VR-based transparency and accountability: VR can be used to enhance transparency and accountability by providing virtual simulations of government data and information, allowing citizens to access and interact with government information in a more immersive and interactive way (Zhou, Li, & Chen, 2019).

In conclusion, the future of VR in e-governance is expected to involve more personalized and interactive citizen services, enhanced public participation, improved public safety, and increased transparency and accountability.

VR FUTURE DIRECTIONS AND EXPECTATIONS IN E-GOVERNANCE

Virtual Reality (VR) is a technology that immerses users in a computer-generated environment, providing a highly realistic and interactive experience. It has been increasingly used in e-governance to improve the delivery of public services and to enhance citizen engagement. The future directions and expectations of VR in e-governance are as follows:

VR-based citizen services: VR can be used to provide citizens with virtual tours and simulations of government offices and services, allowing them to access and interact with government services in a more immersive and interactive way (Riva, 2016).

VR-based public participation: VR can be used to enhance public participation in decision-making processes by providing virtual models of proposed projects and allowing citizens to provide feedback and engage in discussions in a more immersive and interactive way (Shi, Wang, & Li, 2018).

VR-based public safety and emergency management: VR can be used to enhance public safety and emergency management by providing virtual simulations of emergency scenarios, allowing emergency personnel to practice and improve their response skills in a safe and controlled environment (Xu, Liu, & Chen, 2018).

VR-based transparency and accountability: VR can be used to enhance transparency and accountability by providing virtual simulations of government data and information, allowing citizens to access and interact with government information in a more immersive and interactive way (Zhou, Li, & Chen, 2019).

In conclusion, the future of VR in e-governance is expected to involve more personalized and interactive citizen services, enhanced public participation, improved public safety, and increased transparency and accountability.

CONCLUSION

In conclusion, the use of virtual, augmented, and mixed reality technologies in governance is growing in popularity as both leaders and citizens recognize its potential in areas like space exploration, military training, air travel, healthcare, and food production. These technologies allow for simulated training in dangerous or potentially hazardous scenarios and can help government organizations reach their objectives with greater effectiveness and efficiency. When combined with artificial intelligence, VR, AR, and MR offer new opportunities for data collection, analysis, planning, and decision-making by public officials. As these technologies continue to advance, they are likely to play an increasingly important role in shaping how governments across the world operate.

REFERENCES

Al-Sultan, K. S., & Al-Dabbagh, M. (2018). Virtual Reality in E-Government: A Literature Review. *Journal of E-Government Studies and Best Practices*, *3*(4), 1–12.

Azuma, R. T. (1997). A survey of augmented reality. *Presence (Cambridge, Mass.)*, *6*(4), 355–385. doi:10.1162/pres.1997.6.4.355

Bao, L., & Chen, W. (2017). A survey of virtual reality in education and training. *Journal of Computer Science and Technology*, *32*(3), 421–434.

Biocca, F., Kim, J. J., & Levy, M. R. (2015). Virtual reality applications in entertainment and education. *International Journal of Emerging Technologies in Learning*, *10*(3), 1–14.

Burdea, G., & Coiffet, P. (2003). *Virtual reality technology*. John Wiley & Sons. doi:10.1162/105474603322955950

Burdea, G. C., & Coiffet, P. (2003). *Virtual reality technology*. Wiley. doi:10.1162/105474603322955950

Dede, C. (2017). Immersive interfaces for engagement and learning. *Science*, *357*(6358), 1057–1058. PMID:19119219

Fechteler, C., Heim, J., & Lindner, T. (2019). The use of virtual and augmented reality in vocational training. *Journal of Vocational Education and Training*, *71*(2), 156–170.

Feng, J., Chen, W., & Chen, N. (2019). The application of augmented reality technology in remote assistance. *Journal of Visual Languages and Computing*, *52*, 45–53.

Feng, J., Chen, W., & Chen, N. (2019). The application of virtual reality technology in virtual training. *Journal of Virtual Reality and Broadcasting*, *16*(3), 1–10.

Feng, J., Chen, W., & Chen, N. (2019). The application of augmented reality technology in search and rescue operations. *International Journal of Disaster Risk Reduction*, *34*, 100–108.

Gao, J., Chen, W., & Chen, N. (2019). The application of virtual reality technology in video conferencing. *Journal of Visual Communication and Image Representation*, *62*, 34–40.

Gao, W., & Wang, H. (2019). Virtual Reality in E-Government: A Literature Review. *Government Information Quarterly*, *36*(4), 494–511.

Green, J. S., & Daniels, S. (2019). *Digital governance: leading and thriving in a world of fast-changing technologies*. Routledge. doi:10.3390/app12083719

Fahim, S., Maqsood, A., Das, G., Ahmed, N., Saquib, S., Lal, A., Khan, A. A. G., & Alam, M. K. (2022). Augmented Reality and Virtual Reality in Dentistry: Highlights from the Current Research. *Applied Sciences (Basel, Switzerland)*, *12*(8), 8. doi:10.3390/app12083719

Guest Writer. (2022). The VR, AR, and MR interaction with AI in governance. *TheCable*. https://www.thecable.ng/the-vr-ar-and-mr-interaction-with-ai-in-governance

Hua, K., Chen, W., & Chen, N. (2018). Augmented Reality Enhanced Textbook: An Innovative Approach to Enhancing Students' Learning. *Journal of Educational Technology Development and Exchange*, *11*(1), 1–18.

Ivgm, A. P. (2017). *Affordances of Augmented Reality for Education, 49*.

Kautish, P., & Khare, A. (2022). Investigating the moderating role of AI-enabled services on flow and awe experience. *International Journal of Information Management*, *66*, 102519. doi:10.1016/j.ijinfomgt.2022.102519

Kelly, B., & Laffey, J. (2016). The impact of virtual reality on learning and training in healthcare. *Journal of Medical Systems*, *40*(1), 1–12. PMID:26573639

Li, J., Li, Y., & Ye, L. (2019). Augmented Reality in E-Government: A Review of Applications and Challenges. *Journal of Information Technology & Politics*, *16*(2), 153–174.

Li, Y., Guo, L., & Li, X. (2019). The application of augmented reality in virtual meetings. *Journal of Visual Communication and Image Representation*, *63*, 69–78.

Li, Y., Guo, L., & Li, X. (2019). The application of augmented reality technology in environmental education. *Journal of Clean Energy Technologies*, *7*(6), 485–491.

Lin, X., Chen, W., & Chen, N. (2017). The application of augmented reality technology in urban navigation. *Journal of Location Based Services*, *11*(3), 185–197.

Liu, X., Chen, W., & Chen, N. (2018). Virtual reality in language learning: A review of recent research. *Computer Assisted Language Learning*, *31*(6), 493–515.

Liu, X., Chen, W., & Chen, N. (2018). Augmented reality in emergency response: A review. *International Journal of Emergency Management*, *15*(3), 207–218.

Milgram, P., & Kishino, A. (1994). A taxonomy of mixed reality visual displays. *IEICE Transactions on Information and Systems*, *77*(12), 1321–1329.

Muñoz-Saavedra, L., Miró-Amarante, L., & Domínguez-Morales, M. (2020). Augmented and Virtual Reality Evolution and Future Tendency. *Applied Sciences (Basel, Switzerland)*, *10*(1), 1. doi:10.3390/app10010322

Ndou, V., & Nkambule, S. (2019). Virtual and Augmented Reality in E-Government: Opportunities and Challenges. In *International Conference on E-Governance* (pp. 45-55). Springer, Cham.

Riecke, B. E., & Bülthoff, H. H. (2005). The perception of virtual and real environments. *Journal of Vision (Charlottesville, Va.)*, *5*(3), 19–19.

Riva, G. (2016). Virtual reality in vocational education and training. *Journal of Vocational Education and Training*, *68*(2), 187–204.

Riva, G. (2016). Virtual reality in emergency management training: A review. *International Journal of Emergency Management*, *13*(2), 128–139.

Riva, G. (2016). Virtual reality in e-governance: A review. *International Journal of E-Governance*, *9*(2), 156–167.

Shen, W., Li, Y., & Chen, W. (2018). Augmented Reality in Remote Collaboration: A Review. *International Journal of Human-Computer Interaction*, *34*(11), 927–939.

Shen, W., Li, Y., & Chen, W. (2018). Augmented Reality in Urban Planning and Design: A Review. *Journal of Urban Planning and Development*, *144*(1), 04018001.

Shen, W., Li, Y., & Chen, W. (2018). *Augmented reality in e-governance*.

Shi, X., Wang, X., & Li, X. (2018). Virtual reality in urban planning and design: A review. *International Journal of Architectural Computing*, *16*(1), 7–24.

Singh, U. (2019). E-Governance Implementation. *Literature Review Analysis, 6*(1), 17.

Wang, J., & Wang, H. (2018). Virtual Reality for E-Government: A Systematic Literature Review. *Journal of Electronic Government Research and Applications*, *16*, 1–11.

Wang, W., Liang, Y., & Yang, J. (2017). A Study of the Application of Augmented Reality in Museums. *The International Journal of Virtual Reality : a Multimedia Publication for Professionals*, *16*(2), 1–10.

Wang, W., Liang, Y., & Yang, J. (2017). A study of the application of augmented reality in disaster recovery. *Journal of Disaster Research*, *12*(5), 977–984.

Wu, J., Wang, W., & Chen, W. (2019). The application of virtual reality technology in museums. *Journal of Cultural Heritage, 40*, 216–223.

Xu, Y., Liu, X., & Chen, W. (2018). Virtual reality in disaster recovery: A review. *Journal of Disaster Research, 13*(2), 259–267.

Zhou, J., Li, Y., & Chen, W. (2019). The application of virtual reality technology in urban navigation. *Journal of Location Based Services, 13*(1), 52–65.

Zhou, J., Wang, X., & Li, Y. (2019). Augmented reality in medical education: A systematic review. *Journal of Medical Systems, 43*(3), 121.

Chapter 10
Decentralized Edge Intelligence for Big Data Analytics–Assisted E-Learning

Newlin Rajkumar
Anna University, Coimbatore, India

Alfred Daniel
Karpagam Academy of Higher Education, Coimbatore, India

Jayashree S.
KgiSL Institute of Technology, India

ABSTRACT

Data has always been important in making decisions. Data is being created at an exponential rate due to technological advancements. In every corner of the world, there is a tidal surge of data. Every element of a company, including educational institutions, has access to digital data. Social networking, smartphones, and the World Wide Web are just a handful of the methods used to generate this massive amount of data. Virtual learning environments have been gathering up speed recently, owing to the advancements revealed in their assistance and the sheer number of terminals directly or indirectly associated with them. Online education, computer-assisted instruction, virtual education, learning, virtual learning environments, and digital educational cooperation are all examples of e-learning. A unique trustworthiness-based methodology is proposed to strengthen data security in computer-supported collaborative learning environments, taking into account the vital security-related concerns in e-learning.

INTRODUCTION

Virtual learning environments have been gathering up speed recently, owing to the advancements revealed in their assistance and the sheer number of terminals directly or indirectly associated with them. It essentially means that an ever-increasing number of clever gadgets play a role in this admirable Web

DOI: 10.4018/978-1-6684-7697-0.ch010

of Things situation. These interconnected articles are supposed to deliver an ever-increasing number of massive surges of information, themselves created at special rates, once in a while to be broken down practically continuously. Concerning instructive conditions, this means another kind of large information stream, which can be named instructive enormous information streams. Here, snippets of data from various sources require precise examination and mining procedures to recover productive and all-around coordinated experiences from them (Mangaroska et al., 2021).

Intelligent educational systems that use big data and AI techniques can collect accurate and detailed personal information. Students' learning patterns can be revealed via data analytics, and their individual needs can be identified (Gobert & Sao Pedro, 2017; Mislevy et al., 2020). As a result, big data and AI have the potential to provide personalized learning and precision instruction (Lu et al., 2018). We envision the following growing trends, research gaps, and debates in integrating big data and AI into education research. A deep and rigorous understanding of individual variations may be used to tailor learning in real-time and at scale.

EDGE INTELLIGENCE

The convergence of AI and Edge Computing has given rise to Edge Intelligence, which uses the computer and communication capabilities of end devices and edge servers to process data closer to where it is produced, allowing for large-scale and efficient AI deployment. The privacy-preserving machine learning paradigm known as Federated Learning (FL), which allows data owners to conduct model training without submitting their raw data to third-party servers, is one of the enabling technologies of Edge Intelligence. On the other hand, the FL network is expected to include thousands of heterogeneous dispersed devices. As a result, ineffective communication remains a significant obstacle (Dahdouh et al., 2020). The Hierarchical Federated Learning (HFL) framework has been developed to mitigate node failures and device dropouts by designating cluster chiefs to assist data owners through intermediate model aggregation. The reliance on a central controller, such as the model owner, is reduced with this decentralized learning strategy.

Intelligent personal assistants, context-related and personalized purchase advice, automated video monitoring, and smart appliances are just a few of the intelligent applications that have emerged from recent breakthroughs in AI. Such applications swiftly rose to prominence and garnered significant popularity in a short period because they improved the productivity and overall efficiency of human-based activities, positively impacting people's lives. With the rise of mobile, pervasive computing, and the Internet of Things, the cloud's position as the greatest data concentrator is eroding. Given the phenomenon's scale, transferring massive amounts of data to a wholly centralized AI is inconceivable. The edge ecosystem is critical for developing intelligent apps and systems that begin at the edge and interface with centralized AI systems.

E-learning and intelligent education are developing fields that allow the rapid integration of smart technologies, smart environments, and smart learning and teaching methods. Teachers and students benefit from the advantages of cloud computing, the primary paradigm on which the future of education is based, to deliver more effective learning content within an integrated environment.

BIG DATA ASSISTED E- LEARNING

In learning and teaching, e-learning encompasses all forms of educational technology. Online education, computer-assisted instruction, virtual education, learning, virtual learning environments, and digital educational cooperation are all examples of e-learning. Education ministries can store electronic instructional content for institutions on cloud servers since cloud computing allows users to control and access data. Students will not only be able to use online instructional resources, but they will also be able to access data from home or anywhere else. It will result in the widespread use of e-learning. The need for low latency, increased data storage capacity, and data analysis capabilities prompted the development of fog computing, which large software development firms backed. Fog computing is not meant to replace the cloud in e-learning; rather, it is meant to complement and extend existing functions. Fog and cloud share many of the same resources, systems, and characteristics. Smart learning environments often use a three-tier architecture that comprises cloud, fog, and edge computing. Teachers and students are both concerned about the fog-based e-learning paradigm (Sindhwani et al., 2023).

Teachers can speak with other teachers and pupils in a fog environment, providing powerful social interconnectivity features. They can locate colleagues who share their interests and research fields. Encryption techniques can assist in achieving the aims of data confidentiality and availability in E-learning systems.

Figure 1. Big data and e-learning

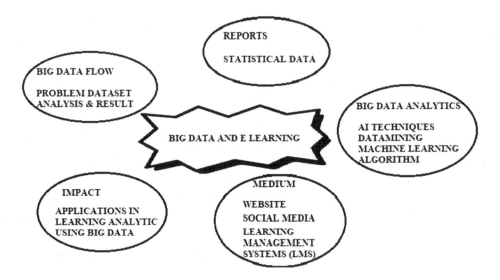

LMS

Learning management systems (LMS) are widely utilized in education and have evolved. It resulted in a large amount of data from the pupils' activities while consuming the online content. It generates a significant amount of discarded and underused data, which standard learning analytics cannot process or support. Big Data is a sophisticated technology that has also become a contemporary trend related to data-driven decision-making. Big data analytics is called, and it is essential to apply for e-Learning in a higher education institution. Big Data Analytics has been proven to be a successful strategy for educational data mining and learning analytics.

Cloud Based E-Learning Schemes

Nowadays, teaching and learning methods use new technology that allows for more efficient interactions between professors and pupils. Cloud-based solutions have been shown to expand the availability of educational services, including course and document sharing between teachers and between teachers and students and reusing pedagogic tools for collaboration. Many traditional top institutions are incorporating cutting-edge technologies such as e-learning, remote learning, and web-based learning into their instructional techniques, attracting an increasing number of students. Universities are becoming more mixed by combining traditional lectures with the delivery of courses to faraway learners via digital platforms. Many, significant colleges make their courses open to the public; the Massive Open Online Course (MOOC) is gaining traction across the higher education sector. It is a web-based course that focuses on large-scale interactive engagement and open access (Lee, 2020).

As a result, MOOCs are becoming a valuable addition to traditional distance education. Even though MOOCs can assist non-subscribed university students in obtaining an e-learning certificate, enrolled students must gain marks in the course to receive a diploma, which is not the case with MOOCs. A unique trustworthiness-based methodology is proposed to strengthen data security in computer-supported collaborative learning environments, taking into account the vital security-related concerns in e-learning. Furthermore, writers have developed a smart campus architecture that incorporates cloud computing and IoT for the smart campus concept. Their multilayer architecture is designed to provide high security and data secrecy. Universities are another example that provides services to help students with their studies and keeps up with the latest innovations in the deployment of e-learning services. Students can now access educational services from their teachers and the e-learning centre from anywhere and at any time. The cloud-based e-learning system is accessed by students using their Username and Password. Despite its positive contributions to the remote learning environment, the literature above failed to consider the security issue and the flexibility in obtaining content learning. When users want to access a course stored on a remote cloud-based system, MOOCs, VLEs, and intelligent campuses rely on standard access protocols like login/password and RBAC. These methods are incompatible with the concept of learn-on-the-go, which allows students to participate in live classes while on the move. A secure fog-assisted e-learning system was created to address these issues. It can allow fine-grained education data exchange for suitable pupils by re-encrypting educational data.

APPLICATIONS

Several colleges and institutions are now taking advantage of information technology to improve and develop their educational programs and attract more students. As a result, universities and service providers have implemented technologies such as distance learning (e-learning) and learning-on-the-go to provide a more flexible education system. E-learning is gaining traction worldwide, with an increasing number of students enrolling in online courses. The prospects given by Cloud Computing are primarily to blame for this development. The security aspect of sharing educational content in a cloud-based educational setting is significant. It faces various security issues, such as fine-grained access control and content learning security preservation. Furthermore, a new idea known as User-Fog-Cloud architecture has emerged to bring services closer to the client. A new fog computing e-learning technique is presented in this research. The proposed method extends learning content from the cloud to the network's edge (Bernardi, 2021). It can improve learning data analysis efficiency, reduce encryption burden in terms of computation cost on user devices by offloading part of the encryption cost to fog servers, and provide fine-grained access control to learning content by encrypting the course and the exam with different cryptographic techniques like IBBE and CP-ABE.

Figure 2. Significance of big data assisted e-learning

SIGNICANCE OF BIG DATA ASSISTED E-LEARNING

> EFFICIENT TECHNIQUE	> CONCEPTUAL EXPERTISE
> ECONOMICAL EXECUTION	> RISK SPECULATION
> DATA VISUALISATION	> DECISION MAKING
> SCHEDULED AND WELL PLANNED FRAMEWORKS	> COLLABORATION OF STUDENTS
> SOCIAL NETWORK ANALYSIS	> STUDENT SKILL ASSESSMENT
> INTELLIGENT EVALUTAION	> BEHAVIOUR PATTERN
> APPROPRIATE COURSEWARE	> COURSE RECOMMENDATION

LITERATURE SURVEY

Decentralized Edge Intelligence: A Dynamic Resource Allocation Framework for Hierarchical Federated Learning

Federated Learning, FL is one of the promising technologies in Edge Intelligence. It uses the computing and communication functions of edge servers and end devices to interpret data closer to where it was generated. The convergence of Edge Computing and AI has enabled Edge Intelligence to facilitate dynamic and efficient AI deployments. With the help of this machine learning model that protects privacy, data owners may train models without submitting their raw data to a server operated by a third party. On the other hand, the FL network should have thousands of networking equipment. As a result, the inability to communicate effectively continues to be a major obstacle. Hierarchical federated learning (HFL) reduces node and device downtime by appointing team leaders to support data operators through multimodal aggregation. Thanks to distributed learning, a central controller acting as the model owner is no longer required. However, the HFL paradigm fails to address incentive design and resource allocation issues. The two-step problem of resource allocation and incentive design will be examined in this article. At the lowest level, the data owner may select which cluster to join, and the team leader is compensated for their involvement. More specifically, it simulates cluster selection dynamics using evolutionary game theory. Each cluster leader can give the model owner better priority service, but the model owner must bid for the cluster head's attention (Hui et al., 2020). In light of this, we provide a unique deep learning-based bidding process to rate every cluster head's advantages. The recommended scalable game's uniqueness and dependability and the benefits of deep learning-oriented auctions are highlighted through performance scores.

Edge Learning: The Enabling Technology for Distributed Big Data Analytics in The Edge

Machine learning (ML) has shown promise in several areas, such as self-driving cars and smart cities, that profoundly change how people live, work, and interact. All training data from various sources must be uploaded to a remote data server as part of a traditional centralized learning framework, resulting in large communication payloads, service delays, and data problems. A new learning concept called Edge Learning (EL) is on the rise to further push the boundaries of the learning model. By allowing distributed edge nodes to collaboratively train models and draw conclusions using their locally cached data, it complements big data analytics techniques cloud based. We provide a thorough evaluation of the most current research efforts on EL to examine the novel characteristics and prospective futures of EL. In particular, we first describe the context and inspiration (Sudirtha et al., 2022). The difficult problems in EL are discussed from computation, data, and communication perspectives. We also review the technologies that make EL possible, such as inference, model training, privacy protection, security assurance, and incentive mechanisms. Finally, we go through potential areas for EL study in the future. This survey, in our opinion, will give a thorough overview of EL and inspire further successful surveys in this area.

Architecting Analytics Across Multiple E-Learning Systems to Enhance Learning Design

Due to the spread of distributed learning environments, more learning approaches are now available. Given a chance to combine data from several learning monitoring data sources, it may be feasible to understand better learner attributes and the complexity of the learning procedure. We contend, integrating data from several virtual learning platforms broadens learning chances in remote areas and aids in assessing how well instructional strategies work. To do this, the three different online learning systems included in this study's learning ecosystem were examined as a method to expand the scope of a single learning domain. This article presents a paradigm for new cross-system data-driven analyses and approach which addresses the significance of cross-platform learning analytics. A cross-platform structure is provided that gathers, combines, and saves information from the learning ecosystem related to learning. We produced interpretable models with analytics by using regression and classification approaches, demonstrating the practicality and benefits of the cross-platform architecture. These models can help educators understand learner behaviour and how the teaching strategy influences student achievement. The findings indicate integration of data from the three learning processes increases the veracity rate by a factor of five correlated to the data from the single learning structure.

Using Cobots, Virtual Worlds, And Edge Intelligence to Support On-Line Learning

This project aims to provide a shared social environment for the learning community using artificial intelligence and virtual reality technology. It aims to provide an e-learning environment where students can connect and participate. It is comparable to a classroom or learning atmosphere. It can be compared to a multi-user online environment like "Second Life," where online students can communicate and create their locations. The abilities a student can develop in the virtual world are influenced by how they behave in the classroom. Their robot mentor's suggestions determine how they can function in that area. The associated Virtual World may remain after the learning session has ended, giving students motivation to do well to gain points that transfer into abilities there. Several courses or learning sessions may share that Virtual World offers a more extensive learning domain. The entire method is bilateral since each Robot mentor may discover information concerning the student's conduct in a classroom or learning setting. The Instructor Robot Learning Unit as a supervisor converts the learner's actions into attention ratings for use in the Virtual World with IRLU. The Supervisor is responsible for recording academic success and compiling a social interaction ethnography of the neighbourhood. The fundamental overview of the way the group of students uses the environment will be provided by this online user ethnography. The Supervisor can adjust the robot's engagement with the students using this knowledge, and the cycle can start over. The authors have previously researched this method with a single learner (Mangaroska et al., 2021).

Incorporating Intelligence Into E-Learning

E-learning is a vital tool for educational institutions to track the performance of their students and professors. It is also beneficial for businesses to raise employee performance. Since it is very difficult to locate, access, display, and preserve the information needed by a broad range of users on the World Wide Web, it is necessary to enhance the information that is already accessible with machine-processable semantics. Personalized and semantic learning services with the help of tactics like semantic web technologies backed by semantic E-learning. Thus, it serves five distinct purposes. The Semantic Web and Semantic E-learning approaches are the first areas of study as promising technology for achieving E-learning objectives. Second, it concentrates on Semantic E-learning knowledge representation approaches. Thirdly, it places much emphasis on talking about the structure of the framework for semantic e-learning and the different phases of an intelligent e-learning scenario. The study also focuses on intelligent information retrieval techniques based on Semantic Web technology. The analysis of several semantic markup languages according to predetermined criteria is also demonstrated in this study ().

Metaverse Framework: An E-Learning Environment Case Study (ELEM)

The term "metaverse" is wide and can refer to any future digital item. To maintain their accessibility and endurance, systems in the field of education as a life domain should be redirected to embrace this concept. The metaverse, its uses, and the historical processes that led to the metaverse's status have all been covered in several publications. However, how the metaverse is organized and what exactly makes up each part is still unknown. Although the need for e-learning systems has increased as technology has developed, the architecture of the methods now available on the market based on the metaverse is either inadequately detailed or, in the best-case scenario, is only a 3D environment. This study looks at earlier studies to determine the unique technologies the metaverse framework should offer (Bernardi, 2021). Then, we discuss the metaverse framework used as an E-Learning environment. Because the recommended architecture will allow for the smooth operation of virtual learning environments on the metaverse, future metaverse-based apps will be easy to develop. Additionally, e-learning will be a more engaging and delightful experience for the students in case of offline classes.

A Distributed Agent-Based Approach for Supporting Group Formation in P2P E-Learning

P2P, the Peer-to-peer technology, is perhaps utilized to construct cooperative e-learning systems, allowing students to get knowledge from professors and other students with similar preferences. Creating user groups that conform to individual user boundaries and share common interests is crucial in such a situation. In this study, we provide a unique approach based on the HADEL overlay network of software agents (Hyperspace Agent-based E-Learning). It uses the overlay network's topology and observable characteristics as a small-world system. Our method protects user privacy by enabling local maintenance of private user information and inferring the features required to identify the groups utilizing agents that function as personal assistants. The outcomes of certain experiments conducted in simulated e-Learning settings demonstrate our strategy's effectiveness (Asim et al., 2020).

An Introduction to Key Technology in Artificial Intelligence and Big Data Driven E-Learning And E-Education

With the quick advancement of computer and communication technology comes the age of big data and Artificial Intelligence, and the new technological advancements usher in a new era of education (Mangaroska et al., 2021). The fragmentation of teaching and mobile learning are emerging themes. Mobile network technologies and artificial intelligence in education are also growing in popularity (Dahdouh et al., 2020). Traditional education is evolving thanks to long-distance learning, which offers several advantages. However, there are still many scientific and engineering issues in it. One of the most important problems to be solved involves mobile networks and education-based information technology. Additionally, the newest IT in education and mobile networks are increasingly predominant in analysis fields. Meanwhile, there are several issues with long-distance learning and data-driven by big data and AI (Liu & Wang, 2009). To address these, academics must invest a lot of time and effort.

Towards A New Access Control Model Based on Trust-Level For E-Learning Platform

E-learning is becoming increasingly popular as more individuals enrol in online courses. It turns into a pressing necessity. A new architecture for these systems will be needed due to the rise in resources available in e-learning systems. Multi-agent system integration has been crucial in enhancing search quality, providing fresh approaches, and streamlining the completion of extremely difficult jobs. While much effort has been made to offer infrastructure and deliver content in the multi-agent system and e-learning sectors, security and trust problems have scarcely been considered. Since it might be difficult to tell if agents can be trusted and that external accesses are secure, it is necessary to be aware that some behaviours in multi-agent systems with agent characteristics (autonomous, social, etc.) will be dangerous and unreliable. The use of a control access policy, which is in charge of securing communication with agents and strengthening it via the incorporation of trust, is directly related to the security aspects of the current study. The proposed work will concentrate on fusing two RBAC-based access models:

T-SR and TrustBAC, also known as "Multi-Agent System Dynamic RBAC with Trust-Satisfaction and Reputation." The major objective in the case is to create a novel archetype that combines the benefits of the two designs to optimize security in multi-agent system-based e-learning platforms (Ren et al., 2021). Utilizing the "MotOrbac" tool, the proposed technique is put into practice and evaluated through simulation to determine its applicability context and deployment-scale limits.

Cloud Computing Technologies' Effects On E-Learning

Distributed computing, Grid computing, virtualization technologies, and parallel computing form the foundation of the modern computer architecture known as cloud computing. The foundational framework and platform of E-learning, particularly in education, is cloud computing. It serves as the future network computing platform's core technology. It provides dependable computing power, simple internet access, and safe data storage. The research of cloud computing's utilization in educational settings is the main subject of discussion today. Moreover, the machine learning models that are deployed along with the cloud helps in automizing the Learning material contents for the students. The study's results demonstrate the cloud platform's importance in helping teachers and students meet course objectives. The nature, advantages, and cloud computing services are discussed in the study as a platform for an online learning environment.

Personalized E-Learning System with Self-Regulated Learning Assisted Mechanisms for Promoting Learning Performance

Web based learning is progressively replacing traditional computer-assisted education (CAL) in light of the Internet's rapid development of new technologies. Unlike traditional classroom settings, web-based learning focuses on the individual student, and most web-based learning systems impart customized learning methods. Additionally, in the conventional classroom setting, teachers frequently base their teaching strategies on the professional disciplines of all students in the class. However, in the typical classroom setting, the needs of individual students are routinely disregarded. One major issue is that learners commonly engage in online learning environments even if there are no instructors to keep an eye on their attitudes and conduct while studying. It follows that how well students do in a web-based learning environment is significantly impacted by their capacity to manage their learning. In a setting of online learning, it may be applied to enhance each student's learning performance. However, how to successfully support students in developing these abilities is a crucial research challenge in self-regulated learning. Students can build their capacity for self-regulated learning with the help of the specially designed e-learning system. Students can acquire autonomous self-regulated learning abilities and become lifelong learners with the aid of the indicated self-regulated learning processes. Four distinct forms of self-regulated learning are also offered based on an evaluation of self-regulated learning ability and an indicator of self-regulated performance in education. According to experimental findings, self-regulating support mechanisms of learning help students learn more effectively by accelerating the development of these skills in a customized e-learning environment (Baig et al., 2020).

Proposed System For E-Learning Using Edge Based Decentralized System

With the expansion of the distributed learning platforms, the E-Learning assistance helps in providing learners with the materials related to the study content and course of study. The proposed system helps in identifying the related study content along with storing and retrieving capabilities provided with the Edge based platform. The big data analytics used in the system along with the edge systems helps in analysing vast data content across the web so that the Learner could use the system as the single platform for the entire course of study or research. The database stores the different e-learning content across platforms and also narrows down the related content using the models of data analytics combined with the selected resource utilization. Moreover, with this system, the AR/VR contents along with the personalized learning environment could be established at much lower cost. The edge-based mechanism of storing and retrieving content of the learning materials helps the learners in accessing the content quickly apart form waiting for others to post the contents. Using this system could enhance the users in gaining knowledge from collective domains and across different platforms. Some of the paid versions of learning sites and domains for the learning environments could be replaced with the edge-based learning that is more effective in terms of latency with the content and also with the throughput experienced by the learners.

The latency of the system and its improvement compared to the existing traditional learning platforms could be represented by the formula:

$$\text{Latency} = D_{\text{from PLA to Edge}} + D_{\text{BD Analytics}} + D_{\text{Edge to PLA}}$$

PLA= Personal Learning Assistant

D=Duration

Hence with the above formula, the Latency calculation could be done as the combination of the communication duration from the Personal Learning Assistant to the Edge, duration of Big Data analytics and the Duration of data from the Edge to the Personal Learning assistant.

Thus, the proposed system could outperform the traditional system of the e-learning environment with the effective deployment of the three successful layers and the reduced time duration of communication between the layers. Data storage done at the edge and fog layers help in easy retrieval of data from the environment and posting of content to the Learning resource. Thus, helping the learners in easy upload and download of the materials.

ARCHITECTURE

The architecture described below is the proposed system architecture that comprises of the three different layers of the allocated functionalities of each. The effective communication between the proposed layers helps in overcoming delayed latency as expected in the traditional learning approaches. Three Layers that are present in the architecture are the Cloud computing Layer, Edge Layer and the Network Layer.

The Network Layer is responsible for getting consumer Input Request, it is loaded with the personalized Learning Framework that takes care of the Learning modules that are required especially for the E-Learning Mechanism. The resource availability is checked and after that the resource allocation methods are used in allocating resources to the users of the E-Learning systems. The resource allocation deals with the nature of devices used at the learners end as like the desktop, laptops or the mobile devices.

Since the platform orientation of the devices might be different, different versions of the materials might be used. After completing all the allocations, the E-Learning Applications such as the Virtual Labs, AR/ VR systems and the Smart board access are provided to the users of the system. The laboratory demos and demos related to the equipment modelling could be easily done with the help of AR/VR simulations that paves way to an effective learning material associated with the E-Learning platforms rather than allocating separate platforms for each learning models.

In the Edge layer, the materials of learning are stored and could be retrieved easily on user need. This layer is responsible for the Processor memory allocation along with the Computation storage and database connectivity. The memory requirement for the AR/VR simulations and other software related demonstration modules might be different and, on the whole, might be of large capacity and hence, memory space allocated to these types of materials could be modified. Here both Fog and Edge connectivity comes into play as per the user needs since they are used in effective data connectivity and enhanced security related to data.

Figure 3. PDA architecture with distributed edge based system

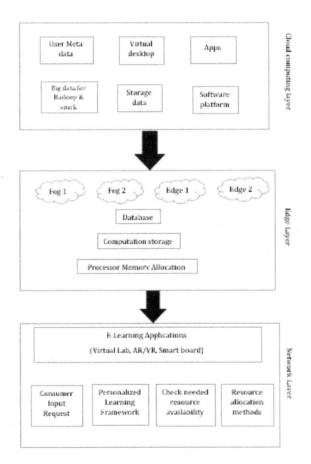

The Cloud computing layer has the Software Platform required for the E-Learning Resources and the applications files. along with that it provides support to the database and Virtual Desktop applications.

On the Whole the above architecture serves in establishing the communications between the Learners and the related materials that are available in the E-Learning Platform. more specialized and improvised learning is possible with the implementation of the edge-based resources since it involves the decentralization of materials that are available on the internet and minimal time is required to search and download the contents from the available resources. Moreover, precise content selection and enabling of various study peer groups could be made possible by this E-Learning method and hence sustainability along with availability of the content online could be enhanced. Some of the recent technological developments in the learning environments such as the AR/VR contents and the smart board utilization could be easily enabled and tracked down back to the classrooms and hence improvising teaching and Learning process.

RESULTS

Figure 4. TLA vs PDA- latency, precision, and energy consumption

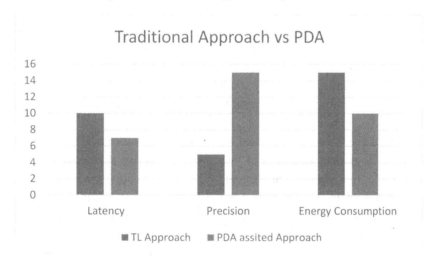

The above graph represents the Latency, Precision and Energy consumption comparison of the Traditional Learning approach and the Personal Digital Learning approach that is implemented with the use of Edge based distributed learning system. It identifies the PDA approach outperforms the Traditional Learning approach in terms of the aspects like reduced Latency duration between the server and the end device. It also has the reduced energy consumption since the latency was low and exhibits high precision ratio.

The above graph represents the comparison of the accuracy of the Proposed PDA method along with the Traditional Approach which denotes that the PDA outperforms the Traditional approach in terms of Privacy and end to end Delay as the Enhanced privacy is provided with the Edge based approach and eventually the accuracy also increases with the same condition.

Figure 5. TLA vs PDA- accuracy and end to end delay

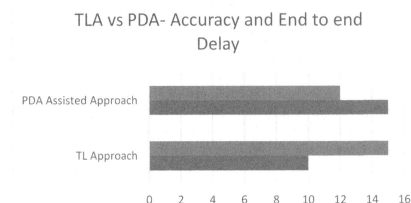

FUTURE DIRECTIONS

Future research should focus on theory-based precision education, cross-disciplinary application, and the effective use of educational technology. The government should encourage lifelong learning, provide teacher education programs, and safeguard personal information. In order to improve academia-industry collaboration, reciprocal and mutually beneficial ties should be formed in the education industry (Ben Amor et al., 2020).

In terms of the future growth of big data and AI, we call for a more in-depth dialogue between supporters of "cold" technology and advocates of "warm" humanity so that technology users can benefit from its capabilities rather than seeing it as a threat to their livelihood. Over reliance on technology may lead to underestimating the role of humans in education, which is an equally vital issue. Keep in mind the school's primary function: it serves as a great equalizer and a vital socializing agent. In addition to cognitive processing, we need to better understand the role of social and affective processing (e.g., emotion, motivation) in student learning success (or failures). After all, human learning is a social behaviour, and our brains are wired to be socially engaged in several critical areas.

CONCLUSION

E-learning eliminates the barriers to traditional education and provides advantages over typical attendance groups by allowing students to access learning content at any time and from any location. One such example could be dated back to the pandemic times caused by COVID where students of the rural areas and isolated places cannot access the classes and the materials could not be tracked down easily for the student requirements. Learning content can be transported and evaluated throughout the cloud-fog-edge three-tier architecture—the fog assists in controlling and managing transmitted data to and from edge users. We presented a safe data sharing and profile matching fog-assisted technique for an e-learning data system to ensure data confidentiality and fine-grained access (Asim et al., 2020). Big data and artificial intelligence (AI) offer enormous potential for achieving very effective learning and teaching. They generate new research questions and ideas, take advantage of cutting-edge data collection and analysis technology, and eventually become a mainstream research paradigm.

REFERENCES

Asim, M., Wang, Y., Wang, K., & Huang, P.-Q. (2020). A Review on Computational Intelligence Techniques in Cloud and Edge Computing. IEEE Transactions on Emerging Topics in Computational Intelligence, 4(6), 742-763. doi:10.1109/TETCI.2020.3007905

Baig, M. I., Shuib, L., & Yadegaridehkordi, E. (2020). Big data in education: A state of the art, limitations, and future research directions. *Int J Educ Technol High Educ*, 17(1), 44. doi:10.118641239-020-00223-0

Ben Amor, A., Abid, M., & Meddeb, A. (2020). Secure Fog-Based E-Learning Scheme. *IEEE Access : Practical Innovations, Open Solutions*, 8, 31920–31933. doi:10.1109/ACCESS.2020.2973325

Bernardi, M. L. (2021). Keynote: Edge Intelligence - Emerging Solutions and Open Challenges. In *2021 IEEE International Conference on Pervasive Computing and Communications Workshops and other Affiliated Events (PerCom Workshops)*, (pp. 160-160). IEEE. 10.1109/PerComWorkshops51409.2021.9431071

Dahdouh, K., Dakkak, A., Oughdir, L., & Ibriz, A. (2020). Improving Online Education Using Big Data Technologies. In The Role of Technology in Education. IntechOpen. doi:10.5772/intechopen.88463

Hui, L. Geczy, P., Lai, H., Gobert, J., Yang, S. J. H., Ogata, H., Baltes J., Rodrigo, G., Li, P., Tsai, C. (2020). Challenges and Future Directions of Big Data and Artificial Intelligence in Education, Frontiers in Psychology, 11. . doi:10.3389/fpsyg.2020.580820

Moharm, K., Eltahan, M. (2020). The Role of Big Data in Improving E-Learning Transition. *IOP Conf. Ser.: Mater. Sci. Eng.*

Kusuma, S. M., Veena, K. N., Kavya, K. S., & Vijaya Kumar, B. P. (2023). Intelligence and Cognitive Computing at the Edge for IoT: Architecture, Challenges, and Applications. In N. Sindhwani, R. Anand, M. Niranjanamurthy, D. Chander Verma, & E. B. Valentina (Eds.), *IoT Based Smart Applications. EAI/ Springer Innovations in Communication and Computing*. Springer. doi:10.1007/978-3-031-04524-0_19

Lee, K. (2020). Openness and innovation in online higher education: A historical review of the two discourses. *Open Learning*, 36(2), 1–21. doi:10.1080/02680513.2020.1713737

Liu, Y., & Wang, H. (2009). A comparative study on e-learning technologies and products: From the East to the West. *Systems Research*, 26(2), 191–209. doi:10.1002res.959

Mangaroska, K., Vesin, B., Kostakos, V., Brusilovsky, P., & Giannakos, M. N. (2021, April 1). Architecting Analytics Across Multiple E-Learning Systems to Enhance Learning Design. *IEEE Transactions on Learning Technologies*, 14(2), 173–188. doi:10.1109/TLT.2021.3072159

Plastiras, G., Terzi, M., Kyrkou, C., & Theocharidcs, T. (2018). Edge Intelligence: Challenges and Opportunities of Near-Sensor Machine Learning Applications. *2018 IEEE 29th International Conference on Application-specific Systems, Architectures and Processors (ASAP)*, (pp. 1-7). IEEE. 10.1109/ASAP.2018.8445118

Ren, S., Kim, J.-S., Cho, W.-S., Soeng, S., Kong, S., & Lee, K.-H. (2021). Big Data Platform for Intelligence Industrial IoT Sensor Monitoring System Based on Edge Computing and AI," *2021 International Conference on Artificial Intelligence in Information and Communication (ICAIIC)*, , pp. 480-482, 10.1109/ICAIIC51459.2021.9415189

Sudirtha, I. G., Widiana, I. W., & Adijaya, M. A. (2022). The Effectiveness of Using Revised Bloom's Taxonomy-Oriented Learning Activities to Improve Students' Metacognitive Abilities. *Journal of Education and E-Learning Research*, *9*(2), 55–61. doi:10.20448/jeelr.v9i2.3804

Zhen, C., & Hu, K. (2022, June 14). Design of Edge Computing Online Classroom Based on College English Teaching. *Computational Intelligence and Neuroscience*, *7068923*, 1–11. doi:10.1155/2022/7068923 PMID:35747728

Chapter 11
FinTech and Artificial Intelligence in Relationship Banking and Computer Technology

Vipin Jain
Teerthanker Mahaveer University, India

Anshu Chauhan
Teerthanker Mahaveer University, India

Mohit Rastogi
Teerthanker Mahaveer University, India

Pankhuri Agarwal
Teerthanker Mahaveer University, India

J. V. N. Ramesh
Koneru Lakshmaiah Education Foundation, India

Sabyasachi Pramanik
Haldia Institute of Technology, India

Ankur Gupta
Vaish College of Engineering, Rohtak, India

ABSTRACT

Banks cannot afford to be complacent in their operations. Due to the dramatic changes brought about by improvements in computer technology (IT) as well as competitive intensity from FinTech businesses, they must re-evaluate their competing advantages. A major point of emphasis in this essay is that banks must not abandon relationship banking that encourages direct interaction with bank clients. Orienting relationship banking on the long term simplifies incentives while also supporting bank clients' long-term requirements and objectives. However, because to the availability of IT-driven economy of scale as well as rivalry by FinTech start-ups and IT corporations, banks may be tempted to enter the transaction banking business. In this context, the paper evaluates the importance of distance, AI, and behavioural inclinations in the decision-making process. The suggestions for banking stability are analyzed in detail. The authors believe that relationship banking has the potential to reduce its disadvantages, but it should conform to the newer facts to flourish.

DOI: 10.4018/978-1-6684-7697-0.ch011

INTRODUCTION

Banks cannot afford to be complacent in their operations. Due to the dramatic alterations caused by improvements in computing technology as well as competing demands from FinTech businesses, they should re-assess their competing benefits. As a result of technological advances in big data analytics, social networks, telecommunications and AI, societies are on the cusp of undergoing a profound shift. Knowing banking in these turbulent times is a difficult undertaking. It is a contention that the economics of banking has not altered. The purpose of banks has always been, and will remain, the reduction of asymmetric facts between lenders and depositors (Lai et al., 2019). When estimating the trustworthiness of bank customers, banks must analyse minimal data, which is often difficult to quantify, due to the fact that their motivations may be fundamentally mismatched with those of the bank. Relationship banking, build intimate links with the clients via continuing collaboration must not be regarded as outmoded in an environment characterised by information asymmetries. A relationship bank lessens information asymmetries via the intensive possession of soft information—information that is challenging to measure, accumulate, and communicate in unbiased manner (Ogura, Y. 2014)—that is private in essence, generally all through the long-term relationship including its clients (Moro, S. et. al., 2015). A relationship bank's ability to respond on soft information is based on its considerable flexibility and discretion, as well as its reliance on secrecy and trust.

As a result of IT-driven advancements, however, relationship banking is facing significant problems that must be addressed and highlighted by (Backhaus, K. et al.,2019). The initial possible issue of relationship banking is that it is less efficient than transaction-driven technology when compared to traditional banking. IT advancements have boosted effectiveness in bank transaction (particularly in transactions, payment and settlement, transactional lending and online banking), hence altering the duties of isolations in the financial services industry. With artificial intelligence computers doing transaction banking operations, a slew of issues have been raised about the role of human financiers, who are critical to the development of long-term relationships with customers. Human beings are still required in banks, but bankers must rethink their position in the industry. Understanding people's thoughts and actions is becoming more crucial as time goes on. Banks must be aware of behavioural biases, herding behaviour, limited rationality, and people's emotional states in order to operate effectively. Because information travels swiftly across social networks, society is more susceptible to herding, information manipulation, and baseless panics than it has ever been. Perfect reason, in this context, may seem to be an unduly straightforward idea. The growth of information technology has increased competition in banking, which has had an impact on the strategic decision of banks between relationship banking and transactional banking. When it comes to transaction banking, scaling up is simple, which makes leveraging relationships a problem. We believe that information technology is becoming more conducive to interpersonal connections.

For example, some FinTech businesses have scaled their relationship banking technologies to great success. Melese, F. (Melese, F. 2021) explain the "hold-up issue", which is a downside of relationship banking in which relationship banks leverage private information for personal gain and make borrowers unduly reliant on them. Competition then works to alleviate this disadvantage. The implications of these approaches for stability are discussed. Risks arising from information technology-based developments in banking must be thoroughly investigated in order to avoid a detrimental influence on bank stability.

The following is the structure of this article. The section under "Relationship Banking and External Influences in Financial Aspects" describes relationship banking along with examining exterior factors within the banking atmosphere, respectively. The section "How far one may keep going for relationship banking?" examines how the role of remoteness has changed as a result of technological advancements. The section "Does human banker need a part for performing at the advent of AI?" explores the function of the human bankers in the context of artificial intelligence aided lending and is divided into three sections. The section "IT firms, Financial Technology, and Relationship banking: Allies or adversaries?" examines the perspectives of Financial Technologies businesses on the changing characteristics of relationship banking and the implications of these perspectives. The section titled "IT innovations, competitiveness, and relationship banking" explores the feasibility of relationship banking in the face of intense IT-based competing compulsion and other factors. The section titled "Suggestions for the Stability of the System" examines the influence of relationship banking along with information technology advancements on the security of the financial system. The "Conclusions" section brings the article to a close.

RELATIONSHIP BANKING AND EXTERNAL INFLUENCES IN FINANCIAL ASPECTS

Following a short discussion of the primary tasks of a bank in the perspective of technological advancements, one can define relationship banking and outlining the social alterations caused by technology which have shaped the financial environment.

The Reason for Existing of Banking and Information Technology Innovations

Prior to describing relationship banking, it is useful to concisely outline the function of banks as proposed by modern financial intervention hypothesis, as well as to highlight the influence of information technology advancements in the financial services industry. Intermediaries in the financial sector promote contacts and transactions between suppliers and consumers of financial resources (Musso et al.,2008). In the most basic sense, a commercial bank is a financial middleman since it takes deposits, which are normally withdrawn on demand, in order to finance illiquid loans. Illiquidity in loan markets emerges as a result of the knowledge asymmetry that exists between customers and their financial institutions. Banks gather personal data about their borrowers throughout the loan application screening process and subsequent loan monitoring. A significant competitive advantage may be gained via the use of proprietary information, which is associated with relationship banking.

The banking business has been transformed as a result of technological advancements. The expense of banks has increased as a result of technological advancements. (Worthington et al.,2011) make the case for the benefits of economizing scale in payment implementation, clearing and settlement systems, and other financial services. Additional cost reductions may be realised via the use of internet and digital access channels, as well as mobile and digital payment systems and better transaction financing procedures. According to Villar et al.,(Villar et al.,2021) better communications, decision-making, automation, and empowerment of bank clients are among the fundamental aspects across which information technology innovations are redesigning banks.

While the current empirical research have shown the presence of economies of scale and scope in banking that may be connected to information technology improvements, there has been little investigation into how information technology influences the banking business (Rajnak et al.,2021). In this context, it is necessary to pay more attention to how information technology advancements impact information asymmetries in banking, as well as to the mediating function that intimate connections play in banking.

The value of connections in banking continues to be emphasised despite cost reductions brought about by information technology. We also discuss the effect of distance, automated conclusion-making in borrowing, and the Financial Technology business.

Relationship Banking

The term "relationship banking" denotes the sort of engagement that takes place between banks and their customers. During the course of a relationship banking transaction, banks may connect with consumers on a regular basis across a variety of services, goods, and/or access channels in order to acquire and utilize proprietary details, which are frequently insignificant or soft in essence, and for establishing close connections with them. One of the most conventional examples of relationship banking is a good bank providing a line of credit to a long-period customer, which is often a small business. Transaction-oriented banking, on the other hand, refers to services that are tailored for a single encounter associating a bank customer; for e.g., planning an initial public offering (IPO) considering a major corporation.

It is difficult to draw a clear line connecting relationship banking and transaction banking activities. Transaction providing automations might depend on a mix of soft and hard facts to make their decisions. Wasim et al.,(2021) and Lesani M. (2014) disintegrate transaction lending automations into the following categories: judgment-based lending, monetary statement lending, asset-based contribution; small-size company credit scoring; fixed-asset lending and leasing; and factoring. An individual lending automation provides a specific benefit to a bank, with the ability to enable financing to small along with medium business organizations. Taking the example of judgment-dependent contribution, which is a transaction lending strategy, soft information is used to make decisions depending on the judgement of a loan official who is depending on his or her expertise and training. Additionally, although relationship lending is often linked with data and information, this does not rule out the possibility of using quantitative information in the context of relationship financing.

Relationship banking involves a larger range of operations than relationship lending and includes additional banking transactions where lengthy relationships with bank customers are desired. A bank collects proprietary information via analysing payment data or by observing a bank customer's long-term deposit-taking activities over an extended period of time (like credit line usage, cash inflows and limit violations). In certain cases, ties may even be established with customers who are looking for investment banking services, like the acquisition and merger.

Changes in Society As A Result Of Information Technology

Societies are confronted with significant economic issues. Society is actually modified by information technology breakthroughs such as full-time connection, IoT and social networks, in conjunction with artificial intelligence (Kaushik, D. et al.,2021). A plethora of information and data-operated decision-making procedures are removing few information barriers that have existed between economic actors who are challenging the traditional management methods. Company information is now simpler to locate, assess, and send than it was before. Despite the fact that a large amount of measurable data is accessible, determining its reliability is critical.

In addition, customers are evolving. They are looking for a low-cost solution that is available from any location and at any time, as well as one that is tailored to their specific requirements. They are looking for a multi-channel experience as well as gaming. They want to be included in the decision-making process and be given the ability to make decisions. All of these shifts have resulted in an increase in short-termism. With the advent of new media vehicles, information is communicated instantly, and consumers are able to coordinate their ideas and behaviours. Customer behaviour is influenced by peer pressures. Customers' tendency to think just on the short term may result in herding, banking crises, and stock market disasters. The conclusion drawn from these considerations is that despite the fact that banks' fundamental competitive advantage has persisted in the mitigation of information issues, the business situation has altered. Financial crises, societal shifts, and technological advancements are all putting pressure on economies. In this context, this essay examines the changing nature of the function of relationship banking.

HOW FAR ONE MAY KEEP GOING FOR RELATIONSHIP BANKING?

In recent years, information technology improvements have made it simpler to conduct banking across longer distances, thanks to (i) more convenient access to banking facilities via cell phone and online banking frameworks, as well as e-payments, and (ii) improved transactions lending automations.

To begin, cell phones and internet banking provide continuous accessibility of bank goods and facilities except geographical limits. This increases bank benefits by reducing costs and raising revenue. Is it possible that internet and mobile banking are displacing the function of the bank branch network, which serves as a primary entry point for relationship banking? At their height in 2008, the number of bank branches in the Eurozone reached 186.255, but by 2016, the figure had dropped to 149.353. When compared to other countries, the number of branches in the United States has witnessed a relatively moderate reduction, falling from 83,600 in 2012 to 80,638 in 2016. 1

In accordance with many research, online banking serves as an enhancement rather than a replacement for the traditional branch network. The findings of (Tsai, CH et al.,2021) demonstrate that online banking users who live in locations with a dense population of branches participate in more aggressively in product purchases and transactional actions than internet banking clients who live in other places. Customers who used online banking were much less likely to abandon their accounts with the bank. (Malhotra, N. et al.,2021) discovered that internet banking enhances the value of a branch network while decreasing the importance of lesser customised dispatch channels (e.g., the ATM network).

Long-distance banking has been made easier thanks to electronic payments. Despite the fact that e-payments are, in essence, a transaction banking system and the payment data must be entered manually.

1. Information obtained from the American Principal Bank's Statistical Information Repository (https://www.federalreserve.gov) and the Federal Deposit Insurance Corporation's website supply a great deal of useful confidential information regarding the credit condition and requirements of bank clients. Santosa, A. D. et al.,(Santosa, A. D. et al.,2021) demonstrates that good payment methods encourage banks to build tight, everlasting connections with the clients. The use of a greater number and a greater variety of retail digital payments is certainly associated to bank profits.

2. Moreover, banks should think about establishing a strong social media existence. The authors (Pengji et al., 2021) suggest that active Facebook connections favour local smaller banks by generating more interest earnings. The link with a social media existence and relationship banking still is being examined by banks and scholars, and there is much more work to be done.

It seems that online banking is still a supplement to relationship-oriented branch communication networks rather than a substitute for them, as shown by these reasons. In order to cater to the younger breed of online adaptable consumers, banks must adapt their relationship banking services to include an online version as a complementary service.

For the second time, the physical barriers between financial institutions and their debtors have widened (Hanoon et al., 2021). Transaction financing strategies have proliferated as a result of technological advancements, and they are always improving (Kaur et al. 2021). In their study, Portela et al., (Portela et al., 2004) confirm that the rise in distances was operated by technological advancements and that it corresponded with advancements in credit scoring lending methodologies.

The quantity of knowledge that is accessible on the internet is enormous. Information on bank customers is exchanged via credit bureaus, and information about banks is taken into consideration by press, credit rating organisations and researchers (Yan, D., et al. 2021). Agrawal, P. et al.,(Agrawal, P. et al.,2021) demonstrates that international banks may employ transaction assessment methods to mitigate their information drawbacks as well as a scarcity of local knowledge about borrowers. Is it possible for relationship lending to challenge having methodical transaction lending approaches enabled by information technology? Relationship lending is characterised by a substantial body of research that emphasises the significance of proximity and a branch network. According to (Ju, L. *et al.* 2021), relational information is more readily accessible when people are close together. Banks use geographical pricing discrimination to increase the amount of rent they get (Zhang et al., 2020). A bank bifurcated network moreover serves to combine the lending and borrowing markets of a financial institution (Atkins, R., et al.,2022). A bifurcated network enables liquidity in moving from areas where it is abundant to areas and there is a strong demand for information-intensive lending services.

In the new social systems that have emerged as a result of social networks, geographical nearness is progressively being substituted by nearness. This means that relationship banking can act as a supplement to social, ethnic and religious closeness in a variety of circumstances. When loan officers have a close cultural relationship with their borrowers, communication frictions in lending are reduced, resulting in increased lending quantity, better quality, and lesser costs of lending. The advantages of ethnic closeness combine with the advantages of hard along with soft knowledge obtained via relationship banking to create a win-win situation.

It is important in banking to be accessible to consumers. The geographical and cultural proximity of lending officers to their clients results in better loan choices, which benefits both the bank and the borrowers. The banker must have adequate flexibility and caution to integrate ethnic expertise into decision-taking in order for this to occur. A mix of relationship banking and ethnic closeness is then used to enhance the quality of bank loan choices in the next step.

Does Human Banker Need a Part for Performing at The Advent Of AI?

With the growth of artificial intelligence, it is necessary to re-evaluate the role of people in the banking industry. Beyond the banking, personal computers have outperformed human beings in chess game, the game show named Jeopardy, and sometimes even poker (Moreau, A. et al.,2020). Is a human being banker is nevertheless required, such as a loan official who gathers local information via direct contact with anyone who borrows (Rostamkalaei, A., 2020), or will computer systems take charge of with preprogrammed transaction lending based on the plethora of data applicable regarding bank borrowers and other financial institutions? To put it another way, can computers outperform humans in the banking industry when it comes to mitigating information asymmetry concerns (such as moral hazard and adverse selection hazard difficulties)?

Despite technological advancements, relationship banking continues to provide advantages (Polak, P. et al.,2020). Credit controlling rises for opaque businesses which are paired with transaction-aligned banks as opposed to opaque firms which are linked with relationship-oriented banks, according to the study (Sakawa, H. et al.,2020). Borrowers with strong management skills and integrity have greater negotiating power when providing on soft information rather than when lending on hard facts, according to research (Segawa, E., 2020).

In light of the fact that computers may readily take over for people in modifiable, repetitive jobs which follow distinct processes (Micheler, E. et al.,2020), the issue becomes that however much freedom against rules loan official's need in their lending. As shown by Nasrallah, N. et al. (Nasrallah, N. et al. 2021), foresight is particularly useful for opaque and tiny businesses, as well as for minor insecure loans and when a company is situated far away from a moneylender. However, instead of in the procedure of loan origination, loan officers' discretion is most frequently employed in the pricing of loans. Homo economics is a fictional agent who is entirely rational and self-interested. Artificially intelligent machines are capable of evaluating and responding to the acts of this agent (Santosh, K. C. et al.,2020). Humans, on the other hand, do not always behave logically in complicated situations characterized by knowledge asymmetry, like bank lending. There are two factors that should be taken into consideration. The first refers to the "human" conduct of a loan official, while the second refers to the "human" behaviour of a debtor, respectively.

Firstly, loan commissioners are inspired by their individual goals while at job. Loan officials' lending choices is demonstrated to be affected by their attitude (Tarchouna, A., et al.,2021), arrogance (Hsu, A., et al.,2022), and professional worries (Cortés and colleagues 2016). (Cole et al. 2015). Individual features of loan aspirants, such as attractiveness, race, and age-groups, may impact the sense of loan lenders (Gafni, H., 2021). Loan officials may also distort soft information and taking precedence over factual facts in order to achieve their personal goals (Younas, W., 2021). Loan officers are encouraged to manipulate and exaggerate credit rating evaluations when they are paid on a flat-based basis and have substantial incentives for loan acceptance (Cole et al. 2015).

The purpose of information technology improvements may also be to better match the incentive of loan servicers with the aims of the bank. According to (Sartzetakis, E.S. 2021), changes in bank lending occur as a result of the adoption of a newer credit scoring system. The authors demonstrate that credit boards use more endeavour when dealing with loan applications that hard-to-assess. The use of credit scoring minimizes the likelihood of default on loans while simultaneously increasing loan benefits. They contend that the access to credit ratings reduces the likelihood of incentive conflicts within credit committees.

Communication channels facilitated by information technology may also boost the intensity of communication across hierarchical levels and geographical distances inside a financial institution. According to current research, interpersonal communication is very important (Adam, M., et al.,2021). Communications between such a mortgage lender and the director of a particular bank branch are reduced, which helps to enhance credit standard evaluation (Bussmann, N., et al.,2021). In view of the widespread use of the WWW and intelligent mobile gadgets, enhanced communication quality inside businesses may allow for more dependence on subjective information, even while communicating over longer distances than before.

Second, debtors may also act in a homo economic manner in order to profit themselves personally. They have the ability to misrepresent their financial situation. To acquire loans and cut the borrowing costs they were charged, financially strapped borrowers exerted influence on the assessment technique at their banks (Ochatt, S., 2021). Residential borrowers, who live in locations with poor financial knowledge or social capital, and those who are more certainly to be default on their loans, underreport their individual assets (Stix, H. 2021). Information, both hard and soft, can be modified, and the two are inclined to the impact of borrowers.

Relationship lending and transaction lending may be used in conjunction with one another (Fiordelisi, F., 2014). The soft information collected via relationship lending, according to this point of view, should be used in conjunction with transaction lending strategies. For instance, despite the abundance of factual facts accessible, the reliability of this knowledge is becoming increasingly elusive. Borrowers have the ability to alter hard information. In certain cases, soft information obtained via relationship banking may serve to restrict the potential for misuse of hard information gathered through other means.

Romay, M.C., (Romay, M.C., 2013) investigate the evolution of the information environment around bank borrowers and the consequences of this evolution for bank lending operations. After the implementation of a credit registry which allows lenders to exchange information on a subgroup of bank debtors, one bank reacted by delegating significant responsibilities to its loan officials. The hardening of data resulted in a shift away from transactional banking toward greater relationship banking (Majumdar, S., et al.,2021). When a bank invests extensively in information and communications technology (ICT), Mocetti and colleagues (Mocetti, S., et al.,2017) discover that the bank delegated greater power to a local branch manager. Having gained increased power, the local branch manager is able to devote more resources to the gathering of data and information (Serrat, O. et al.,2017). Instead, a strong existence across products is essential, and the advantages of bank-borrower connections may be maximized by cross-selling transaction-based items to existing customers (Sengupta, S., et al.,2003).

IT FIRMS, FINANCIAL TECHNOLOGY, AND RELATIONSHIP BANKING: ALLIES OR ADVERSARIES?

As FinTech startups and major IT corporations like Amazon, Apple, Facebook, Google, and PayPal make forays into the conventional banking market, banks must contend with greater competition from these new and emerging competitors. This raises the issue of whether or not banks can learn anything new regarding relationship banking via their new rivals. The concept of relationship banking may be embraced by non-bank rivals, who may bring fresh views to the table.

Various web-based lending platforms fuelled by advancements in big data analysis, scalable IT infrastructures and cloud computation (Bansal, R.et al.,2021), have turned to crowds to get soft knowledge on their borrowers and customers. Consumers may operate as borrowers or lenders on peer-to-peer lending frameworks like Stilt, Lending Club, Prosper Marketplace and SoFi and they may strive to assess certified and overcome information asymmetries in their own way. The trustworthiness of their peers is determined by evaluating soft and non-standard data such as money borrowed and text descriptions provided by non-expert persons who operate as lending institutions. When analyzing lower-quality borrowers, soft and non-standard data is very necessary to consider (Schebesch, K.B., et al.,2005). Borrowers who are ethically and topographically closer to lenders and who have a greater impression of trustworthiness are more likely to get loans and to do so at low interest rates (Aiyar, S., et al.,2015).

A large network of web-based acquaintances increases access to finance, decreases interest amounts, and has a negative relationship with ex-post default amounts, according to research (Bolton, P., et al.,2011). In peer-to-peer lending, having an offline buddy network is a significant factor in determining borrowers' success (Liu et al. 2015). Using offline connections to obtain initial loan, give endorsements via bidding, and encourage herding behaviour among other lenders are all effective strategies.

These considerations show that the business plan of online lending portals is based in part on the collection of soft information via frequent contacts, which are essential components of the relationship banking model. Aforementioned possibly demonstrates is that soft information may be gathered and utilized by anybody other than qualified bankers. Therefore, the essential concern in relationship banking is by what method to pick the people who are the most successful at extracting and judging soft information, how to incentivize them, and how to increase the size of their knowledge.

The excitement and novelty adjacent to newer projects must not be allowed to obscure the challenges that exist under the surface. Investors in peer-to-peer lending are motivated by a variety of factors. When incentives are mismatched, savvy investors may take advantage of less experienced investors (Fang, L.H., et al.,2014). Crowdfunding frameworks can potentially take advantage of people's confirmation bias (Peters, U. 2021). Herding behaviour and product hype, rather from being a by-product of the layout of crowdfunding platforms, might instead be purposefully induced for increasing the performance of the platforms' operations.

FinTech start-ups like Square, Stripe, and existing Information Technology corporations like PayPal are all attempting to agitate the traditional banking industry of accepting payments. Money transfers are supported by Facebook. Mobile payment services like as Walmart, Apple Pay, Google and Android Pay are growing in popularity. According to Rysman and Schuh (2016), the most recent developments in consumer payment are divided into three categories: mobile payments, speedier payouts, and digital currencies.

Banks must exercise caution in order to avoid losing the payments business. It is not just the costs that are important, but also the information that is obtained via payments. The information gained through watching activities in mobilize savings is used to assist in the screening and subsequent monitoring of borrowers, as well as the reduction of loan defaults (Puri et al. 2017).

For the sake of conclusion, even if IT-driven transaction banking poses significant challenges to relationship banking, a deep grasp of the individual person's nature of bank borrowers and bank officials continues to be essential. Relationship banking, on the other hand, must adapt and figure out how to take use of technological advancements to its own advantage.

IT ADVANCES, COMPETITIVENESS, AND RELATIONSHIP BANKING ARE ALL FACTORS TO CONSIDER

We have demonstrated that technological advancements have enabled banks to service more distant customers, hence enhancing competition in the banking industry. FinTech businesses have exacerbated the competitive pressures already present in the banking industry. Changes in political conditions may have an even greater impact on competitiveness. (Tambunan, T. et al.,2008) reports that interventionist government assistance to banks in the course of financial crisis has altered the competing environments in the banking industry. The concern here is if increased competitiveness would cause relationship banking to become obsolete.

An unambiguous response to the question of how competitiveness and relationship banking are intertwined is still awaiting discovery. According to Schnabl, G., et al.,(Schnabl, G., 2011), in an inter-transitory situation, banks have limited motivation for engaging in relationship banking since they know that future rivalry would diminish forthcoming relationship banking revenues (Angelakopoulos, G., 2011). Chiorazzo, V., et al.,(Chiorazzo, V., 2008), on the other hand, demonstrate that banks, in reaction to increasingly severe competition, turn to relationship banking in order to maintain rents that are disappearing, particularly in the transactional banking market. The findings of Qin, X., et al.,(Qin, X., et al.,2021), who conducted an empirical study, reveal that bank branches use better relationship lending when they are subjected to additional severe local competition.

As Roy, A. (Roy, A. et al.,2008) suggest, the organization framework of the banking industry is the driving force behind the link between competitiveness and relationship banking practices. The dominance of big and distant banks in the credit markets means that increased competition is detrimental to the practice of relationship banking. On the contrary, when smaller, local banks constitute the bulk of the banking industry, increased competition encourages banks to develop deep and extended connections with their borrowers.

Information Technology advancements reduce transmission obstacles across countries and have a direct impact on information transfer inside global financial institutions. According to the research, multilayered and cross-border banks perform much poorer at acquiring and transferring soft information contained in lending across the management framework in comparison to smaller, locally based financial institutions (Deloof, M. and La Rocca, M. 2015). If borderlines are weakened, remote banks will have lesser trouble participating in relationship banking activities in the future. Other boundaries, rather than being drawn along national lines, may be drawn on culture, religious, and ethnic boundaries. Extending relationship loans is something that multinational banks avoid doing when they have branches in more distant cultural and geographical locations from the main headquarters.

More than just gathering unique information about specific borrowers, lending specialty in relationship banking extends above and beyond that. Entrepreneurs borrow from banks which are specialized in their export business, and banks that are specialized in their export market get market-specific information (Kontokosta, C.E. et al.,2015). If technological advancements continue to diminish the significance of borders, so encouraging transnational and worldwide commerce bank knowledge of export industries can become always crucial.

An associated subject concern the impact of competing with the advantages of relationship banking to bank borrowers, which is discussed in more detail below. By removing geographical barriers to financial institution development, small businesses may borrow at less interest rate, without having corresponding effect on the quantity of money that smaller businesses borrow (Ortiz-Molina, H., et al.,2008). Small and medium-sized businesses benefit from cooperative banks because they encourage new firm formation and make it easier for them to obtain bank financing, whereas large corporations' benefit from the presence of cooperative banks because they increase the performance of smaller and midsize enterprises (Li, Y., et al.,2015).

Relationship banking has many advantages, but it also has certain difficulties that must be handled appropriately in order to gain the benefits. For instance, a relationship bank which gains market dominance over borrowers may engage in significant rent extraction, putting the borrower at a competitive disadvantage, as in Pastore, P., et al.,(Pastore, P., et al.,2020). When faced with a hold-up situation, the most common remedy is to boost competition in the banking industry. According to Cheung, M.WL., et al.,(Cheung, M.WL., et al.,2016), who conducted a meta-analysis, the advantages of relationship banking are much more obvious when bank rivalry is strong.

Suggestions for the Stability of the System

We are now assessing the effect of information technology-driven developments in banking on the stability of the financial system. A disproportionate dependence on information technology (IT) solutions may result in increased risky behaviour and even systems risk in the financial system. Couchman, N., et al.,(Couchman, N., et al.,2003) demonstrate that mathematical models under-pricing default risk in a systematic way prior to the global financial crisis, particularly for debtors for whom soft information was more important. Using computer simulations which manage for risk in the very same manner that humans does, and making the same errors, might lead to systemic risk problems if they are relied upon.

Because of globalization and advancements in information technology, financial markets have undergone unprecedented levels of integration (Jordà, Ò., et al.,2019). The bad news that travels swiftly via the social networks, (Garz, M. 2014) has the potential to cause bank run and undermine financial stability. In this context, the importance of relationships with bank investors becomes apparent. Investors having an everlasting connection with a bank are much little likely to run away from their accounts (Degryse, H., et al.,2012), and they are more supportive of relationship lending (Hernández-Cánovas, G. and Martínez-Solano, P., 2010). Relationship banking, by depending on a varied pool of soft knowledge, may be able to serve as a stabilizing force in an information-driven society.

The ability to scale transaction-oriented banking operations as a result of technological advancements presents a problem for regulators. The rapid growth enabled by IT innovations has the chance of leading to excess taking risks in banking (Hall, B.H., et al., 2009). Iannotta, P.G. (Iannotta, P.G., 2010) examine the dis-synergies that exist within relationship banking along with other riskier banking operations, as well as whether or not a division of the two is necessary. Performing financial market activities, like as trading on a stock exchange, provides advantages to relationship banks primarily when they are small in scale. The scale of trading activities means that financial institutions cannot devote the entire assets to relationship banking ex-post, hence hindering their capacity to create connections ex-ante. According to Alhassan et al. (Alhassan at al., 2016), increased bank profitability might encourage the growth of riskier side operations, hence boosting bank risk taking. Consequently, information technology improvements that boost the profit of bank core business may indirectly support riskier bank growth inside businesses, according to this viewpoint. Innovations in information technology may have worsened hazards associated with financial markets, such as disinformation resulting from complex information networks, greater volatility associated with transactional speed, along with speculative trading behaviour, among other things (Ma and McGroarty 2017).

According to Yan et al., (Yan et al., 2013), wholesale financing may be troublesome and may result in enormous liquidation of capital. These analyses highlight the need to protect relationship banking against destabilizing pressures such as short-term finance, enormous leveraging, or scaled transaction-based bank operations. Relationship banking is particularly vulnerable to these influences (Calomiris & Pornrojnangkool, 2009).

The implementation of a regulatory overhaul, such as the Basel Committee for capital and liquidity legislation and systemic regulation which differentiates core banking functionalities from unsafe trading schemes, may not only contribute to increased reliability, but it may also start imposing extra expenditures on long-established financial institutions as well. In many cases, FinTech businesses are functioning outside of the modulated banking system, so appealing in administrative investment and profiting from the situation. Barberis et al., (Barberis et al., 2016) demonstrate that FinTech shadow banks have developed significantly in recent years, not just as a result of their better online lending technology, but also as a result of increased regulatory burdens that have placed regular banks at a disadvantage in the marketplace. However, as seen by the current financial crisis, systemic risk may accrue in the shadow banking structure as a result of this (Adrian et al., 2016).

While radical advances in FinTech can increase the performance, the business incentive of FinTech firms must not be linked with the requirement in long-term security. For instance, the strength of the payment system (more broadly, the strength of the financial system framework) is critical to the functioning of the actual economy. Payroll system innovations may have an influence on system stability, and system problems need more managerial attention (Ruozi & Ferrari, 2013). The question of how to maintain a fair playing field while not strangling innovation and new entrance by FinTech companies is thus a critical quandary that regulators must resolve.

The ideals of sharing data and trust are increasingly being challenged by technological advancements. The cryptocurrency Bitcoin, for example, is constructed on top of block chain technology, which provides for a decentralized way to authenticating transactions and asset holdings. Because of its long-term emphasis, relationship banking may be able to maintain a competitive edge in the sphere of trust. The manner in which proprietary information (such as payouts, deposits and lending) and is protected and made available to third party companies would become more important in future, and will correlate to the core subject of banking—the establishment of reliability and security (Pramanik & Raja, 2019).

The possibility of relationship banks operating as guardianship of privileged data which may be shared to other parties with the knowledge and agreement of bank clients are conceivable in the future. A smooth integration of banking processes having financial technology clarifications is facilitated through application programming interfaces (APIs), which link banking and financial technology applications together. The authorities are keeping track on technical advancements. In the US, data exchanging is governed by the Data Sharing Agreements that is aimed at facilitating the entry of non-bank actors into the financial system. After then, the difficulty pertains to merging data that relationship banks acquire and incorporating it into decision-making, or even transferring this information to collaborative FinTech suppliers.

Another source of concern is the impact of information technology-driven advancements in banking and consumer rights issues. Assuming that computers can defeat the finest humans at a range of games, will they also retrieve rents from borrowers who are uneducated in financial matters, poor, or otherwise excluded from the financial system? Inequality may rise as a result of redlining, which is the use of computer algorithms to identify and exploit existing inequalities. According to Hornuf et al., (Hornuf et al., 2021), the effect of technology in borrowing on inequality is widely undefined, and the question of how to protect humans from computers may merit further investigation. 5

The population's financing requirements are increasing as people live longer lives and as the income and expenditure necessities of bank customers fluctuate more widely throughout their life cycles. According to Friedline et al., (Friedline et al., 2021), young and mature persons are much more vulnerable to poor monetary decisions than middle-aged persons, and they are also more susceptible to unfair lending practises like lending practices, enormous credit card fees, and loans. The establishment of manageable information systems will be the initial step, but much more must be done. As McGee, R.W. et al. (McGee et al., 2010) demonstrate in the occurrence of insider trading avoidance, compliance cannot take the place of ethics.) It is still being investigated how to incorporate ethical considerations into artificially intelligent lending programmes.

According to the risk management literature, the successful implementation of new information technology systems is dependent on the care taken during the process. Among the critical risk factors that have an effect on the benefit of an IT project, Al-Shammari, et al. (Al-Shammari, et al. 2021) strategies and develop risk elements and organisational risks, like senior management involvement and user involvement, as the most important. They contend that having close attention to risks may help to minimize the negative impact of risk on task achievements in the long run. According to a recent study, interpersonal skills in risk management are critical for project completion. Thaler et al., (Thaler et al., 2016) provide evidence to support this claim.

The ramifications for the financial industry are obvious. The distinction between IT-dependent transaction banking and relationship banking may be a bit of a figment of the imagination. Instead, effective relationship banking is dependent on the proper deployment of IT-dependent solutions, with a strong emphasis on soft skills, as well as the incorporation of soft information in the process.

CONCLUSION

The purpose of this article is to offer an overview as to how relationship banking is changing in the face of disruptive, information technology-driven advances. We propose that relationship banks may still provide a competitive advantage when contending against transaction-based banks or FinTech enterprises.

Because of technological advancements, expandable transaction banking has become more cost-efficient. In conjunction with transaction lending procedures, mobile and internet banking make it possible to maintain ongoing access to financial services even across long distances. Artificial intelligence-based decision-making is made easier by a greater dependence on factual, measurable information accessible online and via credit bureaus. Despite the many advantages of information technology in banking, there are also possible drawbacks. Hard information is more vulnerable to managing and gaming than soft information. Transaction lending strategies may fail to adequately reflect the motives of human bankers, banking borrowers, and bank depositors that may result in greater marketability, herding, and, as a result, increased systemic risk in the financial system. It is possible that IT-based systems may overlook ethical considerations in lending.

IT advancements do not only alter the way banks operate, but they may also reshape whole social structures. Other sorts of community organisation are taking the place of geographical boundaries. Spreading rumours, hype, and fashion fads through social media can encourage herding behaviour and improve volatility in the financial markets. Individuals may not always make decisions on the provision of factual evidence, rationality, and scientific findings, as has been demonstrated in numerous studies. As a result, the capacity to comprehend the behaviour of bank clients may become a critical competence in the field of relationship banking.

We believe that excellent connections are still a competitive edge in the banking industry today. Because of the advantages of a branch network which come from being geographically and culturally close to bank customers, human bankers may not be totally substituted by AI algorithms in the loan process for the time being, at least not yet. According to the findings, more IT assistance does not lessen the importance of relationship banking, but rather enhances it by increasing the amount of soft information that is acquired. We believe that the way forward for relationship banks is to leverage information technology to expand on their existing relationships. It is necessary for relationship banks to accept new technology, adapt to changing client expectations, and comply with regulatory requirements.

REFERENCES

Adam, M., Wessel, M., & Benlian, A. (2021). AI-based chatbots in customer service and their effects on user compliance. *Electronic Markets*, *31*(2), 427–445. doi:10.100712525-020-00414-7

Adrian, T., & Ashcraft, A. B. (2016). Shadow banking: a review of the literature. In: Jones, G. (ed) Banking Crises. Palgrave Macmillan. doi:10.1057/9781137553799_29

Agrawal, P., Chaudhary, D., Madaan, V., Zabrovskiy, A., Prodan, R., Kimovski, D., & Timmerer, C. (2021). Automated bank cheque verification using image processing and deep learning methods. *Multimedia Tools and Applications*, *80*(4), 5319–5350. doi:10.100711042-020-09818-1

Aiyar, S., Calomiris, C., & Wieladek, T. (2015). Bank Capital Regulation: Theory, Empirics, and Policy. *IMF Economic Review*, *63*(4), 955–983. doi:10.1057/imfer.2015.18

Al-Shammari, M., & Mili, M. (2021). A fuzzy analytic hierarchy process model for customers' bank selection decision in the Kingdom of Bahrain. *Oper Res Int J*, *21*(3), 1429–1446. doi:10.100712351-019-00496-y

Alhassan, A. L., Tetteh, M. L., & Brobbey, F. O. (2016). Market power, efficiency, and bank profitability: Evidence from Ghana. *Economic Change and Restructuring*, *49*(1), 71–93. doi:10.100710644-015-9174-6

Angelakopoulos, G., & Mihiotis, A. (2011). E-banking: Challenges and opportunities in the Greek banking sector. *Electronic Commerce Research*, *11*(3), 297–319. doi:10.100710660-011-9076-2

Atkins, R., Cook, L., & Seamans, R. (2022). Discrimination in lending? Evidence from the Paycheck Protection Program. *Small Business Economics*, *58*(2), 843–865. doi:10.100711187-021-00533-1

Backhaus, K., & Awan, A. (2019). The Paradigm Shift in Customer Analysis: Marketing or IT-Driven? In K. Bergener, M. Räckers, & A. Stein (Eds.), *The Art of Structuring*. Springer. doi:10.1007/978-3-030-06234-7_32

Bansal, R., Obaid, A. J., Gupta, A., Singh, R., & Pramanik, S. (2021). Impact of Big Data on Digital Transformation in 5G Era. *2nd International Conference on Physics and Applied Sciences (ICPAS 2021)*. IOP Science. .10.1088/1742-6596/1963/1/012170

Barberis, J., & Arner, D. W. (2016). FinTech in China: From Shadow Banking to P2P Lending. In: Tasca, P., Aste, T., Pelizzon, L., Perony, N. (eds) Banking Beyond Banks and Money: New Economic Windows. Springer, Cham. doi:10.1007/978-3-319-42448-4_5

Bolton, P., & Jeanne, O. (2011). Sovereign Default Risk and Bank Fragility in Financially Integrated Economies. *IMF Economic Review*, *59*(2), 162–194. doi:10.1057/imfer.2011.5

Bussmann, N., Giudici, P., Marinelli, D., & Papenbrock, J. (2021). Explainable Machine Learning in Credit Risk Management. *Computational Economics*, *57*(1), 203–216. doi:10.100710614-020-10042-0

Calomiris, C. W., & Pornrojnangkool, T. (2009). Relationship Banking and the Pricing of Financial Services. *Journal of Financial Services Research*, *35*(3), 189–224. doi:10.100710693-009-0058-7

Cheung, M. W. L., & Vijayakumar, R. (2016). A Guide to Conducting a Meta-Analysis. *Neuropsychology Review*, *26*(2), 121–128. doi:10.100711065-016-9319-z PMID:27209412

Chiorazzo, V., Milani, C., & Salvini, F. (2008). Income Diversification and Bank Performance: Evidence from Italian Banks. *Journal of Financial Services Research*, *33*(3), 181–203. doi:10.100710693-008-0029-4

Couchman, N., & Tsolacos, S. (2003). Explaining standard retail yields in UK locations. *Journal of Retail & Leisure Property*, *3*(3), 211–222. doi:10.1057/palgrave.rlp.5090177

Cowling, M., Marlow, S., & Liu, W. (2020). Gender and bank lending after the global financial crisis: Are women entrepreneurs safer bets? *Small Business Economics*, *55*(4), 853–880. doi:10.100711187-019-00168-3

(2021). D. K.aushik, M. Garg, Annu, A. Gupta and S. Pramanik, Application of Machine Learning and Deep Learning in Cyber security: An Innovative Approach. InGhonge, M., Pramanik, S., Mangrulkar, R., & Le, D. N. (Eds.), *Cybersecurity and Digital Forensics: Challenges and Future Trends*. Wiley.

Degryse, H., de Goeij, P., & Kappert, P. (2012). The impact of firm and industry characteristics on small firms' capital structure. *Small Business Economics*, *38*(4), 431–447. doi:10.100711187-010-9281-8

Deloof, M., & La Rocca, M. (2015). Local financial development, and the trade credit policy of Italian SMEs. *Small Business Economics*, *44*(4), 905–924. doi:10.100711187-014-9617-x

DeYoung, R., Hunter, W. C., & Udell, G. F. (2004). The Past, Present, and Probable Future for Community Banks. *Journal of Financial Services Research*, *25*(2/3), 85–133. doi:10.1023/B:FINA.0000020656.65653.79

Fang, L. H., & Yasuda, A. (2014). Are Stars' Opinions Worth More? The Relation Between Analyst Reputation and Recommendation Values. *Journal of Financial Services Research*, *46*(3), 235–269. doi:10.100710693-013-0178-y

Fiordelisi, F., Monferrà, S., & Sampagnaro, G. (2014). Relationship Lending and Credit Quality. *Journal of Financial Services Research*, *46*(3), 295–315. doi:10.100710693-013-0176-0

Gafni, H., Hudon, M., & Périlleux, A. (2021). Business or Basic Needs? The Impact of Loan Purpose on Social Crowdfunding Platforms. *Journal of Business Ethics*, *173*(4), 777–793. doi:10.100710551-020-04530-4

Garz, M. (2014). Good news and bad news: Evidence of media bias in unemployment reports. *Public Choice*, *161*(3-4), 499–515. doi:10.100711127-014-0182-2

Hall, B. H., Lotti, F., & Mairesse, J. (2009). Innovation and productivity in SMEs: Empirical evidence for Italy. *Small Business Economics*, *33*(1), 13–33. doi:10.100711187-009-9184-8

Hannoon, A., Al-Sartawi, A. M. A. M., & Khalid, A. A. (2021). Relationship Between Financial Technology and Financial Performance. In A. M. A. Musleh Al-Sartawi (Ed.), *The Big Data-Driven Digital Economy: Artificial and Computational Intelligence. Studies in Computational Intelligence* (Vol. 974). Springer. doi:10.1007/978-3-030-73057-4_26

Hernández-Cánovas, G., & Martínez-Solano, P. (2010). Relationship lending and SME financing in the continental European bank-based system. *Small Business Economics, 34*(4), 465–482. doi:10.1007/11187-008-9129-7

Hsu, A., Lee, C. F., & Liu, S. (2022). Book-tax differences, CEO overconfidence, and bank loan contracting. *Review of Quantitative Finance and Accounting, 58*(2), 437–472. doi:10.1007/11156-021-00992-3

Iannotta, P. G. (2010). Mergers and Acquisitions: Definitions, Process, and Analysis. In *Investment Banking*. Springer. doi:10.1007/978-3-540-93765-4_7

Jordà, Ò., Schularick, M., Taylor, A. M., & Ward, F. (2019). Global Financial Cycles and Risk Premiums. *IMF Economic Review, 67*(1), 109–150. doi:10.1057/41308-019-00077-1

Ju, L. (2021). Relational Subsets Knowledge Distillation for Long-Tailed Retinal Diseases Recognition. In Medical Image Computing and Computer Assisted Intervention – MICCAI 2021. Springer, Cham. doi:10.1007/978-3-030-87237-3_1

Kaur, S. J., & Ali, L. (2021). Understanding bank employees' perception towards technology enabled banking: A developing country perspective. *Journal of Financial Services Marketing, 26*(3), 129–143. doi:10.1057/41264-021-00100-5

Kontokosta, C. E. (2015). A Market-Specific Methodology for a Commercial Building Energy Performance Index. *The Journal of Real Estate Finance and Economics, 51*(2), 288–316. doi:10.1007/11146-014-9481-0

Lai, S. T., Leu, F. Y., & Lin, J. W. (2019). A Banking Chatbot Security Control Procedure for Protecting User Data Security and Privacy. In L. Barolli, F. Y. Leu, T. Enokido, & H. C. Chen (Eds.), Advances on Broadband and Wireless Computing, Communication and Applications. BWCCA 2018: Lecture Notes on Data Engineering and Communications Technologies (Vol. 25). Springer. doi:10.1007/978-3-030-02613-4_50

Lesani, M., & Palsberg, J. (2014). Decomposing Opacity. In F. Kuhn (Ed.), Lecture Notes in Computer Science: Vol. 8784. *Distributed Computing. DISC 2014*. Springer. doi:10.1007/978-3-662-45174-8_27

Li, Y., Youtie, J., & Shapira, P. (2015). Why do technology firms publish scientific papers? The strategic use of science by small and midsize enterprises in nanotechnology. *The Journal of Technology Transfer, 40*(6), 1016–1033. doi:10.1007/10961-014-9391-6

Majumdar, S., & Pujari, V. (2021). Exploring usage of mobile banking apps in the UAE: A categorical regression analysis. *Journal of Financial Services Marketing*. doi:10.1057/41264-021-00112-1

McGee, R. W. (2010). Analyzing Insider Trading from the Perspectives of Utilitarian Ethics and Rights Theory. *Journal of Business Ethics, 91*(1), 65–82. doi:10.1007/10551-009-0068-2

Melese, F. (2021). Insights from Transaction Cost Economics for Government Organizations: An Application to the U.S. Department of Defense (DoD). *Atlantic Economic Journal*, *49*(1), 109–111. doi:10.100711293-021-09705-6

Micheler, E., & Whaley, A. (2020). Regulatory Technology: Replacing Law with Computer Code. *European Business Organization Law Review*, *21*(2), 349–377. doi:10.100740804-019-00151-1

Mocetti, S., Pagnini, M., & Sette, E. (2017). Information Technology and Banking Organization. *Journal of Financial Services Research*, *51*(3), 313–338. doi:10.100710693-016-0244-3

Moreau, A., Sévigny, S., Giroux, I., & Chauchard, E. (2020). Ability to Discriminate Online Poker Tilt Episodes: A New Way to Prevent Excessive Gambling? *Journal of Gambling Studies*, *36*(2), 699–711. doi:10.100710899-019-09903-7 PMID:31679089

Moro, S., Cortez, P., & Rita, P. (2015). Using customer lifetime value and neural networks to improve the prediction of bank deposit subscription in telemarketing campaigns. *Neural Computing & Applications*, *26*(1), 131–139. doi:10.100700521-014-1703-0

Musso, P., & Schiavo, S. (2008). The impact of financial constraints on firm survival and growth. *Journal of Evolutionary Economics*, *18*(2), 135–149. doi:10.100700191-007-0087-z

Nasrallah, N., & El Khoury, R. (2021). Proxy Measure for SMEs Financial Performance in Opaque Markets. In B. Alareeni, A. Hamdan, & I. Elgedawy (Eds.), *The Importance of New Technologies and Entrepreneurship in Business Development: In the Context of Economic Diversity in Developing Countries. ICBT 2020. Lecture Notes in Networks and Systems* (Vol. 194). Springer. doi:10.1007/978-3-030-69221-6_108

Ochatt, S., Lambardi, M., Panis, B., Pathirana, R., Revilla, M. A., & Wang, Q.-C. (2021). Cryopreservation and In Vitro banking: A cool subject – Preface from the editors. *Plant Cell, Tissue and Organ Culture*, *144*(1), 1–5. doi:10.100711240-020-01985-1

Ogura, Y., & Uchida, H. (2014). Bank Consolidation and Soft Information Acquisition in Small Business Lending. *Journal of Financial Services Research*, *45*(2), 173–200. doi:10.100710693-013-0163-5

Ortiz-Molina, H., & Penas, M. F. (2008). Lending to small businesses: The role of loan maturity in addressing information problems. *Small Business Economics*, *30*(4), 361–383. doi:10.100711187-007-9053-2

Pastore, P., Ricciardi, A., & Tommaso, S. (2020). Contractual networks: An organizational model to reduce the competitive disadvantage of small and medium enterprises (SMEs) in Europe's less developed regions. A survey in southern Italy. *The International Entrepreneurship and Management Journal*, *16*(4), 1503–1535. doi:10.100711365-019-00616-2

Pengji, W., & McCarthy, B. (2021). What do people like on Facebook? Content marketing strategies used by retail bank brands in Australia and Singapore, *29*(2). doi:10.1016/j.ausmj.2020.04.008

Peters, U. (2021). An argument for egalitarian confirmation bias and against political diversity in academia. *Synthese*, *198*(12), 11999–12019. doi:10.100711229-020-02846-2

Polak, P., Nelischer, C., Guo, H., & Robertson, D. C. (2020). "Intelligent" finance and treasury management: What we can expect. *AI & Society*, *35*(3), 715–726. doi:10.100700146-019-00919-6

Portela, M., Thanassoulis, E., & Simpson, G. (2004). Negative data in DEA: A directional distance approach applied to bank branches. *The Journal of the Operational Research Society*, *55*(10), 1111–1121. doi:10.1057/palgrave.jors.2601768

Pramanik, S., & Raja, S. S. (2019). Analytical Study on Security Issues in Steganography. Think-India, 22(35), 106-114, .

Rajnak, V., & Puschmann, T. (2021). The impact of blockchain on business models in banking. *Information Systems and e-Business Management*, *19*(3), 809–861. doi:10.100710257-020-00468-2

Romay, M. C., Millard, M. J., Glaubitz, J. C., Peiffer, J. A., Swarts, K. L., Casstevens, T. M., Elshire, R. J., Acharya, C. B., Mitchell, S. E., Flint-Garcia, S. A., McMullen, M. D., Holland, J. B., Buckler, E. S., & Gardner, C. A. (2013). Comprehensive genotyping of the USA national maize inbred seed bank. *Genome Biology*, *14*(6), R55. doi:10.1186/gb-2013-14-6-r55 PMID:23759205

Rostamkalaei, A., Nitani, M., & Riding, A. (2020). Borrower discouragement: The role of informal turndowns. *Small Business Economics*, *54*(1), 173–188. doi:10.100711187-018-0086-5

Roy, A. (2008). Organization Structure and Risk Taking in Banking. *Risk Manag*, *10*(2), 122–134. doi:10.1057/palgrave.rm.8250043

Ruozi, R., & Ferrari, P. (2013). Liquidity Risk Management in Banks: Economic and Regulatory Issues. In *Liquidity Risk Management in Banks. SpringerBriefs in Finance*. Springer. doi:10.1007/978-3-642-29581-2

Sakawa, H., & Watanabel, N. (2020). Main bank relationship and accounting conservatism: Evidence from Japan. *Asian Business & Management*, *19*(1), 62–85. doi:10.105741291-019-00071-5

Santosa, A. D., Taufik, N., Prabowo, F. H. E., & Rahmawati, M. (2021). Continuance intention of baby boomer and X generation as new users of digital payment during COVID-19 pandemic using UTAUT2. *Journal of Financial Services Marketing*, *26*(4), 259–273. doi:10.105741264-021-00104-1

Santosh, K. C. (2020). AI-Driven Tools for Coronavirus Outbreak: Need of Active Learning and Cross-Population Train/Test Models on Multitudinal/Multimodal Data. *Journal of Medical Systems*, *44*(5), 93. doi:10.100710916-020-01562-1 PMID:32189081

Sartzetakis, E. S. (2021). Green bonds as an instrument to finance low carbon transition. *Economic Change and Restructuring*, *54*(3), 755–779. doi:10.100710644-020-09266-9

Schebesch, K. B., & Stecking, R. (2005). Support Vector Machines for Credit Scoring: Extension to Non-Standard Cases. In: Baier, D. & Wernecke, KD. (eds) Innovations in Classification, Data Science, and Information Systems. Studies in Classification, Data Analysis, and Knowledge Organization. Springer, Berlin, Heidelberg. doi:10.1007/3-540-26981-9_57

Schnabl, G., & Zemanek, H. (2011). Inter-temporal savings, current account trends and asymmetric shocks in a heterogeneous European Monetary Union. *Inter Economics*, *46*(3), 153–160. doi:10.100710272-011-0377-4

Segawa, E., Schalet, B., & Cella, D. (2020). A comparison of computer adaptive tests (CATs) and short forms in terms of accuracy and number of items administrated using PROMIS profile. *Quality of Life Research: An International Journal of Quality of Life Aspects of Treatment, Care and Rehabilitation*, *29*(1), 213–221. doi:10.100711136-019-02312-8 PMID:31595451

Serrat, O. (2017). Social Network Analysis. In *Knowledge Solutions*. Springer. doi:10.1007/978-981-10-0983-9_9

Stix, H. (2021). Ownership, and purchase intention of crypto assets: Survey results. *Empirica*, *48*, 65–99. doi:10.100710663-020-09499-x

Tambunan, T. (2008). SME development, economic growth, and government intervention in a developing country: The Indonesian story. *Journal of International Entrepreneurship*, *6*(4), 147–167. doi:10.100710843-008-0025-7

Tarchouna, A., Jarraya, B., & Bouri, A. (2021). Do board characteristics and ownership structure matter for bank non-performing loans? Empirical evidence from US commercial banks. *The Journal of Management and Governance*. doi:10.100710997-020-09558-2

Thaler, T. A., Priest, S. J., & Fuchs, S. (2016). Evolving inter-regional co-operation in flood risk management: Distances and types of partnership approaches in Austria. *Regional Environmental Change*, *16*(3), 841–853. doi:10.100710113-015-0796-z

Tsai, C. H., & Su, P. C. (2021). The application of multi-server authentication scheme in internet banking transaction environments. *Information Systems and e-Business Management*, *19*(1), 77–105. doi:10.100710257-020-00481-5

Villar, A. S., & Khan, N. (2021). Robotic process automation in banking industry: A case study on Deutsche Bank. *J BANK FINANC TECHNOL*, *5*, 71–86. doi:10.100742786-021-00030-9

Waseem, M., Liang, P., Márquez, G., Shahin, M., Khan, A. A., & Ahmad, A. (2021). A Decision Model for Selecting Patterns and Strategies to Decompose Applications into Microservices. In H. Hacid, O. Kao, M. Mecella, N. Moha, & Hy. Paik (Eds.), Lecture Notes in Computer Science: Vol. 13121. *Service-Oriented Computing. ICSOC 2021*. Springer. doi:10.1007/978-3-030-91431-8_62

Worthington, A. C., & Higgs, H. (2011). Economies of scale and scope in Australian higher education. *Higher Education*, *61*(4), 387–414. doi:10.100710734-010-9337-3

Yan, N., & Sun, B. (2013). Coordinating loan strategies for supply chain financing with limited credit. *OR-Spektrum*, *35*(4), 1039–1058. doi:10.100700291-013-0329-4

Younas, W., & Kalimuthu, K. R. (2021). Telecom microfinance banking versus commercial banking: A battle in the financial services sector. *Journal of Financial Services Marketing*, *26*(2), 67–80. doi:10.105741264-020-00085-7

Zhang, M., Huang, C., Zhang, J., Qin, H., Ma, G., Liu, X., & Yin, J. (2020). Accurate discrimination of tea from multiple geographical regions by combining multi-elements with multivariate statistical analysis. *Food Measure*, *14*(6), 3361–3370. doi:10.100711694-020-00575-1

Chapter 12
Recent Developments of Medical Image Processing Techniques and Challenges

Kannadhasan Suriyan

iD https://orcid.org/0000-0001-6443-9993

Study World College of Engineering, India

Nagarajan R.

iD https://orcid.org/0000-0002-4990-5869

Gnanamani College of Technology, India

Manjushree Kumari J.

Gnanamani College of Technology, India

Jisha Chandra C.

Gnanamani College of Technology, India

ABSTRACT

Medical image collaboration may be accomplished for medical practise and education by bringing the idea of CSCW to the medical imaging field. Medical pictures may be examined and diagnosed by groups of people, and individuals can talk about them on a chat system while exchanging visual image data on their terminals. The process of generating visible pictures of inside body structures for scientific and medicinal research and therapy, as well as a visible view of the function of internal tissues, is known as medical imaging. The goal of this procedure is to identify and treat disorders. This procedure generates a database of the organs' normal structure and function, making it simple to spot abnormalities. Organic and radiological imaging, using electromagnetic energy (X-rays and gamma), sonography, magnetic scopes, and thermal and isotope imaging are all part of this process.

DOI: 10.4018/978-1-6684-7697-0.ch012

INTRODUCTION

The image is a measurement of a perceived sight's characteristics, such as lighting or color. Lower processing costs, simpler storage and transfer, rapid quality assessment, repeated copying while preserving quality, fast and affordable reproduction, and flexible editing are just a few benefits of using digital photos. Digital images have a number of downsides, including copyright infringement, difficulties resizing while preserving quality, the need for vast amounts of memory, and the need for a rapid CPU for processing. Image processing is the use of a computer to modify a digital image. This approach has various benefits, such as adaptation, flexibility, data storage, and communication. Thanks to the development of various picture scaling techniques, images may be retained effectively. This strategy calls for simultaneously applying a lot of different criteria to the images.

Such techniques have a number of disadvantages in comparison to methods that produce images. Worldwide, billions of photographs are taken each year for a variety of medical purposes. Nearly half of them utilize radiation therapy, both ionizing and non-ionizing. Without invasive procedures, medical imaging may provide images of the inside organs. Fast computers and the mathematical and logical conversion of energy into signals were used to produce such images. The impulses are then converted to digital images. These signals show the many tissue types that comprise the human body. Digital photos are essential in everyday life. The phrase "medical imaging processing" describes the process of modifying images using a computer. A few of the techniques and actions used in this processing include image capture, storage, display, and transmission (Kasban et al., 2015; Matthews & Jezzard, 2004; Suetens, 2017; Webb, 2017; Wen, 2019).

Pictures in 2D and 3D can manage several dimensions. Image processing techniques were created in the 1960s. These techniques have been used to a number of fields, including as television visual improvement, therapeutic purposes, the arts, and space exploration. Picture processing grew speedier and less costly in the 1970s as a result of advancements in computer systems. Throughout the 2000s, image processing became quicker, more affordable, and simpler. One of the most complex systems ever created is the visual system of humans. Living things need this system to organize and grasp the many intricate parts that make up their environment. The visual system is made up of the eye, which transforms light into neural signals, and the brain's related areas, which process those signals and extract significant information. Two cylinder-shaped structures that are anteriorly located in the skull make form the human eye. The eyeballs measure 2.5 cm both longitudinally and transversally. The centre of the eyeball has a darkened feature called the pupil. This system enables light to enter the eye. This system narrows when exposed to a stronger light source. This enhances the visual process and reduces the quantity of light that reaches the retina. Several muscles that surround the eye are in charge of controlling the pupil's enlargement. The sclera, or eye's supporting tissues, are constantly there. A ligamentous structure, the lens is joined to the cornea via the corneal stroma.

As an interdisciplinary research field bringing together specialists from applied mathematics, computer science, engineering, statistics, physics, biology, and medicine, biomedical image processing has expanded quickly. Today, computer-assisted diagnostic processing is a common practice in clinical settings. The flurry of new high-tech development and the use of various imaging modalities brings up new challenges, such as how to process and analyze a vast number of images in order to provide high-quality information for sickness diagnosis and treatment. This course's major objectives are to introduce students to the basic concepts and techniques of medical image processing and to stimulate their interest in further research and study in this area. Discussions of recent advancements in biological signal processing and image processing are frequent (Elmogy, 2017; Gill & Sharma, 2016; Marcel et al., 2012; Qu & Xu, 2020; van Sloun et al., 2019).

The classification of pixel and voxel data processing methods, such as image segmentation, or their applications in diagnosis, treatment planning, and follow-up research often serve as the inspiration for such review publications. On the other hand, this essay focuses on the challenges of processing massive amounts of medical image data. In recent years, the amount of medical imaging data has grown from Kilobytes to Terabytes. This is mostly because of improvements in the medical picture gathering technology, which now has greater pixel resolution and faster reconstruction processing. For instance, the high resolution micro computed tomography (CT) reconstructs images with 8,000 8,000 pixels per slice and detectability of 0.7 m isotropic detail, while the latest Sky Scan 2011 x-ray nano-tomograph has a resolution of 200 nm per pixel. Consequently, each slice is 64 Megabytes in size (MB). In modern CT and magnetic resonance imaging (MRI) systems, the image resolution and reconstruction time may be scaled. This resolution may result in scans of the whole human body using several Gigabytes (GB) of data. Massive volumes of image data from a single data set and big amounts of image data from hundreds of images, as in picture archiving and communication systems (PACS), are two instances of large medical image data.

An image is made up of measurements taken in two-dimensional (2-D) or three-dimensional (3-D) space. These measurements, often known as "image intensities" in medical images, include things like radio frequency (RF) signal amplitude in MRI, acoustic pressure in ultrasound, and radiation absorption in X-ray imaging. Every point in an image that is measured using a single measurement is referred to as a scalar picture. Medical imaging has experienced a revolution as a result of the development of speedier, more accurate, and less invasive technologies in the last ten years. This sparked the development of matching software, which in turn sparked the invention of cutting-edge signal and image processing methods. Many of these techniques are based on curvature-driven flows and partial differential equations, which are the main topics of this overview article. Mathematical models are the cornerstone of biomedical computers. In experimental, clinical, biological, and behavioral research, building such models using data gathered from images is still a critical way to progress science. Modern medical imaging techniques go much beyond the visible light photographs and microscope images of the early 20th century. They encompass all biological scales. The spatial variation of hemoglobin deoxygenation during brain metabolism or water molecule transport through and inside tissue are just two examples of the many physical processes that can be measured by modern medical images, which can be conceptualized as geometrically organized arrays of data samples. We have significantly improved our capacity to use new processing techniques and combine multiple data channels into sophisticated and complex mathematical models of physiological function and dysfunction as a result of the increasing use of imaging to organize our observations of the biophysical world. Both the creation of biomedical engineering ideas based on strong mathematical foundations and the development of general-purpose software approaches that may be implemented into complete treatment delivery systems are significant research topics (Fan et al., 2005; Gonzalez & Woods, 2002; Khandare, 2014; Khan, 2014). Such devices may improve the efficacy of several image-guided therapies, including biopsy, minimally invasive surgery, and radiation therapy.

MEDICAL IMAGE PROCESSING

The field of medicine relies heavily on medical images. Medical image analysis' main objective is to gather data from images taken by tools like X-rays, CT scans, MRIs, and PET-CT scans. There are vast amounts of organized and unstructured data. A growing number of countries have been actively involved in medical information reform because big volumes of unstructured data and large amounts of data provide substantial challenges for healthcare systems. Accurate and personalized health care services may be provided by integrating image processing technology into the medical and health sector as well as using classification and analysis technology to analyze medical data and integrate it with traditional medical data. In clinical applications, image processing technology may be used to analyze illness patterns, compare clinical effects, examine susceptibility populations, create customized treatments, provide clinical decision support, and monitor patients remotely. In order to spread medical knowledge and boost the effectiveness and caliber of the medical industry, medical data should be used to the fullest extent possible. The four distinct imaging modalities are as follows.

Supervised learning techniques that learn a mapping from input data to output (labels) from a set of training examples have showed great promise in the interpretation of medical images. Based on parameters defining local image appearance, pattern categorization has been used for decades to detect and define anomalies in chest radiographs and mammograms. With improvements in computing power, it is now feasible to train more complex models on bigger datasets, and supervised learning has seen greater use lately in the segmentation, identification, and registration of images. In many cases, trained appearance models are taking the role of basic intensity and gradient models as a component in segmentation systems, while statistical shape models that describe the typical shape and shape variations in a collection of training shapes have replaced free form deformable models. A number of emerging strategies enable data-driven diagnosis by immediately converting imaging data to a diagnosis using multivariate classification or regression. In terms of diagnostic accuracy, these approaches often outperform more traditional quantitative analyses based on fundamental volume or density measurements since they are not bound by current knowledge of disease-related radiological patterns.

In addition to aiding in diagnosis, supervised quantification approaches are increasingly being used to predict the beginning or course of future illnesses. Then, utilizing data from longitudinal studies where the sickness condition is known years after the baseline image was collected, models are developed. A significant aspect is probably the availability of large datasets with diagnostic labels, such as the Alzheimer's Disease Neuroimaging Initiative (ADNI) and the Open Access Series of Imaging Studies (OASIS). Another illustration of how the availability of data has altered the course of research is the detection of diabetic retinopathy in retinal fundus photographs. The improvement of retinal vascular identification and segmentation was the subject of several early investigations, for which there are many smaller public datasets that include ground truth. An industry-changing Kaggle competition on the detection of diabetic retinopathy made 35000 images accessible for training with professional visual assessments. Data scientists from all around the world who have little to no experience with medical image processing have become interested in it. Despite using little to no pre-processing or segmentation, several of the 661 participating teams still produced exceptional results. The best contributions received performance ratings that were greater than those previously noted for human experts because they made use of several convolution network topologies and extensive data augmentation to increase the amount of training data even further.

It's crucial to keep in mind that this specific work utilizes 2D images. Deferential diagnosis or quantification based on entire 3D or 4D, possibly multi-modal, imaging data will need much larger training sets to accurately characterize all biological variety. Many times, more domain-specific knowledge will still be needed. However, this example shows that massive volumes of training data may significantly enhance general purpose machine learning algorithms' current state-of-the-art performance in medical image analysis and computer aided diagnosis. As direct digital imaging methods for medical diagnosis become more widespread, digital image processing is becoming increasingly crucial in healthcare. Analogue imaging modalities like endoscopy and radiography increasingly use digital sensors in addition to initially digital methods like computed tomography (CT) or magnetic resonance imaging (MRI). Digital photographs have separate brightness or color values assigned to each individual pixel (this acronym is derived from the phrases "image" and "element"). They may be quickly processed, impartially reviewed, and made accessible in several places simultaneously by employing the right communication networks and protocols, such as Picture Archiving and Communication Systems (PACS) and the Digital Imaging and Communications in Medicine (DICOM) protocol. Thanks to digital imaging techniques, the whole spectrum of image processing is now useable in medicine.

The complexity of biological images makes it difficult to communicate medical a priori knowledge in a manner that it can be directly and easily integrated into automated image processing methods. The semantic gap is a phrase used in the literature to refer to the discrepancy between a doctor's high-level cognitive interpretation of a diagnostic image and the fundamental makeup of discrete pixels utilized in computer systems to represent an image (low level). Three significant barriers stand in the way of narrowing the gap in the medical field: The heterogeneity of images Medical images depict living tissue, organs, and biological parts. The size, shape, and internal structures of these objects can vary significantly even when they are captured using the same modality and in accordance with a standard acquisition protocol, not only between patients (inter-subject variation), but also between different views of the same patient and similar views of the same patient taken at different times (intra-subject variation). In other words, both inside and between people, biological structures may alter. Universal a priori knowledge formulation is thus not possible.

Since the whole image comprises the crucial element for diagnosis or treatment, biological structures are sometimes difficult to discern from the background. Biomedical images may show identifiable objects, but segmentation is challenging since the shape or border is fuzzy or only partly represented. Consequently, things that are pertinent to medicine are often abstracted at the texturing level. The medical industry requires certain requirements for the reliability and robustness of medical processes and, when employed in routine, image processing algorithms, in addition to the inherent qualities of medical images that limit high-level processing. Automated image analysis in medicine should, in most situations, not provide findings that are incorrect. That suggests that images that can't be processed correctly must be automatically recognized as such, rejected, and taken out of the processing loop. All photos that haven't been rejected must thus be fairly evaluated. The number of rejected images cannot go too high since the majority of medical imaging procedures are risky and cannot be repeated owing to image processing errors.

The majority of afflicted countries have sealed their borders and banned travel and transportation services as part of the rapid and overwhelming global response to halt COVID-19 from spreading. In order to completely control the disease and stop the cycle that has caused this pandemic, the World Health Organization (WHO) and the Centers for Disease Control and Prevention (CDC) have issued structured recommendations for individuals, governments, and national and multinational corporations to abide by. The five steps of the WHO's global response strategy for COVID-19 are: mobilizing all facets of society to uphold social distance and hygiene; controlling sporadic cases to prevent community spread; stifling community transmission by enacting pertinent restrictions; providing healthcare services to reduce mortality; and developing COVID-19 vaccines and therapeutics.

The World Health Organization and the Centers for Disease Control and Prevention have recognized and recorded symptoms such as fever, a dry cough, vomiting, diarrhea, and myalgia (CDC). In order to reduce morbidity rates, the general public in all countries has been made aware of the need of receiving treatment as soon as feasible. Governments have started to invest freely and ardently in the research and development of the COVID-19 vaccine. In addition to this endeavor, the COVID-19 pandemic is the subject of extensive study and development. Machine learning (ML) and deep learning (DL) techniques have become popular for identifying various illnesses. The use of image processing in the healthcare sector has skyrocketed, especially for cancer detection in smart cities. This made these techniques the ideal choice for COVID-19 study. The present study emphasizes how deep learning and medical image processing techniques may help fight the COVID-19 pandemic, and it offers a thorough analysis of the cutting-edge frameworks built with these tools.

The uniqueness of this study lies in its attempt to highlight significant DL and image processing techniques proposed in the detection of COVID-19, as well as the difficulties associated with such implementations, in order to open up particular research directions that have not yet been explored or taken into account. The techniques described are taken from several published articles by respected publishers, which helps in the formation of a serious set of recommendations for the scientific community and administrative authorities in the battle against the sickness. One of the key issues in COVID-19 research is the lack of reliable and adequate data. Due to a restriction on the number of tests run, several death cases and virus-related diseases go undetected. It's difficult to determine if the COVID-19 infection detection failure factor is three, 300, or even higher. No country in the globe has been able to provide precise figures on the prevalence of the virus in a sample of the general population. Information fusion is essential because research and development efforts must continue. Information fusion is defined technically as "the process of integrating and associating information from one or more sources to offer important information for the detection, identification, and characterization of a certain entity," according to the text's contents. The accuracy of the conclusions depends on the availability of large-scale, high-quality datasets in machine learning and deep learning applications. Information fusion makes it possible to mix several datasets and utilize them in DL models to increase prediction accuracy. For instance, information fusion has integrated CT scans from Xi'an Jiaotong University, Nanchang First Hospital, and Xi'an No. 8 Hospital and put the combined data into AI and DL models.

In order to solve health-related issues involving medical images and their usage in biomedical research, clinical care, and other applications, medical image analysis develops computational and numerical methodologies. Medical imaging often uses images to assess the severity of an infection or to rank the risk level of a disease. There are several ways for establishing image accuracy as well as numerous approaches for monitoring 2D or 3D image sequences in the medical field. A customized Medical Image Tracking Toolbox (MITT) is created in the medical field to identify various diseases. This procedure is known as medical image grading. The articulation of elements associated with the pattern of images used for personal identification has resulted in substantial breakthroughs in several fields, including biometrics. The objects must be photographed close to a Led or CCD, and the recorded data must be transformed to digital data in order to get the object's pattern. A sparse representation approach is used to determine the recognition rate and data accuracy of the various types of biometric scanners that are often employed in security systems.

The capacity of tissue force disseminations of medical images to have various levels of measurable dispersion is known as heteroscedasticity. The imaging properties and processing techniques of CT scans are identical to those of MR images. The specific region of interest was mapped, and various markers were automatically expected. Neural networks collect features and convert input to binary codes to recognize numerous images. Deconstructing the arrangement data using a supervised learning system yields a capacity estimate that can be used to mapping new precedents. The language will be changed into a hypothetical situation where the algorithm will work out the marks for concealed occurrences. The "sensibly" designed learning algorithm conceals the background knowledge. Despite the widespread use of frames from unsigned burn (8-bit) to 32-bit skim, the binarization approach is used to increase performance. Information is often presented in essential form by using short, designated sentences (16-bit). The technology being utilized, such as a CT scan that gathers radio density measures or an MRI scan that gathers T1 or T2-weighted images, determines the significance of the data.

An information solution is analyzed by a supervised learning algorithm to determine capacity, which may then be utilized to map new precedents. MRI improves picture quality and boosts performance for sensitive data. MRI scans also provide better imaging. Many techniques have been developed to reduce noise in multichannel samples. The spatial affectability of various slope encoding loops is used by the medical sector to minimize the quantity of information checks required for recreation. Earlier, a number of strategies, such as conventional affectability encoding, to precisely rebuild MR images from under-inspected multichannel information have been proposed (SENSE). One of the most crucial imaging modalities employed in today's medical facilities and institutions is processed computed tomography (CT). Since x-rays may induce genetic damage and trigger the sickness indicated in the radiation section, potential radiation dangers to patients are a typical occurrence. Using a number of learning techniques, denoising the image is performed with enhanced quality and performance. In medical image grading, a supervised learning approach collects existing informational categories and known reactions to the information (yield), then develops the model to give plausible predictions for the response to new information. As part of the implementation of supervised learning models, finger-vein extraction techniques based on distinguishing line-like highlights are being reviewed and researched. In a certain neighborhood area, a vein pattern belonging to this class should have a surface that resembles a line, and finger-vein extraction techniques depend on locating valley highlights. The cross-sectional profile of a vein pattern has a valley shape because the pixel values of vein patterns are lower than those of foundation in clear portions of the finger-vein image. As a consequence, many strategies for finding the valley have been proposed. The World Health Organization (WHO) estimates that diabetes affects millions of people globally. Medical professionals often utilize a fasting plasma glucose test to identify diabetes in their patients. With the aid of a non-intrusive capturing device, images are captured and corrected. The early detection of illnesses may be achieved by using a variety of imaging techniques. To create an appearance model, one RGB vector is mapped to another using the Munshell color checker. Texture representation is necessary to calculate a picture's texture value.

MEDICAL IMAGE TECHNOLOGIES

More data storage is required due to the expanding use of Electronic Health Records (EHR) and the growth in diagnostic medical imaging worldwide. When a professional sees and analyses medical images remotely in order to make a diagnosis, it could be necessary to transport massive data sets over the network for processing. Moving huge data quantities may cause unwelcome delays, break service level agreements (SLAs), and negatively impact other users on the same infrastructure's network performance. Using cutting-edge imaging technologies like synchrotron-based X-Ray microscopy and micro spectroscopy, as well as computed tomography, research experts may quickly gather images of sub-cellular components and have a fresh dynamic view on life. Reconstruction, pre-processing, and measurement of large image datasets are thus in high demand. Medical image analysis often involves the interleaving of many tools from various sources, which causes problems with file formats, data interoperability, and communication with multi-processing computer systems. Image processing is now widely used, not only in the technological world but also in everyday life. Modern personal computers can handle enormous volumes of graphics and images with ease.

Thanks to the quick network infrastructure and modem transfer rate, images may be sent in a fraction of the time. Image editing software has become a standard item on personal computers. The Image Processing Toolbox in MATLAB, for instance, provides a comprehensive set of reference-standard algorithms and graphical tools for image processing, analysis, visualization, and method design. The user may easily do image enhancement, DE blurring, noise reduction, feature identification, image segmentation, geometric transformations, and image registration.

Numerous clinical applications, including tumor segmentation, identification, and quantification, 3D pathology modelling, the production of normal and aberrant templates (atlases), diagnosis, and therapy evaluation, call for accurate analysis of medical images. There are still a lot of issues and challenges, however, because to the enormous and complex data volume that has to be managed. Additionally, creating effective algorithms is difficult due to the enormous size of the information and the variety of anatomical shape and appearance within and across classes. On the other hand, it is impossible to manually draw the boundaries of specific locations in medical imaging. A reliable and well-automated process is thus necessary. In order to get over these present limitations, we focus on creating an efficient hybrid framework for the task of image segmentation in this research. Our core idea is based on the idea that high performance may be achieved by working together multiple complementary algorithms created from variation models, statistical classification techniques, and atlas guided procedures. According to our research, combining the proper approaches into a single, sturdy structure may help in achieving superior results. Therefore, in order to further improve the projected results, our main contribution is to create an affective hybrid solution.

Modern personal computers can handle enormous volumes of graphics and images with ease. Thanks to the quick network infrastructure and modem transfer rate, images may be sent in a fraction of the time. Image editing software has become a standard item on personal computers. The Image Processing Toolbox in MATLAB, for instance, provides a comprehensive set of reference-standard algorithms and graphical tools for image processing, analysis, visualization, and method design. The user may easily do image improvement tasks as deblurring, feature identification, noise reduction, segmenting images into groups, geometric manipulations, and image registration. Segmenting brain tumors is a relatively recent research area in the biomedical field. Image segmentation is the process of breaking a picture up into different groups. Without respect to the image's domain, the goal of image segmentation is to divide a picture into several components, such as color, intensity, brightness, textures, and so on. An important step in segmentation is the extraction of the area of interest in which we are interested. A brain tumor is the uncontrolled growth of ill or abnormal brain cells. A brain tumor affects the white matter (WM), grey matter (GM), and cerebrospinal fluid (CSF) areas, raising the intracranial pressure within the skull (CSF). The brain serves as the centre of thoughts, emotions, wisdom, communication, and coordination of muscular activities from sense organs (pain, taste, sight, hear, and touch), among other functions. It is the most sophisticated bio-computing system in the world. The size, kind, and location of the tumor all affect the symptoms of a brain tumor. Any section of the brain may be affected by tumors, and the effects vary depending on the affected area. Brain tumors come in two varieties: benign and malignant tumors.

A key advantage of using computers for medical imaging is the use of image processing techniques for quantitative analysis. Although the majority of medical images are visual in nature, human observers' ability to analyze them visually is often constrained by inter-observer variations and errors brought on by fatigue, distractions, and inexperience. Despite the fact that an expert's evaluation of a photograph is based on his or her expertise and experience, there is often always some element of subjectivity. Computer analysis has the power to provide the expert's interpretation objective support when carried out with care and reason. As a consequence, even a specialist with many years of experience may increase the confidence and accuracy of their diagnosis. In the field of imaging science, segmentation, registration, and visualization are three distinct but related topics. Segmentation, particularly in three dimensions, continues to be the pinnacle of image analysis. It is the vital but elusive ability to recognize and characterize each unique object in a visual situation. Registration is the process of identifying the change that brings several images of the same object into precise spatial (and/or temporal) congruence. Additionally, visualization involves showing, adjusting, and computing image data. In this work, the differentiation and fusion of images is a constant theme. To enhance our understanding of life processes and illness, automatic tissue segmentation and classification provide the essential differentiation, while the fusion of complementary images offers the necessary integration. The ability to quantify shape and function, both at the overall image level and at the pixel level, as well as the capacity to show and manipulate digital images, are requirements for the ability to extract clinical information from biological images. The need for innovative techniques grows as imaging technology advances and more complex things can be scanned and simulated.

The fundamental tactic that has to be adopted is problem-solving. But understanding the problem often requires a lot of upfront work. The programs included for this book are typical of those used in medical imaging; they are meant to act as examples rather than as an exhaustive list. It is anticipated that many of the suggestions made will apply to other problems. Each application begins with a description of the issue and includes illustrations based on actual instances. The methods for processing images are discussed, starting with extremely simple generic methods, and moving up to more intricate methods customized for that specific problem. The benefits and challenges of transitioning from a research-based solution to a clinical one are also covered. Biomedical imaging is mostly an applied science that uses imaging ideas to diagnose and treat disease as well as get a basic understanding of how life functions. Developing such abilities is a time-honored practice in research labs. Making novel technologies available outside of the lab where they were developed is tough so that others may use them and modify them for other purposes. A broader community may then benefit from the ideas, talents, and skills of certain individuals, making it simpler to translate effective research methods into routine clinical use. Techniques for nonlinear signal and image processing have become more and more common during the last three decades. There are four different categories of nonlinear filters: order statistic, morphological, homomorphic, and polynomial. The 1970s invention of homomorphic filters is based on a development of the superposition concept. The polynomial filters, which are based on traditional nonlinear system theory, use the Volterra series. In many ways, linear system and filter analysis and design and homomorphic and polynomial filter analysis and design are the same. Extensions of linear methods, on the other hand, are useless for analyzing the order statistic and morphological filters. One type of order statistic filter is the median filter, which is arguably the most well-known and frequently used.

CONCLUSION

This article examines medical image processing, including the challenges it faces in the MATLAB environment and all of its benefits. The rest of the document is organized as follows: This research is divided into six sections. The first section provides an overview of the research. It provides a thorough review of technology for medical image processing and visualization. The second section of the essay describes the aim of the research and the challenges of processing medical images. The third section goes into the various tools and how they are used to the study. The latter two portions of the essay offer the results, conclusions, and future developments. Mathematical morphology, a subset of set algebra, serves as the foundation for morphological filters. Since morphological filters use extreme order statistics (minimum and maximum values) within a filter window, they are closely related to order statistic filters. While order statistic filters are often chosen using more heuristic methods, the methods used to define homomorphic and polynomial filters are employed to create and assess them. Because of this, the behavior of the median filter and other comparable filters was unclear for a long time. The root signals, a class of signals invariant to median filtering, were found using a unique approach that was developed in the early 1980s as a result of significant results on the statistical behavior of the median filter.

REFERENCES

Elmogy, A. M. (2017). Image noise detection and removal based on enhanced gridLOF algorithm. *Image*, *8*(12).

Fan, J., Zeng, G., Body, M., & Hacid, M. (2005). Seeded region growing: An extensive and comparative study. *PatternRecog. Lett.*, *26*(8), 1139-56.

Gill, N. K. & Sharma, A. (2016). Noise Models and De-noising Techniques in Digital Image Processing. *International Journal of Computer & Mathematical Sciences, 5*(1), 21-25.

Gonzalez, R., & Woods, R. (2002). *Digital Image Processing.* Prentice Hall.

Kasban, El-Bendary, & Salama. (2015). A comparative study of medical imaging techniques. *International Journal of Information Science and Intelligent System, 4*(2), 37–58.

Khandare, S. T. (2014). A Survey Paper on Image Segmentation with Thresholding. *International Journal of ComputerScience and Mobile Computing, 3*(1), 441–446.

Marcel, J., & Soruba, AJayachandran, GSundararaj, K. (2012). An efficient algorithm for removal of impulse noise using Adaptive Fuzzy Switching Weighted Median Filter. *International Journal of Computer Technology and Electronics Engineering, 2*(2).

Matthews, P. M., & Jezzard, P. (2004). Functional magnetic resonance imaging. *Journal of Neurology, Neurosurgery, and Psychiatry, 75*(1), 6–12. PMID:14707297

Khan, M. (2014). A Survey: Image Segmentation Techniques. *International Journal of FutureComputer and Communication, 3*(2).

Qu, J., & Xu, J. (2020). Image salt and pepper noise adaptive based on fuzzy median filtering. In *Twelfth International Conference on Digital Image Processing* (vol. 11519). International Society for Optics and Photonics. 10.1117/12.2573114

Shrimali, S. (2009). Current trends in segmentation of medical ultrasound B-mode images: A review. *IETE Tech. Rev, 1*(8), 26.

Suetens, P. (2017). *Fundamentals of medical imaging*. Cambridge University Press. doi:10.1017/9781316671849

van Sloun, RCohen, REldar, Y. (2019). Deep learning in ultrasound imaging. *Proceedings of the IEEE, 108,* 11-29.

Webb, A. G. (2017). *Introduction to biomedical imaging*. John Wiley & Sons.

Wen, H. (2019). Biomedical X-Ray Phase-Contrast Imaging and Tomography. In *Springer Handbook of Microscopy* (pp. 2–2). Springer. doi:10.1007/978-3-030-00069-1_30

Chapter 13
Smart Healthcare Application Implementation of AI and Blockchain Technology

B. Satheesh Kumar

https://orcid.org/0000-0001-7964-616X

Karpagam Academy of Higher Education, Coimbatore, India

K. Sampath Kumar

Galgotias University, India

ABSTRACT

Patients can control, share, and manage their health records with family, friends, and healthcare professionals utilizing electronic health records (EHRs), which use an open channel, or the Internet. When a lot of data is available, DL methods show promise in these health applications. A distributed blockchain-based IoT system would benefit greatly from these ideas. This research proposes novel technique in Healthcare Data Based Feature Selection and Classification Using Blockchain and Machine Learning Architectures. The network has been secured using centralized blockchain sensor network. Here the input sensor-based healthcare data has been collected and processed for noise removal and smoothening. Then the processed data feature has been selected using Greedy Mixed Forward Colony Optimization feature selection. The suggested framework's superiority is supported by security research and experimental findings using the IoT-Botnet and ToN-IoT datasets. Proposed technique attained acc of 95%, precision of 85%, recall of 76%, F1 score of 63%, sec rate of 95%, DT Rate of 85%.

INTRODUCTION

Recent years have seen a tremendous increase in efforts to automate the processes used to collect and evaluate healthcare data specific to humans. There are numerous technologies in use to gather data specifically related to health, as well as analysis tools to examine the types of data that determine the state of human health (Mansour, 2022). Biomedical data analysts have faced a significant hurdle as a result.

DOI: 10.4018/978-1-6684-7697-0.ch013

There are many new data types relating to health that have been discovered in contemporary biomedical research, including text, visual patterns, sound records, sensor data, and other electronic health records. These data kinds are all evolving into more complicated entities. We need to complete two processes using conventional data mining and statistical analysis methods in order to (a) recover highly efficient and reliable characteristics from recorded data, and (b) thereafter create models for predictions. We face numerous obstacles and require adequate subject knowledge due to the complexity of the data (Ambika, 2020). Deep learning techniques have recently been actively offering ways to handle such complicated data employing numerous efficient learning models with such problems. EHRs can now record a variety of data, such as a patient's medical history, laboratory test results, demographics, drug and allergy information, immunisation status, radiological pictures, and vital signs, in addition to basic patient information and administrative activities. Doctors, healthcare professionals, and public health professionals used EHRs in the past to store as well as extract patient data for clinical care (Ashima et al., 2021). Secondary use of EHR data for tool creation intends to enable medical professionals as well as policy makers launch or adjust therapies, comprehend the progression of disease, and propose or enhance policies to help avoid disease (Gladence et al., 2020). It is challenging to create effective analytical models using traditional statistical analysis techniques because patient information in EHRs is very variable and contains dimensions, class unbalanced data, and missing data (Sherasiya et al., 2016). When smart devices are constrained and must convey essential data for some critical scenarios when a choice must be made precisely and on time, idea of trust, as well as security, becomes even more important Patients value a safe as well as high-quality healthcare service above everything else. As a result, healthcare data security and patient privacy are critical concerns that will have a significant impact on blockchain IoT future success (Imran et al., 2021). The protection of privacy is one of the most pressing concerns in IIoT-based healthcare system. A healthcare service provider, in general, collects data from its users as well as shares it with registered clinics or healthcare professionals. Data may also be distributed to health insurance companies as well as pharmaceutical firms by the provider. Furthermore, during cloud transfer or synchronisation with associated devices, patient data may be accessible to hackers. As a result, we must protect sensitive data from illegal access, which could result in public disclosure of personal data or interference with life-saving medical equipment, such as a pacemaker. A breach in the security of a patient's monitoring equipment as well as data could result in social embarrassment, mental illnesses, or negative physical consequences such as a fatal heart attack. As a result, in an blockchain IoT-based healthcare system, data protection in form of watermarking as well as authentication is critical. The capacity to anticipate disease start with high accuracy is made feasible by the availability of EHRs, advancements in hardware (such as CPUs and GPUs), and computer algorithms. Regarding diabetes, the majority of studies utilising EHRs assessed significance of typical ML methods in predicting the course of diabetes. To overcome these difficulties, non-parametric modelling techniques from the literature on machine learning may be used. A programme that "learns to perform a task or make a decision automatically from data, rather than having the behaviour explicitly programmed," is what is meant by machine learning. In actuality, these algorithms or programmes fall along a spectrum, ranging from totally machine-driven to fully human-guided. Use of SVM to determine flu-related tweets to discover influenza trends, use of RF and LSTM networks to detect credit card fraud, and use of DCNN to recognise and classify objects in images are just a few examples of successful ML applications based on non-EHR data (Awotunde et al., 2021).

Contribution of this research is as follows:

1. To propose novel method in Healthcare Data Based Feature Selection and Classification Using Blockchain and Machine Learning Architectures for smart applications.
2. The network has been secured using centralized blockchain sensor network. Then the processed data feature has been selected using Greedy Mixed Forward Colony Optimisation feature selection.
3. The selected feature has been classified using Fuzzy Bayesian adversarial vector machine.

RELATED WORKS

Numerous research teams have attempted to use DL techniques in medical big data analysis in recent years (Adeniyi et al., 2021). In order to improve brain state decoding, Work (Amit & Chinmay, 2021) first examines brain state signal. However, there is a lot of noise data and the algorithm does not analyse the brain state signal well. Author (Ayo et al., 2020) created a deep learning architecture to categorise the findings of data analysis. The deep learning framework's extensive layer count contributes to the algorithm's poor time performance. In order to assess medical images, work (Abdulraheem et al., 2021) suggested using supervised as well as unsupervised learning algorithms to learn properties of deep convolution images. However, the system can only process medical picture data and not medical text data. Based on data from medical transcripts, author (Bakhtawar et al., 2021) analyses data using a DL network as well as generalised estimation equations to assess efficacy of diabetic management. The extended estimating equation's assumptions are more exacting, though, and the model is not transferable. Work (Rao et al., 2022) highlights how medical big data might offer clinical researchers information in unprecedented quantities. But there is no practical way to examine medical data. Work (Balyan et al., 2022) suggests an automated data analysis approach that examines information from heart failure patients who are hospitalised and makes precise predictions about the likelihood of mortality and pre-hospitalization within the next 30 days. While using a less involved strategy to assess the data, this approach concentrates on the probabilistic predictions that come afterwards. The tensor decomposition technique is used by the author (14), who examines each patient's physical health state and test indicators. However, the relationship between the images cannot be examined, which could lead to incorrect evaluation of the recognition outcome. In work (Nguyen et al., 2021), a cognitive approach based on natural language processing was investigated for study as well as recognition of patient illness states. This approach, however, is unable to examine the link between an image's constituent pieces and its subtleties, and it is also unable to handle text records of arbitrary sizes (Nadeem et al., 2021). DL is capable of automatically learning represented features from input data, which minimizes need for feature engineering (Imran et al., 2021). This is in contrast to classical ML (DT, RF, and SVM (Vijai & Wisetsri, 2021)) and statistical methods for prediction of patient mortality utilizing hazard ratios (survival analysis (Zhang et al., 2022)) and onset of diabetes utilising risk factors (logistic regression (Das et al., 2022)). In (Gupta et al., 2020), a two-way convergence of blockchain with ML was discussed. Blockchain with ML features provided security and reliability. ML was the tool used for optimizing blockchain networks. In (Pokhrel, 2020), present blockchain based on AI techniques were examined for energy-cloud management, were the security and privacy issues were listed out. In(Singh et al., 2020), a comprehensive study on blockchain-AI applications was presented along with their relationship in IoT-enabled ecosystem. But, MEC which is a key technology of evolving 5G networks were not concentrated. In (Rametta & Schembra, 2017), blockchain techniques in 5G networks were discussed and a short survey was presented. Three major challenges were identified namely identity authentication, privacy, and trust management along with few blockchain-based solutions. In (García-Magariño et al., 2019), a short survey on blockchain enabled federated model was described. In (Hattab & Cabric, 2020), motivation to integrate MEC with blockchain was presented. Edge computing was employed to enable mobile blockchains.

SYSTEM MODEL

This section discusses novel technique in Healthcare Data Based Feature Selection and Classification Using Blockchain and Machine Learning Architectures for smart applications. The network has been secured using centralized blockchain sensor network. Here the input sensor based healthcare data has been collected and processed for noise removal and smoothening. Then the processed data feature has been selected using Greedy Mixed Forward Colony Optimisation feature selection. The selected feature has been classified using Fuzzy Bayesian adversarial vector machine. the proposed architecture is shown in figure 1.

Figure 1. Overall proposed architecture

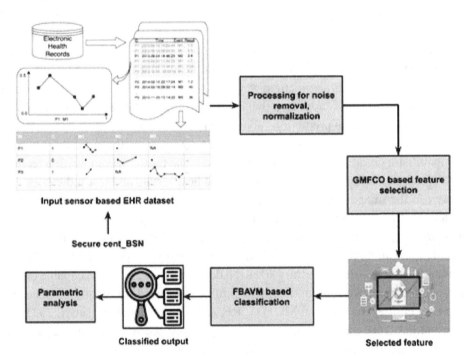

Each sample in raw data belongs to a particular patient as a time-ordered sequence of EHR events $E=(e_1,e_2,...,e_T)$, where e t is an observed event ordered by t ∈ 1, ..., T. Each vector entry is further converted as seen in the second phase. Numerical features are standard normalised, categorical characteristics are transformed into their respective one-hot binary feature vectors. Thus, a highly sparse, 80,000-dimensional vector et—not necessarily one-hot—results from the vectorization of a particular event et.

Greedy Mixed Forward Colony Optimisation (GMFCO) Feature Selection

The choice of an evaluation criterion is a crucial decision because it has an immediate impact on the outcomes. The widely used modularity, which is typically designated as Q and was first suggested by Newman, is the fitness function employed in this research. It is possible to write the fitness function as eq. (1)

$$\text{fit}\ (-) = Q = \frac{1}{2m} \sum_{\bar{i}}^{n} \left(A_{\bar{i}} - \frac{k_i - k_i}{2m} \right) \delta (i, j) \tag{1}$$

where n and m refer to a network's nodes and edges, respectively; ki is a node's degree; if I and j are in the same group, $\delta(i,j)$ otherwise, $\delta(i,j)$ Modularity has been demonstrated to be a useful metric for assessing the quality of a partition. Typically, we presume that the division is better the higher the value of Q. First, using r1 parameters as an equation, p observations are linearly produced. (2):

$$y = Cz \tag{2}$$

Here, observation vector, parameter vector, and supplied measurement matrix are designated as y $\in$ R p, z $\in$ R r1 and C $\in$ R p×r1, respectively. It should be observed that Eq (3) makes the assumption that noise does not exist. (1). A pseudo-inverse operation by eq(3) can be used to acquire estimated parameters z.

$$y = \begin{cases} C^{\mathrm{T}} \left(CC^{\mathrm{T}} \right)^{-1} y, & p < r_1, \\ \left(C^{\mathrm{T}} C \right)^{-1} C^{\mathrm{T}} y, & p \geq r_1. \end{cases} \tag{3}$$

Considered is uncorrelated Gaussian noise with zero mean and constant variance across all observation points. For the case p $\geq$ r1, Joshi and Boyd unmistakably shown an objective function to construct optimum evaluation method. They sought to maximise the logarithm of Fisher data matrix's determinant, which, according to Eq. (4), realised least ellipsoid volume of anticipated estimation error z z.

$$\text{maximize logdet}(C^{\mathrm{T}} C) \tag{4}$$

In Eq. (3) the measurement matrix (4) changes to C = HC, with C serving as a total measurement matrix best places to place sensors by figuring out H if C is known. A greedy selection was proven using the U1:r1 matrix to seek Eq, as illustrated in Algorithm 1.. Singular value decomposition (SVD) in equation provides the reduced-order representation of a data matrix X $\in$ R n×m (n > m) and its reduced-order form. (5):

$$X = U\Sigma V^{\mathrm{T}}$$

$$= \begin{bmatrix} U_{1:r_1} & U_{(r_1+1):m} \end{bmatrix} \begin{bmatrix} \Sigma_{1:r_1} & 0 \\ 0 & \Sigma_{(r_1+1):m} \end{bmatrix} \begin{bmatrix} V_{1:r_1}^{\mathrm{T}} \\ V_{(r_1+1):m}^{\mathrm{T}} \end{bmatrix}$$

$$= U_{1:r_1}\Sigma_{1:r_1}V_{1:r_1}^{\mathrm{T}} + U_{(r_1+1):m}\Sigma_{(r_1+1):m}V_{(r_1+1):m}^{\mathrm{T}} \tag{5}$$

$$\equiv X_{1:r_1} + X_{(r_1+1):m}$$

$$\approx X_{1:r_1}.$$

The notation Ai:j for a given matrix A represents a low-rank representation of A, utilising the ith-to-jth singular values or vectors. $\Sigma \in \mathbb{R}^{m \times m}$ and $V \in \mathbb{R}^{m \times m}$ are diagonal matrices representing the singular values and temporal modes, respectively. It should be highlighted that POD can be processed by SVD if the data have undergone uniform spatial and temporal desensitisation. Additionally, notation A I k for a given quantity A designates that the amount's kth component will be examined in this stepwise selection, with (k1) components provided by (k1) selected sensors. Following kth selection phase, Ak is built using k sensors chosen. C I k and Ck, for instance, are written as eq. (6):

$$C_k^{(i)} = \begin{bmatrix} u_{i_1}^{\mathrm{T}} & u_{i_2}^{\mathrm{T}} & \cdots & u_{i_{k-1}}^{\mathrm{T}} & u_i^{\mathrm{T}} \end{bmatrix}^{\mathrm{T}}$$

$$C_k = C_k^{(i)}\Big|_{i=i_k}, \tag{6}$$

Network is referred to as a weighted graph in the proposed approach (G). G consists of edges between vehicles and within vehicles. Eq displays a depiction of G. 7.

$$G = (V, R) \tag{7}$$

where R stands for a group of edges known as the route between vehicles and V = {1...., n} denotes the group of cars in G. The route structure is displayed in Equation 8.

$$R = \{(i,j): i, j \in V\} \tag{8}$$

The m ants are distributed randomly across these n cities, and di j is used to indicate the distance between any two cities di j (,). The set of ant pheromone concentrations between two cities is known as i j, τ The initial pheromone concentration is the same in both cities. The probabilities of a transition for an ant k moving from city I to city j at time t are given by eq. (9):

$$\Delta\tau_{i,j}(t) = \sum_{k=1}^{m} \Delta\tau_{i,j}^k(t) \tag{9}$$

Wherein "k allowed" refers to the group of cities that "k allowed" is allowed to travel to next. When ants choose a path, the symbol symbolises the pheromone's level of influence. After the m ants have completed traversing all n cities in order, update the pheromone in order to prevent the heuristic from having no effect due to an excess of residual pheromone in the path. The pheromone update formula is thus as eq., (10) in the time t n.:

$$\tau_{i,j}\left(t+n\right)=\left(1-\rho\right)\tau_{i,j}\left(t\right)+\rho\cdot"\tau_{i,j}\left(t\right)$$

$$\Delta\tau_{i,j}\left(t\right)=\sum_{k=1}^{m}\Delta\tau_{i,j}^{k}\left(t\right) \tag{10}$$

The degree of pheromone volatilization is indicated by the expression $\rho(0<\rho<1)$ i in the formula above. The number 1 denotes the pheromone's remaining strength. The sum of the residual pheromone increase throughout the route for this iteration is represented by $\Delta\tau_{i,j}(t)$. Set Initial Time is, $\Delta\tau_{i,j}(0)=0$ represents amount of pheromone left behind by ant k along the route $\Delta\tau_{i,j}^{k}\left(t\right)$. A typical computational model is depicted in eq. (11):

$$\Delta\tau_{i,j}^{k}\left(t\right)=\begin{cases}Q/D_{k}, & \text{the route of } k \text{ ant in this iteration}\\0, & \text{other}\end{cases} \tag{11}$$

Q is a constant that, to some extent, affects the rate of convergence. In this iteration, DK is the path length by ant k.

Fuzzy Bayesian Adversarial Vector Machine

The largest classification interval is equivalent to minimising $\|w\|^2$, which is the normal vector of the classification plane. To correctly categorise all samples, a classification plane is necessary. Equation (12) provides the constraint condition:

$$yi(\omega x_i + b) - 1 \geq 0 \tag{12}$$

Resulting IT2FM ($\varphi 0(\sigma)$) for $\sigma \in$ (Mansour, 2022) can be formulated as eq. (13):

$$\phi_o(\sigma) = P\sigma k(\sigma) \tag{13}$$

where $k(\sigma)$ is defined as eq. (14)

$$k\left(\sigma\right)=\frac{1}{2}\left(\frac{1}{\alpha+\sigma-\alpha\sigma}+\frac{-1+\alpha}{-1+\alpha\sigma}\right) \tag{14}$$

Table 1. Algorithm of GMFCO

Algorithm of GMFCO:
Input: parent_one, parent_two, dist
Output: Child one, child two, start_c
For i=1 to n do
Start child one, child two
Update child one, determine right_one and right 2 cities the parent individual 6
If dist(right one 6)< dist (right_two,6) then
Else
Update element at second position of child one to right two
End if
Delete city 6 from parent as well as update parent
Similarly update child two
End for
$i_1 = \operatorname{argmax}_{i \in S} u_i u_i^T$
$C_1 = u_{i_1}$
for $k= 2,\ldots,r_1,\ldots,p$ do
if $k \leq r_1$ then
$i_k \qquad = \operatorname{argmax}_{i \in S \setminus S_k} \det\left(C_k^{(i)} C_k^{(i)T} \right)$
$= \operatorname{argmax}_{i \in S \setminus S_k} \det\left(\begin{bmatrix} C_{k-1} \\ u_i \end{bmatrix} \begin{bmatrix} C_{k-1}^T & u_i^T \end{bmatrix} \right)$
$= \operatorname{argmax}_{i \in S \setminus S_k} u_i \left(I - C_{k-1}^T \left(C_{k-1} C_{k-1}^T \right)^{-1} C_{k-1} \right) u_i^T$
else
$i_k = \operatorname{argmax}_{i \in S \setminus S_k} \det\left(\boldsymbol{C}_k^{(i)T} \boldsymbol{C}_k^{(i)} \right)$
$= \operatorname{argmax}_{i \in S \setminus S_k} \det\left(\begin{bmatrix} C_{k-1}^T & u_i^T \end{bmatrix} \begin{bmatrix} C_{k-1} \\ u_i \end{bmatrix} \right)$
$= \operatorname{argmax}_{i \in S \setminus S_k} \left(1 + u_i \left(C_{k-1}^T C_{k-1} \right)^{-1} u_i^T \right)$
end if
$C_k = \begin{bmatrix} C_{k-1}^T & u_{ik}^T \end{bmatrix}^T$
end for

A type-2 fuzzy set M~ Q ij is given as eq. (15)

$$\tilde{M}_{ij}^{Q} = \left\{ \left(p_{ij}, \mu_{M_{ij}^{Q}} \right), \mu_{\tilde{M}_{ij}^{Q}} \left(p_{ij}, \mu_{M_{ij}^{Q}} \right) \; \forall p_{ij} \in I \right.$$

$$\left. \forall \mu_{M_{ij}^{Q}} \in J_{p_{ij}} \subseteq [0,1] \right\} \tag{15}$$

$$m_k\left(X_{ij}^{Q}\right)=\begin{cases}\dfrac{1}{2k-1}\sum_{i=q-k+1}^{q+k-1}x_i & \text{for odd } n\\[4pt]\dfrac{1}{2k}\sum_{i=q-k+1}^{q+k}x_i & (n=2q-1)\\[4pt] & \text{for even } n\\[4pt] & (n=2q)\end{cases}\tag{16}$$

Each element of the type-1 fuzzy set, X Q ij = {x1, x2, x3, ..., xn}, in a window of size $(2Q+1)\times(2Q+1)$ has an associated GMF defined as eq. (17)

$$\mu_{M_{ij}}^{(Q,k)}\left(x_n\right)=e^{-\left(x_n-v_{ij}^{(Q,k)}\right)^2/2\left(\sigma_{ij}^{Q}\right)^2}.\tag{17}$$

Then, q distinct means are produced as eq using the k-middle mean. (18)

$$v_{ij}^{(Q,k)}=m_k\left(X_{ij}^{Q}\right),\ k=1,2,3,\ldots q\tag{18}$$

Equation (19) is used to calculate standard deviation for k-middle means in a window.

$$\sigma_{ij}^{Q}=m_h\left(\Omega_{ij}^{Q}\right)$$

$$\Omega_{ij}^{Q}=\left|x_n-v_{\text{avg}}\right|,\ \ \forall x_n\in X_{ij}^{Q}\tag{19}$$

$$v_{\text{avg}}=\frac{1}{q}\sum_{k=1}^{q}v_{ij}^{(Q,k)}$$

Second sub step involves obtaining a matrix Δij utilising the q membership values for every window's dominant convolved feature. Matrix Δij can be written as eq., (20) in mathematics.

$$\Delta_{ij}=\begin{bmatrix}\mu_{M_{ij}}^{(Q,1)}\left(x_1\right) & \mu_{M_{ij}}^{(Q,1)}\left(x_2\right) & \cdots & \mu_{M_{ij}}^{(Q,1)}\left(x_n\right)\\[4pt]\mu_{M_{ij}}^{(Q,2)}\left(x_1\right) & \mu_{M_{ij}}^{(Q,2)}\left(x_2\right) & \cdots & \mu_{M_{ij}}^{(Q,2)}\left(x_n\right)\\[4pt]\cdots & \cdots & \cdots & \cdots\\[4pt]\mu_{M_{ij},q}^{(Q,q)}\left(x_1\right) & \mu_{M_{ij}}^{(Q,q)}\left(x_2\right) & \cdots & \mu_{M_{ij}}^{(Q,q)}\left(x_n\right)\end{bmatrix}\tag{20}$$

Interval Type-2 Fuzzy Membership becomes eq. (21),

$$\underline{u}_j(x_i) = \begin{cases} \dfrac{\sum_{k=1}^{C}\left(\left(d_{ji}/d_{ki}\right)+\alpha\left(d_{ji}/d_{ki}\right)\delta\right)^{2/(m_1-1)}}{\sum_{k=1}^{C}\left(\left(d_{ji}/d_{ki}\right)+\alpha\left(d_{ji}/d_{ki}\right)\delta\right)^{2/(m_1-1)}} \\[4pt] \text{if } \dfrac{1}{\sum_{k=1}^{C}\left(d_{ji}/d_{ki}\right)} \geq \dfrac{1}{C} \\[4pt] \dfrac{\sum_{k=1}^{C}\left(\left(d_{ji}/d_{ki}\right)+\alpha\left(d_{ji}/d_{ki}\right)\delta\right)^{2/(m_2-1)}}{\sum_{k=1}^{C}\left(\left(d_{ji}/d_{ki}\right)+\alpha\left(d_{ji}/d_{ki}\right)\delta\right)^{2/(m_2-1)}} \\[4pt] \text{otherwise} \end{cases} \tag{21}$$

Type reduction and hard-partitioning can be acquired as eq. (22)

$$u_j(x_i) = \frac{u_i^{R}(x_i)+u_j^{L}(x_i)}{2}, j=1,\ldots,C,$$

$$u_j^{R}(x_i) = \frac{\sum_{l=1}^{M}u_{il}(x_i)}{M},$$

where

$$u_{jl}(x_i) = \begin{cases} \overline{u}_j(x_i), & \text{if } x_{il} \text{ uses } \overline{u}_j(x_i) \text{ for } v_j^{R}, \\ \underline{u}_j(x_i), & \text{otherwise}, \end{cases} \tag{22}$$

Figure 2. Type-2 system of the fuzzy logic system

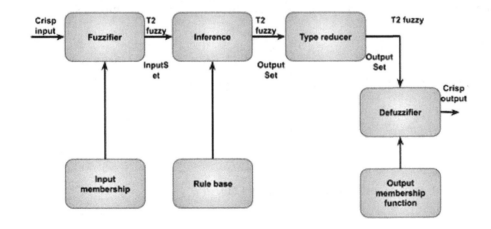

A method of empirical selection is used to determine the Upper Membership values function. As shown in Figure 2, our approach offers an additional set of configurable parameters that are dependent on the Type-2 Fuzzy Logic Systems (FLS) Centroid-type for reduction method ().

The concept is analogous to solving eq., (23) mathematically.

$$\frac{1}{2}\mathbf{w}^T\mathbf{w} + C\sum_{i=1}^{n}\xi_{i,t}$$

subject to $\quad y_i\left(\mathbf{w}^T\mathbf{s}\left(\mathbf{x}_i\right)+b\right) \geq 1-\xi_{i,t},$

$$\xi_{i,1} \geq 0, \text{ for } i = 1,\ldots,n, \tag{23}$$

$$\text{Max}_a \sum_{i=1}^{n}\alpha_i - \frac{1}{2}\sum_{i=1}^{n}\sum_{j=1}^{n}\alpha_i\alpha_j y_i y_j K\left(\mathbf{x}_i,\mathbf{x}_j\right)$$

subject to $\sum_{i=1}^{n}\alpha_i y_i = 0, 0 \leq \alpha_i \leq C, i = 1,2,\ldots,n$ (24)

$$\sum_{i\in SV}a_i y_i K\left(\mathbf{x}_i,\mathbf{x}\right)+b = 0. \tag{25}$$

Consequently, sign(D(x)), with eq, (26) assigns the label of an instance x.

$$D\left(\mathbf{x}\right) = \sum_{i\in SV}\hat{a}_i y_i K\left(\mathbf{x}_i,\mathbf{x}\right)+b \tag{26}$$

where the projected value of an is represented by a. The bias term bj is theoretically shown to be the same for every instance in the SV (Gupta et al., 2020).

$$b_j = y_j - \sum_{i\in SV}\hat{a}_i y_i K\left(\mathbf{x}_i,\mathbf{x}_j\right) \tag{27}$$

a k-category classification issue where the value of class label, yi, comes from 1. . . Generally speaking, k is broken down into a series of one-versus-all binary classification problems. m-th binary classification, when m = 1. . . as, Kk, and m-th kernel form by eqn (28)

$$D_m\left(\mathbf{x}\right) = \sum_{i\in SV_m}a_i^{(m)} y_i^{(m)} K_m\left(\mathbf{x}_i,\mathbf{x}\right)+b^{(m)} \tag{28}$$

A majority voting approach can be used to determine final class label for an instance utilizing evaluated decision functions from all m-th binary classifications. There are many common kernels available for the SVM process. Gaussian RBF kernel, for example, has radial kernel K (x, x 0) = f(kx x 0k 2/2) by eqn (29),

$$K\left(\mathbf{x},\mathbf{x}'\right)=\exp\left(-\mathbf{x}-\mathbf{x}'^{2}/2\sigma^{2}\right) \tag{29}$$

A different kind of kernel, such as a polynomial kernel with degree d eq., (30), has form of inner product K (x, x 0) = f (x, x 0 >).

$$K\left(\mathbf{x},\mathbf{x}'\right)=\left(1+\mathbf{x},\mathbf{x}'\right)^{d} \tag{30}$$

For example, in two-dimensional scenario, eq. (31) will transfer a minor changed(x) in input space to ds(x) in feature space.

$ds(x) = \nabla s \bullet dx$

$$\nabla\mathbf{s}=\left(\frac{\partial\mathbf{s}\left(\mathbf{x}\right)}{\partial\mathbf{x}}\right)=\begin{pmatrix}\dfrac{\partial s_{1}\left(\mathbf{x}\right)}{\partial x_{1}} & \cdots & \dfrac{\partial s_{1}\left(\mathbf{x}\right)}{\partial x_{p}} \\ \vdots & \vdots & \vdots \\ \dfrac{\partial s_{1}\left(\mathbf{x}\right)}{\partial x_{1}} & \cdots & \dfrac{\partial s_{1}\left(\mathbf{x}\right)}{\partial x_{p}}\end{pmatrix} \tag{31}$$

As a result, squared length of ds(x) is expressed as eq., (32) in quadratic form.

$$\| \, \mathbf{ds}\left(\mathbf{x}\right)\|^{2}=\left(\mathbf{ds}\left(\mathbf{x}\right)\right)^{T}\mathbf{ds}\left(\mathbf{x}\right)=\sum_{ij}s_{ij}\left(\mathbf{x}\right)dx_{i}\,dx_{j}, \\ s_{ij}\left(\mathbf{x}\right)=\left(\nabla\mathbf{s}\right)^{T}\cdot\left(\nabla\mathbf{s}\right). \tag{32}$$

Finding approximate locations of support vectors as well as initial bounds at this step is crucial. The adaptive data dependent kernel transformation function is described as eq., (33) which is analogous to concept of conformal transformation in binary case.

$$c\left(\mathbf{x}\right)=\begin{cases}\exp\left(-p_{1}\left(\mathbf{x}\right)\big|D_{1}\left(\mathbf{x}\right)\big|\right), & \text{if }\mathbf{x}\in S_{1} \\ \exp\left(-p_{2}\left(\mathbf{x}\right)\big|D_{2}\left(\mathbf{x}\right)\big|\right), & \text{if }\mathbf{x}\in S_{2} \\ \cdots \\ \exp\left(-p_{k}\left(\mathbf{x}\right)\big|D_{k}\left(\mathbf{x}\right)\big|\right), & \text{if }\mathbf{x}\in S_{k}\end{cases} \tag{33}$$

where m = 1 and pm(x). . ., k, are data functions that will be chosen to regulate decay rates and therefore impact the classifier's performance.

PERFORMANCE ANALYSIS

Three open-source broker software solutions that were deployed utilizing VMs were used to examine each of the distinct monitoring situations on version 3.1. Three VMs used to deploy broker software were hosted by Oracle Virtual Box (Oracle, 2018) on a Windows 10 computer with 64GB RAM, an Intel Core i7-5820K processor, six physical CPUs, and twelve virtual CPUs operating at 3.30GHz.

Dataset description: Over 98% of people in UK are registered with a general practise (GP), which serves as initial point of contact for medical needs under UK National Health Service. CPRD is a service that gathers longitudinal primary care data from a network of UK general practitioners that have been deidentified and linked to secondary care, other health databases, and administrative databases for specific geographic areas. Hospital Episode Statistics, Office of National Statistics, Public Health England, and Index of Multiple Deprivation are a few examples of these linked databases. Nearly one in ten GP units provide data to CPRD. It combines primary care records with mortality data from national death registries and discharge diagnoses from Hospital Episode Statistics (Nadeem et al., 2021) in a manner that is comparable to WHO International Classification of Diseases-10th Revision (ICD-10). National Patient Register (Das et al., 2022) as well as Civil Registration System (Gupta et al., 2020) data, which contain data of a more contextual nature, were merged with the EHR data. These data were utilized to incorporate contextual factors in addition to information on age, marital status, and comorbidities that had been registered prior to the present admission. The information was taken from the "CROSSTRACKS" research project.

Table 2. Comparative analysis between proposed and existing technique based on various dataset

Parameters	Techniques	Accuracy	Precision	Recall	F1_Score	Security rate	Data transmission rate
CPRD	CNN	81	71	64	51	85	72
	SVM	85	73	65	53	88	75
	HDFS_MLA	88	75	68	55	89	77
ICD-10	CNN	82	76	65	52	88	75
	SVM	89	79	69	57	91	79
	HDFS_MLA	92	81	72	59	93	82
National Patient Register	CNN	85	79	69	55	89	79
	SVM	89	82	73	59	93	83
	HDFS_MLA	95	85	76	63	95	85

The above table-1 shows comparative analysis between proposed and existing technique based on various healthcare dataset. Here the parameters analyzed are accuracy, precision, recall, F-1 score, security rate, data transmission rate. Accuracy calculation is done by the general prediction capability of projected DL method. For calculating F-score, number of images processed are EEG signal for both existing and proposed technique. The F-score reveals each feature ability to discriminate independently from other features. For the first feature, a score is generated, and for the second feature, a different score is obtained. However, it says nothing about how the two elements work together. Here, calculating the F-score using exploitation has determined the prediction performance. It is created by looking at the harmonic component of recall and precision. If the calculated score is 1, it is considered excellent, whereas a score of 0 indicates poor performance. The actual negative rate is not taken into consideration by F-measures. The accuracy of a class is calculated by dividing the total items classified as belonging to positive class by number of true positives. Probability that a classification function will produce a true positive rate when present. It is also known by the acronym TP amount. In this context, recall is described as ratio of total number of components that genuinely fall into a positive class to several true positives. How well a method can recognize Positive samples is calculated by recall. Recall increases as more positive samples are determined.

Figure 3. Comparative analysis between proposed and existing technique for CPRD dataset

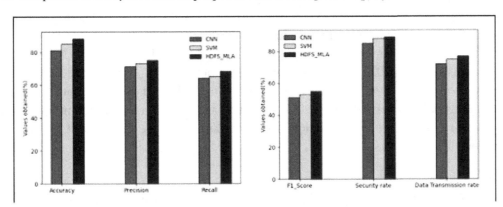

The above figure-3 shows comparative analysis between proposed and existing technique for CPRD dataset. Here proposed technique attained accuracy of 88%, precision of 75%, recall of 68%, F-1 score of 55%, security rate of 89%, data transmission rate of 77%; CNN attained accuracy of 81%, precision of 71%, recall of 64%, F-1 score of 51%, security rate of 85%, data transmission rate of 72%; SVM attained accuracy of 85%, precision of 73%, recall of 65%, F-1 score of 53%, security rate of 88%, data transmission rate of 75%.

Figure 4. Comparative analysis between proposed and existing technique for ICD-10 dataset

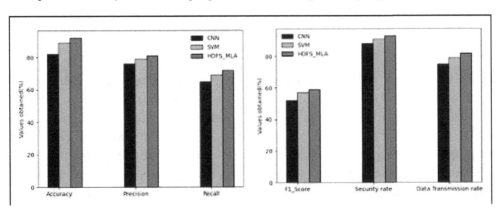

From above figure-4 shows comparative analysis between proposed and existing technique for ICD-10 dataset. Here proposed technique attained accuracy of 92%, precision of 81%, recall of 72%, F-1 score of 59%, security rate of 93%, data transmission rate of 82%; CNN attained accuracy of 82%, precision of 76%, recall of 65%, F-1 score of 52%, security rate of 88%, data transmission rate of 75%; SVM attained accuracy of 89%, precision of 79%, recall of 69%, F-1 score of 57%, security rate of 91%, data transmission rate of 79%.

Figure 5. Comparative analysis between proposed and existing technique for national patient register dataset

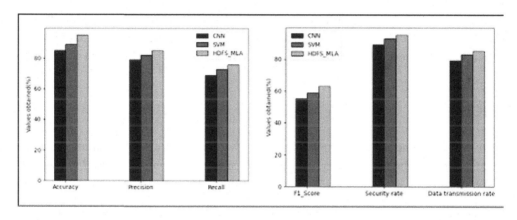

The above figure-5 shows comparative analysis between proposed and existing technique for National Patient Register dataset. Here the proposed technique attained accuracy of 95%, precision of 85%, recall of 76%, F-1 score of 63%, security rate of 95%, data transmission rate of 85%; CNN attained accuracy of 85%, precision of 79%, recall of 69%, F-1 score of 55%, security rate of 89%, data transmission rate of 79%; SVM attained accuracy of 89%, precision of 82%, recall of 73%, F-1 score of 59%, security rate of 93%, data transmission rate of 83%.

DISCUSSION

By using an open channel, like the Internet, patients can control, share, and manage their health records with family members, friends, and healthcare professionals. Therefore, privacy, confidentiality, and data consistency present significant difficulties in such a setting. Even though cloud-based EHRs deal with aforementioned issues, they are still vulnerable to numerous harmful assaults, trust management, and server non-repudiation. Therefore, blockchain-based EHR solutions are the most widely used to foster consumers' confidence, security, and privacy. Motivated from aforementioned discussions, we propose Healthcare Data Based Feature Selection and Classification Using Blockchain and Machine Learning Architectures.

CONCLUSION

In this chapter discussed different selection methods for processed data feature has been using Greedy Mixed Forward Colony Optimization feature selection. After the feature selections the classification is done by Fuzzy Bayesian based adversarial vector machine classification method. In book chapter we will discuss in detail about healthcare data science, blockchain technique, machine learning technique for smart applications. The Proposed application are compare and analysis with the existing technique by comparing of in terms of accuracy, precision, recall, F-1 score, security rate and data transmission rate. the proposed technique attained accuracy of 95%, precision of 85%, recall of 76%, F-1 score of 63%, security rate of 95%, data transmission rate of 85%. In comparison to other blockchain data transmission protocols already in use, simulation results demonstrate that suggested method accurately replies to query with fast speed retrieval of classified results. In order to achieve effective ledgering of the addresses, ML or DL optimization may one day be employed to enhance modelling of blockchain in a distributed ledger.

REFERENCES

Abdulraheem, M., Awotunde, J. B., Jimoh, R. G., & Oladipo, I. D. (2021). An efficient lightweight cryptographic algorithm for IoT security. In *Communications in Computer and Information Science* (pp. 444–456). Springer.

Adeniyi, E. A., Ogundokun, R. O., & Awotunde, J. B. (2021). IoMTbased wearable body sensors network healthcare monitoring system. In IoT in Healthcare and Ambient Assisted Living. Springer.

Ali, A., Pasha, M. F., Ali, J., Fang, O. H., Masud, M., Jurcut, A. D., & Alzain, M. A. (2022). Deep Learning Based Homomorphic Secure Search-Able Encryption for Keyword Search in Blockchain Healthcare System: A Novel Approach to Cryptography. *Sensors (Basel)*, *22*(2), 528. doi:10.339022020528 PMID:35062491

Ambika, P. (2020). Machine learning and deep learning algorithms on the Industrial Internet of Things (IIoT). *Advances in Computers*, *117*(1), 321–338. doi:10.1016/bs.adcom.2019.10.007

Amit, K., & Chinmay, C. (2021). Artificial intelligence and Internet of Things based healthcare 4.0 monitoring system. *Wireless Personal Communications*, 1–14.

Ashima, R., Haleem, A., Bahl, S., Javaid, M., Mahla, S. K., & Singh, S. (2021). Automation and manufacturing of smart materials in Additive Manufacturing technologies using the Internet of Things towards the adoption of Industry 4.0. *Materials Today: Proceedings*, *45*, 5081–5088. doi:10.1016/j.matpr.2021.01.583

Awotunde, J. B., Jimoh, R. G., Folorunso, S. O., Adeniyi, E. A., Abiodun, K. M., & Banjo, O. O. (2021). Privacy and security concerns in IoT-based healthcare systems. Internet of Things, pp. 105–134. doi:10.1007/978-3-030-75220-0_6

Ayo, F. E., Folorunso, S. O., Abayomi-Alli, A. A., Adekunle, A. O., & Awotunde, J. B. (2020). Network intrusion detection based on deep learning model optimized with rule-based hybrid feature selection. Information Security Journal: A Global Perspective, *29*(6), 267–283. doi:10.1080/19393555.2020.1767240

Bakhtawar, A., Abdul, R. J., Chinmay, C., Jamel, N., Saira, R., & Muhammad, R. (2021). Blockchain and ANFIS empowered IoMT application for privacy preserved contact tracing in COVID-19 pandemic. *Personal and Ubiquitous Computing*. PMID:34312582

Balyan, A. K., Ahuja, S., Sharma, S. K., & Lilhore, U. K. (2022, February). Machine Learning-Based Intrusion Detection System for Healthcare Data. In 2022 IEEE VLSI Device Circuit and System (VLSI DCS) (pp. 290-294). IEEE. doi:10.1109/VLSIDCS53788.2022.9811465

Das, S., Das, J., Modak, S., & Mazumdar, K. (2022). Internet of Things with Machine Learning-Based Smart Cardiovascular Disease Classifier for Healthcare in Secure Platform. In *Internet of Things and Data Mining for Modern Engineering and Healthcare Applications* (pp. 45–64). Chapman and Hall/CRC. doi:10.1201/9781003217398-4

García-Magariño, I., Lacuesta, R., Rajarajan, M., & Lloret, J. (2019). Security in networks of unmanned aerial vehicles for surveillance with an agent-based approach inspired by the principles of blockchain. *Ad Hoc Networks*, *86*, 72–82. doi:10.1016/j.adhoc.2018.11.010

Gladence, L. M., Anu, V. M., Rathna, R., & Brumancia, E. (2020). Recommender system for home automation using IoT and artificial intelligence. *Journal of Ambient Intelligence and Humanized Computing*, 1–9. doi:10.100712652-020-01968-2

Gupta, R., Shukla, A., &Tanwar, S. (2020). BATS: A Blockchain and AI-empowered Drone-assisted Telesurgery System towards 6G. *IEEE Transactions on Network Science and Engineering*. IEEE.

Hattab, G., & Cabric, D. (2020). Energy-efficient massive IoT shared spectrum access over UAV-enabled cellular networks. *IEEE Transactions on Communications*, *68*(9), 5633–5648. doi:10.1109/TCOMM.2020.2998547

Imran, M., Zaman, U., Imtiaz, J., Fayaz, M., & Gwak, J. (2021). Comprehensive survey of iot, machine learning, and blockchain for health care applications: A topical assessment for pandemic preparedness, challenges, and solutions. *Electronics (Basel)*, *10*(20), 2501. doi:10.3390/electronics10202501

Mansour, R. F. (2022). Artificial intelligence based optimization with deep learning model for blockchain enabled intrusion detection in CPS environment. *Scientific Reports*, *12*(1), 1–14. doi:10.103841598-022-17043-z PMID:35902617

Nadeem, M. W., Goh, H. G., Ponnusamy, V., Andonovic, I., Khan, M. A., & Hussain, M. (2021, October). A fusion-based machine learning approach for the prediction of the onset of diabetes. [). MDPI.]. *Health Care*, *9*(10), 1393. PMID:34683073

Nguyen, G. N., Le Viet, N. H., Elhoseny, M., Shankar, K., Gupta, B. B., & Abd El-Latif, A. A. (2021). Secure blockchain enabled Cyber–physical systems in healthcare using deep belief network with ResNet model. *Journal of Parallel and Distributed Computing*, *153*, 150–160. doi:10.1016/j.jpdc.2021.03.011

Pokhrel, S. R. (2020, September). Federated learning meets blockchain at 6g edge: A drone-assisted networking for disaster response. In *Proceedings of the 2nd ACM MobiCom Workshop on Drone Assisted Wireless Communications for 5G and Beyond* (pp. 49-54). 10.1145/3414045.3415949

Rametta, C., & Schembra, G. (2017). Designing a softwarized network deployed on a fleet of drones for rural zone monitoring. *Future Internet*, *9*(1), 8. doi:10.3390/fi9010008

Rao, T. P., Rao, M. N., Arul, U., & Balajee, J. (2022). Detection of MRI Medical MRI Images of Brain Tumors Using Deep Learning & Secure the Transfer of Medical Images Using Blockchain. *Journal of Algebraic Statistics*, *13*(3), 374–377.

Sherasiya, T., Upadhyay, H., & Patel, H. B. (2016). A survey: Intrusion detection system for internet of things. *International Journal on Computer Science and Engineering*, *5*(2), 91–98.

Singh, P., Nayyar, A., Kaur, A., & Ghosh, U. (2020). Blockchain and fog based architecture for internet of everything in smart cities. *Future Internet*, *12*(4), 61. doi:10.3390/fi12040061

Vijai, C., & Wisetsri, W. (2021). Rise of artificial intelligence in healthcare startups in India. *Advances in Management*, *14*(1), 48–52.

Zhang, G., Zhang, X., Bilal, M., Dou, W., Xu, X., & Rodrigues, J. J. (2022). Identifying fraud in medical insurance based on blockchain and deep learning. *Future Generation Computer Systems*, *130*, 140–154. doi:10.1016/j.future.2021.12.006

Compilation of References

A, G., AF, C., & A, I. D. S. (2017). *Blockchain in Education* (Issue KJ-NA-28778-EN-N). Publications Office of the European Union. doi:10.2760/60649

Abdulraheem, M., Awotunde, J. B., Jimoh, R. G., & Oladipo, I. D. (2021). An efficient lightweight cryptographic algorithm for IoT security. In *Communications in Computer and Information Science* (pp. 444–456). Springer.

Adam, M., Wessel, M., & Benlian, A. (2021). AI-based chatbots in customer service and their effects on user compliance. *Electronic Markets*, *31*(2), 427–445. doi:10.100712525-020-00414-7

Adamu, J., Hamzah, R., & Rosli, M. M. (2020). Security issues and framework of electronic medical record: A review. *Bulletin of Electrical Engineering and Informatics*, *9*(2), 565–572. doi:10.11591/eei.v9i2.2064

Adeniyi, E. A., Ogundokun, R. O., & Awotunde, J. B. (2021). IoMTbased wearable body sensors network healthcare monitoring system. In IoT in Healthcare and Ambient Assisted Living. Springer.

Adrian, T., & Ashcraft, A. B. (2016). Shadow banking: a review of the literature. In: Jones, G. (ed) Banking Crises. Palgrave Macmillan. doi:10.1057/9781137553799_29

Agrawal, P., Chaudhary, D., Madaan, V., Zabrovskiy, A., Prodan, R., Kimovski, D., & Timmerer, C. (2021). Automated bank cheque verification using image processing and deep learning methods. *Multimedia Tools and Applications*, *80*(4), 5319–5350. doi:10.100711042-020-09818-1

Ahmad, A., Ahmad, T., Ahmad, M., Kumar, C., Alenezi, F., & Nour, M. (2023). A complex network-based approach for security and governance in the smart green city. *Expert Systems with Applications, 214*. doi:10.1016/j.eswa.2022.119094

Ahmad, K., Maabreh, M., Ghaly, M., Khan, K., Qadir, J., & AlFuqaha, A. (2020). Developing future human-centered smart cities: Critical analysis of smart city security, interpretability, and ethical challenges. arXiv preprint. doi:10.1111/deci.12451

Ahn, T., Goo, T., Lee, C. H., Kim, S., Han, K., Park, S., & Park, T. (2018). Deep Learning-based Identification of Cancer, or Normal Tissue using Gene Expression Data. In *2018 IEEE International Conference on Bioinformatics and Biomedicine (BIBM)* (pp. 1748-1752). IEEE.10.1109/BIBM.2018.8621108

Aiyar, S., Calomiris, C., & Wieladek, T. (2015). Bank Capital Regulation: Theory, Empirics, and Policy. *IMF Economic Review*, *63*(4), 955–983. doi:10.1057/imfer.2015.18

Akram, S. V., Singh, R., AlZain, M. A., Gehlot, A., Rashid, M., Faragallah, O. S., El-Shafai, W., & Prashar, D. (2021). Performance Analysis of IoT and Long-Range Radio-Based Sensor Node and Gateway Architecture for Solid Waste Management. *Sensors (Basel)*, *21*(8), 2774. doi:10.339021082774 PMID:33920008

Akram, S. V., Singh, R., Gehlot, A., Rashid, M., AlGhamdi, A. S., Alshamrani, S. S., & Prashar, D. (2021). Role of Wireless Aided Technologies in the Solid Waste Management: A Comprehensive Review. *Sustainability*, *13*(23), 13104. doi:10.3390u132313104

Alabdulatif, A., Khalil, I., & Saidur Rahman, M. (2022). Security of Blockchain and AI-Empowered Smart Healthcare: Application-Based Analysis. *Applied Sciences (Basel, Switzerland)*, *12*(21), 11039. doi:10.3390/app122111039

Al-Besher, A. & Kumar, K. (2022). Use of artificial intelligence to enhance e-government services. *Sensors, 24*. doi:10.1016/j.measen.2022.100484

Alexopoulos, C., Lachana A Androutsopoulou, Z., Diamantopoulou, V., Charalabidis, Y., & Loutsaris, M. A. (2019). How Machine Learning is Changing e-Government. ICEGOV '19, Melbourne, Australia.

Alhassan, A. L., Tetteh, M. L., & Brobbey, F. O. (2016). Market power, efficiency, and bank profitability: Evidence from Ghana. *Economic Change and Restructuring*, *49*(1), 71–93. doi:10.100710644-015-9174-6

Ali, A., Pasha, M. F., Ali, J., Fang, O. H., Masud, M., Jurcut, A. D., & Alzain, M. A. (2022). Deep Learning Based Homomorphic Secure Search-Able Encryption for Keyword Search in Blockchain Healthcare System: A Novel Approach to Cryptography. *Sensors (Basel)*, *22*(2), 528. doi:10.339022020528 PMID:35062491

Ali, Z., Imran, M., & Shoaib, M. (2022). An IoT-based smart healthcare system to detect dysphonia. *Neural Computing & Applications*, *34*(14), 11255–11265. doi:10.100700521-020-05558-3

Alla, S., & Soltanisehat, L. (2018). *Blockchain Technology in Electronic Healthcare System*.

Al-Mushayt, O. S. (2019). Automating E-Government Services with Artificial Intelligence. IEEE Access, 7, 146821-146829. doi:10.1109/ACCESS.2019.2946204

Al-Shammari, M., & Mili, M. (2021). A fuzzy analytic hierarchy process model for customers' bank selection decision in the Kingdom of Bahrain. *Oper Res Int J*, *21*(3), 1429–1446. doi:10.100712351-019-00496-y

Alshomrani, Q. (2013). Cloud based e-Government: Benefits and Challenges. *International Journal of Marketing and Sales Education*, *4*(6), 15–19.

Al-Sultan, K. S., & Al-Dabbagh, M. (2018). Virtual Reality in E-Government: A Literature Review. *Journal of E-Government Studies and Best Practices*, *3*(4), 1–12.

Ambesange, S., Vijayalaxmi, A., & Sridevi, S., Venkateswaran, & Yashoda, B. S. (2020). Multiple Heart Diseases Prediction using Logistic Regression with Ensemble and Hyper Parameter tuning Techniques. *2020 Fourth World Conference on Smart Trends in Systems, Security and Sustainability (WorldS4)*, 827–832. 10.1109/WorldS450073.2020.9210404

Ambika, P. (2020). Machine learning and deep learning algorithms on the Industrial Internet of Things (IIoT). *Advances in Computers*, *117*(1), 321–338. doi:10.1016/bs.adcom.2019.10.007

Amit, K., & Chinmay, C. (2021). Artificial intelligence and Internet of Things based healthcare 4.0 monitoring system. *Wireless Personal Communications*, 1–14.

Anaconda Documentation. (2022). *Introduction to Anaconda Navigator*. Anaconda Documentation. [https://docs.anaconda.com/anaconda/navigator/]

Androulaki, E. (2018). Hyperledger Fabric: A Distributed Operating System for Permissioned Blockchains. In *Proceedings of the 13th EuroSys Conference, EuroSys 2018*. ACM. 10.1145/3190508.3190538

Angelakopoulos, G., & Mihiotis, A. (2011). E-banking: Challenges and opportunities in the Greek banking sector. *Electronic Commerce Research*, *11*(3), 297–319. doi:10.100710660-011-9076-2

Ashima, R., Haleem, A., Bahl, S., Javaid, M., Mahla, S. K., & Singh, S. (2021). Automation and manufacturing of smart materials in Additive Manufacturing technologies using the Internet of Things towards the adoption of Industry 4.0. *Materials Today: Proceedings, 45*, 5081–5088. doi:10.1016/j.matpr.2021.01.583

Ashish, S. (2021). Now is the time for smart meter adoption in India. *Times of India.* https://timesofindia.indiatimes.com/blogs/voices/now-is-the-time-for-smart-meter-adoption-in-india/

Asim, M., Wang, Y., Wang, K., & Huang, P.-Q. (2020). A Review on Computational Intelligence Techniques in Cloud and Edge Computing. IEEE Transactions on Emerging Topics in Computational Intelligence, 4(6), 742-763. doi:10.1109/TETCI.2020.3007905

Atkins, R., Cook, L., & Seamans, R. (2022). Discrimination in lending? Evidence from the Paycheck Protection Program. *Small Business Economics, 58*(2), 843–865. doi:10.100711187-021-00533-1

Aung, Y. N., & Tantidham, T. (2017). Review of Ethereum: Smart home case study. *2017 2nd International Conference on Information Technology (INCIT)*, 1–4. 10.1109/INCIT.2017.8257877

Awotunde, J. B., Jimoh, R. G., Folorunso, S. O., Adeniyi, E. A., Abiodun, K. M., & Banjo, O. O. (2021). Privacy and security concerns in IoT-based healthcare systems. Internet of Things, pp. 105–134. doi:10.1007/978-3-030-75220-0_6

Ayo, F. E., Folorunso, S. O., Abayomi-Alli, A. A., Adekunle, A. O., & Awotunde, J. B. (2020). Network intrusion detection based on deep learning model optimized with rule-based hybrid feature selection. Information Security Journal: A Global Perspective, 29(6), 267–283. doi:10.1080/19393555.2020.1767240

Azuma, R. T. (1997). A survey of augmented reality. *Presence (Cambridge, Mass.), 6*(4), 355–385. doi:10.1162/pres.1997.6.4.355

Backhaus, K., & Awan, A. (2019). The Paradigm Shift in Customer Analysis: Marketing or IT-Driven? In K. Bergener, M. Räckers, & A. Stein (Eds.), *The Art of Structuring.* Springer. doi:10.1007/978-3-030-06234-7_32

Baig, M. I., Shuib, L., & Yadegaridehkordi, E. (2020). Big data in education: A state of the art, limitations, and future research directions. *Int J Educ Technol High Educ, 17*(1), 44. doi:10.118641239-020-00223-0

Bakhtawar, A., Abdul, R. J., Chinmay, C., Jamel, N., Saira, R., & Muhammad, R. (2021). Blockchain and ANFIS empowered IoMT application for privacy preserved contact tracing in COVID-19 pandemic. *Personal and Ubiquitous Computing.* PMID:34312582

Balyan, A. K., Ahuja, S., Sharma, S. K., & Lilhore, U. K. (2022, February). Machine Learning-Based Intrusion Detection System for Healthcare Data. In 2022 IEEE VLSI Device Circuit and System (VLSI DCS) (pp. 290-294). IEEE. doi:10.1109/VLSIDCS53788.2022.9811465

Bansal, R., Obaid, A. J., Gupta, A., Singh, R., & Pramanik, S. (2021). Impact of Big Data on Digital Transformation in 5G Era. *2nd International Conference on Physics and Applied Sciences (ICPAS 2021).* IOP Science. .10.1088/1742-6596/1963/1/012170

Bao, L., & Chen, W. (2017). A survey of virtual reality in education and training. *Journal of Computer Science and Technology, 32*(3), 421–434.

Barberis, J., & Arner, D. W. (2016). FinTech in China: From Shadow Banking to P2P Lending. In: Tasca, P., Aste, T., Pelizzon, L., Perony, N. (eds) Banking Beyond Banks and Money: New Economic Windows. Springer, Cham. doi:10.1007/978-3-319-42448-4_5

Behrendt, A., Odenwälder, P., Müller, N., & Schmitz, C. (2020). *Industry 4.0 Demystified—Lean's Next Level McKinsey*. McKinsey. https://www.mckinsey.com/business-functions/operations/our-insights/industry-4-0-demystified-leans-next-level (accessed on 9 January 2020).

Ben Amor, A., Abid, M., & Meddeb, A. (2020). Secure Fog-Based E-Learning Scheme. *IEEE Access : Practical Innovations, Open Solutions*, 8, 31920–31933. doi:10.1109/ACCESS.2020.2973325

Bernardi, M. L. (2021). Keynote: Edge Intelligence - Emerging Solutions and Open Challenges. In *2021 IEEE International Conference on Pervasive Computing and Communications Workshops and other Affiliated Events (PerCom Workshops)*, (pp. 160-160). IEEE. 10.1109/PerComWorkshops51409.2021.9431071

Bhattacharya, S., Singh, A., & Hossain, M. M. (2019). Strengthening public health surveillance through blockchain technology. *AIMS Public Health*, 6(3), 326–333. doi:10.3934/publichealth.2019.3.326 PMID:31637281

Biocca, F., Kim, J. J., & Levy, M. R. (2015). Virtual reality applications in entertainment and education. *International Journal of Emerging Technologies in Learning*, 10(3), 1–14.

Bitcoin. (n.d.). *Frequently Asked Questions*. https://bitcoin.org/en/faq

BMBF-Internetredaktion. (2016). *Zukunftsprojekt Industrie 4.0 - BMBF*. Bmbf.de.

Bolton, P., & Jeanne, O. (2011). Sovereign Default Risk and Bank Fragility in Financially Integrated Economies. *IMF Economic Review*, 59(2), 162–194. doi:10.1057/imfer.2011.5

Brad, S., Murar, M., & Brad, E. (2018, March). Design of smart connected manufacturing resources to enable changeability, reconfigurability and totalcost-of-ownership models in the factory-of-the-future. *International Journal of Production Research*, 56(6), 2269–2291. doi:10.1080/00207543.2017.1400705

Broto, L. M. & Indiarto, B. (2021). Issues and Challenges in Implementing Industry 4.0 for the Manufacturing Sector. *Indonesia International Journal of Progressive Sciences and Technologies*, 25, 650-658.

Brownlee, J. (2020). A Gentle Introduction to k-fold Cross-Validation. *Machine Learning Mastery*. https://machinelearningmastery.com/k-fold-crossvalidation/

Burdea, G., & Coiffet, P. (2003). *Virtual reality technology*. John Wiley & Sons. doi:10.1162/105474603322955950

Bussmann, N., Giudici, P., Marinelli, D., & Papenbrock, J. (2021). Explainable Machine Learning in Credit Risk Management. *Computational Economics*, 57(1), 203–216. doi:10.100710614-020-10042-0

Calomiris, C. W., & Pornrojnangkool, T. (2009). Relationship Banking and the Pricing of Financial Services. *Journal of Financial Services Research*, 35(3), 189–224. doi:10.100710693-009-0058-7

Chakrabarty, N. (2019). Application of Synthetic Minority Over-sampling Technique (SMOTE) for Imbalanced Datasets. *Medium*. https://medium.com/towards-artificial-intelligence/application-of-syntheticminority-over-sampling-technique-smote-for-imbalanced-data-sets-509ab55cfdaf

Chang, S. E., Chen, Y.-C., & Lu, M.-F. (2019). Supply chain re-engineering using blockchain technology: A case of smart contract-based tracking process. *Technological Forecasting and Social Change*, 144, 1–11. doi:10.1016/j.techfore.2019.03.015

Chatterfee, A. (2022). India gets its first High Throughput Satellite Broadband Service. *The Hindu*. https://www.thehindu.com/sci-tech/technology/india-gets-its-first-high-throughput-satellite-broadband-service/article65889436.ece

Cheung, M. W. L., & Vijayakumar, R. (2016). A Guide to Conducting a Meta-Analysis. *Neuropsychology Review*, 26(2), 121–128. doi:10.100711065-016-9319-z PMID:27209412

Chiorazzo, V., Milani, C., & Salvini, F. (2008). Income Diversification and Bank Performance: Evidence from Italian Banks. *Journal of Financial Services Research*, *33*(3), 181–203. doi:10.100710693-008-0029-4

Christidis, K., & Devetsikiotis, M. (2016). Blockchains and smart contracts for the internet of things. *IEEE Access : Practical Innovations, Open Solutions*, *4*, 2292–2303. doi:10.1109/ACCESS.2016.2566339

Chui, K. T., Alhalabi, W., Pang, S. S. H., Pablos, P. O. D., Liu, R. W., & Zhao, M. (2017). Disease Diagnosis in Smart Healthcare: Innovation, Technologies and Applications. *Sustainability*, *9*(12), 2309. doi:10.3390u9122309

Cornelius, C. A., Qusay, H. M., & Mikael, E. (2019). Blockchain technology in healthcare: A systematic review. *Health Care*, *7*(2), 56. doi:10.3390/healthcare7020056 PMID:30987333

Couchman, N., & Tsolacos, S. (2003). Explaining standard retail yields in UK locations. *Journal of Retail & Leisure Property*, *3*(3), 211–222. doi:10.1057/palgrave.rlp.5090177

Cowling, M., Marlow, S., & Liu, W. (2020). Gender and bank lending after the global financial crisis: Are women entrepreneurs safer bets? *Small Business Economics*, *55*(4), 853–880. doi:10.100711187-019-00168-3

Dahdouh, K., Dakkak, A., Oughdir, L., & Ibriz, A. (2020). Improving Online Education Using Big Data Technologies. In The Role of Technology in Education. IntechOpen. doi:10.5772/intechopen.88463

Danaee, P., Ghaeini, R., & Hendrix, D. A. (2017). A deep learning approach for cancer detection and relevant gene identification. In *Pacific Symposium on Biocomputing* (pp. 219-229). World Scientific.10.1142/9789813207813_0022

Das, S., Das, J., Modak, S., & Mazumdar, K. (2022). Internet of Things with Machine Learning-Based Smart Cardiovascular Disease Classifier for Healthcare in Secure Platform. In *Internet of Things and Data Mining for Modern Engineering and Healthcare Applications* (pp. 45–64). Chapman and Hall/CRC. doi:10.1201/9781003217398-4

Datta, S. P. A. (2017). Cybersecurity-Personal Security Agents for People, Process, Atoms & Bits. *Journal of Innovation Management, 5*(1), 4-13.

Dede, C. (2017). Immersive interfaces for engagement and learning. *Science*, *357*(6358), 1057–1058. PMID:19119219

Degryse, H., de Goeij, P., & Kappert, P. (2012). The impact of firm and industry characteristics on small firms' capital structure. *Small Business Economics*, *38*(4), 431–447. doi:10.100711187-010-9281-8

Deloof, M., & La Rocca, M. (2015). Local financial development, and the trade credit policy of Italian SMEs. *Small Business Economics*, *44*(4), 905–924. doi:10.100711187-014-9617-x

Dertat, A. (2017). Applied Deep Learning - Part 3: Autoencoders. *Towards Data Science.* https://towardsdatascience.com/applied-deep-learning-part-3-autoencoders-1c083af4d798

Devi, P. D., Mirudhula, S., & Devi, A. (2021). Advanced Library Management System using IoT. In *Fifth International Conference on I-SMAC (IoT in Social, Mobile, Analytics and Cloud) (I-SMAC)*, (pp. 150-154). IEEE. 10.1109/I-SMAC52330.2021.9640697

DeYoung, R., Hunter, W. C., & Udell, G. F. (2004). The Past, Present, and Probable Future for Community Banks. *Journal of Financial Services Research*, *25*(2/3), 85–133. doi:10.1023/B:FINA.0000020656.65653.79

Dhule, C., Agrawal, R., Dorle, S., & Vidhale, B. (2021) Study of Design of IoT based Digital Board for Real Time Data Delivery on National Highway. In *6th International Conference on Inventive Computation Technologies (ICICT)*, (pp. 195-198). IEEE. 10.1109/ICICT50816.2021.9358560

Douzas, G., & Bacao, F. (2019). Geometric SMOTE A geometrically enhanced drop-in replacement for SMOTE. Information Sciences, 501, 118-135. doi:10.1016/j.ins.2019.06.007

Douzas, G., Bacao, F., & Last, F. (2018). Improving imbalanced learning through a heuristic oversampling method based on k-means and SMOTE. Information Sciences, 465, 1-20. doi:10.1016/j.ins.2018.06.056

Dudhpachare, A. K., Kuthe, T. V., Lalke, C. V., Wyawahare, N. P., Agrawal, R., & Daigavane, P. (2022). Process of RO's Wastewater Reuse & Water Management in Society by Using IOT Automation. In *International Conference on Applied Artificial Intelligence and Computing (ICAAIC)*, (pp. 1546-1550). IEEE. 10.1109/ICAAIC53929.2022.9792805

Dutta, S., & Saini, K. (2020). Blockchain and Social Media. In Blockchain Technology and Applications (pp. 101-114). Auerbach Publications. doi:10.1201/9781003081487-6

Dutta, S., & Saini, K. (2021). Statistical Assessment of Hybrid Blockchain for SME Sector. *WSEAS Transactions on Systems And Control, 16*. doi:10.37394/23203.2021.16.6

Dutta, S., & Saini, K. (2021). Securing Data: A Study on Different Transform Domain Techniques. *WSEAS Transactions on Systems And Control, 16*, 110–120. doi:10.37394/23203.2021.16.8

Du, X., Chen, B., Ma, M., & Zhang, Y. (2021, January 12). Research on the Application of Blockchain in Smart Healthcare: Constructing a Hierarchical Framework. *Journal of Healthcare Engineering, 6698122*, 1–13. doi:10.1155/2021/6698122 PMID:33505644

Dwivedi, A., Pant, R.P., Khari, M., Pandey, S., & Pande, M. (2019). E-Governance and Big Data Framework for e-Governance and Use of Sentiment Analysis. SSRN doi:10.2139/ssrn.3382731

Elmogy, A. M. (2017). Image noise detection and removal based on enhanced gridLOF algorithm. *Image, 8*(12).

Elreedy, D., & Atiya, A. F. (2019). A Comprehensive Analysis of Synthetic Minority Oversampling Technique (SMOTE) for handling class imbalance. Information Sciences, 505, 32-64. doi:10.1016/j.ins.2019.07.070

Ervural, B., & Ervural, B. (2017). Overview of Cyber Security in the Industry 4.0 Era. *Industry 4.0: Managing The Digital Transformation, 267–284*.

ETTelecom. (2022). *Tata's Nelco, Telesat successfully conduct LEO satellite internet trial in India*. ETTelecom. https://telecom.economictimes.indiatimes.com/news/tatas-nelco-telesat-successfully-conduct-leo-satellite-internet-trial-in-india/91640942

Fan, J., Zeng, G., Body, M., & Hacid, M. (2005). Seeded region growing: An extensive and comparative study. *PatternRecog. Lett., 26*(8), 1139-56.

Fang, L. H., & Yasuda, A. (2014). Are Stars' Opinions Worth More? The Relation Between Analyst Reputation and Recommendation Values. *Journal of Financial Services Research, 46*(3), 235–269. doi:10.100710693-013-0178-y

Fechteler, C., Heim, J., & Lindner, T. (2019). The use of virtual and augmented reality in vocational training. *Journal of Vocational Education and Training, 71*(2), 156–170.

Federal Government of Germany. (n.d.). *Information on Industrie 4.0*. Federal Government of Germany. www. bmwi. de/ Redaktion/ DE/Dossier /industrie -40.html

Feng, J., Chen, W., & Chen, N. (2019). The application of augmented reality technology in remote assistance. *Journal of Visual Languages and Computing, 52*, 45–53.

Feng, J., Chen, W., & Chen, N. (2019). The application of augmented reality technology in search and rescue operations. *International Journal of Disaster Risk Reduction, 34*, 100–108.

Feng, J., Chen, W., & Chen, N. (2019). The application of virtual reality technology in virtual training. *Journal of Virtual Reality and Broadcasting, 16*(3), 1–10.

Ferdous, M., Debnath, J., & Chakraborty, N. R. (2020). Machine Learning Algorithms in Healthcare: A Literature Survey. *2020 11th International Conference on Computing, Communication and Networking Technologies (ICCCNT)*, 1–6. 10.1109/ICCCNT49239.2020.9225642

Fiordelisi, F., Monferrà, S., & Sampagnaro, G. (2014). Relationship Lending and Credit Quality. *Journal of Financial Services Research*, *46*(3), 295–315. doi:10.100710693-013-0176-0

Gafni, H., Hudon, M., & Périlleux, A. (2021). Business or Basic Needs? The Impact of Loan Purpose on Social Crowd-funding Platforms. *Journal of Business Ethics*, *173*(4), 777–793. doi:10.100710551-020-04530-4

Gao, J., Chen, W., & Chen, N. (2019). The application of virtual reality technology in video conferencing. *Journal of Visual Communication and Image Representation*, *62*, 34–40.

Gao, W., & Wang, H. (2019). Virtual Reality in E-Government: A Literature Review. *Government Information Quarterly*, *36*(4), 494–511.

García-Magariño, I., Lacuesta, R., Rajarajan, M., & Lloret, J. (2019). Security in networks of unmanned aerial vehicles for surveillance with an agent-based approach inspired by the principles of blockchain. *Ad Hoc Networks*, *86*, 72–82. doi:10.1016/j.adhoc.2018.11.010

Garz, M. (2014). Good news and bad news: Evidence of media bias in unemployment reports. *Public Choice*, *161*(3-4), 499–515. doi:10.100711127-014-0182-2

Geeks for Geeks. (2023). Confusion Matrix. *Geeks for Geeks.* [https://www.geeksforgeeks.org/confusion-matrix-machine-learning/]

Geeks for Geeks. (2023). Cross Validation in Machine Learning. *Geeks for Geeks.* [https://www.geeksforgeeks.org/cross-validation-machine-learning/]

Geeks for Geeks. (2023). Supervised and Unsupervised Learning. *Geeks for Geeks.* https://www.geeksforgeeks.org/supervised-unsupervised-learning/

Gil-Garcia, J. R., Zhang, J., & Puron-Cid, G. (2016). Conceptualizing smartness in government: An integrative and multi-dimensional view. *Government Information Quarterly*, *33*(3), 524–534. doi:10.1016/j.giq.2016.03.002

Gill, N. K. & Sharma, A. (2016). Noise Models and De-noising Techniques in Digital Image Processing. *International Journal of Computer & Mathematical Sciences, 5*(1), 21-25.

Giraldo, J., Sarkar, E., Cardenas, A. A., Maniatakos, M., & Kantarcioglu, M. (2017). Security and privacy in cyber-physical systems: A survey of surveys. *IEEE Des. Test*, *34*(4), 7–17. doi:10.1109/MDAT.2017.2709310

Gladence, L. M., Anu, V. M., Rathna, R., & Brumancia, E. (2020). Recommender system for home automation using IoT and artificial intelligence. *Journal of Ambient Intelligence and Humanized Computing*, 1–9. doi:10.100712652-020-01968-2

Gonzalez, R., & Woods, R. (2002). *Digital Image Processing.* Prentice Hall.

Green, J. S., & Daniels, S. (2019). *Digital governance: leading and thriving in a world of fast-changing technologies.* Routledge. doi:10.3390/app12083719

Gröger, C. (2018). Building an industry 4.0 analytics platform. *Datenbank-Spektrum: Zeitschrift fur Datenbanktechnologie: Organ der Fachgruppe Datenbanken der Gesellschaft fur Informatik e.V, 18*(1), 5–14. doi:10.100713222-018-0273-1

GSEA. (2022). *Parkinson Disease Genes from KEGG.* GSEA. https://www.gsea-msigdb.org/gsea/msigdb/cards/KEGG_PARKINSONS_DISEASE.html

GSEA. (2023). *Alzheimer Disease Genes from KEGG*. GSEA. https://www.gsea-msigdb.org/gsea/msigdb/cards/KEGG_ALZHEIMERS_DISEASE.html

Guest Writer. (2022). The VR, AR, and MR interaction with AI in governance. *TheCable*. https://www.thecable.ng/the-vr-ar-and-mr-interaction-with-ai-in-governance

Gupta, R., Shukla, A., &Tanwar, S. (2020). BATS: A Blockchain and AI-empowered Drone-assisted Telesurgery System towards 6G. *IEEE Transactions on Network Science and Engineering*. IEEE.

Gupta, N., Mangal, N., Tiwari, K., & Mitra, P. (2006). Mining Quantitative Association Rules in Protein Sequences. In G. J. Williams & S. J. Simoff (Eds.), *Data Mining: Theory, Methodology, Techniques, and Applications* (pp. 273–281). Springer Berlin Heidelberg. doi:10.1007/11677437_21

Hall, B. H., Lotti, F., & Mairesse, J. (2009). Innovation and productivity in SMEs: Empirical evidence for Italy. *Small Business Economics*, *33*(1), 13–33. doi:10.100711187-009-9184-8

Hannoon, A., Al-Sartawi, A. M. A. M., & Khalid, A. A. (2021). Relationship Between Financial Technology and Financial Performance. In A. M. A. Musleh Al-Sartawi (Ed.), *The Big Data-Driven Digital Economy: Artificial and Computational Intelligence. Studies in Computational Intelligence* (Vol. 974). Springer. doi:10.1007/978-3-030-73057-4_26

Hattab, G., & Cabric, D. (2020). Energy-efficient massive IoT shared spectrum access over UAV-enabled cellular networks. *IEEE Transactions on Communications*, *68*(9), 5633–5648. doi:10.1109/TCOMM.2020.2998547

Hemant Mishra/Mint. (2022). DoT okays BSNL to provide satellite-based services using gateway installed in India. *Mint*. https://www.livemint.com/companies/news/dot-okays-bsnl-to-provide-satellite-based-services-details-here-11652010859939.html

Hercko, J. (2015). Industry 4.0 – New Era Of Manufacturing. In Conference: InvEnt. Demänovská.

Hermann, M. P. & Otto, B. (2015). *Design Principles for Industrie 4.0 Scenarios: A Literature Review*. Technische Universität Dortmund Fakultät Maschinenbau Audi Stiftungslehrstuhl Supply Net Order Management.

Hermann, P. O. (2016). *Design Principles for Industrie 4.0 Scenarios*. Academic Press.

Hernández-Cánovas, G., & Martínez-Solano, P. (2010). Relationship lending and SME financing in the continental European bank-based system. *Small Business Economics*, *34*(4), 465–482. doi:10.100711187-008-9129-7

He, S., Ren, W., Zhu, T., & Choo, K.-K. R. (2020, February). BoSMoS: A BlockchainBased Status Monitoring System for Defending Against Unauthorized Software Updating in Industrial Internet of Things. *IEEE Internet of Things Journal*, *7*(2), 948–959. doi:10.1109/JIOT.2019.2947339

Hosseini Bamakan, S. M., Ghasemzadeh Moghaddam, S., & Dehghan Manshadi, S. (2021). Blockchain-enabled pharmaceutical cold chain: Applications, key challenges, and future trends. *Journal of Cleaner Production*, *302*, 127021. doi:10.1016/j.jclepro.2021.127021

Hsu, A., Lee, C. F., & Liu, S. (2022). Book-tax differences, CEO overconfidence, and bank loan contracting. *Review of Quantitative Finance and Accounting*, *58*(2), 437–472. doi:10.100711156-021-00992-3

Hua, K., Chen, W., & Chen, N. (2018). Augmented Reality Enhanced Textbook: An Innovative Approach to Enhancing Students' Learning. *Journal of Educational Technology Development and Exchange*, *11*(1), 1–18.

Hui, L. Geczy, P., Lai, H., Gobert, J., Yang, S. J. H., Ogata, H., Baltes J., Rodrigo, G., Li, P., Tsai, C. (2020). Challenges and Future Directions of Big Data and Artificial Intelligence in Education, Frontiers in Psychology, 11. . doi:10.3389/fpsyg.2020.580820

Iannotta, P. G. (2010). Mergers and Acquisitions: Definitions, Process, and Analysis. In *Investment Banking*. Springer. doi:10.1007/978-3-540-93765-4_7

Imran, M., Zaman, U., Imtiaz, J., Fayaz, M., & Gwak, J. (2021). Comprehensive survey of iot, machine learning, and blockchain for health care applications: A topical assessment for pandemic preparedness, challenges, and solutions. *Electronics (Basel)*, *10*(20), 2501. doi:10.3390/electronics10202501

Ismagilova, E., Hughes, L., Rana, N. P., & Dwivedi, Y. K. (2022). Security, Privacy and Risks Within Smart Cities: Literature Review and Development of a Smart City Interaction Framework. *Information Systems Frontiers*, *24*(2), 393–414. doi:10.100710796-020-10044-1 PMID:32837262

Ivgm, A. P. (2017). *Affordances of Augmented Reality for Education, 49*.

Jadhav, B., Patankar, A. B., & Jadhav, S. B. (2018). A Practical approach for integrating Big data Analytics into E-governance using Hadoop. *2018 Second International Conference on Inventive Communication and Computational Technologies (ICICCT)*, Coimbatore, India. 10.1109/ICICCT.2018.8473353

Jagatheesaperumal, S. (2021). The Duo of Artificial Intelligence and Big Data for Industry 4.0. *Review of Applications, Techniques, Challenges, and Future Research Directions*.

Jordà, Ò., Schularick, M., Taylor, A. M., & Ward, F. (2019). Global Financial Cycles and Risk Premiums. *IMF Economic Review*, *67*(1), 109–150. doi:10.105741308-019-00077-1

Ju, L. (2021). Relational Subsets Knowledge Distillation for Long-Tailed Retinal Diseases Recognition. In Medical Image Computing and Computer Assisted Intervention – MICCAI 2021. Springer, Cham. doi:10.1007/978-3-030-87237-3_1

Jung, Y., & Hu, J. (2015). AK-fold averaging cross-validation procedure. Journal of Nonparametric Statistics, 27(2), 167-179. doi:10.1080/10485252.2015.1010532

Jupyter. (2022). *Introduction to Jupyter*. Jupyter. https://jupyter.org/

Kansal, I., Popli, R., Verma, J., Bhardwaj, V., & Bhardwaj, R. (2022) Digital Image Processing and IoT in Smart Health Care -A review. *International Conference on Emerging Smart Computing and Informatics (ESCI)*, 1-6. 10.1109/ESCI53509.2022.9758227

Karabulut, E. M., & Ibrikci, T. (2017). Discriminative deep belief networks for microarray-based cancer classification. *Journal of Biomedical Research*, *28*(3). doi:10.1016/j.patcog.2010.12.012

Kasban, El-Bendary, & Salama. (2015). A comparative study of medical imaging techniques. *International Journal of Information Science and Intelligent System*, *4*(2), 37–58.

Kashyap, H. (2022). *Elon Musk's Starlink Applies for DoT Licence To Bring Satellite Broadband To India. INC 42*. inc42. com/buzz/elon-musks-starlink-applies-dot-licence-bring-satellite-broadband-india/#:~:text=The%20competition%20 within%20India's%20%2413,satellite%2Dbased%20broadband%20to%20India

Kaur, J. (2022). *Jio Gets DoT Nod To Launch Satellite-Based Broadband Services: Report*. INC 42. https://inc42.com/ buzz/jio-gets-dot-nod-to-launch-satellite-based-broadband-services-report/

Kaur, S. J., & Ali, L. (2021). Understanding bank employees' perception towards technology enabled banking: A developing country perspective. *Journal of Financial Services Marketing*, *26*(3), 129–143. doi:10.105741264-021-00100-5

Kautish, P., & Khare, A. (2022). Investigating the moderating role of AI-enabled services on flow and awe experience. *International Journal of Information Management*, *66*, 102519. doi:10.1016/j.ijinfomgt.2022.102519

Kelly, B., & Laffey, J. (2016). The impact of virtual reality on learning and training in healthcare. *Journal of Medical Systems*, *40*(1), 1–12. PMID:26573639

Khandare, S. T. (2014). A Survey Paper on Image Segmentation with Thresholding. *International Journal of ComputerScience and Mobile Computing*, *3*(1), 441–446.

Khedkar, V.S. & Patel, S. (2021). Diabetes prediction using machine learning: A bibliometric analysis, *Library Philosophy and Practice, 4751*.

Kontokosta, C. E. (2015). A Market-Specific Methodology for a Commercial Building Energy Performance Index. *The Journal of Real Estate Finance and Economics*, *51*(2), 288–316. doi:10.100711146-014-9481-0

Koo, D., Shin, Y., Yun, J., & Hur, J. (2018). Improving Security and Reliability in Merkle Tree-Based Online Data Authentication with Leakage Resilience. *Applied Sciences (Basel, Switzerland)*, *8*(12), 2532. doi:10.3390/app8122532

Ktari, J., Frikha, T., Amor, N. Ben, Louraidh, L., Elmannai, H., & Hamdi, M. (2022). *IoMT-Based Platform for E-Health Monitoring Based on the Blockchain.*

Ktari, Jalel and Abid, M. (2008). A Low Power Design Methodology Based on High Level Models. *ESA*, 10--15.

Kumari, K., & Saini, K. (2019). CFDD (CounterFeit Drug Detection) using Blockchain in the Pharmaceutical Industry. *International Journal of Engineering Research & Technology, 8*(12), 591-594.

Kusuma, S. M., Veena, K. N., Kavya, K. S., & Vijaya Kumar, B. P. (2023). Intelligence and Cognitive Computing at the Edge for IoT: Architecture, Challenges, and Applications. In N. Sindhwani, R. Anand, M. Niranjanamurthy, D. Chander Verma, & E. B. Valentina (Eds.), *IoT Based Smart Applications. EAI/Springer Innovations in Communication and Computing*. Springer. doi:10.1007/978-3-031-04524-0_19

Lai, S. T., Leu, F. Y., & Lin, J. W. (2019). A Banking Chatbot Security Control Procedure for Protecting User Data Security and Privacy. In L. Barolli, F. Y. Leu, T. Enokido, & H. C. Chen (Eds.), Advances on Broadband and Wireless Computing, Communication and Applications. BWCCA 2018: Lecture Notes on Data Engineering and Communications Technologies (Vol. 25). Springer. doi:10.1007/978-3-030-02613-4_50

Lasi, H., Hans-Georg, K, Fettke, P., Feld, T., & Hoffmann, M. (2020). Industry 4.0. Business & Information Systems Engineering, 4 (6), 239-242.

Lee, J., Bagheri, B., & Kao, H. A. (2015). A cyber-physical systems architecture for industry 4.0-based manufacturing systems. *Manufacturing Letters*, *3*, 18–23. doi:10.1016/j.mfglet.2014.12.001

Lee, K. (2020). Openness and innovation in online higher education: A historical review of the two discourses. *Open Learning*, *36*(2), 1–21. doi:10.1080/02680513.2020.1713737

Lesani, M., & Palsberg, J. (2014). Decomposing Opacity. In F. Kuhn (Ed.), Lecture Notes in Computer Science: Vol. 8784. *Distributed Computing. DISC 2014*. Springer. doi:10.1007/978-3-662-45174-8_27

Leyva-Mayorga, I., Soret, B., Roper, M., Wubben, D., Matthiesen, B., Dekorsy, A., & Popovski, P. (2020). LEO Small-Satellite Constellations for 5G and Beyond-5G Communications. *IEEE Access : Practical Innovations, Open Solutions*, *8*, 184955–184964. doi:10.1109/ACCESS.2020.3029620

Lezzi, M., Lazoi, M., & Corallo, A. (2018). Cybersecurity for Industry 4.0 in the current literature: A reference framework. *Computers in Industry*, *103*, 97–110. doi:10.1016/j.compind.2018.09.004

Li, J., Li, Y., & Ye, L. (2019). Augmented Reality in E-Government: A Review of Applications and Challenges. *Journal of Information Technology & Politics*, *16*(2), 153–174.

Lin, X., Chen, W., & Chen, N. (2017). The application of augmented reality technology in urban navigation. *Journal of Location Based Services*, *11*(3), 185–197.

Liu, G., Bao, H., Han, B. (2018). A stacked autoencoder-based deep neural network for achieving gearbox fault diagnosis. *Article in Mathematical Problems in Engineering*, 23-33. doi:10.1155/2018/5105709

Liu, X., Chen, W., & Chen, N. (2018). Augmented reality in emergency response: A review. *International Journal of Emergency Management*, *15*(3), 207–218.

Liu, X., Chen, W., & Chen, N. (2018). Virtual reality in language learning: A review of recent research. *Computer Assisted Language Learning*, *31*(6), 493–515.

Liu, Y., & Wang, H. (2009). A comparative study on e-learning technologies and products: From the East to the West. *Systems Research*, *26*(2), 191–209. doi:10.1002res.959

Li, Y., Guo, L., & Li, X. (2019). The application of augmented reality in virtual meetings. *Journal of Visual Communication and Image Representation*, *63*, 69–78.

Li, Y., Guo, L., & Li, X. (2019). The application of augmented reality technology in environmental education. *Journal of Clean Energy Technologies*, *7*(6), 485–491.

Li, Y., Shan, B., Li, B., Liu, X., & Pu, Y. (2021, August 13). Literature Review on the Applications of Machine Learning and Blockchain Technology in Smart Healthcare Industry: A Bibliometric Analysis. *Journal of Healthcare Engineering*, *9739219*, 1–11. doi:10.1155/2021/9739219 PMID:34426765

Li, Y., Youtie, J., & Shapira, P. (2015). Why do technology firms publish scientific papers? The strategic use of science by small and midsize enterprises in nanotechnology. *The Journal of Technology Transfer*, *40*(6), 1016–1033. doi:10.100710961-014-9391-6

LotusArise. (2020). *Satellite Frequency Bands: L, S, C, X, Ku, Ka-band.* Lotus Arise. https://lotusarise.com/satellite-frequency-bands-upsc/

Ma, C. (2021). Smart city and cyber-security; technologies used, leading challenges and future recommendations, *Energy Reports, 7*, 7999-8012. doi:10.1016/j.egyr.2021.08.124

Majumdar, S., & Pujari, V. (2021). Exploring usage of mobile banking apps in the UAE: A categorical regression analysis. *Journal of Financial Services Marketing*. doi:10.105741264-021-00112-1

Mangaroska, K., Vesin, B., Kostakos, V., Brusilovsky, P., & Giannakos, M. N. (2021, April 1). Architecting Analytics Across Multiple E-Learning Systems to Enhance Learning Design. *IEEE Transactions on Learning Technologies*, *14*(2), 173–188. doi:10.1109/TLT.2021.3072159

Mansour, R. F. (2022). Artificial intelligence based optimization with deep learning model for blockchain enabled intrusion detection in CPS environment. *Scientific Reports*, *12*(1), 1–14. doi:10.103841598-022-17043-z PMID:35902617

Martin-Gutierrez, L., Peng, J., Thompson, N. L., Robinson, G. A., Naja, M., Peckham, H., Wu, W., J'bari, H., Ahwireng, N., Waddington, K. E., Bradford, C. M., Varnier, G., Gandhi, A., Radmore, R., Gupta, V., Isenberg, D. A., Jury, E. C., & Ciurtin, C. (2021). Stratification of Patients With Sjögren's Syndrome and Patients With Systemic Lupus Erythematosus According to Two Shared Immune Cell Signatures, With Potential Therapeutic Implications. *Arthritis & Rheumatology (Hoboken, N.J.)*, *73*(9), 1626–1637. doi:10.1002/art.41708 PMID:33645922

McGee, R. W. (2010). Analyzing Insider Trading from the Perspectives of Utilitarian Ethics and Rights Theory. *Journal of Business Ethics*, *91*(1), 65–82. doi:10.100710551-009-0068-2

Melese, F. (2021). Insights from Transaction Cost Economics for Government Organizations: An Application to the U.S. Department of Defense (DoD). *Atlantic Economic Journal, 49*(1), 109–111. doi:10.100711293-021-09705-6

Meshram, C., Obaidat, M. S., Tembhurne, J. V., Shende, S. W., Kalare, K. W., & Meshram, S. G. (2021). A Lightweight Provably Secure Digital Short-Signature Technique Using Extended Chaotic Maps for Human-Centered IoT Systems. *IEEE Systems Journal, 15*(4), 5507–5515. doi:10.1109/JSYST.2020.3043358

Micheler, E., & Whaley, A. (2020). Regulatory Technology: Replacing Law with Computer Code. *European Business Organization Law Review, 21*(2), 349–377. doi:10.100740804-019-00151-1

Milgram, P., & Kishino, A. (1994). A taxonomy of mixed reality visual displays. *IEICE Transactions on Information and Systems, 77*(12), 1321–1329.

Mocetti, S., Pagnini, M., & Sette, E. (2017). Information Technology and Banking Organization. *Journal of Financial Services Research, 51*(3), 313–338. doi:10.100710693-016-0244-3

Moharm, K., Eltahan, M. (2020). The Role of Big Data in Improving E-Learning Transition. *IOP Conf. Ser.: Mater. Sci. Eng.*

Moreau, A., Sévigny, S., Giroux, I., & Chauchard, E. (2020). Ability to Discriminate Online Poker Tilt Episodes: A New Way to Prevent Excessive Gambling? *Journal of Gambling Studies, 36*(2), 699–711. doi:10.100710899-019-09903-7 PMID:31679089

Moro, S., Cortez, P., & Rita, P. (2015). Using customer lifetime value and neural networks to improve the prediction of bank deposit subscription in telemarketing campaigns. *Neural Computing & Applications, 26*(1), 131–139. doi:10.100700521-014-1703-0

Muneer, S., & Raza, H. (2022). *An IoMT enabled smart healthcare model to monitor elderly people using Explainable Artificial Intelligence (EAI). 1*(June), 16–22.

Muñoz-Saavedra, L., Miró-Amarante, L., & Domínguez-Morales, M. (2020). Augmented and Virtual Reality Evolution and Future Tendency. *Applied Sciences (Basel, Switzerland), 10*(1), 1. doi:10.3390/app10010322

Musso, P., & Schiavo, S. (2008). The impact of financial constraints on firm survival and growth. *Journal of Evolutionary Economics, 18*(2), 135–149. doi:10.100700191-007-0087-z

Nadeem, M. W., Goh, H. G., Ponnusamy, V., Andonovic, I., Khan, M. A., & Hussain, M. (2021, October). A fusion-based machine learning approach for the prediction of the onset of diabetes. []. MDPI.]. *Health Care, 9*(10), 1393. PMID:34683073

Nakamoto, S. (2008). *Bitcoin: A peer-to-peer electronic cash system.* Bitcoin.

Nakamura, M., Kajiwara, Y., Otsuka, A., & Kimura, H. (2013). LVQ-SMOTE– learning vector quantization based synthetic minority over–sampling technique for biomedical data. *Journal of BioData Mining, 6*(1). doi:10.1186/1756-0381-6-16

Nasrallah, N., & El Khoury, R. (2021). Proxy Measure for SMEs Financial Performance in Opaque Markets. In B. Alareeni, A. Hamdan, & I. Elgedawy (Eds.), *The Importance of New Technologies and Entrepreneurship in Business Development: In the Context of Economic Diversity in Developing Countries. ICBT 2020. Lecture Notes in Networks and Systems* (Vol. 194). Springer. doi:10.1007/978-3-030-69221-6_108

Ndou, V., & Nkambule, S. (2019). Virtual and Augmented Reality in E-Government: Opportunities and Challenges. In *International Conference on E-Governance* (pp. 45-55). Springer, Cham.

NeGP Website. "About NeGP". NeGP Website. Retrieved 17 July, 2014.

Nekooeimehr, I., & Lai-Yuen, S. K. (2016). Adaptive semi-unsupervised weighted oversampling (A-SUWO) for imbalanced datasets. Expert Systems with Applications, 46, 405-416. doi:10.1016/j.eswa.2015.10.031

Nguyen, G. N., Le Viet, N. H., Elhoseny, M., Shankar, K., Gupta, B. B., & Abd El-Latif, A. A. (2021). Secure blockchain enabled Cyber–physical systems in healthcare using deep belief network with ResNet model. *Journal of Parallel and Distributed Computing, 153*, 150–160. doi:10.1016/j.jpdc.2021.03.011

Niranjane, V., Shelke, U., Shirke, S., & Dafe, S. (2022). IoT based Digital Production Counting System. In *International Conference on Electronics and Renewable Systems (ICEARS),* (pp. 452-455). IEEE. 10.1109/ICEARS53579.2022.9752399

Nishadi, A. S. T. (n.d.). Predicting Heart Diseases in Logistic Regression of Machine Learning Algorithms by Python Jupyterlab. *International Journal of Advanced Research and Publications* . https://www.kaggle.com

Ochatt, S., Lambardi, M., Panis, B., Pathirana, R., Revilla, M. A., & Wang, Q.-C. (2021). Cryopreservation and In Vitro banking: A cool subject – Preface from the editors. *Plant Cell, Tissue and Organ Culture, 144*(1), 1–5. doi:10.100711240-020-01985-1

Octaviani, T. L., & Rustam, Z. (2019). Random forest for breast cancer prediction. *AIP Conference Proceedings, 2168*, 020050. doi:10.1063/1.5132477

Ogura, Y., & Uchida, H. (2014). Bank Consolidation and Soft Information Acquisition in Small Business Lending. *Journal of Financial Services Research, 45*(2), 173–200. doi:10.100710693-013-0163-5

Oladimeji, O. (2023). Machine Learning in Smart Health Research: A Bibliometric Analysis. *International Journal of Information Science and Management, 21*(1), 119–128. doi:10.22034/ijism.2022.1977616.0

Ortiz-Molina, H., & Penas, M. F. (2008). Lending to small businesses: The role of loan maturity in addressing information problems. *Small Business Economics, 30*(4), 361–383. doi:10.100711187-007-9053-2

Pandimurugan, V., Mandviya, R., Gadgil, A., Prakhar, K., & Datar, A. (2021). IoT based Smart Beekeeping Monitoring system for beekeepers in India. In *4th International Conference on Computing and Communications Technologies (ICCCT),* (pp. 65-70). IEEE. 10.1109/ICCCT53315.2021.9711901

Pardakhe, N. V., & Deshmukh, V. M. (2019). Machine Learning and Blockchain Techniques Used in Healthcare System. *2019 IEEE Pune Section International Conference (PuneCon)*, Pune, India. 10.1109/PuneCon46936.2019.9105710

Pardini, K., Rodrigues, J. J. P. C., Kozlov, S. A., Kumar, N., & Furtado, V. (2019). IoT-Based Solid Waste Management Solutions: A Survey. *Journal of Sensor and Actuator Networks, 8*(1), 5. doi:10.3390/jsan8010005

Pastore, P., Ricciardi, A., & Tommaso, S. (2020). Contractual networks: An organizational model to reduce the competitive disadvantage of small and medium enterprises (SMEs) in Europe's less developed regions. A survey in southern Italy. *The International Entrepreneurship and Management Journal, 16*(4), 1503–1535. doi:10.100711365-019-00616-2

Pengji, W., & McCarthy, B. (2021). What do people like on Facebook? Content marketing strategies used by retail bank brands in Australia and Singapore, 29(2). doi:10.1016/j.ausmj.2020.04.008

Pereira, G. V., Charalabidis, Y., Alexopoulos, C., Mureddu, F., Parycek, P., Ronzhyn, A., & Wimmer, M. A. (2018). Scientific foundations training and entrepreneurship activities in the domain of ICT-enabled governance. In *Proceedings of the 19th Annual International Conference on Digital Government Research: Governance in the Data Age,* (p. 98). ACM. 10.1145/3209281.3209316

PeterJ. (2017). https://blogs.oracle.com/bigdata/machine-learningtechniques

Peters, U. (2021). An argument for egalitarian confirmation bias and against political diversity in academia. *Synthese*, *198*(12), 11999–12019. doi:10.100711229-020-02846-2

Picciano, A. G. (2012). The Evolution of Big Data and Learning Analytics in American Higher Education. *Journal of Asynchronous Learning Networks*, *16*(3), 9–20. doi:10.24059/olj.v16i3.267

Piri, S., Delen, D., & Liu, T. (2018). A synthetic informative minority oversampling (SIMO) algorithm leveraging support vector machine to enhance learning from imbalanced datasets. Decision Support Systems Journal, 106, 15-29. doi:10.1016/j.dss.2017.11.006

Plastiras, G., Terzi, M., Kyrkou, C., & Theocharides, T. (2018). Edge Intelligence: Challenges and Opportunities of Near-Sensor Machine Learning Applications. *2018 IEEE 29th International Conference on Application-specific Systems, Architectures and Processors (ASAP)*, (pp. 1-7). IEEE. 10.1109/ASAP.2018.8445118

Pokhrel, S. R. (2020, September). Federated learning meets blockchain at 6g edge: A drone-assisted networking for disaster response. In *Proceedings of the 2nd ACM MobiCom Workshop on Drone Assisted Wireless Communications for 5G and Beyond* (pp. 49-54). 10.1145/3414045.3415949

Polak, P., Nelischer, C., Guo, H., & Robertson, D. C. (2020). "Intelligent" finance and treasury management: What we can expect. *AI & Society*, *35*(3), 715–726. doi:10.100700146-019-00919-6

Portela, M., Thanassoulis, E., & Simpson, G. (2004). Negative data in DEA: A directional distance approach applied to bank branches. *The Journal of the Operational Research Society*, *55*(10), 1111–1121. doi:10.1057/palgrave.jors.2601768

Pramanik, S., & Raja, S. S. (2019). Analytical Study on Security Issues in Steganography. Think-India, 22(35), 106-114, .

PTI. (2021). SIA-India for unleashing full potential of all satellite bands for IoT. *Economic Times*. https://economictimes.indiatimes.com/tech/tech-bytes/sia-india-for-unleashing-full-potential-of-all-satellite-bands-for-iot/articleshow/82219179.cms

Qureshi, A., Batra, S., Vats, P., Singh, S., & ... (2022). A Review of Machine Learning (ML) in the Internet of Medical Things (IOMT) in the Construction of a Smart Healthcare Structure. *Journal of ...*, *13*.

Rahaman, Md.Mahbobor & Haque, Afruza & Hasan, Md. (2021). *Challenges and Opportunities of Big Data for Managing the E-Governance. 1.* 490-499.

Rajnak, V., & Puschmann, T. (2021). The impact of blockchain on business models in banking. *Information Systems and e-Business Management*, *19*(3), 809–861. doi:10.100710257-020-00468-2

Raj, P., Saini, K., & Surianarayanan, C. (Eds.). (2020). *Blockchain Technology and Applications*. CRC Press. doi:10.1201/9781003081487

Rakshit, P., & Srivastava, P. K. (2021). Cutting Edge IoT Technology for Smart Indian Pharma. In *International Conference on Advance Computing and Innovative Technologies in Engineering (ICACITE)* (pp. 360-362). IEEE. 10.1109/ICACITE51222.2021.9404627

Rametta, C., & Schembra, G. (2017). Designing a softwarized network deployed on a fleet of drones for rural zone monitoring. *Future Internet*, *9*(1), 8. doi:10.3390/fi9010008

Rao, T. P., Rao, M. N., Arul, U., & Balajee, J. (2022). Detection of MRI Medical MRI Images of Brain Tumors Using Deep Learning & Secure the Transfer of Medical Images Using Blockchain. *Journal of Algebraic Statistics*, *13*(3), 374–377.

Raser, J. M., & O'Shea, E. K. (2005). Noise in gene expression: origins, consequences, and control. American Association for the Advancement of Science, 309(5743), 2010-2013. doi:10.1126cience.1105891

Rehse, J.-R., Mehdiyev, N., & Fettke, P. (2019). Towards explainable process predictions for industry 4.0 in the dfki-smart-lego-factory. KIKunstliche Intelligenz, 33(2), 181–187. doi:10.100713218-019-00586-1

Ren, S., Kim, J.-S., Cho, W.-S., Soeng, S., Kong, S., & Lee, K.-H. (2021). Big Data Platform for Intelligence Industrial IoT Sensor Monitoring System Based on Edge Computing and AI," *2021 International Conference on Artificial Intelligence in Information and Communication (ICAIIC)*, , pp. 480-482, 10.1109/ICAIIC51459.2021.9415189

Riecke, B. E., & Bülthoff, H. H. (2005). The perception of virtual and real environments. *Journal of Vision (Charlottesville, Va.)*, 5(3), 19–19.

Riva, G. (2016). Virtual reality in e-governance: A review. *International Journal of E-Governance*, 9(2), 156–167.

Riva, G. (2016). Virtual reality in emergency management training: A review. *International Journal of Emergency Management*, 13(2), 128–139.

Riva, G. (2016). Virtual reality in vocational education and training. *Journal of Vocational Education and Training*, 68(2), 187–204.

Romay, M. C., Millard, M. J., Glaubitz, J. C., Peiffer, J. A., Swarts, K. L., Casstevens, T. M., Elshire, R. J., Acharya, C. B., Mitchell, S. E., Flint-Garcia, S. A., McMullen, M. D., Holland, J. B., Buckler, E. S., & Gardner, C. A. (2013). Comprehensive genotyping of the USA national maize inbred seed bank. *Genome Biology*, 14(6), R55. doi:10.1186/gb-2013-14-6-r55 PMID:23759205

Rostamkalaei, A., Nitani, M., & Riding, A. (2020). Borrower discouragement: The role of informal turndowns. *Small Business Economics*, 54(1), 173–188. doi:10.100711187-018-0086-5

Routray, S. & Mohammed, H. (2019). *Satellite Based IoT Networks for Emerging Applications.* Springer.

Routray, S. K., Javali, A., Sahoo, A., Sharmila, K. P., & Anand, S. (2020). Military Applications of Satellite Based IoT. In *Third International Conference on Smart Systems and Inventive Technology (ICSSIT)* (pp. 122-127). IEEE. 10.1109/ICSSIT48917.2020.9214284

Routray, S. K., Tengshe, R., Javali, A., Sarkar, S., Sharma, L., & Ghosh, A. D. (2019). Satellite Based IoT for Mission Critical Applications. In *2019 International Conference on Data Science and Communication (IconDSC)* (pp. 1-6). IEEE. 10.1109/IconDSC.2019.8817030

Roy, A. (2008). Organization Structure and Risk Taking in Banking. *Risk Manag*, 10(2), 122–134. doi:10.1057/palgrave.rm.8250043

RudinC. (2019). "Stop Explaining Black Box Machine Learning Models for High Stakes Decisions and Use Interpretable Models Instead." ArXiv:1811.10154. https://arxiv.org/abs/1811.10154

Ruozi, R., & Ferrari, P. (2013). Liquidity Risk Management in Banks: Economic and Regulatory Issues. In *Liquidity Risk Management in Banks. SpringerBriefs in Finance.* Springer. doi:10.1007/978-3-642-29581-2

Saini, K. (2020). Next Generation Logistics: A Novel Approach of Blockchain Technology. In *Essential Enterprise Blockchain Concepts and Applications.* CRC Press.

Saini, K., Roy, A., Chelliah, P. R., & Patel, T. (2021). Blockchain 2.O: A Smart Contract. In *International Conference on Computational Performance Evaluation (ComPE)*, (pp. 524-528). IEEE. 10.1109/ComPE53109.2021.9752021

Sakawa, H., & Watanabel, N. (2020). Main bank relationship and accounting conservatism: Evidence from Japan. *Asian Business & Management*, 19(1), 62–85. doi:10.105741291-019-00071-5

Santosa, A. D., Taufik, N., Prabowo, F. H. E., & Rahmawati, M. (2021). Continuance intention of baby boomer and X generation as new users of digital payment during COVID-19 pandemic using UTAUT2. *Journal of Financial Services Marketing*, *26*(4), 259–273. doi:10.105741264-021-00104-1

Santosh, K. C. (2020). AI-Driven Tools for Coronavirus Outbreak: Need of Active Learning and Cross-Population Train/ Test Models on Multitudinal/Multimodal Data. *Journal of Medical Systems*, *44*(5), 93. doi:10.100710916-020-01562-1 PMID:32189081

Sarhaddi, F., Azimi, I., Labbaf, S., Niela-Vilén, H., Dutt, N., Axelin, A., Liljeberg, P., & Rahmani, A. M. (2021). Long-Term IoT-Based Maternal Monitoring: System Design and Evaluation. *Sensors (Basel)*, *21*(7), 2281. Advance online publication. doi:10.339021072281 PMID:33805217

Sartzetakis, E. S. (2021). Green bonds as an instrument to finance low carbon transition. *Economic Change and Restructuring*, *54*(3), 755–779. doi:10.100710644-020-09266-9

Schebesch, K. B., & Stecking, R. (2005). Support Vector Machines for Credit Scoring: Extension to Non-Standard Cases. In: Baier, D. & Wernecke, KD. (eds) Innovations in Classification, Data Science, and Information Systems. Studies in Classification, Data Analysis, and Knowledge Organization. Springer, Berlin, Heidelberg. doi:10.1007/3-540-26981-9_57

Schell, A. (2021). *Fixed Wireless Internet vs. Satellite Internet: What Are The Differences*. Upward Broadband. https://www.upwardbroadband.com/fixed-wireless-internet-vs-satellite-internet-what-are-the-differences/#:~:text=However%2C%20satellite%20and%20fixed%20wireless,tower%20that%20broadcasts%20these%20services

Schnabl, G., & Zemanek, H. (2011). Inter-temporal savings, current account trends and asymmetric shocks in a heterogeneous European Monetary Union. *Inter Economics*, *46*(3), 153–160. doi:10.100710272-011-0377-4

Scholl, H. & Scholl, M. (2014). Smart Governance: A Roadmap for Research and Practice. *iConference 2014 Proceedings*. . doi:10.9776/14060

Segawa, E., Schalet, B., & Cella, D. (2020). A comparison of computer adaptive tests (CATs) and short forms in terms of accuracy and number of items administrated using PROMIS profile. *Quality of Life Research: An International Journal of Quality of Life Aspects of Treatment, Care and Rehabilitation*, *29*(1), 213–221. doi:10.100711136-019-02312-8 PMID:31595451

Sequeira, N. (2020). IoT Applications in Waste Management. *IoT For All*. https://www.iotforall.com/iot-applications-waste-management

Serrat, O. (2017). Social Network Analysis. In *Knowledge Solutions*. Springer. doi:10.1007/978-981-10-0983-9_9

Shahnaz, A., Qamar, U., & Khalid, A. (2019). Using Blockchain for Electronic Health Records. *IEEE Access : Practical Innovations, Open Solutions*, *7*, 147782–147795. doi:10.1109/ACCESS.2019.2946373

Shen, W., Li, Y., & Chen, W. (2018). *Augmented reality in e-governance*.

Shen, W., Li, Y., & Chen, W. (2018). Augmented Reality in Remote Collaboration: A Review. *International Journal of Human-Computer Interaction*, *34*(11), 927–939.

Shen, W., Li, Y., & Chen, W. (2018). Augmented Reality in Urban Planning and Design: A Review. *Journal of Urban Planning and Development*, *144*(1), 04018001.

Sherasiya, T., Upadhyay, H., & Patel, H. B. (2016). A survey: Intrusion detection system for internet of things. *International Journal on Computer Science and Engineering*, *5*(2), 91–98.

Shi, X., Wang, X., & Li, X. (2018). Virtual reality in urban planning and design: A review. *International Journal of Architectural Computing, 16*(1), 7–24.

Simon, J., Perić, N., Mayer, S., Deckert, J., Gorwood, P., Pérez, V., Reif, A., Ruhe, H., Veltman, D., Morriss, R., Bilderbeck, A., Dawson, G., Dourish, C., Dias, R., Kingslake, J., & Browning, M. (2019). PMH21 cost-effectiveness of the predict test: results and lessons learned from a European multinational depression trial. *Value in Health, 22*, S684. doi:10.1016/j.jval.2019.09.1495

Singh, U. (2019). E-Governance Implementation. *Literature Review Analysis, 6*(1), 17.

Singh, P., Nayyar, A., Kaur, A., & Ghosh, U. (2020). Blockchain and fog based architecture for internet of everything in smart cities. *Future Internet, 12*(4), 61. doi:10.3390/fi12040061

Singhvi, R. K., Lohar, R. L., Kumar, A., Sharma, R., Sharma, L. D., & Saraswat, R. K., Singhvi, R. L., Lohar, A., Kumar, R., Sharma, L. D., & Saraswat, R. K. (2019). IoT BasedSmart Waste Management System: India prospective. In *4th International Conference on Internet of Things: Smart Innovation and Usages (IoT-SIU)* (pp. 1-6). IEEE. 10.1109/IoT-SIU.2019.8777698

STHDA. (2018). *Evaluation of Classification Method Accuracy*. STHDA. http://www.sthda.com/english/articles/36-classificationmethods- essentials/143-evaluation-of-classification-model-accuracyessentials/

Stix, H. (2021). Ownership, and purchase intention of crypto assets: Survey results. *Empirica, 48*, 65–99. doi:10.100710663-020-09499-x

Subash, C., Mahapatra, Das, R., & Patra, M. (2008). *Current e-Governance Scenario in Healthcare sector of India.*

Sudirtha, I. G., Widiana, I. W., & Adijaya, M. A. (2022). The Effectiveness of Using Revised Bloom's Taxonomy-Oriented Learning Activities to Improve Students' Metacognitive Abilities. *Journal of Education and E-Learning Research, 9*(2), 55–61. doi:10.20448/jeelr.v9i2.3804

Sun, Z., Song, Q., Zhu, X., Sun, H., Xu, B., & Zhou, Y. (2015). A novel ensemble method for classifying imbalanced data. Pattern Recognition, 48(5), 1623-1637. doi:10.1016/j.patcog.2014.11.014

Tambunan, T. (2008). SME development, economic growth, and government intervention in a developing country: The Indonesian story. *Journal of International Entrepreneurship, 6*(4), 147–167. doi:10.100710843-008-0025-7

Tarchouna, A., Jarraya, B., & Bouri, A. (2021). Do board characteristics and ownership structure matter for bank non-performing loans? Empirical evidence from US commercial banks. *The Journal of Management and Governance.* doi:10.100710997-020-09558-2

Tay, L., Te Chuan, A. H., Aziati, N. (2018). An Overview of Industry 4.0: Definition, Components, and Government Initiatives. *Journal of Advanced Research in Dynamical and Control Systems.*

Tech Stocks. (2023). *Tech Stocks*. Investopedia. https://www.investopedia.com/terms/d/deep-learning.asp

Tele2. (2021). The Role of IoT in Smart Waste Management. *Tele2*. https://tele2iot.com/article/the-role-of-iot-in-smart-waste-management/

Teli, T. A., Yousuf, R., & Khan, D. A. (2022). Ensuring Secure Data Sharing in IoT Domains Using Blockchain. In *Cyber Security and Digital Forensics: Challenges and Future Trends* (pp. 205–221). Wiley. doi:10.1002/9781119795667.ch9

Tensor Flow. (2022). Introduction to TensorFlow and Keras. *TensorFlow*. https://www.tensorflow.org/

Thaler, T. A., Priest, S. J., & Fuchs, S. (2016). Evolving inter-regional co-operation in flood risk management: Distances and types of partnership approaches in Austria. *Regional Environmental Change, 16*(3), 841–853. doi:10.100710113-015-0796-z

Tien Tuan Anh, D., Ji, W., Gang, C., Rui, L., & Blockbench, A. (2017). Framework for Analyzing Private Blockchains. *Proceedings of the 2017 ACM International Conference on Management of Data,* Chicago, IL, USA, 14–19.

Tsai, C. H., & Su, P. C. (2021). The application of multi-server authentication scheme in internet banking transaction environments. *Information Systems and e-Business Management, 19*(1), 77–105. doi:10.100710257-020-00481-5

UCI. (2016). *Default of Credit Card Clients Data Set.* UCI. https://archive.ics.uci.edu/ml/datasets/default+of+credit+card+clients

Underwood, S. (2016). Blockchain beyond Bitcoin. *Communications of the ACM, 59*(11), 15–17. doi:10.1145/2994581

Varma Kakarlapudi, P., Mahmoud, Q. H., & Systematic, Q. A. (2021). *healthcare A Systematic Review of Blockchain for Consent Management.* doi:10.3390/healthcare

Vijai, C., & Wisetsri, W. (2021). Rise of artificial intelligence in healthcare startups in India. *Advances in Management, 14*(1), 48–52.

Villar, A. S., & Khan, N. (2021). Robotic process automation in banking industry: A case study on Deutsche Bank. *J BANK FINANC TECHNOL, 5,* 71–86. doi:10.100742786-021-00030-9

Vishnu, S., Ramson, S. R. J., Senith, S., Anagnostopoulos, T., Abu-Mahfouz, A. M., Fan, X., Srinivasan, S., & Kirubaraj, A. A. (2021). IoT-Enabled Solid Waste Management in Smart Cities. *Smart Cities, 4*(3), 1004–1017. doi:10.3390martcities4030053

Vyas, S., Gupta, M., & Yadav, R. (2019). Converging Blockchain and Machine Learning for Healthcare. *2019 Amity International Conference on Artificial Intelligence (AICAI),* Dubai, United Arab Emirates. 10.1109/AICAI.2019.8701230

Wang, J., & Wang, H. (2018). Virtual Reality for E-Government: A Systematic Literature Review. *Journal of Electronic Government Research and Applications, 16,* 1–11.

Wang, S., Wan, J., Li, D., & Zhang, C. (2016). Implementing Smart Factory of Industrie 4.0: An Outlook. *International Journal of Distributed Sensor Networks, 12*(1), 3159805–3159810. doi:10.1155/2016/3159805

Wang, W., Hoang, D. T., Hu, P., Xiong, Z., Niyato, D., Wang, P., Wen, Y., & Kim, D. I. (2019). A Survey on Consensus Mechanisms and Mining Strategy Management in Blockchain Networks. *IEEE Access : Practical Innovations, Open Solutions, 7,* 22328–22370. doi:10.1109/ACCESS.2019.2896108

Wang, W., Liang, Y., & Yang, J. (2017). A study of the application of augmented reality in disaster recovery. *Journal of Disaster Research, 12*(5), 977–984.

Wang, W., Liang, Y., & Yang, J. (2017). A Study of the Application of Augmented Reality in Museums. *The International Journal of Virtual Reality : a Multimedia Publication for Professionals, 16*(2), 1–10.

Waseem, M., Liang, P., Márquez, G., Shahin, M., Khan, A. A., & Ahmad, A. (2021). A Decision Model for Selecting Patterns and Strategies to Decompose Applications into Microservices. In H. Hacid, O. Kao, M. Mecella, N. Moha, & Hy. Paik (Eds.), Lecture Notes in Computer Science: Vol. 13121. *Service-Oriented Computing. ICSOC 2021.* Springer. doi:10.1007/978-3-030-91431-8_62

Wenhua, Z., Qamar, F., Abdali, T.-A. N., Hassan, R., Jafri, S. T. A., & Nguyen, Q. N. (2023). Blockchain Technology: Security Issues, Healthcare Applications, Challenges and Future Trends. *Electronics (Basel)*, *12*(3), 546. doi:10.3390/electronics12030546

Worthington, A. C., & Higgs, H. (2011). Economies of scale and scope in Australian higher education. *Higher Education*, *61*(4), 387–414. doi:10.100710734-010-9337-3

Wu, J., Wang, W., & Chen, W. (2019). The application of virtual reality technology in museums. *Journal of Cultural Heritage*, *40*, 216–223.

Xu, Y., Liu, X., & Chen, W. (2018). Virtual reality in disaster recovery: A review. *Journal of Disaster Research*, *13*(2), 259–267.

Yan, N., & Sun, B. (2013). Coordinating loan strategies for supply chain financing with limited credit. *OR-Spektrum*, *35*(4), 1039–1058. doi:10.100700291-013-0329-4

Younas, W., & Kalimuthu, K. R. (2021). Telecom microfinance banking versus commercial banking: A battle in the financial services sector. *Journal of Financial Services Marketing*, *26*(2), 67–80. doi:10.105741264-020-00085-7

Yu, H., Sun, H., Wu, D., & Kuo, T. T. (2020, March 4). Comparison of Smart Contract Blockchains for Healthcare Applications. *AMIA ... Annual Symposium Proceedings - AMIA Symposium. AMIA Symposium*, *2019*, 1266–1275. PMID:32308924

Yulu. (2021). Pi Machine learning in Governments: Benefits, Challenges and Future Directions. *eDEM 13*(1), 203-219. http://www.jedem.org doi:10.29379/jedem.v13i1.625

Yusuf, H., & Surjandari, I. (2020). Comparison of Performance Between Kafka and Raft as Ordering Service Nodes Implementation in Hyperledger Fabric. *Int. J. Adv. Sci. Technol.*, *29*(7), 3549–3554.

Zhang, G., Zhang, X., Bilal, M., Dou, W., Xu, X., & Rodrigues, J. J. (2022). Identifying fraud in medical insurance based on blockchain and deep learning. *Future Generation Computer Systems*, *130*, 140–154. doi:10.1016/j.future.2021.12.006

Zhang, M., Huang, C., Zhang, J., Qin, H., Ma, G., Liu, X., & Yin, J. (2020). Accurate discrimination of tea from multiple geographical regions by combining multi-elements with multivariate statistical analysis. *Food Measure*, *14*(6), 3361–3370. doi:10.100711694-020-00575-1

Zhao, Z. Z., Chen, H. P., Huang, Y., Zhang, S. B., Li, Z. H., Feng, T., & Liu, J. K. (2017). Bioactive polyketides and 8, 14-seco-ergosterol from fruiting bodies of the ascomycete Daldinia childiae. *Phytochemistry*, *142*, 68–75. doi:10.1016/j.phytochem.2017.06.020 PMID:28686900

Zhen, C., & Hu, K. (2022, June 14). Design of Edge Computing Online Classroom Based on College English Teaching. *Computational Intelligence and Neuroscience*, *7068923*, 1–11. doi:10.1155/2022/7068923 PMID:35747728

Zheng, Z., Xie, S., Dai, H., Chen, X., & Wang, H. (2017). An Overview of Blockchain Technology: Architecture, Consensus, and Future Trends. In *Proc. - IEEE 6th Int. Congr. Big Data*. IEEE. 10.1109/BigDataCongress.2017.85

Zhou, K., Liu, T., & Zhou, L. (2015). Industry 4.0: Towards Future Industrial Opportunities and Challenges. In *12th International Conference on Fuzzy Systems and Knowledge Discovery*. IEEE. 10.1109/FSKD.2015.7382284

Zhou, J., Li, Y., & Chen, W. (2019). The application of virtual reality technology in urban navigation. *Journal of Location Based Services*, *13*(1), 52–65.

Zhou, J., Wang, X., & Li, Y. (2019). Augmented reality in medical education: A systematic review. *Journal of Medical Systems*, *43*(3), 121.

Zhu, L., Yu, F. R., Wang, Y., Ning, B., & Tang, T. (2018). Big data analytics in intelligent transportation systems: A survey. *IEEE Transactions on Intelligent Transportation Systems*, *20*(1), 383–398. doi:10.1109/TITS.2018.2815678

About the Contributors

Chamundeswari Arumugam is a Professor of Computer Science and Engineering department at Sri Sivasubramaniya Nadar College of Engineering, Chennai, India.

R. Athilakshmi is currently working as an Assistant Professor in the Department of Computational Intelligence at SRM Institute of Science and Technology, SRM University, KTR Campus, Chennai. She acquired her Ph.D. degree in 2022 at Anna University. During her Ph.D. research, she worked on a DST-SERB-funded project "Investigation on the effect of gene and Protein in Neurodegenerative Brain disorders" for 2 years. Her research interests cover Data Mining, Bioinformatics, Deep Learning, and Computer Vision. She has delivered guest lectures in the fields of Artificial Intelligence and Bioinformatics.

Anshu Chauhan is currently working as Assistant Professor at Teerthanker Mahaveer Institute of Management & Technology TMU Moradabad, U.P. India. She has more than 11 years of teaching experience. She has done MBA, MBA Economics, and Qualified UGC NET. Apru student counsellor at tmimt, tmu mouradabad

Ankur Gupta has received the B.Tech and M.Tech in Computer Science and Engineering from Ganga Institute of Technology and Management, Kablana affiliated with Maharshi Dayanand University, Rohtak in 2015 and 2017. He is an Assistant Professor in the Department of Computer Science and Engineering at Vaish College of Engineering, Rohtak, and has been working there since January 2019. He has many publications in various reputed national/ international conferences, journals, and online book chapter contributions (Indexed by SCIE, Scopus, ESCI, ACM, DBLP, etc). He is doing research in the field of cloud computing, data security & machine learning. His research work in M.Tech was based on biometric security in cloud computing.

Aswini J. received the M.E. degree in Computer Science and Engineering from Anna University, Chennai in 2011. She has completed her Ph.D. in Computer Science and Engineering at Meenakshi Academy of Higher Education and Research, Chennai during the year 2020 and is a Professor in Department of AIML at Saveetha Engineering College, Autonomous, Affiliated to Anna University, Chennai. Her research interests include Cloud Computing, IoT and Machine Learning. She has published 20 papers in international journals and conferences.

Vipin Jain is Director/Principal of Teerthanker Mahaveer Institute of Management and Technology (TMIMT) & Department of Hospital Administration, Officiating Dean of College of Law and Legal Studies and Chairperson of Center for Jain Studies. He is appointed as Chief Proctor of the University in April 2021. Formerly he was Head of Department, Department of Economics, Banking and Finance, College of Business, Hospitality and Tourism Studies, Fiji National University, Fiji Islands. Formerly he was Head of Department, Maharishi Arvind Institute of Science and Management (MAISM), Jaipur. He is having 23 years of experience in Teaching, Research, Consultancy and Administration. 9 research scholars have been awarded PhD under him and currently guiding 8 research scholars. Published 81 research papers (out of which 35 Scopus, ABDC-2 A Category and 5 B Category), 30 patents (17 International Patent and 15 National Patent). His Google Scholar detail is as follows: h-index = 10, i10-index= 10 & Citations =659. His Scopus detail is as follows: Documents – 34; Citation – 123; H – Index – 4. His Publon detail as follows: Articles – 55; Citation – 188; H- Index – 5.

J. Brintha Jei got a BDS from Rajas dental college under The TamilNadu Dr.MGR Medical University in the year 2005 and topped the periodontics subject in final year. MDS post-graduation from Vinayaka missions Shankaracharya Dental College and university in the year 2009. From then working in the department of Prosthodontics at SRM Dental College, Ramapuram and currently she is an Associate Professor in the same department. She is in postgraduate teaching profession from 2009 till date. She has several publications in national and international standard indexed journals, published few patents and contributed as authors to few textbooks. Has presented guest lectures and demonstrations, conducted preconference courses in state and national level scientific forums. She is a peer reviewer in national scientific journals. Currently she is also an executive committee of Indian Prosthodontic Society Tamilnadu &Pondicherry Branch and web and networking chairman in Indian Society of Prosthodontics –Restorative –Periodontics. She has been a significant part of organizing committee member in conduction of many state and national conferences, CDE programs, trainings and workshops. At present she is pursuing her PhD in the field of dentistry.

Jayashree K. is an Engineer by qualification, having completed her Doctorate in the area of Web Services Fault Management from Anna University, Chennai and Masters in Embedded System Technologies from Anna University and Bachelor's in Computer Science and Engineering from Madras University. She is presently working as Professor in the Department of Artificial Intelligence and Data Science at Panimalar Engineering College, affiliated to Anna University Chennai. Her areas of research interest include Web services, Cloud Computing, Data Mining, Data Analytics and Image Processing. She is a member of ACM, CSI.

Vijay K. is working as Assistant Professor (SG) in the department of Computer Science and Engineering, Rajalakshmi Engineering College, Chennai. B.Tech., M.E., graduate and pursuing PhD in Anna University, Chennai in the area of cloud computing. Having 16+ years of experience in teaching.

Jyothi K. C. is currently a final year student pursuing her B.Tech in Computer Science specialization in Data Science at Vellore Institute of Technology(VIT) , Vellore, Tamil Nadu.

Neelu Khare is presently working as Professor in the School of Information Technology and Engineering at VIT, Vellore, India from 2012. Overall she has 16 years of Academic and Research experience. She has completed Ph.D degree from Maulana Azad National Institute of Technology Bhopal, India in the year 2011. She has published 53 research papers in International Journals and conferences and 5 Book Chapters. She has guided 5 Ph.D students. She filed 2 patents and working on the research project funded by King Saud university SA worth 20 lacks for 6 month duration. Her areas of interest are Data Science, Machine Learning, Deep Learning, Soft computing techniques, Network Intusion Detection, IoT and Bio-informatics.

Reshmy Krishnan is working as an Assistant Professor in the Department of Computational Intelligence, School of Computing, SRM Institute of Science and Technology, Chennai, TamilNadu, India. She has more than 18 years of experience in teaching and research. She has received her Master of Engineering in Systems Engineering and Operations Research from College of Engineering, Guindy, Anna University, Chennai, India. She is a recipient of gold medal for securing first rank in Master of Engineering. She received Professor T.R. Natesan Endowment Award (Gold Medal-Instituted by Operational Research Society of India-Chennai Chapter). She has completed her doctorate (Ph.D in Information and Communication Engineering) from Anna University in the field of Big Data. Her current research focus is on Data Science, Machine Learning. To her credit she has published papers in Scopus Indexed Journal, presented papers in International Conferences and has filed patent. She has served as resource person and chaired conference session. She is Life member of Indian Society of Technical Education (ISTE) and a fellow of Institution of Engineering and Technology (IET).

B. Satheesh Kumar has received a Ph.D., in the Department of Computer Science and Engineering from Annamalai University, Chidambaram, India. He is working as an Assistant Professor in School of Computer Science and Engineering, Galgotias University, deemed to be University, Greater Noida, India. He received his Bachelor of Technology degree in the Department of Computer Science and Engineering from Arunai Engineering College, Thiruvanamalai, Tamilnadu in 2012; his Masters in Engineering in the Department of Computer Science and Engineering from PGP College of Engineering and Technology, Namakkal, Tamilnadu in 2014. His area of research includes, Digital Image Processing and Big Data Analytics, and Computer Vision, Machine learning and Video retrieval. He published article in SCI, SCIE, Scopus Journal and some International Conferences like IEEE, AISE, etc. He as 3 book chapters in IGI, CRC Press and Taylor and Francis and 3 book series in springer. He is also a reviewer in some reputed journals and as an external reviewer in conferences at IMPACT22.

K. Sampath Kumar is a Professor and PhD Coordinator in the School of Computing Science and Engineering, Galgotias University, Greater Noida, UP, Delhi-NCR, India. He has complete his Ph.D. in Big Data Mining from Anna University, Chennai, Tamil Nadu India and obtained his ME from Sathyabama University, Chennai, Tamil Nadu, India. He has over 23 years of teaching experience and more than 10 years in research work. He published more than 70 research articles in the international Journals and Conferences also published more than 4 Book and Book Chapters. He published more than 18 patens (National & International patents). His expertise in Big Data, Cloud, IOT and Artificial Intelligence.

R. Nagarajan received his B.E. in Electrical and Electronics Engineering from Madurai Kamarajar University, Madurai, India, in 1997. He received his M.E. in Power Electronics and Drives from Anna University, Chennai, India, in 2008. He received his Ph.D in Electrical Engineering from Anna University, Chennai, India, in 2014. He has worked in the industry as an Electrical Engineer. He is currently working as Professor of Electrical and Electronics Engineering at Gnanamani College of Technology, Namakkal, and Tamilnadu, India. His current research interest includes Power Electronics, Power System, Soft Computing Techniques and Renewable Energy Sources. He is published more than ninety research papers in various referred international journal.

Sabyasachi Pramanik is a Professional IEEE member. He obtained a PhD in Computer Science and Engineering from Sri Satya Sai University of Technology and Medical Sciences, Bhopal, India. Presently, he is an Associate Professor, Department of Computer Science and Engineering, Haldia Institute of Technology, India. He has many publications in various reputed international conferences, journals, and online book chapter contributions (Indexed by SCIE, Scopus, ESCI, etc). He is doing research in the field of Artificial Intelligence, Data Privacy, Cybersecurity, Network Security, and Machine Learning. He is also serving as the editorial board member of many international journals. He is a reviewer of journal articles from IEEE, Springer, Elsevier, Inderscience, IET, and IGI Global. He has reviewed many conference papers, has been a keynote speaker, session chair and has been a technical program committee member in many international conferences. He has authored a book on Wireless Sensor Network. He has edited 8 books from IGI Global, CRC Press EAI/Springer and Scrivener-Wiley Publications.

Babu R. is currently working as an Assistant Professor in the Department of Computational Intelligence, School of Computing, SRM Institute of Science and Technolgy.. He has completed his Masters in Software Engineering with a merit of 2nd rank in the Anna University and Bachelors in Computer Science and Engineering from Rajalakshmi Engineering College affiliated to Anna University. His areas of interest include Web Services, Service Oriented Architecture, Cloud Computing, Big Data Analytics and Internet Of Things. He is a life member of Computer Society of India (CSI) and served as a Management Committee Member for three years. He has received Active Participation Award – Youth and Significant Contribution Award from CSI. He also received Faculty Excellence Award from Infosys in Faculty Enablement Program for three successive years.

S. Sam is a Ph.D (Computer Science) from Anna University in the year 2007, have several Scopus indexed publications in national and International journals. contributed chapters in few books and presently working as Assistant Professor of Computer Science.

Prithi Samuel is currently working as an Assistant Professor in the Department of Computational Intelligence at SRM Institute of Science and Technology, Kattankulathur Campus, Chennai. She has completed her Ph.D. in Information and Communication Engineering from Anna University, Chennai. She has got over 15 years of teaching experience in reputed engineering colleges in Coimbatore and Chennai. She is a pioneer researcher in the areas of Automata Theory, Big Data, Machine Learning, Computational Intelligence Techniques, and Natural language Processing. She has published papers in leading International Journals and International Conferences and published books and book chapters in Wiley, Taylor and Francis, Springer and Elsevier.

Siva Subramanian is an Associate Professor in department of Computer Science and Engineering at S.A. Engineering College, Chennai. He has completed his under graduate and Post Graduate in Information Technology. He has completed his Ph.D in Information and communication Engineering from Anna University, Chennai. His research interests include Data mining, Big Data Analytics and Customer Analysis. He has published many papers in International journals and conferences

Bramha S. Tripathi is working as an Engineer-Firmware in the Depart. Of DBEB in Indian Institute of Technology Delhi. He received the Mtech in VLSI Design & B.E. in Electronics from RGPV University MP and has 9 year experience in Prototype development, R&D, Product Designing, project lead, Teaching. His current research interests are in IIoT, Embedded System, Product Design Technology (3d Printing, Laser cutting, PCB Designing), wireless sensor network.

Ramdhanush Venkatakrishnan is a student in III year CSE at Sri Sivasubramaniya Nadar College of Engineering.

Vishal Venkataramani is a student in III year CSE at Sri Sivasubramaniya Nadar College of Engineering.

Index

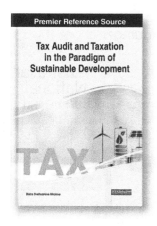

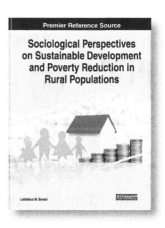

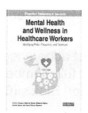

Printed in the United States
by Baker & Taylor Publisher Services